ERROL FLYNN
The Untold Story

BOOKS BY CHARLES HIGHAM

Theatre and Film

HOLLYWOOD IN THE FORTIES
(with Joel Greenberg)
THE CELLULOID MUSE: Hollywood Directors Speak
(with Joel Greenberg)
HOLLYWOOD CAMERAMEN
THE FILMS OF ORSON WELLES
HOLLYWOOD AT SUNSET
ZIEGFELD
CECIL B. DeMILLE: A Biography
THE ART OF THE AMERICAN FILM
AVA
KATE: The Life of Katharine Hepburn
CHARLES LAUGHTON: An Intimate Biography
THE ADVENTURES OF CONAN DOYLE:
The Life of the Creator of Sherlock Holmes
MARLENE: The Life of Marlene Dietrich
CELEBRITY CIRCUS

Poetry

A DISTANT STAR
SPRING AND DEATH
THE EARTHBOUND
NOONDAY COUNTRY
THE VOYAGE TO BRINDISI

Anthologies

THEY CAME TO AUSTRALIA
(with Alan Brissenden)
AUSTRALIANS ABROAD
(with Michael Wilding)
PENGUIN AUSTRALIAN WRITING TODAY

Errol Flynn

THE UNTOLD STORY

Charles Higham

DOUBLEDAY & COMPANY, INC., GARDEN CITY, NEW YORK
1980

ISBN: 0-385-13495-9
Library of Congress Catalog Card Number: 78–22633

For my editors
KEN MCCORMICK,
JEANNE BERNKOPF,
and
RUDY BEHLMER

—I pluck the rose
And love it more than tongue can speak—
Then the good minute goes.

Already how am I so far
Out of that minute? Must I go
Still like the thistle-ball, no bar,
Onward, whenever light winds blow,
Fixed by no friendly star?

Just when I seemed about to learn!
Where is the thread now? Off again.
The old trick! Only I discern—
Infinite passion, and the pain
Of finite hearts that yearn.

> Robert Browning,
> *Two in the Campagna*

"Once in intelligence work one cannot bring oneself to desert it. A spy is like an alcoholic. One espionage act and then another, until he is irretrievably hooked on spying."

> Dr. Hermann Friedrich Erben to
> Captain Frank Farrell of the OSS,
> Shanghai, 1946.

"In Secret Service work one must never be rash. The careful selection of above average collaborators is decisive."

> From the memoirs of Walter Schellenberg,
> head of Gestapo Foreign Intelligence.

MAID MARIAN (to Robin Hood): You speak treason!
ROBIN (smiling): Fluently!

> From *The Adventures of Robin Hood*,
> Banquet-hall scene.

ERROL FLYNN
The Untold Story

Prologue

It was two hours after a summer midnight. I had been sleeping fitfully, disturbed by the insistent drumming of rain on my roof: rain that followed fire and mass evacuation of parts of Los Angeles; disaster following disaster in the disturbed dream state we call California. Now I woke, sitting sharply upright, as though an invisible puppet master had pulled me by a thread. I saw him leaning against the wall. The door glowed white through his body, the narrow corridor was visible beyond his heart. A lamp, accidentally left on, shone through the paperlike thinness of the ghost's face.

He was smiling. That old, insolent smile that said "Fuck you" to the world. The brown eyes twinkled with devilish mischief. White teeth flashed against dark skin. The body still seemed to have the ruthless strength it had enjoyed in physical life. The mouth moved, but the words seemed to come from the whole room, vibrating as though they were spoken underwater. "Well, old sport," he seemed to be saying, "so you've blown my cover, have you? Good luck to you. You know what? I don't give a God damn. Where I am, there are no politics, no sex, no death, no contraband, no theft, no greed —though I've got to admit there are one hell of a lot of Nazis. I lived my fifty years, chum. I don't blame you for getting on to me, old sport. The Feds never did. I got away with everything, and I'm glad. If I had to do the whole bloody thing over again I would. Most Aussies Down Under only dream of conquering the world. I did it. And I didn't leave the stinking bloody world until I'd used up all those God-damned options. And I'll tell you another thing. I left the best way of all. With a young kid who loved me, the nicest girl I ever knew, kissing me on the lips. Smashing, old boy. What?"

Blowing Errol's cover was a difficult task. There was very little to start with. Several worthless biographies simply echoed his own memoirs, *My Wicked, Wicked Ways,* a book written to disguise his dark life by providing a largely fictitious alternative. Other stars' memoirs may be fixed up to enhance their images; none has been as filled with fiction as this. And most of those who have written about Flynn have fallen headlong into the trap he so carefully set for them.

I began from scratch, throwing away almost everything that had been written, knowing its futile source in his imagination and in that of his press agents. I soon found that Errol Flynn was a man who lived out his most dangerous fantasies in reality, performed actions and took risks most of us only imagine or fear, spent almost ten million dollars doing so, and still had a million left at the end.

Dub him, if you will, a cynic, an animal, a pagan, a demon on horseback—but perhaps, guiltily, if you are a man, still feel a twinge of envy for him. Patric Knowles, his friend and fellow actor of the 1930s, says that whatever Errol may have been, whatever he may have done, he would rather have been Errol Flynn than himself. Errol was ahead of his time in his casual amorality, refusal to believe in the work ethic—a deeply Australian trait—political cynicism, joyful laziness, nihilism, and effortless physical glamour. Most men of his time looked shapeless, staid, and dull beside him. He was in a sense a portent: of the triumph of the senses over reason, of self-indulgence over sanity, of chaos over order. Even though the bland, smiling face hid an evil man in many ways—anti-human, chauvinist, parasitical, murderous, traitorous, and predatory—he was also exciting, passionate, and audacious. He was, in other words, a devil whom men can easily understand: a devil many of us hide away in our adolescence and never let out again. He was frozen in that dangerous fascist period of first puberty when the human male feels his oats and is ready to try anything. Perhaps the secret of his charm for men is that so many of us also wish we hadn't had to grow up to bury the devilish Flynn in all of us.

At his best on the screen, in classics like *Captain Blood, The Adventures of Robin Hood, The Sea Hawk,* his animal grace and insolent, anarchic style excite audiences. Warner Brothers had the wit to create piratical vehicles for him. Jack Warner, piratical boss of Warners, lived out a widely shared fantasy of *being* Flynn—in these adventures until his terror of Flynn overcame his dreams.

Writing this book was an adventure in itself. In the first week of work in January 1978, the Warner Brothers files became available to me, making it possible to cover every day and hour of Flynn's film career at the studio from contemporary records. At the same time, I made a call to an obscure archery shop in Glendale, California, to ask about Errol's prowess with bow and arrow. And with that call, everything fell into place. The owner, Hugh Rich, made it possible for me to meet Paul McWilliams, champion archer, Errol's genial friend and stand-in, who followed up countless leads for me. Paul, in turn, happened to run into a woman named Jane Chesis, who once had been a friend and secretary of Flynn's. Through Paul and Jane I reached many others. And soon I also met Errol's pimp and henchman, Johnny Meyer; Jim Fleming, Errol's close friend and associate from 1933 until 1949; Barry Mahon, Errol's manager and mentor from 1950 until 1959; Clelle, Barry's extraordinary wife; Charles Pilleau, Errol's intimate boyhood friend, who first knew of his bisexuality; and over two hundred others.

More and more people talked with me, chief among them the four remarkable women—three married to him, the other not—who dominated Errol's life. Lili Damita, the tempestuous French actress, spoke to me sharply and dismissively about Errol on the telephone from her home in Iowa, indicating harsh bitterness about the past. The loyal Nora Eddington swept into lunch in Beverly Hills in a fury, angered by a column interview I had given on her late husband's bisexuality. We drove in her Mercedes through a storm up a crumbling cliff road to the house she once shared with Errol, Mulholland Farm, where a gospel composer now lived and concocted his pious themes in the room Errol had used for elaborate orgies; Errol's two-way mirror in the ceiling was primly boarded

over. On the verge of tears, Nora walked from room to room, seeing
what time had wrought, while the storm exploded angrily outside the
tall, Manderley-like windows.

Patrice Wymore, Errol's third wife, dropped into Los Angeles on a
two-day visit from Jamaica. She came to check one of her Jamaican
servants into a sanitarium, but she took time off to tell me how she
felt about Errol Flynn. I found her still the cool, witty, and beautiful
woman I hope Errol knew was the best thing that happened to him.
And last, in her simple, sunlit house in Palmdale, in the high, wind-
swept, stinging cold of the California desert, I met Beverly Aadland,
whom Errol had fallen in love with when she was fifteen—still
cute, pretty, bright, miraculously unspoiled by experiences that
would have crushed most people from the outset. Each of these four
women, strong and impressive in very different ways, taught me
much about Errol Flynn.

There was little they told me that shocked me. And I did not discover the most disturbing facts about Flynn until well after I had
seen his wives and his teen-age girl friend.

The greatest shock came almost as a personal blow. Flynn had
been an idol of my boyhood and young manhood. I could have forgiven him almost anything. Anything but the fact that this man who
personified patriotism on the screen was a spy for the Nazis, a collaborator, and a traitor to Britain and America.

I am partly Jewish; my childhood home was bombed by the Germans in World War II; I risked my life firefighting on a school roof-
top as a boy of eleven in the Blitz. When I sat in the National
Archives in Washington, with the evidence of Flynn's Fifth Column
activities staring me in the face, I felt the tears of grief and shock
rolling down my cheeks.

How did I first stumble on this information? It came from an obscure lead that Dr. Hermann Friedrich Erben, known to be Errol's
close friend and mentor, had been a Nazi agent.

In the course of tracking that lead, I solved a mystery that has
puzzled Flynn buffs for years. Ever since the publication of *My
Wicked, Wicked Ways,* its readers have puzzled over the real identity
of two individuals who loom large in its pages: Swartz, the American
film-maker in New Guinea who hired Errol's boat, and Koets, the
Dutchman who accompanied Errol to England. From what I have
learned of Dr. Erben as a personality, it is now clear that Swartz and
Koets are merely Errol's fictionalized portrayals of this Nazi, without

the politics. (Though it is interesting that the treasurer who signed Erben's Nazi Party card was named Schwarz.)

From my first clue about Erben, I followed a complex, labyrinthine trail to the truth about Flynn himself. The second clue lay in Flynn's second closest friend, Freddy McEvoy. McEvoy, I discovered, had been under constant investigation as a Nazi collaborator during the prewar and wartime years, and was involved in U-boat refueling operations.

Later, I found that many of Errol's connections were with very prominent Nazis. His glamorous Swedish mistress, Gertrude Anderson, was so prominent a Nazi agent in the 1940s that the local FBI representatives in Los Angeles still talk of her with awe—and disgust that she escaped from them into Mexico after Pearl Harbor.

I went at once to Washington. There, in the submarinelike bleakness of the file rooms of the National Archives, I found numerous Fifth Column index cards on Erben, McEvoy, Anderson, and—yes—Errol. Soon, I contacted the CIA, the State Department, the intelligence branches of the Army, Navy, and Air Force, the FBI, and every part of the National Archives as well as the Berlin and Viennese documentation centers, the Sûreté and the Moroccan police. After ten months of declassifications, about twelve thousand pages of documents flooded my house. What I discovered forms much of the substance of this book.

I spoke to Colonel William E. Williamson, who was in charge of demilitarizing military zones in Japan under MacArthur, and commander of the repatriation vessel upon which Dr. Erben was shipped from Shanghai to a prison camp in Germany after the war. Williamson had done his own research at the Pentagon and State Department and the CIA to unravel the truth about the connections between Erben and Errol, and had learned that Errol was a spy for the Nazis on a very major scale.

My correspondent in London, Roy Moseley, asked Willi Frischauer, authority on the subject of espionage and naval history, whether he knew that Flynn was a spy for Germany. Frischauer replied that he did and added, "Come and see me tomorrow. This is very dangerous territory. There are people that won't like this found out. Be careful. Tell Mr. Higham to be careful. . . ." Next day, Frischauer was dead, apparently a suicide.

It was, of course, essential to unlock the mystery of Dr. Erben. Could he possibly still be alive? I asked my assistant Peter Lev to check the American Medical Association directories from 1930 to the present day.

Incredibly, Erben was still listed in 1978—as an absentee member in Vienna! The roll call of his addresses was bewildering, and included such unlikely places as China, Afghanistan, Iran, Pakistan, Indonesia, and Saudi Arabia.

I called Dr. Erben's home in Vienna. No reply.

There were weeks of frustration as I called day and night, unable to elicit a response. I had almost given up hope when, one morning at nine, I managed at last to get through. My heart almost stopped.

A woman answered. She said she was Dr. Erben's sister, that she came to his house once a week to collect the mail, and that I was lucky to have caught her in the few minutes she was there. Dr. Erben was not at home. *Where was he then?* The line began to crackle. I thought, If she's cut off now, I'll die. I struggled to hear her heavily accented voice through the static. "S-a-g-a-d-a!" S-a-g-a-d-a? Where in God's name was Sagada? And what in God's name was Dr. Erben doing there? "Philippines," she said. "Luzon Island. He is studying his favorite subject," she replied. My mind raced. "And what is it?" I asked. The answer sliced like a scalpel across several thousand miles. "LEPROSY!"

It was too much. Too extreme, too impossible. Dr. Erben in a *leper hospital?* But then, in the state of before-the-Fall innocence I was in that November, I knew nothing of Dr. Erben's astounding story.

I didn't go to the Philippines myself. I was tempted, but Sagada, the Atlas and guidebooks told me, was in the remotest highlands of the mountain province in Luzon. It was a kind of Shangri-La in reverse where lepers were treated along with victims of other horrifying diseases. A trip to a leper hospital was too extreme for me: my imagination working overtime, I was seized by macabre humors; maybe I would return from the adventure, have my hand shaken by reporters at the airport—and watch it fall off.

No good. No good at all. So I must hire someone courageous to do the job for me. It seemed unlikely I would find anyone in pampered Hollywood to undertake such a trip, and even less likely that I would find anyone who wouldn't talk about it. I asked the Philippine Consulate for a list of journalists in Manila. I looked at the list. Twelve names, none of which meant any more to me than its neighbor. I took out a pin. I punctured a name. Marcos Agayo. I telephoned him.

He was amazed by my call. Agayo turned out to be the closest friend in the world of Dr. Erben! His mother had greeted Dr. Erben in Sagada, and his brother was Dr. Erben's best field worker! The odds against finding the one person in the Philippines who was close to the mysterious doctor were surely forty-seven million to one. And Marcos Agayo flew perilously three times across mountain ranges in a battered plane to his home town of Sagada to bring back for me the last terrifying piece of the jigsaw puzzle that made up the untold story of Errol Flynn.

One

Picture a city some seventy years ago: the last great British port before the South Pole. A city of 65,000 souls, a harbor town, filled with the sound of foghorns or ship's whistles; alive with sparkling sunshine or black with the long winter rains; swept by the terrible winds called the roaring forties.

The architecture is a dour impersonation of England's: red brick houses with eaves and white-painted window sills frowning on the clear Prussian blue or profound gloom of the harbor. Church bells and gardens and dark green lawns are forlorn echoes of a faraway home. It is a cozy colonial bulwark against the knowledge of remoteness. The heart aches for originals. Houses are built, lawns are groomed, businesses are attended, and beer is drunk. Steak and eggs are breakfasted upon. It seems a northern life. But there are strange trees, threatening bushes, birds which are too bright and exotic to fit in. A mountain broods over the city as menacingly as a gigantic stone lion, casting a shadow across it. At the public library, people reverently turn over the pages of newspapers fixed into long wooden handles. They are copies of English papers, six months old, shipped across the world, reporting events that are long since forgotten in the northern hemisphere.

We are in Hobart, Tasmania, 12,000 miles from Europe. It takes a P&O liner six weeks to chug across from England: six weeks of costume parties and Mad Hatters' balls and totes on the ship's run and crossing-the-equator ceremonies with Neptune and his queen in cardboard crowns and flaxen rope curls. From Tilbury dock to Naples and Port Said and the Suez Canal and Aden to Colombo and at last to Perth, Melbourne, and Sydney seems a lifetime of journeying. And then yet another voyage must be undertaken: a night and a day and a night on the stormy Bass Straits from Sydney.

Despite its Victorian office buildings with their copper domes bleeding green in the subtropical rain, Sydney is "American." Its citizens are divided into the far too quick and the very nearly dead. It is tennis parties in white flannels and swimming contests in green ocean pools and sailing on weekends across the vast, iridescent glitter of the harbor. It is ferries with rust-brown hulls and beach picnics and fairs. Hobart despises puffed-up Sydney; Hobart is propriety and order, and it firmly closes its doors on Saturday night; Hobart is denial of sex and worship of business; discussion of royal doings in London and saving for trips by P&O.

We are in 1909. Australia's spirit is swelling with a newly discovered national pride. Her heart has not yet been ripped out by the tragedy of the Somme and the deadly horror of her military defeat at Gallipoli. She is a boisterous nation, defiant of England yet paradoxically yearning for English approval. Her newspapers are full of criticism of effete English ways, yet she still leans to the Privy Council in London for final judgments in litigation. The Commonwealth of Australia has only been in existence for eight years and is still a bawling infant.

Only three things worth mentioning happened to Australia in 1909. One was the fixing of the capital city in the region known as Canberra. The second was the formation of a new government under the aggressive Prime Minister Alfred Deakin. And the third was the birth in Hobart on June 20 of Australia's most famous export apart from the kangaroo.

Errol Leslie Thomson Flynn was a prince of liars. He stoutly maintained that he was born in Ireland, fought for Australia in the

Olympic boxing team and was descended from a noble Irish family, the Flynn O'Flynns. He said that he attended St. Paul's School in London and King's College in Ireland, swam the Irish Channel, had his first erection in the cradle, and could drink twenty-five glasses of ale without slurring a syllable. Lies, all lies.

In fact he was descended on his mother's side from Fletcher Christian and Edward Young of *Bounty* fame, and one of his ancestors, Robert Young, was a slave trader who was murdered by South Seas natives and eaten in a cannibal feast. On his father's side, he was descended from a poor immigrant family from Ireland, one member of which was hanged for sheep stealing. His paternal grandmother was so poor she kept her coal in the bath. Her children bathed at a pump in the yard and had to start earning a living at a very early age.

John Harcourt, who knew the family well, says:

> There was great bitterness through much of the family about the British ill treatment of their Irish ancestors. Also, there was a strong streak of nationalism in Australia when Errol was a child, and Britishers were referred to by the contemptuous term of "pommies." Professor and Mrs. Flynn, Errol's parents, were, like many educated people, pro-British and thought of England as "home." Errol was painfully aware of the cruelty of the British toward his ancestors. I believe that knowledge affected his complete indifference to Britain, even his dislike of it later on. He also hated Australia, dismissing it as "the colonies." And, like his mother, he hated Jews.

The Flynn parents were so oddly matched that one can understand why Errol thought himself a bastard. His father, Theodore Leslie Thomson Flynn, lecturer and later Ralston Professor of Biology at the University of Tasmania in Hobart, sounded like a fake medicine peddler in a carnival, but was in fact an expert on the mating habits of whales. He had a horsy red face and ginger-colored hair which stood straight up from his forehead like the quills of a porcupine. His body seemed to be composed of spare parts borrowed from different people and covered with freckles. He liked to pinch young girls—few young ladies were safe from him—and he was addicted to fishing. He had an odd, disconcerting tendency to take off to the South Pole. He was nearsighted and so shy that he would enter a room containing a group of people, begin an anecdote about whales or dolphins, lose the thread, turn a bright shade of scarlet, and retire from the room in order to compose himself. Then he would return, adjust his tie, clear his throat and continue with his story.

His wife, Lily Mary, more closely resembled Captain Bligh than her ancestor Fletcher Christian. She was an authority on the art of punishment. She thrashed young Errol as regularly as she beat eggs. She was a beauty, with chestnut hair and sharp brown eyes and a winning smile, but the picture was spoiled when she spoke French in a flat Australian twang and gave herself the phony name of Marelle. She was irritable and impatient with her absent-minded husband, and combined her earnest reading of the Bible with a custom of inviting gentleman callers from time to time. She refused to breast-feed Errol because she feared her breasts might be ruined. She gave him bottled milk which had not been pasteurized. As a result, he contracted undulant fever which recurred throughout his adult life.

Errol annoyed his mother by telling her his real father had been a dashing Irish sailor off a cargo boat. She responded by boxing his ears and calling him "Leslie."

What Errol did not know was that he had been born only five months after his parents were married. Evidently, it had been a forced marriage. His mother was underage at sixteen; and once he found this out, his parents were never able to talk puritanically to him again.

Errol showed his character at an early age. A handsome child, with a mop of brown hair, sparkling eyes, and an impish grin, he was an impertinent charmer at the age of four. He built a model of a pirate ship which he sailed in a local pond with a skull and cross-bones flying from the stern. He made a tent with a bed sheet and sticks and lived in it as much as he could, calling himself Robinson Crusoe and naming his Irish terrier Man Friday.

At the same age, he went with his parents to Sydney, where he, his mother, a friend, and his cousin Ronnie dressed up as pierrots in a beach carnival party at Manly. Errol was annoyed by the camera and frowned sulkily at the photographer. But he was unmistakably photogenic even then.

One afternoon, when his parents were out, there was a knock at the door of their home. The housekeeper went to see who it was and Errol followed her.

It was an elderly beggar asking for money and food. The man hadn't eaten for two days. While the housekeeper went to fetch him something to eat, Errol went to his mother's dressing room and took her toilet set—a mirror, brush and comb made of expensive tortoise shell with her initials inscribed on them in silver—and gave it to the old man.

When Lily Mary Flynn returned, she was horrified to discover the toilet set missing. Errol cheerfully announced that it had been stolen.

His conflict with his mother was bitter and constant. Despite her own amorous escapades, she was pious about his behavior. She thrashed him when she caught him masturbating, threatened to evict him when she discovered him dallying with a neighbor's girl, and constantly abused him for his sly mischief. Professor Flynn was so often gone abroad looking for bizarre fish specimens that there was no buffer between mother and child. As a result, Errol's hatred grew and flourished. The only relief in their charged relationship came at the beach or in the river, where they swam together, or at picnics and picnic races when they would sometimes laugh at the same jokes or bet on the same horses.

A contemporary of Errol's, Max Darling, remembers him at the age of six. He says:

> I recall Errol as a plucky, confident little boy whose parents dressed him in pantaloons which he always discarded for knicker-bockers with braces whenever he stayed with my family. Once, on an excursion to Wine Glass Bay near Hobart, I returned with Errol to find two naked men on the sand sunning themselves after a swim. "I hate hairy people," Errol said. "But all people are hairy when they grow up," I replied. To which Errol responded, "Daddy and Mummy are hairy, but I don't like to kiss them the way I do Millie. She doesn't have hair on her body." I've never forgotten this example of Errol's amazing sexual precocity. Millie was a little girl Errol loved to play with. She was about five.

Errol's first school in Hobart was the Albuera. Enid McKoy, a fellow pupil in the lower grades, writes:

> It was a plain brick building but the front doors and windows looked over the lovely Derwent River. It was run with military preci-sion. Everyone had to sit up straight in class. Nobody *ever* dared to speak in class. Not even Errol.
>
> The head teacher, Mr. William Duncomb, was a tall, thin, erect former army officer; when he taught us he wore the medal his only

son would have possessed, if the boy had not been killed in the Great War.

At the time, Errol lived with his family at a place called Battery Point. It was high above the harbor, and the higher you lived, the posher you were. The Flynns lived about half-way up. A great many men in the whaling fleets lived in the lower reaches. The Japanese whalers would come and visit them. They would climb up a steep flight known as the Kelly Steps to the Point. Sailing into Hobart was glorious: no tugs needed, sixty-five feet of water, and boats coming in under their own steam.

Errol loved ships and seamen. He would often look longingly out of the classroom windows. I could tell he was thinking of oceans and places far away.

As he grew, Errol was increasingly neglected by his father. Not only was Professor Flynn frequently away on expeditions of various kinds in search of marine specimens, he was also busy stocking Tasmanian streams with salmon and developing the export of crayfish and scallops to mainland Australia, a business which earned him enough money to obtain a more elaborate home on Upper Davey Street. Meanwhile, his teaching of biology to his class of young girls sometimes went beyond the limits of scholarly instruction. The father of one irate pupil followed him as he left his house and drove wildly after him up a steep road leading around the cliffs of Mount Wellington. When he caught up with the professor, he demanded that Flynn step out of his car. A moment later, the professor found himself flying through the windshield. Next morning, Professor Flynn appeared before his helplessly giggling class with an assortment of adhesives attached to his face. This curious streak of Don Juanism sat oddly with the professor's austere manner, high stiff wing collar, bashful blushes and meticulously polished gold pince-nez.

Mrs. Flynn brought a constant stream of men to the family home in her husband's absence. Errol resented this cuckolding of his father. His resentment affected his attitude toward women for the rest of his life. He was attracted by the figures and faces of young girls, but from the beginning, he found it difficult to relate to women: to understand their needs on the deepest level. It was a failing which flawed his life and destroyed his marriages. Given the double standards of the day, his father's extraordinary promiscuity seems not to have bothered him and may even have made his father something of a hero in his eyes.

Finally, his mother, too, began to neglect him. She traveled frequently to Sydney without him. He resented and brooded over the fact that he was left alone for long periods. He hated the winters of Hobart, with their black skies and months of freezing rain. Now, and for the rest of his life, he had brutal headaches whenever it rained.

He was more or less adopted by neighborhood women who took pity on him, sewed his buttons and mended his pants, and gave him food.

It was at this time that he developed his lifelong kleptomania. He was dismissed from three schools for stealing, beginning at the age of eleven. Yet these dismissals were very quietly arranged in light of Professor Flynn's official position at the university. A more or less conventional psychological explanation might be that, deprived of gifts, sometimes even on birthdays, Errol had to steal candies from stores, books, papers, even clothes and shoes.

In his many hours alone, when he was ill or tired of various jokes, Errol plunged into what became a lifelong habit of somber meditation and bouts of reading. He loved Masefield, Stevenson, and Melville. In Masefield's poem *Sea Fever* he found his greatest solace and the guide to his life:

> *I must go down to the seas again, to the vagrant gypsy life,*
> *To the gull's way and the whale's way, where the wind's*
>   *like a whetted knife,*
> *And all I ask is a merry yarn from a laughing fellow-rover,*
> *And quiet sleep and a sweet dream when the long trick's over.*

Reading *Treasure Island,* he lived passionately among the characters; Long John Silver in particular came alive for him. Reading *Moby Dick,* he was stirred, as only a boy in a whaling port like Hobart could be, by the mystique of the vast creatures sailing along the deep.

He hated the repressive atmosphere of Hobart, with its emphasis on religion and good works, on church-every-Sunday. Hobart made Errol the rebel against organized religion and snobbery that he remained for the rest of his life. He was infuriated by snobbery. His mother insisted on living above her means despite the fact that her

husband was earning only the equivalent of $1,000 a year. She was furious when she caught Errol playing with the son and daughter of a grocer: grocers, she told him, were "trade" and were to be looked down on by gentle-folk. Errol retaliated by playing with the children of a park sweeper.

Mrs. Marie Dechaineux vividly recalls Errol at the time:

There were trams [streetcars] and trains but very few autos in those days after World War I. My family lived five miles up the Derwent River. Father used to have some of the children I knew, including Errol, who was about ten, come to us from Hobart in a horse-drawn carriage for a picnic lunch on Sundays. He would unharness the horse and tie it up outside the stable door. It would be watered while the children had their meal.

The first time he came, Errol noticed that a handyman had left Father's shotgun, which Father used to frighten birds away from the orchard, propped up near the tethered horse at the stable door. When my sister came out to supervise the feeding of Star, the horse, Errol picked up the gun and aimed it at her. Mercifully, though he actually pulled the trigger, he didn't understand the workings of the weapon. It wasn't cocked. If it had been, he might have killed her. My sister finally persuaded him to put it down.

Mrs. Dechaineux continues:

On a second visit, Errol's mother came with him. She danced and sang prettily and kept us all laughing with stories of his escapades. Her lack of humor in telling them made us laugh all the more. She told us that when Errol was six he had been staying with his family at a boarding house and disappeared with a girl age three. Frantic, the Flynns had called the police. After a day and night search, the children were found on a roof in a slum called Wapping. Three years later, Errol had disappeared again. He was found sleeping in a cowshed high on the slopes on Mount Wellington. Another time, Mrs. Flynn told us, a lady came home to find her goats loose in the rose garden. They had completely ruined it. The first thing she asked was, "Has Errol been here today?" "Of course," her children replied in unison.

He could never be left alone. When the tablecloth was completely set for a meal, he could firmly be relied upon to pull it off, bringing all the dishes crashing to the floor.

After leaving the Albuera school in disgrace for stealing, Errol was enrolled at Hutchins, the second-oldest educational institution in Australia. It was a handsome building with cool, gray cloisters and a centerpiece of a massive square tower with battlements. The tower and the Gothic main entrance were covered in ivy that since the school's founding in 1846 had spread over the sandstone main structure.

There were just over three hundred pupils, including some seventy day boys, most of whom were the children of wealthy farmers. Errol was a day boy. One of his best friends was a nervous, sensitive boy named Angus Brammall, who later became a well-known Australian journalist. Errol protected Angus from the rougher, tougher boys. Brammall remembers:

> I first knew Errol when I was eleven. My father was classical languages tutor at Hutchins and a deputy headmaster. Errol was a fine boy. It's true he had a temper and liked to fight but he protected the weak and hit out at the strong and powerful. He was Robin Hood even then.
>
> Errol, I, and a boy named William Lacey used to wander down to the wharves after school and drool over the great liners of the P&O Orient Blue Funnel Lines. "Christ," Errol would say, as he looked up at the beautiful eighteen thousand and twenty thousand ton vessels. "I'd like to get away from this dump on one of those ships."

Brammall continues:

> Flynn and I often walked home together after school and were once assailed by a pack of State School roughnecks. They tagged us fairies ("poofters") because we attended Hutchins which was a school for gentlemen. The "larrikins" set about punching us and Errol's eyes sparkled at the prospect. He loved a fight. When they tried to snatch our magenta and black school caps and tear the metal badges off, Flynn was into them. There were five of them against two of us. He downed the whole pack in double quick time. "That'll teach the fucking bastards," he exulted, straightening his tie.
>
> He refused to wear the mandatory school tie of horizontal magenta and black stripes and always affected a polka dotted bow tie. "Fuck the old school and their tie, too," he would comment. "I like this one."
>
> He didn't give a damn for the dear old school, although the then headmaster, Mr. C. C. Thorold M.A. Oxon, bashed our ears every

morning in assembly about tradition. Errol showed his feelings about the subject one morning by letting off a resounding fart bang in the middle of one of the old man's tedious orations.

After school he remained the same. He and a friend of his named Donald Love once "borrowed" a yacht from the Hobart Yacht Basin and blithely sailed off one night with New Guinea their destination. But they ran the vessel ashore on Tasmania's east coast where they were run in by waiting cops. They were never charged because Flynn's father was a university "big shot" and Love's father owned a department store. Hobart was like that in those days.

When Errol was ten, the Flynns discovered to their surprise that they were going to have another child. A daughter, Rosemary, was born in 1920. Lily Mary decided she did not want the pretty little girl to grow up in Hobart. Since she had a mania for everything French, she dreamed of abandoning her husband and son one day and moving to Paris. Professor Flynn convinced her the baby was too young to be taken away from home. But after an afternoon picnic with both children, she was more determined than ever. It was an icy but sun-drenched winter's day and they were all on a hill overlooking a small frozen lake. Lily Mary was sleeping when Errol took Rosemary and carefully tied her to her sled. He pushed the sled down the side of the hill toward the lake. The baby's screams woke Lily Mary who ran desperately to the foot of the hill, just managing to catch her daughter before the child drowned in the icy water.

From early childhood, Errol had developed a horrifying streak of cruelty to animals. He loved his own dog and yet when a mad dog attacked him, he caught it and glued its eyelids together. He would take a parrot and clip its wings, making it dance on a hot metal tub. He was constantly putting snails on lime and watching them explode, and he liked to trap birds and pluck their wings. And yet he shared his father's love of the preservation of wild creatures. It is scarcely surprising that his parents thought him contradictory enough to be possessed by the devil.

The family moved to Sydney in 1921. Errol spent much of the time with his maternal grandmother a short distance from Manly Beach, a handsome stretch of sand across the harbor from the city proper. One Sunday afternoon, Errol and his cousins took off in a rowboat into Sydney harbor. When they were a mile out, Errol stood up and began rocking the boat, challenging the other children to swim to shore. Fortunately, the rowboat owner, a commercial fisherman, drew up alongside in another boat and rescued the children. In revenge, Errol made spears out of harbor reeds and stabbed them into the owner's fish destined for market. The catch was ruined.

The author John Hammond Moore wrote:

> When a five masted schooner, the *H.K. Hall* was in port excited youngsters swarmed over the vessel. In short order the boy who became Captain Blood a decade later was swinging in the rigging with loud shouts and much bravado. Summoned back to the deck, he sulked for a few moments; then, when no one was looking, he threw all the buckets used by the crew over the side.

In 1921, there was a rift between the Flynn parents. Mrs. Flynn fulfilled her ambition to go to Paris with Rosemary.

Errol and his father commuted to and from Britain, spending most of the time in Australia. In Paris, the socially ambitious Lily Mary worked her way up until she actually enjoyed a brief affair with the Aga Khan. In Sydney, the professor dallied more modestly with the wife of a local merchant.

Errol wasted one full term at South London College. Back in Tasmania, he was a pupil at Hobart High School, where he proved to be a fierce and vigorous tennis player whose style was marred only by a poor backhand. He won many swimming races and became a juvenile lifeguard. He was the Don Juan of the classroom, beloved by everyone.

He gained even greater popularity during a fair, held in the school hall. As the parents, businessmen and their ladies, trooped into the large, echoing room, Errol hid in the balcony. He had an enormous box full of ice creams. With unerring aim, he dropped one ice cream after the other on the ladies' flowered hats and the men's balding heads. There was a chase in which the offended people pursued him up and down stairs and through the corridors. He disappeared into a closet and watched, shaking with silent laughter as they raced past him.

Caught eventually, he was thrashed by the head teacher. Late that night, he stole out of the school dormitory and crept into the kitchen. There, he found a large tub of molasses. He made his way into the parking lot, pried open the door of the head teacher's car, and poured the molasses over the steering wheel. To compound the crime, he stuffed a potato up the exhaust pipe. He walked off laughing.

In 1926, at the age of seventeen, Errol was a magnificent-looking boy. He was a full six feet tall, and would grow another inch before he was eighteen. He weighed one hundred and seventy-five pounds. He had a tennis player's body, with very broad shoulders and chest, muscular arms, narrow waist and hips, and long, slim legs. His golden brown hair with reddish highlights in it was brilliantined, parted, and slicked down in the manner of the time. His skin was tan from the Australian sun. His brown eyes blazed out of his face: they could turn cold as agates if somebody irritated or displeased him. He moved like an animal: lithe and quick and dangerous. Nobody forgot his smile: it was daring and frankly sexual, white teeth flashing wickedly against dark skin.

Girls could not resist him. Indeed, many pursued him avidly and were not disappointed. He was a sexual athlete from the beginning. He had extraordinary staying power and a deep understanding of women's bodies. Perhaps it was a part of his bisexuality that he was inventive and daring in bed. He had the capacity to make women feel they were the most important creatures in the world for the length of time he was with them. He had a surprising ability to flatter. And he had an interest in the feminine: in the color and cut of a dress, the effect of a marcel bob, or a particular perfume.

He was a colorful presence everywhere: at tennis matches, leaping vigorously across the court. In the boxing ring, in scarlet shorts sewn with his initials in gold, slamming brutally at his opponent. In a swimming race, diving into the echoing pale green water in a skin-tight suit. Manning a boat out in rough seas.

In 1926, Errol went to the Sydney Church of England Grammar School. One of Australia's most venerated institutions, the school imposed a uniform of gaudy straw boaters and handsome blazers on its flock. Errol was proud to be at "Shore" or "SCEGS" as it was known, but he rapidly became notorious for his masturbatory activities. He told Johnny Meyer later he acted out a "hambone": a male striptease peculiar to Australia in which a handsome youth would throw off his clothes in a bump and grind while watched in enthusiasm by his fellow pupils, then provoke a large erection at the finish. Or he would plunge into a circle jerk, called a jack-off session in Australia, at which several boys stood in a circle and masturbated —with a prize of a precious box of condoms, imported from France, to the first boy to climax.

At SCEGS Errol was known for his excellence at boxing, football, and cricket. His brilliant lies, complicated dirty stories told in the school dormitory, and ready wit earned him a fast reputation. But he only lasted two terms.

He became fascinated with the daughter of the laundress, and found various places around the school to consummate his interest in her. Finally, he discovered an ideal spot: the coal pile in the cellar.

Late one night, he met the girl at the coal pile and they lay on top of it, energetically making love. It gave way beneath them and they rolled all the way to the bottom, becoming completely covered with coal dust in the process.

As they lay there coughing and sneezing, they heard a footstep on the stairs. A flashlight cast an arc through the darkness. The school nurse stood there, speechless with horror at the sight of the two naked black bodies on the floor. She rushed to the head teacher and got him out of bed. When she told him the name of the male culprit he said: "I'm not surprised. He just stole the slush fund for the tennis team."

His father was asked to pick him up the next day and told that Errol was not to return. It is unlikely that Errol did anything but laugh over the episode. And it is equally likely that his indulgent father congratulated him on being dismissed from the school in such glorious circumstances.

TWO

Since no school, it was painfully clear, could hold Errol Flynn, the professor managed to wangle a job for the boy. Because of his powerful physique, Errol was hired as a wharf laborer for the shipping company of Dalgety's, Ltd., to shift bales of wool and load cranes with a variety of export goods. The romantic names of the ships and the exotic ports for which they were headed acted like wine on Errol's senses. He longed to go to Queensland, the tropical state which lay to the north of New South Wales, and to New Guinea, the island which lay to the north of Australia itself, shaped like a prehistoric lizard, set in the exotic South Seas.

While working on the wharves, stripped to the waist in hot sun, inhaling the scent of tar and copra and spume from the ocean, Errol was entertained by a grand old codger named Happy Harry. Happy Harry had cross eyes and several missing teeth. He spun marvelous tales of adventure in the South Seas. Errol sparked particularly when Harry mentioned the gold that had been discovered in New Guinea. He swore he would travel there one day.

Errol became a man at Dalgety's. He learned to mix with the big, rough, cheerful "wharfies" or wharf laborers, who liked to gather after work in a huge, white-tiled urinal-like bar where they could swill oceans of brown beer. Errol got practice in drinking "schooners," enormous glasses filled to the brim. No sooner was he halfway through one, feeling slightly dizzy, than two more would be set beside it. He would be staggering drunk by the time he had finished the third glass.

The hard work in the damp heat still further developed Errol's body and gave him the sense of being alive and one of a pack. It was a male-dominated society. Women were excluded from the pubs, considered of use only as sexual objects, darners of socks, and sewers-on of buttons.

Yet on weekends, Errol entered another world. Instead of joining his mates for more beer-swilling, he took off into the elegant life of Sydney.

It was one of the pleasantest existences on earth. The rich lived in harborside mansions that were cool and airy and ventilated by giant fans revolving in the ceilings. Windows opened onto pale green lawns that stretched all the way to the brilliant azure water. Scarlet and blue parrots flashed through the feathery eucalyptus trees as the social crowd played lawn tennis or croquet on the long golden afternoons or took off to the country in crowded autos for picnics by the rivers. And in the evening, Professor Flynn, who was often entertained by high society, would take Errol, resplendent in white tie and tails in his mid-teens, to gala balls.

When Errol was promoted to an office job at Dalgety's, a discrepancy was found in the petty cash accounts. Errol had bet the money at Randwick Race Track, hoping to return it by morning. He was fired less than two weeks after he began the job.

The gentle and charming young society blade Ken Hunter-Kerr befriended him. They shared a converted stable with tiny rooms where the horse stalls used to be and with a bathroom in the old hayloft. Girls used to come there in droves, eager for sex with handsome Errol, while the shy Hunter-Kerr would steal off for the evening to oblige his friend.

Another close friend was a teen-ager named Edward Ashley Cooper, later the actor Edward Ashley, the dashing son of a British Royal Navy man. Errol, Ken, and Edward used to date three pretty teen-age girls, Miriam, Naomi, and Cecile, locally famous as the

Dibbs sisters. They were grandnieces of a former premier of New South Wales, and were extremely "social," whirling about in cloche hats and flapper dresses, getting slightly tipsy at parties, chased by all the eligible, sleek-haired young men in derby hats.

Too poor to buy a car, the six teen-agers would dash off on weekends to the rusty trolley car that ground its weary way toward Bondi Beach along grass grown tracks, emitting asthmatic sounds as it did so. Once at the beach—a stretch of perfect white sand bordering the blue Pacific—they were in their element, racing each other into the waves, jumping up and down in the surf, catching the great boomers as they rolled in from the ocean.

The boys were all good swimmers, and Errol joined the Bondi Lifesavers' Club as a lifeguard, marching in military formation, goose-stepping in the soft white sand, dressed in a heroic bathing suit with a sash across it and a bright scarlet cap on his brown hair.

Swimming and tennis—to say nothing of lovemaking—made him a magnificent specimen. Free of all moral restraint, he was an odd man out in that prudish Australian society in which sex was discussed only furtively and young men and women were warned of the dreaded social results of a pregnancy or an attack of gonorrhea. The extreme repressiveness of puritanical Australia worked against the intensely physical, sensual, and passionate feelings aroused by the warmth and erotic appeal of its beaches. At weekends, the sand was filled with people so physically handsome they could have earned a place in a classical Greek frieze. Yet if they dared to embrace each other or lie too close in the sand, beach inspectors, huge men with arms and legs like sides of beef, wearing white straw bowling hats and the body-covering bathing suits of the day, would pull them angrily apart. As a result, every cranny of the granite, wind-riddled cliffs with their mazes of caves, became hiding places for the most sexually determined. At night, the inspectors would cast their flashlights into the caves, sometimes disturbing a couple vigorously making love. Errol was twice flushed from these hiding places, only to dispose of the unwelcome visitor with a swift left uppercut to the genitals.

Back in the city, in the fly-blown, sticky Sydney summers, Puritanism clamped down on everyone. In the heat, men wore heavy gray suits, tight collars, narrow ties, and black patent leather shoes. Even their faces, traditionally bony and clean-cut and brown, were partly hidden by the turned down brims of the nationally worn somber gray felt hats. The ugly flat drone of politicians' speeches, the strictness and lack of fun in business life, the harshness of religious condemnation, the hatred of even the smallest perversity, and the sheer absence of any charm in the somber red brick and green copper domes of the public buildings helped to weigh the spirit down. Only the flash and sparkle of the harbor, the decks of a scudding yacht, the soft white sand and young healthy bodies in the white Australian sun gave relief and pleasure.

At eighteen, in 1927, Errol returned briefly to Hobart and enrolled at the University of Tasmania. He excelled in boxing, fencing, and swimming, but barely managed to scrape through his examinations. He lasted only a year. He went to the university dances wearing white tie and tails and smoking a cigarette through a long holder, in imitation of a photograph of his childhood idol, John Barrymore. All of the other boys were in black tuxedos. His date was his first serious girl friend, a pretty hairdresser from Melbourne named Pat Potter. Tall, willowy and ash blond, she resembled his mother as well as two of the women he later married, Nora Eddington and Pat Wymore. But he was by no means interested in dating her exclusively. A friend of his at the university recalls, "He was wickedly handsome, lazy, and cynical about his studies in those days. His mother leaving him alone so much and his father's peccadillos gave him little respect for the human race."

Errol had taken a biology course to please his father, but he proved to have no aptitude for it. This was not only a disappointment but an embarrassment to his father since Professor Flynn had announced to his fellow faculty members that Errol would undoubtedly follow in his footsteps.

In the summer of 1928, when he was on his way to a horse race, Errol ran into a boy who for four years became a close friend. Charlie Pilleau was a thin, bright, energetic "cobber" or companion who was Errol's age. They met in the men's room on Martin Place in the downtown section of Sydney. Errol said, "I'm on the spot, mate. I'm supposed to go to the track at Randwick today and my car's broken down. The bloody thing is stalled outside the post office."

Charlie replied, "Don't worry, cobber, I'll give you a lift." Errol said, "Thanks. And in return for your help, sport, I'll give you the hottest tip you ever had on a race. Do you have two hundred quid in your pocket?"

Charlie told him he did have that much to spend, wondering how Errol could possibly have known. But, Charlie announced, he was planning to buy his girl friend an engagement ring with the money. Errol told him no woman was worth two hundred pounds. But a bet on a good horse certainly was.

Errol told Charlie that a horse named Olive Bell was going at a hundred to one and that he could guarantee she would come in first. After the race, Charlie could come to his flat where there would be many chorus girls who would gladly help him spend his winnings.

Errol talked Charlie into giving him £150 to bet on the outsider. Charlie left Errol at the track and went to his girl friend's house. They turned the radio to the race. The announcer said, "It's Olive Bell! Olive Bell coming up on the outside! Olive Bell running neck in neck with the champ!" When Olive Bell was announced the winner, Charlie seized his girl and waltzed her around the room. What he did not know was that Errol, while ostensibly patting the horse on the behind, had inserted an enema of bomblike potency in its rectum and the poor creature had hurtled down the track as if a hundred devils were behind it, letting off a stream of ordure which effectively slowed the competition.

Errol was very fond of boxing. When the Oscar-winning actor Victor McLaglen was a boxing promoter in Sydney, he used to present Errol in exhibition matches at the Sydney Stadium on Friday nights. Errol often emerged the victor. Tricky, ruthless, and fast on his feet, he was a master of technique even at the age of seventeen.

He fought at the YMCA on Saturday afternoons, where a man named Hawkins encouraged him, promising to present him in Britain. And he also fought in Melbourne where he was coached by the Sharman troupe, a family of athletes who operated out of the Sydney Showground. They were rough, tough boxers, including the women. The mother and daughters could knock out any man who came up against them. They taught Errol the finer points of pugilism—and a few dirty tricks as well.

Sometimes, Errol would plunge into a wrestling match with one of the Sharman women and emerge mangled from the ordeal. The Sharmans lived in a tent. They encouraged boys to enter the ring and fight with the girls. In minutes, the boys would lie in the dust. The girls would take a bow and the audience would cheer.

Errol entered the New South Wales Amateur Boxing Competition well primed by the Sharmans. He was sure he had won the match and was jumping jubilantly up and down in the ring when he learned the judges' disagreeable decision: they ruled in favor of his opponent, Frank Scarf, because Errol had dodged about so rapidly Scarf hadn't been able to hit him.

With all his ventures, there were times when Errol was so poor that he had to live in a cave in a large forested area on the outskirts of Sydney. He shared the cave with a strange old man whose hair fell to his knees and whose beard joined it in a hopeless tangle. After a few months, Errol's outcrop of hair was equally junglelike, and he looked like the hero of *The Count of Monte Cristo* after imprisonment in the Château d'If. For money, he fished halfpennies from a wishing well and dipped them in a stolen pot of mercury to make them look like silver shilling pieces. With these, he would buy small amounts of food when he was unable to steal it. For several weeks, he and his companion lived on apples and half-empty bottles of beer which had been tossed out in the trash.

Finally, he tired of his appearance and went to an Italian barber. But when the haircut was finished, he skipped out without paying, brandishing an open razor which he took from the barber's table to prevent complaints. The barber pursued him with the account (the equivalent of about thirty cents) for years, until finally Errol sent him in lieu of payment a signed photograph from Hollywood with an inscription on the back saying that the photograph was to be given to the barber's daughter—whom he had seduced.

He had several narrow escapes. He was interested in a fifteen-year-old girl who lived with her grandmother. Since he knew the old lady was in bed with a broken arm and leg, Errol felt safe in going upstairs with the girl and enjoying her. He was in the middle of his visit when he heard a limping footstep on the stair. He jumped out of the window onto a metal awning designed to keep out the rain. He hit it so hard that the wooden supports splintered and he went right through the awning. He was wedged there, unable to go up or down. The old lady called the neighbors and they seized his legs, but still he would not move.

The awning gave way and he found himself sitting in the street in the middle of it. Finally, he wriggled loose, ran to the nearest tram, and tried to board it with a flying leap. He attacked the task with such energy that he was propelled clear through the tram and out the other side. He nursed a sore head for a week.

He concocted an elaborate plan to steal a ferryboat which plied the harbor of Sydney from Circular Quay to Kirribilli, a nearby suburb. He intended sailing it down the coast for some fishing. After the last passenger left at 2 A.M., the ferry was berthed on Kirribilli Wharf. He crept in, accompanied by three friends, and tried to get the ferry started. But there was a notice attached to the engine which read, "We have taken precautions. All fuel has been removed." Despondently, he and his friends spent the rest of the night tying tin cans to the tails of local stray dogs.

Errol and Charlie took off for dreamed-of Queensland in 1928. Errol caused a tremendous commotion. The editor of the Brisbane *Courier-Mail* had a favorite horse that was tethered outside the newspaper office. Errol stroked the beast and gave it sugar only to find himself kicked into a flying arc across the square. He soon obtained his revenge. In a new version of his racetrack trick, he bought a very large fireworks rocket, which, when lit, emitted a shower of sparks. He pushed the rocket into the horse's rear end and, with sparks flying from under its tail, it did everything except fly in its frantic progress through the city streets. It was never seen again.

At a bar in Cairns, Errol heard some talk about a gang of Chinese opium smugglers who were bringing in their wares from Hong Kong aboard a merchant vessel, the *Taiping*. He contacted a gang member and offered to take a small rented outboard motor boat to an agreed-upon point off the coast where the *Taiping* had dropped anchor—beyond the three-mile limit normally patrolled by customs officers.

He carried a hurricane lamp. Attached to it was a complicated device he rigged up, similar to the filters used for color photography. This contraption surrounded the lamp, enabling it to flash alternate green, red, and blue signals. When the Chinese were ready to drop the opium overboard, they semaphored Errol who responded with his own multicolored message. The code had been carefully worked out in advance.

The opium was wrapped in small silk containers and placed in muslin bags packed tight with salt. Three corks were attached by a string to the tops of the bags to enable them to float. When the salt dissolved upon contact with the water, the bags would naturally float on the surface.

As soon as an agreed-upon number of bags was visible in the moonlight, Errol, who was coasting along almost silently in the *Taiping*'s wake, stripped and dived overboard into the shark-infested waters while a friend stayed in the boat and took care of the rudder. With a knife between his teeth, in case he was attacked by sharks, Errol dived under the water and scooped up the bags one by one while only minimally disturbing the surface.

One night as he was dog-paddling, scooping up the bags, a sinister triangular black fin pierced the water not far from him. He just managed to scramble aboard the boat in time.

Errol was caught on one of these expeditions by a local Irish policeman who locked him up in a cell. The policeman was suspicious because his boat had come in without kerosene or provisions and obviously had not been out to sea for any length of time. Charlie was absent from this caper. When Charlie went to visit Errol, he found him sitting cheerfully on a box in the cell chatting with the policeman. Errol was saying to the Irishman, "Just think. You treat me like this, putting me in jail, and I was so considerate of you. I brought you a bottle of Irish whiskey."

The policeman said, "You're a liar, Flynn. You've never seen a bottle of Irish whiskey in your life."

"Oh yes, I have," Errol replied. "Just go and look. Charlie will show you where it is. It's under a tarpaulin in the cabin."

The policeman accompanied Charlie to the boat. Charlie lifted the tarpaulin and showed the bottle of whiskey. Astonished, the policeman returned with it, and soon was happily downing the liquor. Errol said, "I'll bet you can't finish the bottle." The Irishman, put on his mettle, drank every last drop.

As the cop staggered and leaned against the bars, Errol snatched the keys from his pocket, opened the cell door, pushed him in, and locked him up for the night. Then he fled north.

Errol sold the opium for the equivalent of fifteen hundred dollars with a 25 per cent commission. He spent the money quickly in the local bars and brothels.

He decided to arrange a fake welterweight boxing championship in which two well-worn pugs would be in competition. To add fun to the event, he disguised his own contender as a black islander. He obtained a treatment for syphilis known as Condy's Crystals, a horrible blend of potassiums of various kinds which, when dissolved and rubbed on the human skin, turned it completely black. For a fee of several pounds, the pug agreed to be dipped in a bath of this loathsome substance.

Announcing his contender as Bubu, the Black Bomber, Errol staged the fight with a local promoter in an open field at night. The field was lit by hurricane lamps slung from the branches of the overhanging eucalyptus trees. A large crowd of local "yobbos," or hicks, appeared, very drunk, cheering lustily their favorites in the fight. Both boxers wound up knocking each other out in the third round, and the fight was declared a draw. However, as he fell, the Black Bomber was seen to be not so black after all. Some of the pigment had been left off his feet.

With a "Let's get out of here quick!" Errol rushed Charlie into his beaten-up car. They made a getaway down the road in a cloud of dust, leaving the unfortunate promoter to face the music in court the following morning. The Black Bomber remained black for a very long time.

In New South Wales again, Errol had to make his living by more humdrum means. He and Charlie worked in a bottling plant near the town of Kyogle. Their job involved sniffing used bottles to see if they had had kerosene or some other poisonous substance in them; if they had not, then they could be used as fresh bottles. The two men had to put their noses through the tops of the bottles and sniff deeply. If a bottle was contaminated, they would smash it against a wheel and drop the pieces in a box. If the bottle was clean, or had contained only milk or some similarly harmless substance, they would wash it in a tub and put a seal on it with the bottle company's name.

They kept a tally of the number of bottles they had handled by making a mark for each one on the dirt floor of the shed in which they were working. Errol became impatient after two hours of the work and asked Charlie to add some marks in the dirt to his tally to make it appear he had done more than his share. At the end of the day Errol had a large colored ring around his nose which refused to come off despite the most desperate scrubbing. Charlie also had a ring around his nose. When they walked into the trolley car to go to Kyogle that night, the passengers laughed at the strange spectacle of the two disfigured youths. Walking down the street or going to the local pub proved to be a similar ordeal.

In Brisbane, Queensland, Errol used to visit a fortuneteller at the local fairgrounds. She was festooned in beads and wore a robe decorated with the sun, moon, and stars. Usually, she would tell him that his immediate future involved a romance with a woman who had occult powers. He would enter her tent and fulfill her as well as her prophecy.

He loved the atmosphere at night on the Brisbane Bridge. The girls who were available for a price would sway up and down opposite sides of the bridge, dressed very primly in case the police should see them. When a man approached them, they would say, demurely, "How much will you pay for my flowers?" and hold up a small bouquet. The police could do nothing about it.

Errol would thread his way past the streetcars and automobiles and bicycles across the bridge to confer with the girls on both sides. They would call out to each other over the traffic, vying for the favors of the handsome young man with the cheerful grin and no money in his pockets. He would return to Charlie at dawn announcing that he had three "naughties" with the girls of his choice. Then he would empty his pockets of large sums of money which the prostitutes had paid him for his services in bed.

Errol liked to go to a particular ball that was held strictly for the wealthy society of the time. He would stand outside in a borrowed tuxedo and say to the lords and ladies as they stepped from the limousines, "Tickets, please." They would hand him the tickets and ask him why he didn't return the stubs. He said these were "not necessary." After he had collected from two or three couples, he would disappear behind the building. Then he would return in his tuxedo and sail into the hall with his latest girl friend and two or three others, all holding tickets in their hands.

Sometimes, as he had at school, Errol would suggest a "different" strain. Charles Pilleau recalls:

> He said to me one day, "Have you ever tried having sex with men?" I said, "No." He then went on and added, "Why don't you try it? It's an exciting and unusual adventure." I told him I had no interest in it whatever. He laughed that laugh of his and shrugged.

When money ran short, either in Brisbane or Sydney, Errol had several ways of coping. He would move into a rooming house and sell off all the doormats to anyone who would buy them. On rainy days, he and a friend would take the umbrellas people stored in racks at the entrances of the department stores and would sell them in the pubs for a few shillings apiece to people who had been left umbrellaless.

When he played crap, Errol would begin the game with, "Heads I win and tails you lose." Invariably, he would win and would move very fast down the street before the loser realized what had happened.

Despite his numerous escapades, Errol had a way of ingratiating himself. Ken Hunter-Kerr recalls:

> He was a little bit stagy, admittedly: when he entered a room and was introduced to people he hadn't met before, he bowed; he rather noticeably attracted attention without perhaps intending to. He was very formal with the "how do you do's"; he would kiss his hostess' hand which in those days the average young man didn't do; some people scoffed; some said, he genuinely means it; to some it seemed like an affectation, but not to many. His behavior was so natural that even to average people it seemed almost normal.

Three

In 1928, gold strikes in New Guinea attracted Errol's attention, and he told all his friends to come with him and get rich. Busy at various occupations, they were unable to do so. With a small sum of stolen money, he sailed north to the nearby tropical island of New Britain and spent a useless period there doing little more than dancing to the Tropical Troubadours at the Kokopo Hotel in Rabaul or bumming through various useless jobs in and out of the jungle. At one stage, his friend Edward Ashley Cooper recalls, he actually obtained the job of district officer in a small town when the official concerned left on vacation. But the job only lasted a few days when he was found to be trading in native labor on the side.

He worked in a gas station and as a miner but did not find gold. The islands captivated him nevertheless. The odd, formal colonial social life, the tin roofs and gimcrack buildings, girls with flowered dresses and parasols framed against palm-fringed bays, ugly commercial buildings set down on the edge of jungles, and men in pith helmets and shorts created a pleasant picture of indolence and trop-

ical ease. Rabaul on the island of New Britain was an especially
pretty sight: a perfectly formed volcanic peak rose near the edge of
the emerald water of the harbor, which shone back inverted reflec-
tions of the white cruising ships of the P&O Line and the more modest local vessels. The great tin sheds of the customs office, the squat
and ungainly town hall, and the dusty streets threaded through by
battered Fords fascinated him.

His companion at the time was not a particular woman but a
collection of stories by Jack London, who rapidly became his idol
and whose life in some ways compared with his. He loved the thrust
of high adventure in the tales, the constantly moving swiftness of the
sentences, the surge of the dramatic episodes, the powerful theme of
man against nature.

Errol's chief problem in New Britain was the rainy season. The
rain was like a dense curtain that smothered the vegetation and
brought sinister things crawling from the undergrowth. Just as he
had dreaded the rain in Hobart, he dreaded it here. It once more
gave him terrible headaches that made him yell out in agony.
Friends remember that he would groan and hold his head from the
first moment the raindrops that heralded the monsoon thudded on
the thick green leaves. And when the downpour began, he flung himself on his bed, and the tears of pain and terror streamed down his
cheeks.

Once Errol transferred to the more sinister land of New Guinea,
his life became harder and more grueling. It was so vast an island
that it could have swallowed California, Washington, and Oregon
without experiencing indigestion. New Guinea was a suffocating hell
of swamps, impenetrable jungles, and jagged mountain ranges.
Through much of the year, the temperature was over ninety degrees
and the humidity was so intense it seemed to be raining indoors. A
man would rise in the morning and brush aside his mosquito net for
a quick shower under a rusty pump, only to find himself covered
with leeches which he would have to burn off with cigarettes. Large
and alarming insects flew about, banging themselves against bare
light bulbs. Spiders as big as gloves would crawl on windows in the
middle of dinner parties.

In the hinterland, headhunters lingered, ready to kill and devour
any stray natives who wandered off the path. Stuffed human heads
were offered in trade for fishhooks, safety-razor blades, empty ciga-

rette tins, or colorful fabrics to be used for lap-laps or loincloths. Deadly arrows were tipped with carved cassowary breastbones and cassowary claws and barbed porcupine quills or spines from the dorsal fins of fish. The shafts, often made of wild sugar cane, were not feathered; the flight of such arrows was almost always true to the mark, and the death toll was high.

But despite the terror of New Guinea, the black magic rituals and eerie drums that echoed through the hills, the island offered much exotic beauty. The D'Alberti Creeper was an astonishing flower that grew from the root to the crown of the forest trees, swathing them in ropes and coils the color of fire. A hundred feet tall, the creepers bridged glades and shed flourishes of the crimson blossoms in the clearings. Orchids grew by the thousand, wild and brilliant, and housewives festooned their verandas with the white and pink and yellow and brown blossoms. Lilies were as large as summer hats, their pistils the size of bananas.

The extreme exoticism of the environment fascinated Errol. He loved the town of Salamaua's hotel, which was on stilts so precarious that during squalls it would rock violently to and fro like a ship at sea and the guests would carry their beds into the garden. He enjoyed dances conducted by hurricane lamp to the tune of a wind-up phonograph, and magic shows at the children's schools when he helped out the Chinese magicians with concealed devices.

He made his living largely by recruiting native labor for trips to and from the gold fields. Crossing the jungle terrain was a major ordeal. Squadrons of mosquitoes attacked the flesh. Malaria and black-water fever parasites lurked in the streams. Food and drink grew moldy in a matter of hours. Fungus settled on the skin, and lice crawled in the body hairs.

Men were men in New Guinea. Few white women existed there, and there was little to do except get drunk and fornicate with the native women. Errol tried to find excitement running a small sloop up and down the river and helping a visiting National Geographic team.

Errol planned to import some of the headhunters to Sydney, but he was quickly disabused of this idea when, on a preliminary venture, an arrow went through his hat. Instead, he took some of his gold and returned to the more moderate climes of New South Wales.

He stayed in Sydney long enough to buy and fit up a beaten-up yawl called the *Sirocco* for a pleasure trip back to New Guinea. His mother had returned briefly to Australia. She grew so impatient with his pleas she grudgingly supplied the three hundred dollars he needed to make the purchase.

Almost fifty years old, the vessel was in very poor condition and had to be extensively refitted. Errol stole some loose canvas left by a Sydney traveling circus and raised it as sails.

To earn additional money for the trip, Errol obtained a job modeling suits for R. C. Hargon, Ltd., and that became his first screen exposure: their advertisements were flashed on the screens of motion picture theatres between the first and second half of the bill.

In February 1930, at age twenty-one, Errol and four friends took off into Sydney Harbor on the first leg of the voyage to New Guinea only to be hit by a wind so violent they almost rammed into the northernmost headland of the entrance. Following much refitting, they proceeded on a voyage which took them a full six months. The young men, Trelawney Adams, Ken Hunter-Kerr, Charlie Pilleau (also known as Charlie Burt), and Rex Long-Innes, were inexperienced sailors and could barely tell port from starboard. They spent as much time as possible wenching and drinking in the local ports or cheating at poker sufficiently to earn enough to repair the miserably choking engine of the vessel. They charmed their way north, swimming, descending on islands in the Great Barrier Reef to seduce the local talent, and enjoying horse races, rodeos, and lassoing cattle. In one town, a touring troupe of girls came aboard for a binge, and in another the entire group wound up in jail after making off with stolen gold dust.

Sirocco sailed comfortably up the mountainous coast of New Guinea and made landfall in Port Moresby in late August.

Errol began a long career of writing in New Guinea. He contributed a series of articles to *The Bulletin,* Australia's venerated weekly newspaper, a hideous legal-sized publication of pink and white paper with tiny cramped print, edited out of a dusty rabbit warren of offices in Sydney. People who wanted to be paid for their contributions had to arrive at the office and ask for the money in person.

His articles were crisply written and covered such pressing matters as the tobacco tariff, the medicine men and their bizarre seances in which they would bring dogs back to life.

Errol also wrote of the terrifying activities of the Kuku-Kukus Tribe in the jungle. He described their stone-age customs in interesting detail. He told of an episode in the village of Hanuabada, near Port Moresby:

> The medical officer . . . was confronted by a deaf and dumb native. That native had been as garrulous and able to hear as any other Papuan a week or so previous, so the M.O. inquired of the village constable how he became affected. "Well," answered the gentleman cautiously, "I understand it was a punishment for blasphemy. The man would not listen to the talk of Tau, the missionary, and one day, in Tau's presence, he tore a page from the Bible to use as cigarette paper. So Tau said he would ask God to strike him deaf and dumb. And God did."

Errol wrote colorfully of the people known as the Goiaribari:

> In addition to being filthy in all their habits, and eaters of snakes, snails, and crocodiles, their treatment of their womenfolk relegates them to a cultural status little above that of the beast. A Coiaribari will prostitute his wife and daughter to anyone for three sticks of trade tobacco, sell her outright to the highest bidder, or hire her out by the week or month. It is necessary that young men of this tribe about to marry should first do some brave deed. This is how he usually qualifies: He purchases from her father, who knows exactly what will happen to her, a girl about twelve years old, and then gathers round him six or seven cronies. The party, armed with spears, stone axes and other weapons, journey into the bush for a week or longer. The girl is, for several days, subjected to unmentionable barbarities. Then, at last, the stalwart braves form a circle about her and, at a signal, all rush in to hack and batter her to pulp. She is then cut into small pieces, cooked in sections of bamboo and eaten. Such a case occurred only a month ago and the murderers are still at large.

During 1931 and part of 1932, Errol was in the Port Moresby area growing tobacco on a fifteen-acre lease at the nearby Laloki Plantation. There, he became friendly with a genial official named Jack Hides and Hides's sister-in-law Eileen, a nurse at the European hospital. He spent much of his time looking futilely for female company, swimming in the local baths, playing cards with the hatchet-faced local policeman or boxing in exhibition matches with Hides. He piled up an enormous number of debts. When a friend of his, Mrs. Giblin, won a lease on a gold mine at Wau, a small local settlement, in a lottery, she asked Errol to recruit some native labor and work the claim for her. Instead of using the shillings she had given him to acquire the native boys, he resorted to his old trick and dipped halfpennies in quicksilver as imitation shillings. The lease was a failure and finally was sold by Mrs. Giblin for the equivalent of ten thousand dollars.

He became fascinated in 1932 by the German population in Rabaul. New Guinea had for many years been in part a German colony. And a number of Germans had moved to New Britain, where they had a German club, a German beer hall, and occasional concerts of German music. Errol liked to enjoy a stein of beer with these people. A German friend of his at the time, Carl Schencke, recalls:

> It was at the time when we were aware of the first stirrings of Nazism in Europe. Many of us were Jews and were afraid of what was coming. Errol was excited by the whole German mystique, by the sexual fascination of Nazism. I regret to say it but I did not blame him at the time.

The basis of another abiding interest was discovered that same year. Two American film-makers, George Dromgold and James Shackleford, arrived in Port Moresby to film background footage for jungle movies. They hired a lugger, the *Veimauri,* from a Captain Fitch, and made a coastal voyage past Port Moresby to the southernmost tip of New Guinea. They obtained the governor's permission to film natives in simulated war and action scenes, but they were forbidden to stage native combat involving hand to hand fights, to depict weapons in native hands, to show natives laying hands on white men, or to show white women with natives in any circumstances. They shot advancing canoes, a mass simulated attack by hill tribes on a marine village, scenes of a war canoe attacking the movie hero's lugger, and the looting of a shipwreck on a reef, as well as pearl-diving sequences.

In their book, *Two Lugs on a Lugger* (Hutchinson, London, 1938) Dromgold wrote:

> Our last evening in Port Moresby proved to be a very pleasant one despite . . . a torrential downpour which lasted through the night. Dinner with Mr. William Dupaine and family at their comfortable home alongside the Burns-Philp Building where Mr. Dupaine presides over the firm's local business.

During the evening a young chap by the name of Errol Flynn dropped in, or to be more explicit he practically washed in, for the sloping street before the house was a rushing torrent at the time of his arrival. He appeared to be quite interested in moving pictures and asked us many questions about Hollywood's studios and personalities.

On one of his visits to Sydney in 1932, Errol heard that the best-known film-making team in Australia, Charles and Elsa Chauvel, were planning to make *In the Wake of the Bounty:* the story of the *Bounty* mutineers. There are several versions of the way in which he obtained the part of Fletcher Christian, his long dead ancestor. Charles Chauvel said he had seen a photograph of Errol with a wrecked boat on the Queensland coast. Elsa Chauvel remembers her husband running into him in a bar in Sydney. The casting director, John Warwick, says he spotted Errol's physique at Bondi Beach. Charlie Pilleau remembers a more colorful story:

While visiting Melbourne, Errol was told that Elsa Chauvel had been attending a period play when she saw a man on the stage whom she was convinced was perfect for the part of Fletcher Christian. She had gone backstage and talked to the man, John Hampden, inviting him to come to Sydney to sign the contract the following week. He agreed to arrive by train on that Sunday.

Errol was several steps ahead of him. When Hampden arrived on the train, he was greeted by two of Errol's friends, one disguised as a chauffeur, the other as a studio official. The two men greeted Hampden warmly then took his luggage and drove him over to the offices of Universal Studios, where Errol knew the janitor.

Hampden expressed surprise that the office was open on Sunday. But the two men said that Errol Flynn, the chief executive, would be at his office in person to greet the new arrival.

Each office door had a gold wooden marker indicating the name and title of the occupant. Errol had fashioned one with the aid of a carpenter and a coat of paint and had put it on the door of the men's room, with his name and imaginary position inscribed on it.

When John Hampden arrived with the two men, Errol came out of the men's room and greeted them. He said, "Delighted you're here, Mr. Hampden. Do come in. But no. You look very tired. Why don't you go to your hotel and rest, and we'll sign the contract tomorrow."

Hampden thanked him and the "chauffeur" and "executive" took

him to the hotel they had selected. They had already removed the room telephone. They locked him in firmly.

Errol knew that the Chauvels were shooting a picture that Sunday at Cinesound Studios. Chauvel was on the sound stage and Elsa was in her office. Errol, after bribing a couple of officials along the way, contrived to enter her office.

"Who are you?" she asked him as he walked in.

He fell to his knees in an exact replica of a gesture made in the period play by John Hampden and said, "Don't you recognize me? It's me, Hampden."

"Oh!" Elsa exclaimed. "You look so different without your makeup and costume."

Errol had little time to waste. "Where's the contract?" he asked.

She handed it to him. He signed it, "Errol Flynn."

"But I thought your name was John Hampden," Elsa Chauvel said.

"That's my stage name!" he replied.

A few hours later, the irate John Hampden managed to get out of the hotel. By this time, Errol was on the train to Melbourne. Elsa tried to get out of the contract. But it was too late. He called in his solicitors, Campbell, Campbell, and Campbell, who pointed out that a contract was a contract was a contract. The Chauvels had no alternative but to use Errol in the picture.

Errol proved to be strong-willed on the set of the movie, insisting on lines being changed to suit his character. He acted with a naturalness and ease which surprised everyone. Despite the amateurism of the direction, he emerged with credit, giving a convincing portrait of anger and desperation which compares interestingly with Clark Gable's later interpretation of the same role. The reviews were favorable. Errol's acting was called "convincing and natural." Only his own stately *Bulletin* panned him and the picture. But the film made little money, since Australians preferred Hollywood movies.

Errol seemed not to be disappointed. He did not take his brief movie appearance seriously. Instead, he became involved in a romantic affair with a society woman. She taught him oral sex, and arranged for him to remove her pearls so that she could collect the insurance money and escape from her husband. Soon the pearls and he disappeared rapidly to Queensland, where he obtained a job "lamb-

ing the hogget." This involved desexing lambs by cutting open the scrota and sucking out the testicles into the mouth. Errol varied this disagreeable activity with dalliance with the daughter of the sheep rancher. Surprised by her father, he fled to New Guinea with the pearls.

He spent much of 1933 in Salamaua. It was there he began to keep a diary, written in a composition book which was cut in half in order to fit into the pocket of his bush jacket. He described the life of the island in more detail but with less proficiency than he had done in his earlier articles for the *Bulletin*. A typical excerpt reads:

> Essay on Several Don'ts in "The Art and Niceties of Seduction." Compromising positions to avoid—avenues of escape must be arranged first. Avoid betraying astonishment at credulity of victim— even in the dark. Draw analogy between the mention of the word marriage and he who uses dynamite in exasperation after having failed with dry fly. Use of alcohol is to be deprecated except as a last resort.

He also wrote a description of a mission he visited:

> Colored prints of Christ are regarding me dolefully from every angle in the room. He is portrayed in a large variety of postures. Rebuking (or confusing) the Elders who have the longest and whitest beards I've ever seen; conferring blessings, etc.; why is that Christ is never shown smiling? He must have laughed sometimes.

He talked of his joy in reading, a joy which remained with him to the end of his life:

> One can never become a skillful reader, or acquire the ability to appreciate books, unless once first cultivates a keen sense of the relative value of things; for this sense is the quintessence of true education and culture. To learn what is worth one's while is the largest part of the Art of Life.
>
> Time, for example, just one hour of time is far more important than money, for time is life. Whenever you waste your time over printed words that neither enlighten or amuse you, you are in a sense, committing suicide. The value, the intrinsic value, of our actions, emotions, thoughts, possessions, occupations, of the manner in which we are living; this is the first thing to be determined; for unless we are *satisfied* that any of these things have a true value, even if

only relative, our lives are futile, and there is no more hopeless reali-
zation than this.

. . .

Have just finished reading "The Good Companions." Wonderful.
Can Priestley ask for anything more from life than that gift of expression? I felt I knew personally every one of these characters at the
end. Especially Micham Moreton—if he had been drawn from old
Simpson, ex-actor-manager, now sandalwood king in Papua, he
couldn't have been described more faithfully.

The most significant passage in the diary reflects a new fascination
with the Orient:

I am going to China because I wish to live deliberately. New
Guinea offers me, it is true, satisfaction for the tastes I have acquired
which only leisure can satisfy. I am leaving economic security and I
am leaving it deliberately.

By going off to China with a paltry few pounds and no knowledge
of what life has in store for me there, I believe that I am going to
front the essentials of life to see if I can learn what it has to teach
and above all not to discover, when I come to die, that I have not
lived.

We fritter our lives away in detail but I am not going to do this. I
am going to live deeply, to acknowledge not one of the so-called social forces which hold our lives in thrall and reduce us to economic
dependency. The best part of life is spent in earning money in order
to enjoy a questionable liberty during the least valuable part of it.

. . .

To hell with money! Pursuit of it is not going to mould my life for
me. I am going to live sturdily and Spartan like; to drive life into a
corner and reduce it to its lowest terms, and if I find it mean, then
I'll know its meanness, and if I find it sublime I shall know it by experience, and not make wistful conjectures about it, conjured up by
illustrated magazines. I refuse to accept the ideology of a business
world which believes that man at hard labour is the noblest work of
God. Leisure to use as I think fit!

By 1933, Errol was tired of New Guinea. Among his few consola-
tions were letters from his father, now professor of biology at the
Queen's University, Belfast. Charlie Pilleau joined him for a time;
Pilleau recalls:

It was hot, stinking, nothing but sandflies and blowflies. We seemed to be running into an endless nothingness. I said, "Let's go back. Back to civilisation. At least we can get a bath, fresh clothes, food that's better than pig shit." And he replied, "It's an adventure. What does it matter if we eat raw fish?" But then he finally had enough. One night we were on a river boat. It was very late, no stars or moon, the heat suffocating. He smoked for a while in silence and suddenly he said, "I've had it here, with this God forsaken place. It took God six days to create the world. Late on Saturday night, God said, 'I'll take all the trees and mountains and swamps that are no good, that are left over from everywhere else and I'll make New Guinea with them.'" I'll never forget Errol saying that.

If Errol had any lingering doubts about his departure from New Guinea, they were quickly settled. His career as a slave trader or "blackbirder" came to a rapid end when members of a savage tribe realized they had been cheated and put a curse on him. He fled, declining to pay his bill at the Salamaua Hotel. When the owners who had befriended him asked him for the money, he instead offered to leave his large trunk as "security."

Years later, the couple went to a shack in the jungle to see a film without knowing what it was. They were astonished when their former star boarder appeared on the screen, waving a cutlass as Captain Blood. Instantly, they decided to return to the hotel and examine the trunk, which had lain in the cellar gathering mold for two years.

They managed to open the rusty lock. They discovered stuffed into the trunk, all of the missing hotel sheets and towels. Underneath the moldy linen they found the sawed-off diary.

There was a warrant out for Errol's arrest on charges of illegally procuring native labor when he left New Guinea for neighboring New Britain. In April 1933, he persuaded an Australian woman in Salamaua to let him sail her lugger to Rabaul, where, he said, he would trade on her behalf.

Instead, he stole the vessel and hired a crew of three, whom he paid in false coin. On his way across, the lugger was hit by a freak storm, and driven onto a reef. She foundered. Errol saved his own life while letting the three native crewmen drown.

Drenched to the skin, exhausted, his clothes in shreds, Errol clambered up the side of a cliff on the northern coast of New Britain. His knife had vanished in the shipwreck; he had to force his way through the undergrowth with his hands. Fortunately, he was immensely strong, with a wrestler's arms. But still, the vegetation swarmed in, a menacing green; he feared he would be lost forever.

Just as he was abandoning hope, the storm cleared up. He saw a sudden glimmer—a beam slanting through an unexpected jungle clearing. He heard the welcome babble of native voices. He stumbled into watery sunlight.

He was in a small native village. Lepers with their strange, silvery skins and stunted limbs wandered about. Almost at once Errol became aware of an extraordinary presence: a powerful man standing against the trees. He was six feet tall and weighed over two hundred and thirty pounds. He had a shock of light brown hair shot through with reddish gold. His eyes were enormous, penetrating, a clear sharp blue. His beard was fair and covered most of his face. He was clad in khaki-colored tropical clothes, with puttees and heavy brown leather boots. A heroic belly swelled over his trouser belt. A deep scar slashed one cheek beginning on the cheekbone, and a vertical slit on one thumb ran from the knuckle to the base. When he smiled, he had a gap between his front teeth. Thick glasses in horn rims gave him a mysterious, almost sinister look.

The man greeted Errol in a loud, clear, aggressive, utterly commanding voice: the most riveting sound Errol had ever heard. In a thick Austrian accent, he announced himself as Dr. Hermann Friedrich Erben. Errol responded with his own name—telling of the near fatal mishap on the reef and saying weakly, that he had "to get out of the country at once." Erben was impressed by this ragged castaway's looks, presence, intelligence, bearing.

It was a momentous meeting. Dr. Erben was to become a forceful and extraordinary influence on Errol's life from that moment. It was indeed a touch of fate that they should have met on that particular day when Errol was on the verge of going to the larger world. The twenty-four-year-old man was still raw and unformed, politically ignorant, cynical about everything. He was open to influence and eager for experience. And he was overpowered at that moment by the most amazing personality he would ever meet.

Four

Dr. Hermann Friedrich Erben was one of the most important and ingenious Nazi agents of the twentieth century. He was also a pioneer in the field of tropical medicine, an adventurer of the seven seas, a soldier of fortune, and a legionnaire of the human spirit whose loyalties could be divided whenever he was in danger and who many times turned double agent on behalf of America when he found it convenient. His anti-Semitism and love of Hitler were the overpowering impulses of his life. A lesser but still powerful impulse caused him to mystify, disturb, and confuse the FBI, the State Department, the military and naval intelligence branches, and the police of several countries.

At the time Errol met him, in April 1933, Erben was a passenger aboard the North German Lloyd *Friderun,* a 2,464-ton tramp steamer that wallowed like a sick whale through the South Seas, picking up and delivering mail, small amounts of cargo, and copra.

Erben had been born in Vienna, Austria, on November 15, 1897. From the first, his character was marked by a mischievous humor, a diabolically brilliant intelligence, and an antic, cynical adventurousness. He served as a lieutenant in the Austrian field artillery reserve against Britain and America in World War I and was honorably discharged in 1918. He grew up in the fiercely anti-Semitic atmosphere of Vienna that also stimulated Hitler. A recurrent theme of the many Washington files stamped HF ERBEN—ESPIONAGE is his manic hatred of the English. He was reported dead in action, and in an incident that became legendary in Vienna, walked into his astonished family days after his name appeared on the death lists.

Erben worked for a time at Count Sascha Kolowrat's movie studios, Saschafilm, in Vienna, as a doctor for the crew and actors. There he treated two people prominent in Errol's life: the actress Lili Damita, who married Errol, and Errol's best-known director, Michael Curtiz. Erben graduated from the medical school of the University of Vienna and worked as a tropical-medicine specialist abroad. He claimed to have worked for the Rockefeller Institute and the Australian Department of Aborigines, although neither body has any record of his employment. He traveled to Queensland in Australia to study rare diseases and took home with him to Vienna a rare, cockroachlike creature preserved in a glass jar. He sailed to South America for the Pacific Institute of Tropical Medicine's revered Dr. Alfred C. Reed.

And along with his important journeys in search of the origins and symptoms of leprosy, polio, and yaws, work which could have made him a world figure in science, some streak of perversity in him drove him to a profoundly different career. He joined the Nazi Party in 1922. This was one year before Himmler—who later became, as head of the Gestapo, his supreme commander. He once boasted he was in prison for three months in Vienna by mistake for Hitler, to whom, in his younger days, he bore a very marked resemblance.

The Nazi Party became illegal in 1923. He rejoined the party on July 23, 1926, and was issued a new Austrian party card.

Two years before he rejoined the party, Erben took up residence in America. He became a citizen five days before his thirty-third birthday, on November 10, 1930, in San Francisco, swearing allegiance to a country he almost consistently betrayed from that moment on.

During the early 1930s, Dr. Erben began a series of feverish battles with the State Department passport division. He was working for the Pacific Institute of Tropical Medicine attached to the University of California in San Francisco in 1930–31. On a voyage for the Institute aboard the *West Notus* in Montevideo, Uruguay, he obtained a new passport. But this was strictly illegal, since he already had one. He was accused of securing his second passport on false pretenses. He claimed that he had forwarded the original to Louisiana in connection with his application to become a doctor there, but this statement was regarded with suspicion. It was believed he had obtained the second passport in order to travel freely as a drug smuggler if the first one should be impounded.

In 1932, he sailed from Italy to China aboard the Dollar Lines vessel *President Garfield*. An attractive investigator for the Federal Bureau of Narcotics named Helen Haskin, disguised as an Italian government publicity woman, was aboard to find out the particulars of Dr. Erben's alleged trading in morphine. She flirted with him and made an assignation with him in his cabin. He proposed marriage to her, despite the fact that he was already married, claiming he had considerable sources of income. When pressed to reveal what these sources were, he told her, she said, that he was dealing with narcotics in Marseilles, Manila, Shanghai, and Singapore and that these insured his future financially. Erben was posing as a White Russian: he apparently sensed that she was an agent, because he later claimed that her entire story was based on her fury at being rejected by him. But her account convinced the authorities and Erben remained on the proclaimed list of suspected drug smugglers for six years.

In Shanghai, Erben's closest friend was Dr. Albert von Miorini, a former classmate of his at the University of Vienna. Von Miorini had himself been suspected of drug smuggling and Gestapo work for many years. His chamber music evenings were famous in Shanghai. In later years, they were attended by an extraordinary group of people, including Erben himself: Gerhardt Kahner, the Gestapo chief of Shanghai; Richard Sorge, famous spy for Russia against Japan; and Ignatius Trebitsch Lincoln, celebrated World War I agent and British MP who had become a Buddhist monk as Abbot Chao Kung.

Erben was a man after Errol's own heart. He evidently relished running two steps ahead of the law, existing cheerfully in the shadow of the world's suspicions. He was obsessed by the sea. He loved exotic ports and ships. Consider the list of some vessels he sailed on: *Parrakoola, Ussukuma, Koko Maru, Heiyo Maru, Chichibu Maru, West Mahwah, Triton, West Notus, Esperanza, Friderun, City of Rayville, Steel Seafarer, Conte Verde, Sarcoxie.*

Erben had a habit, annoying to consular officials, of shaving his beard or growing it again after new passport photographs were taken, so that he was barely recognizable. Like a figure in an animated cartoon, he seemed to be in a permanent state of fluidity and self-concealment, mischievously evading arrest, a professional man of mystery, flitting like a witty, dangerous shadow round the darkest edges of the world.

Shortly before he met Errol in 1933, Erben had sailed from San Francisco to Shanghai. Only three days after he arrived, he had to leave because the police were probing into his drug activities. A friend who was in charge of North German Lloyd's offices arranged for him to get away aboard the *Friderun* bound for New Guinea and South Sea ports. He used the opportunity to take many films and still photographs of New Guinea tribesmen, and to confer with village doctors on the treatment of tropical diseases.

The idea of meeting an exotic Nazi scientist, explorer, and wild adventurer excited Errol. He wrote in an early letter to his father (May 8, 1933) "Nürmunger [his nickname for Erben] will take a Nazi belt to hit a Communist . . . but he will still devote himself to medicine."

He and Erben had much in common. Errol inherited his anti-Semitism from his mother, but his mother was not alone in hating Jews. Tasmania was as racist as Austria. In the early days of the colony, white settlers wiped out virtually every Aborigine in the horrifying Black Wars. For almost two centuries, Australia maintained an all-white policy in defiance of every principle of democracy. In Hobart, Jews were tortured at school, eliminated from businesses if found out. They were forbidden to work in politics or the police department, and their shops and offices were smashed by hoodlums. There were strange, militaristic clubs whose members donned uniforms and jackboots—almost like Nazis themselves. Australia emphasized physical strength and despised traditional culture. It was filled with disgruntled Irish expatriates. The country, male-dominated, chauvinist, worshiping the male body, had an undercurrent of sadomasochistic repressed homosexuality to which Errol responded. It was a breeding ground of incipient fascism: Errol, like many Australians, associated Jews with decadent Europe; with authority.

He had his own hatred of democratic authority thanks to the repression he had felt in provincial Hobart. He despised Western society with its safe standards and humdrum morals. As an Australian colonial of Irish extraction, he certainly had no love of the British. He could easily be a friend to someone steeped in Nazi philosophy: he too enjoyed the discipline of the body, military uniforms, the philosophy of Nietzsche, the somber romanticism of Wagner's music.

For two days, Errol hid out with Erben, watching fascinated as the doctor worked on the sick and dying. It is one of the most incredible aspects of Erben's character that he belonged to the most murderous of political groups and at the same time devoted himself utterly to the saving of life. It was as though Himmler and Dr. Schweitzer had been combined in one personality.

Errol was hypnotized and enthralled by the sight of the big German, in his pith helmet, toiling in the primitive huts in the midst of the dense jungle, filled with chattering birds, huge moths and crawling lizards, and the pale gray silvery lepers. But he had to get out of the country as soon as possible. He would have been in jeopardy if it had been found out that he had allowed his crew to drown while he escaped from the wreck of his lugger. Fortunately, Erben had to return to the *Friderun,* which was due to be back in Rabaul in less than a week.

They sailed together on the *Friderun* to Rabaul, where Errol miraculously obtained a passport despite his lack of identification papers. Errol's passport was issued on April 21, and that very same afternoon, at 4 P.M., he was back on board the *Friderun,* bound for Hong Kong with Erben on Hitler's birthday.

And how did Errol get onto the *Friderun* without funds? Erben was a close friend of the ship's captain. He got Errol aboard by a technical device of great ingenuity: as a distressed Australian seaman. Vessels at sea were not able to refuse distressed seamen, but in this case, Erben's influence was needed because Errol had no seaman's protection certificate in his possession.

The day after the two men left, the police in Rabaul checked the wreck, made their deductions about the drowning of the crew whose bodies were found washed ashore several miles up the coast, and turned up at the agency handling the *Friderun* for North German Lloyd with a warrant for Errol's arrest. Local records show that the warrant remained in existence for many years, but that every effort to have the American government act upon manslaughter charges failed.

Errol cabled his father in Northern Ireland and asked him to send funds to Hong Kong. They were waiting for him when he arrived on May 5.

Errol was overwhelmed by Hong Kong. In 1933, the island colony was at the height of its raffish corrupt beauty. The papers were full of the rise of Hitler. During the four days he was there, Errol met an individual who, though he never saw him again, was a major influence on Errol's life. The man was Abbot Chao Kung. His background was amazing. He was born Ignatius Trebitsch Lincoln in Hungary in 1879 and was educated as a rabbi. Converted to the Lutheran Church, he then changed his religion again and became the Anglican curate of Appledore, a village in Kent, England. He became the secretary to the chocolate tycoon, Seebohm Rowntree, and amazingly rose to be member of Parliament for Darlington in 1910. During World War I, he became a German agent and served three years in prison for forgery. In Shanghai, he was involved in double agentry between government and revolutionary forces. His son was executed for murder. In 1931, he changed his name to Chao Kung and became a Buddhist monk at a monastery near Peiping.

When Errol met him, Chao Kung was on his way back to Shanghai after an unsuccessful trip to Germany to establish a Buddhist monastery there. He was intensely pro-Nazi and believed that Hitler would be the savior of the world. Along with Erben, he became a prime mover in Errol's linking up with the Nazis at the time.

On May 9, Errol and Erben sailed aboard the Messageries Maritimes liner *D'Artagnan* for Saigon in French Indochina. They visited friends in the colonial service. They met French Foreign Legion soldiers, former criminals; Errol questioned these men closely on the free and dangerous life they led, thinking for a moment he might want to become one of them. There was something irresistible about the idea of men in uniform who owed allegiance only to themselves.

He thrilled the Saigon ladies by giving high-diving exhibitions in an elegant swimming pool, twisting and turning his body and double somersaulting from each of the four diving boards. He not only conquered their hearts but their racquets by beating them at excellent games of tennis.

From Saigon—talking of life as discipline and challenge and struggle—the two men sailed to Colombo in Ceylon where they visited the Hagenbeck Wild Animal Reserve and took photographs. Hagenbeck, the owner, specialized in acclimatizing the creatures for shipping to temperate zones and national zoos by placing them in cool environments against the stifling tropical heat. On the edge of the reservation lived a very proper English lady who rejoiced in the name of Miss Spittel and entertained visitors with afternoon tea. After Errol and Erben had sought their own entertainment with several local ladies, they happened to pass the house. "Well, old pal," Errol said in a "British" drawl, "I suppose we'll have to pass up Miss Spittel, won't we?"

From Colombo, the travelers sailed to India. They took a train going north, but could not afford first class. When the conductor came, he was astonished to find the two men in first class boldly carrying third-class tickets. Erben recalls:

> Instead of panicking, Errol simply showed our tickets and told the conductor very haughtily, "It's perfectly all right, my dear man, perfectly all right." The conductor was so hypnotized by Errol's charm he must have assumed Errol was traveling in some official capacity. The conductor simply saluted him, touched his cap to me and moved on. Errol's smile and manner were amazing. I was impressed by Errol's gift of controlling his voice, his facial expression, his entire body. It was the first inkling I had of what the young and impoverished man I had befriended might one day become.

After visiting a number of temples at Madura, the pair proceeded to Djibouti in French Somaliland. Together with a number of travelers on the French vessel, they embarked on a tour of the kräals or native villages. A native policeman thrust Errol harshly in line for the two-horse carriages, and Errol knocked him out cold. When the passengers stared in horror, expecting an immediate lynching, Errol said suavely, "I don't let anyone interfere with my dignity." Even the French police were frozen by this manner and he was allowed to proceed unmolested.

From Djibouti, Errol and Erben went to Marseilles where they parted, exchanging addresses and promising to keep in touch. Erben returned to Vienna and trouble with the law over drugs and illegal Nazi activities.

Errol continued by train and channel steamer to England in that late July of 1933. He hoped to enroll at the Old Vic, but failed his reading test and received no encouragement to try again.

He took an advertisement in *Spotlight,* a publication announcing the qualifications of performers for film and stage parts. Just before he bought the ad, he had obtained a brief walk-on part—wearing white tie and tails, dancing at the Savoy Hotel—in a low-budget feature called *I Adore You,* made at Warner Brothers in Teddington with Margot Grahame as its star.

Despite his outrageous self-confidence, Errol soon realized he wasn't ready for a career in the West End. He began to make plans to travel to the provinces. But in the meantime, his audacious social climbing earned him a remarkable reward. He succeeded in meeting one of his idols: the celebrated and immensely rich Fascist the Duke of Alba.

Even at that stage, the Duke of Alba was an ardent supporter and friend of Adolf Hitler, and later in the 1930s and during the war became a dangerously subversive ambassador for General Franco to the Court of St. James. The idea of an obscure Australian actor hobnobbing at Claridge's with so distinguished a gentleman may seem peculiar. But Errol had formed a liaison or friendship with the Woolworth heiress, Barbara Hutton, who knew Errol and was also a close friend of the Duke. She arranged the introduction, and later in the 1930s introduced Errol to Ribbentrop at her famous house in Regents Park.

The Duke of Alba proved to be as strong an influence on Errol as Erben and Trebitsch Lincoln had been. Hawk-faced and autocratic, he claimed descent from the Stuarts in a direct line from James II of England. He even used the name James Stuart in his long list of titles. It was believed by some that should the Germans ever attack England, he would seek the restoration of the Stuart line and assume the throne.

Many English aristocrats were already at that early stage infatuated with Hitler. German officials in London were received socially everywhere and were eagerly questioned on Hitler's rise to power. Some British women even traveled to Berlin to have their hands kissed by Hitler. Soon the Cliveden set and Unity Mitford would make world headlines for their pro-Nazi activities. According to the late Benn W. Levy, a well-known playwright who knew Errol, Errol was the darling of the Fascist Mayfair set and hugely enjoyed their company.

Errol's hatred of Jews found a ready ear in those grossly anti-Semitic circles. His looks ensured him attention from rich women, whom he unhesitatingly used for his own gain. Most Englishmen seemed weedy and effete in comparison to his bronzed, raw masculinity. He sold his body cheerfully, his sexual skills quickly earning him the reputation he wanted.

In early October, he drove up to Northampton, where the local repertory company had been advertising for new performers.

The head of the repertory company was a Mr. Robert Young, a gentle and civilized man who had made the small company one of the best respected in the nation. Mr. Young recalls:

One Sunday in October, 1933, I was finishing my coffee after lunch at my lodging when the bell rang and the housemaid came into my room to tell me that a very tall and handsome man stood at the door. He had asked to see me. I was not pleased because after a strenuous week of rehearsing I was jealous of my private time and rest. However, I went to the door and was confronted by a vivid red sports car and a young man whose description was not exaggerated. He asked to see me and I invited him in.

He told me he was an Australian and had come to England to act. He admitted he had not had any experience of stage work but felt confident that if only I could give him a chance he would justify my decision to engage him. He told me he was a keen swimmer and amateur boxing champion of Australia. The confident boasts made with engaging modesty, backed up by a tall, handsome presence and a pleasant voice with, regrettably, an Australian accent, gradually impressed me, and remembering that the company could do with a young man of athletic appearance, I offered him an engagement at the minimum salary of three pounds per week.

He accepted this idea with enthusiasm and I asked him to attend a rehearsal on Friday at 10:30 A.M. He thanked me profusely and drove away. I soon realized he knew nothing of the technique of acting so I arranged for him to attend private lessons in stage technique two afternoons a week. I trained him in walking the stage, in easy, graceful movements and in voice technique. He rapidly improved.

He played small parts in four months of work with surprisingly good results. Due mainly to his natural attractiveness, his powerful and pleasing presence, he aroused the interest of many young lady playgoers and our attendances rose dramatically.

The distinguished English actress Freda Jackson was at that time in the repertory company. She remembers:

> We were all in a flap when we first met him. He was like a burst of sunshine in our dark grey world. Here was this beautiful creature. There were no superlatives big enough to describe his perfection. He was a Greek god. Not beefcake. His was a delicate beauty. Gorgeous. The young men didn't like him because they knew he was going to wipe the stage with them and walk off with all the pretty girls. He did.

Errol's first part was in a play called *The Thirteenth Chair*. It was a mystery melodrama in which a man was killed during a seance. Errol was cast as the victim. He had to enter, dressed in a tuxedo, make a bow to his hostess, and take his seat at the table. Then the lights would go out and he would be discovered dead.

It was a simple enough assignment, but Errol caused a riot at the first rehearsal when he ran on stage bent double like a chimpanzee. He had to return and make his entrance several times before Robert Young was satisfied.

He was more successful in tights as the wicked Prince Donzil in *Jack and the Beanstalk*. He went on to play slightly larger parts in such reliable repertory items as *Yellow Sands* and *The Farmer's Wife*.

On many nights after the performance, young girls would wait for Errol at the stage door and follow him back to his lodgings. Usually, they would fight over which one would go up to his room. He would line them up and make a selection. One night, when a particularly determined group had refused to go away and announced they would follow the winner up the stairs in relays, he drew back the curtains, slowly stripped naked, and showed them a large erection. This episode caused a considerable flurry in staid Northampton. Some offended mothers reported his action to the police and he was warned very politely not to do it again.

It is likely that his period at Northampton was the happiest of his life. He was added to a new play every few days. He enjoyed the

simple meals of sausage rolls, fish and chips wrapped up in a newspaper, and gallons of tea and coffee, resenting only the warm beer
served in the local pubs. He was always sober onstage. He was
prompt and reliable, and quickly learned to be professional. He
never forgot lines, and he was never clumsy.

He fell in love with a local girl, the daughter of a politician, and
promised her in a reckless moment that he would take her to London to co-star with her in the West End. Unhappily, she believed
him sufficiently to live with him. It led to a difficult affair.

Errol's one problem in the repertory company was the woman
stage manager, the wife of Robert Young. Another actress in the
company, Zillah Gray, says:

> Mrs. Young was a disciplinarian. She rode him so hard that he
> would talk loudly in the wings or tread heavily upstairs and slam
> doors just to annoy her. Finally, when the end of the season came
> he waited till the last performance was over and then intercepted her
> on the stairs. He slapped her so hard she fell all the way down to
> the bottom of the steps. He could easily have killed her. She stood
> up and hailed him with abuse.

Because of his conflict with Mrs. Young, Errol took off and joined
another company in Malvern. He was there from July to August
1934, playing *The Moon in the Yellow River* as an Irish soldier; in
A Man's House; and in *Doctor Faustus.*

He frequently understudied the well-known actor Geoffrey Toone,
whom he referred to as "Melodious Toone." He shared rooms in
Malvern with Toone and two other actors. Toone says:

> Many Americans came to Malvern to see the plays and there was a
> garden party every Monday. Errol would beat us all finding young
> and nubile girls and they flung themselves at him. He would just de-
> cide which one he was going to attract for the week.
> He always reached his target. But never bragged. At one time he
> chose two girls and did not know they were sisters. He was successful
> with both and I don't think either sister found out that the other had
> slept with him.

Errol felt he had to crash the West End of London in order to
prove himself as an actor. But although he later boasted he had appeared in two plays on Shaftesbury Avenue, in fact he had not. Una-

ble to find work in the London theatre, where standards were far higher than in the provinces, he went to Teddington Studios and applied for work as an extra. He obtained employment in crowd scenes at seven pounds a week.

He decided immediately that he was going to be a star. He used a trick to become one. Irving Asher was in charge of British production for Warner Brothers Pictures in Hollywood. Errol set out to fascinate Asher's secretary, Mrs. Boyd. He flattered her, brought her perfume and flowers, and begged her to let him have an audience with Asher. Finally, she gave in, and induced her boss to see the determined young man.

Irving Asher will never forget the day that Errol walked into his office. He remembers:

> He was, of course, extraordinary looking. He sat down on the edge of my desk and told me bluntly he intended to be a star. I felt like yawning. Finally, I called my secretary in. I said, "This young man here wants to be a star." She looked him up and down meaningfully and said, "Mr. Asher, I have news for you. He *is* a star!"

Asher decided to include a test of Errol with a test of several other actors for the leading role in a third-rate "quota quickie" or low-budget feature called *Murder at Monte Carlo*. The part called for him to be a dashing hero helping to solve a crime in the Riviera resort.

Asher ran the test, still yawning. But a few minutes later, he wasn't yawning anymore. Errol's presence on the screen was electrifying. He was handsome, debonair, and utterly photogenic. Asher took a gamble and signed him up. Errol received the news with a smile of blasé self-confidence. He had never for a moment thought any of the other actors had a chance.

Asher sent a telegram to Hollywood after seeing the first rushes. He begged Jack Warner to look at the test. Warner ignored the telegram. After several weeks, Asher sent the test over, but there was no response. He cabled again: INSIST YOU LOOK AT ERROL FLYNN TEST. Jack Warner continued to ignore the request. Finally, tired of Asher's further cables, Warner sent a telegram to London which read: ERROL FLYNN IS TERRIFIC. SHIP HER OVER. He believed Errol was a woman because he had an actress called Erin O'Brien Moore under contract.

Asher decided to use Jack Warner's cable to give the young actor an opportunity.

On November 10, 1934, Errol left Southampton for America on board the *Paris*. He paid the difference between the second-class fare supplied by Warner Brothers and the first-class fare which would enable him to meet the rich and the famous who in those days were still to be found mingling in the grand saloons of transatlantic liners. He obtained a "loan" of one hundred and seventy-five pounds from Warners to buy an overcoat, two suits and a new pair of patent leather shoes. He never paid the loan back, and for months the studio argued with him over it. (When he got to Hollywood he sent the overcoat to Jack Warner, asking for "a refund, because it was too hot to wear it in Hollywood.")

He reveled in his social position on board, entertaining his fellow first-class passengers at table with tall tales of New Guinea and the headhunters and slaves of the region. He surprised the crew by talking to them fluently in French.

The crossing was choppy. But rough weather or no rough weather, Errol would not be denied deck tennis, quoits, clay-pigeon shooting, or vigorous laps up and down the pool. Amid the vibrant noises of a ship at sea—slapping waves, throbbing decks, voices beating against metal bulkheads and bouncing and echoing back, cries of people playing games, totes on the ship's daily run—he was constantly to be found sitting stripped down to blue and quite indecently revealing Australian trunks at the indoor pool, regaling a posse of women with his fictitious New Guinea adventures.

In the evening, he strode off to seek sexual pleasure. As always, women were not merely available, they were insistent. He made love as vigorously and ruthlessly as he played deck tennis. Women threw themselves at him, and he loved it.

The South African actor Louis Hayward introduced him to a very gifted, vivacious leading lady who called herself Lili Damita. She had been born Lilliane Carré in Bordeaux. She was a great beauty and a fine actress. Lili had won a beauty contest, and had appeared quite successfully in pictures. She emerged as a sophisticate in comedies about the rich: she was a French precursor of Kay Francis. She starred in three movies for the Hungarian director Michael Curtiz, a fact that was to become highly significant later on.

When Errol met her, she had suffered reverses in her career. A leading player in the films *The Cockeyed World* and *The Bridge of San Luis Rey,* she had been reduced to playing in comedies like *Goldie Gets Along* and *Brewster's Millions.* She was returning to Hollywood to make a movie with James Cagney called *Frisco Kid.*

Lili made an immediate impression on Errol. She exuded an atmosphere of European wit and intelligence, of fire and style and shrewdness. But Errol's animal strength and energy made little impression on her. He was nobody, nothing. He came, almost literally, from another world: from twelve thousand miles away in the South Seas. He was beneath her.

There were no photographers or reporters to greet Errol at the gangway in New York. He left for Hollywood at once.

Five

Errol was met at Los Angeles airport by Dick Carlin, a studio driver; Carlin, who was to become a friend and confidant, drove him to the Knickerbocker Hotel in Hollywood. On the way, Flynn was chiefly interested in asking where he could "get a poke." Dick didn't know what he meant until Errol painstakingly explained that poke was British for fuck.

Dick couldn't help, and Errol checked into the hotel feeling very despondent. He got drunk in the bar and, furious, went to bed alone. Next day, Carlin picked him up and drove him to the studio in Burbank, where Errol signed a contract guaranteeing him one hundred and fifty dollars a week with six monthly options. "Where can I play tennis?" Errol asked Dick, who at once drove him to the Los Angeles Tennis Club. One good thing about Hollywood, Errol decided, was that a man could find plenty of sporting facilities there.

He bought a one-hundred-dollar Chevrolet with a battered top and drove over to see Lili Damita at the Garden of Allah. She agreed reluctantly to play tennis at the Westside Tennis Club and on the studio courts. But there was a problem to their dating: he couldn't keep up with her financially. She had to slip him the money to pay the tab as they went to the Trocadero and the Coconut Grove and Chasen's and the Brown Derby.

Hollywood was a tough factory town. Inside the great, gray, whalelike shapes of the studio factories, the pressure was constant: everyone worked well into Saturday night to pay the shareholders their dividends, the hours were harrowing and the summer heat on the set insufferable.

But on Sundays a handsome young man with a sports car, a fine physique and great sexual skill had nothing to worry about.

Although the suburb called Hollywood was little more than a collection of romantic shacks at the end of a poisoned rainbow, Beverly Hills, Bel Air, and Santa Monica had in those days an authentic glamour. Marlene Dietrich gave superb parties. Errol and Lili spent many Sundays at the magnificent Art Deco home of MGM art director Cedric Gibbons and his wife, the beautiful Dolores Del Rio, near Santa Monica Beach: there was a tennis court, a huge pool, and a cocktail bar, and Dolores recalls Errol was fascinated by a marvelous example of Hollywood nonsense: a secret stairway which Cedric would have to climb at night, middle-aged Romeo to his Dolores' Juliet—before she would grant him her favors.

At first, Warners had no work for Errol, and there was little to do. He used to stand around at the Hollywood Tennis Club bar and tell stories about his amatory exploits with Lili in great detail; not in a prurient manner but with graphic, comic, or theatrical flourishes which had everyone laughing and ordering more rounds of drinks. He was a Tartar on the courts, pitilessly defeating his rivals before flinging his arm around them and inviting them indoors to cool off with beers or scotches on the long, hot, dry December and January afternoons.

Sometimes, Errol would drive to the Hollywood Athletic Club on Sunset Boulevard, where, clad only in a jockstrap and gym shoes, he would work out with weights. Sweat pouring down his body, he would perform a feat which brought applause even in that hard-bitten environment: his head thrown back, he would balance a hundred-pound weight on the bridge of his nose. He formed a close friendship with an Indian named Jim Cody and his brother "Iron

Eyes": Iron Eyes had just come back from Australia with a white parrot and a pet boxing kangaroo.

He also formed a friendship with the character actor Victor Jory, who came from a Welsh-Canadian background. Victor Jory invited him to an elaborate New Year's Day party in San Marino. The rooms were cleared of furniture for slot machines and pinball tables and an orchestra played in the living room. But Errol behaved badly. Every time a married woman came into the bar where he was standing he would make a pass at her. An actor named Charles Lane told Jory: "I'm going to kill that son-of-a-bitch. He just had his hand up my wife's dress."

Jory cautioned Flynn to select only single girls. But soon after, another husband complained. Jory warned Errol, "If you don't stop this, I'll put you out of the house." Errol replied, with a dangerous glint in his eye, "You think you can do that?" Jory's voice was cold as he said, "I haven't the vaguest idea. But I'll sure as hell try."

Errol asked Jory to step outside. As they walked into the garden, Errol said, "I think I should be fair to you. I should tell you I boxed as a light heavyweight on the Irish Olympic Team." Jory was unimpressed by the picturesque lie. He said, "Well, get your ass out on the lawn because *I'm* British Columbia light heavyweight champ. *And* the Army champion for the Western states. Let's find out about you."

He did quickly. Jory was by far the better boxer. He smashed Errol to his knees.

Errol proved to be a good sportsman. Rubbing his jaw ruefully, he grinned, and said, "How about introducing me to some *single* women?"

Despite the evenings spent in dating Lili or in picking up pretty girls in bars, taking them back to the hotel and making love to them obsessively over and over again until dawn, the days on the courts in the sun, the quick showers and long rounds of drinking before dinner, Errol was restless and irritable. He found no pleasure in the arid hot Hollywood spells and shabby palms. He longed to work, and no script was ready for him. He was healthy and handsome and talented and he had told everyone in England he was going to be a star. When the fuck would these Warner bastards give him a job?

At last, in March 1935, they sent him a script. It was an adaptation of an Erle Stanley Gardner Perry Mason mystery, *The Case of the Curious Bride.* He was to play a man named Gregory Moxley. He started to read. There were constant references to Moxley in the script, but soon Errol started to groan and hold his head. Moxley it turned out had been murdered long before the main action of the picture began. And Errol would have only two scenes to play, both of them without dialogue. In the first, he would be seen as a corpse, silhouetted under a sheet in somebody's apartment; in the second, he would struggle with a woman and a man in a fight and be impaled and killed on a jagged piece of glass that had been shattered by a poker.

He told Dick Carlin disappointedly, "I'm not going to have a career in Hollywood." "You're crazy," Carlin replied. "Just look in a mirror! You'll be a star within a year."

Lili was shooting *Frisco Kid* at Warners while *The Case of the Curious Bride* was being prepared there. When Errol finally began work he felt humiliated at once. The director of his picture, Michael Curtiz, was a powerful and vicious Hungarian with a tongue like a cobra's. Lying under the sheet with arc lights beating on him, Errol inadvertently sneezed. Allergic to pollen, he was reacting to a bowl of flowers that stood on a nearby table. "God *damn* you!" Curtiz said. The "corpse" jumped off the table and was barely restrained from punching the director's nose. "Dead corpses don't sneeze," Curtiz said as he ordered Errol to return to the table.

Errol had not met Margaret Lindsay, the star of the picture, until the scene in which she attacked him with a poker and he struck her so violently she fell back against a wall. He was so eager to make an impression in the scene he disregarded the script instructions and Curtiz's screams of rage and snatched the poker from her hand and hit her over the head with it. She fell, bleeding and unconscious, to the floor. Curtiz shouted at Errol, who cradled her head in his arms.

Miss Lindsay was rushed to the hospital. She remembers Errol calling her over and over again to see how she was. A week later she came out with eleven stitches in her head and did the scene again. This time, it went off without a hitch, but Errol almost succeeded in knocking Donald Woods, his other antagonist in a scene, out cold when he failed to pull his punches.

The word at Warners was that Errol Flynn was a "bum" who didn't know how to act. He was rushed into another B-picture, *Don't Bet on Blondes,* directed by a Frenchman, Robert Florey. It was a corny waste of time: he spoke lines this time—in an uneasy transatlantic accent—but he hated the picture and his part in it: he might as well not have been on the screen at all.

In the meantime, Errol and Lili had virtually set up house in her suite at the Garden of Allah. They had become friendly with a flyer named Bud Ernst, a massive six-foot-five, energetic and voluble "character," hard-drinking and fond of wenching, a man after Errol's own heart. But Ernst had been having an affair with an actress named Lyda Roberti. Ernst decided he would fly to Yuma, Arizona, in June to marry Lyda; Errol and Lili were to be best man and bridesmaid. Then Ernst suggested that they make it a double wedding and Flynn agreed nervously. But at the last minute, Lyda was delayed making a picture; and Ernst flew Errol and Lili to Yuma without companions.

Errol was extremely nervous all the way to Yuma, and twice lost the ring in his pockets, which were as full of rubbish as a British schoolboy's, full of crumpled cigarette packages, Wrigley chewing gum, half-read letters, unopened bills.

The plane bumped in for a dusty landing at 2 P.M. that June day. At 3:30 the couple were in the offices of Justice Ernest A. Freeman. Errol balked at the door. Lili led him into the office and the nuptials were completed. Errol trembled in terror as he spoke his vows.

He had cause to be afraid. He was quite unsuited to marriage. He wanted women all the time: of every size, shape, and color. He wanted freedom. He had no money, no credit, he owed everybody in varying amounts. When Lili and he went househunting, it was in her Packard automobile in order to impress the various real estate agents: his battered Chevy would have been a mistake. He felt like a gigolo. Moreover, Lili was possessive and became violent when he strayed from the Garden of Allah for a night of pleasure. She would throw vases, cut-glass ash trays, anything she could lift. He would duck and run out to his car.

At last, he and Lili found a house that suited them. It was up a narrow corkscrew road, called Lookout Mountain Avenue, high over Laurel Canyon at 8946 Appian Way. With shingle roofs and gables, it had a magnificent view over the then still unspoiled spread of the San Fernando Valley. They furnished it together, blending some of Lili's oriental things—a carved ebony dressing table, a Chinese bed with a gold and yellow cover—with modern American furniture.

It was a pleasant, unpretentious house, but it needed servants. Lili hired Jim and Frances Fleming, a couple who had lost their money in the Depression, as live-in houseman and housekeeper. Frances, who had been used to servants of her own, was too "high hat" for the job and hated Lili; they quarreled so seriously that Frances moved to another address. Jim—cool, dark, intelligent—became Errol's friend and stand-in for fifteen years. He briefly assumed the role of business manager for the Flynns. He froze Lili's charge accounts at stores and took over Errol's small income, compelling him to pay his bills at Schwab's Drugstore and arranging credit for him.

Jim Fleming recalls what their marriage was like:

> I chiefly remember jealous quarrels at the house. Lili resented Errol's sex life and drinking buddies. He used to delight in provoking her. He would drive back with me from the studio and have me pick up a couple of condoms from the drugstore. He'd be going to bed that night and he'd pull the condoms out and drop them on the dressing table with his keys and his money. She'd know they were for other women. She'd get wildly upset and throw things. He was pleased.

In many respects, Errol and Lili were suited to each other. They enjoyed music and dancing and social life, and though neither was an intellectual, they enjoyed good books, an uncommon attribute in Hollywood. Lili taught Errol the fundamentals of wine selection and decent French food; he taught her to cook plain, wholesome English fare. Yet they were in many ways incompatible. This was Lili's first marriage and she wanted possession: a man who could be relied on to escort her to parties; who would come home at night and put his feet up and appear at dinner on time, who would sit with her after dinner and listen to records or the radio and dream.

It is astonishing that the marriage lasted as long as it did: for another six years. Dolores Del Rio points out that Lili may have been capable of the unselfishness, the extreme self-sacrifice which love entails; Errol emphatically was not. He loved himself first and foremost, yet he was unfulfilled, insecure, constantly needing food for his nervously unstable ego. It wasn't in Lili's nature to flatter him incessantly; instead, she was far too honest and outspoken. He was in a straitjacket and he longed to get out.

Despite her jealousy of Flynn, Lili was determined to see to it that he obtained decent roles in pictures. She and her friend Dolores Del Rio pestered Jack Warner to give him a break. Nothing was forthcoming, and it seemed that his contract might be terminated. Then quite suddenly, a chance of a lifetime came along.

The writer Casey Robinson, who had met Errol on the set of *The Case of the Curious Bride* and been impressed by his magnetism, had just completed a screenplay version of Rafael Sabatini's novel *Captain Blood*. The studio bosses had decided to give the title role to Robert Donat, a British actor who had enjoyed a triumph in *The Count of Monte Cristo*.

By July of 1935, it was clear that Donat would not be coming to Hollywood. A victim of asthma, he was afraid of the dry air and dusty winds of California, and he was also in love with a girl who would not leave England. He backed out of his contract at the last minute, citing reasons of health. The picture had been fully planned: with Curtiz as director, Hal Mohr as cameraman, and Jean Muir as female star. Now, suddenly, Warners had no male star, and the executives began talking urgently about available British actors, all of whom were obviously too effete. John Barrymore was considered, but MGM would not let him out of his contract. What could be done?

What *must* be done, Lili and Dolores Del Rio, decided, was to obtain the role for Errol. He was "British"; he had the looks to play the young doctor who becomes a pirate and graduates to governor of Jamaica; the part was made for him. Yet the problem seemed insoluble. If Lili or anyone else were to suggest to Jack Warner that an unknown should play the leading role in this expensive production, Warner would have screamed with rage and laughter. Casey Robinson says:

> So I went to Lili and I said, "Why don't you talk with Jack Warner's fiancée, Ann? She's a friend of yours isn't she?" And Lili went to Ann who told her, "Leave it to me." Ann settled the whole thing at a pillow conference with Jack.

Warner called Casey Robinson and associate producer Harry Joe Brown (another early supporter of Flynn's) into his office and said: "Boys, are you blind? Do you walk around this lot and never see anything or anybody? Don't you know that you've got the greatest Captain Blood right here under contract?" The two men said, in unison, "Who? Who?" and Warner snapped back, "Errol Flynn, you bums!" And Robinson and Brown looked at each other; Harry Joe Brown looked at Warner and said, "Only you would have thought of that!"

Errol was indifferent to this elaborate maneuver on his behalf. A pirate picture seemed unimportant to him, an unsatisfactory way to start a career. While Lili and her friends toiled and spun for him, he took off to the ports of the southern coast to chase girls and inspect yachts for possible purchase. He sold the Chevrolet and bought an Auburn at discount from the studio fleet of cars.

He arrived barely on time for the costume and acting tests for *Captain Blood*. Since he was not experienced in fencing, it was decided to test him in a romantic scene with Jean Muir. He seized Miss Muir's shoulder so firmly he almost dislocated it; the director, Curtiz, screamed at him, and he repeated the gesture more gently. He spoke his lines in a soft Australian accent and gazed at Jean Muir as though he had been in love with her for months.

That night, convinced he had been hopeless in the test, Errol got drunk. He disappeared again, and a distracted Lili was unable to find him. In the private screening room of the Executive Building at Warners, Hal Wallis and Jack Warner ran the test. It was electrifying. Errol seemed to leap out of the screen with an animal vitality and intensity which spelled "star." It wasn't exactly a matter of acting or even of correct movement and gesture and expression. It was a mysterious force of personality with which the camera fell in love. He seemed to bloom in the lens. He suggested courage and freedom and laughter and adventure and glamour. He was what mass audience motion pictures were all about. He *was* Captain Blood.

He was hired at once. Lili and the gang celebrated more than he did. He took his new success coolly as his due.

Jean Muir was dropped suddenly because the British representatives in London felt the English public and critics would be irritated by an American accent in a leading lady performing the role of a British subject. Instead, a young British girl named Olivia de Havilland was hired. She was nervous, virginal, and staid—far different from any woman Errol had met. He, too, was a type she had never come across before. She was far too shy to admit her attraction, and he was far too inexperienced and clumsy to succeed in wooing her. They were plunged into an absurd publicity routine. Olivia de Havilland recalls:

Errol and I had a kind of common destiny. We did some photographs together. Me in shorts—ridiculous. And the two of us, in modern dress, carrying rapiers. We had to laugh! All this had nothing to do with his part as a privateer in Jacobean England and mine as a demure lady with long flowing ringlets and billowing skirts, but they thought the shots of us would attract attention in magazines, and I suppose they were right. I looked at Errol and I thought, This is the most attractive, the most charming, the most magnetic man I will ever meet. I still think he was.

Blushingly, Olivia kept her feelings very much to herself. She brushed off Errol so firmly that he told Jim Fleming, "I don't think she has a hole between her legs." He consoled himself with carhops and cocktail waitresses. He borrowed five thousand dollars from Lili (who was generosity itself to him) to buy a decent wardrobe to wear in public in keeping with his new status. He lost most of the money at poker.

Captain Blood began shooting in the suffocating August of 1935. There was no air conditioning in those days and the sound stage doors had to be kept closed because the din of airplanes or automobiles could ruin a take. The heavy costumes, wigs, and makeup made filming an endurance test. Errol frequently ruined a take by snatching off his wig and mopping his face with a handkerchief which was anachronistically stuck in his trouser pocket. The director, Curtiz, would become hysterical because the scene had to be reshot. Between takes, Errol would go to his dressing room and lie down on a couch, naked, running a water-soaked sponge over his body. Sometimes, an available dress extra would drop in for sexual play.

He began acting in a "Shakespearean" manner, striking theatrical poses with one leg extended in front of the other and the toe pointing down sharply to the chalk mark. Curtiz, who was on to Errol, yelled, "Stop acting like a goddam faggot, you no-good Tasmanian bum son-of-a-bitch!" Or, "Stop being a fairy and try to be an American!" Errol screamed back, "Go fuck yourself, you dumb Hungarian!" And he rudely reminded Curtiz of a favorite saying: "A Hungarian and a Rumanian will both sell you their grandmother, but the Rumanian will deliver." Olivia was shocked by these exchanges, and kept fleeing to her dressing room, clapping her hands to her ears.

Errol couldn't sleep well at night. Always an insomniac, he was more restless than ever now that he had to stay at home with Lili and go to bed early. He would pace about at night, cut to the quick by Curtiz's insults. In the daytime, he frequently lost his lines. After a week, Curtiz snarled at his script clerk, Fred Applegate, "This son-of-a-bitch is no damn good. Maybe we should fire him and get some other goddam bum." And he said to his assistant, Sherry Shourds, "This bum should be back playing dead corpses."

Curtiz stormed into Hal Wallis' office and demanded that Errol be removed. He suggested George Brent and Wallis laughed in his face. "Go back to the set, keep to the script, direct Errol Flynn and don't say anything else," Hal Wallis told the recalcitrant director.

As soon as Errol heard that Hal Wallis had told Curtiz off on his behalf, Errol changed. He decided he was now a star and adopted the manner and bearing. He "went Hollywood," and the crew resented it.

Some scenes on the Carribbean shore were shot at Laguna Beach, including a duel to the death between Errol and Basil Rathbone, who played the villain of the piece. It was an especially difficult sequence because the tide was coming in, splashing around the actors' feet and making the rocks so slippery that Errol twice fell to his knees, and on one occasion Rathbone slipped so badly his sword cut Errol's face, causing a small scar. Errol was furious: Curtiz had deliberately removed the small protective knob at the end of the sword which saved the actors' faces from injury. He never forgave Curtiz for risking his chief asset: his male beauty.

Errol was slow and awkward in the climax of the duel, irritated by the scratch on his face and unwilling to respond to the hated director. Curtiz settled on a ploy. He drew Rathbone aside and whispered an instruction in his ear. Obediently, just before they went into the scene, Rathbone taunted Errol, "I'm making forty-five hundred dollars a week more than you are, you dirty little Australian!" Flynn flew at him with the sword, and suddenly the duel came to life.

Often, Curtiz dragged Errol through ten or more takes. The results were worthwhile, and the rushes were extraordinary. Errol looked magnificent: Captain Blood's speech of defiance to the hanging judge who condemns him in Taunton Great Hall, his rallying cry to his crew of cutthroats, his onslaught on Jamaica and his conquest of Port Royal were inspired by his hatred of Curtiz. For Errol, the villainy of colonial rule was translated into the villainy of the martinet director who drove him ruthlessly every day.

In lunch breaks, Errol would escape the misery of shooting the picture and sit at the Green Room table with the writers—the only actor so honored up to that time. Julius Epstein, and his twin brother Philip admired the new star, and listened enthralled to his sexual anecdotes.

Captain Blood was completed in October, 1935.

Errol sweated out the editing, begging Jack Warner in a series of telegrams to give him a chance to appear in a Shakespearean film. In his memoirs he invented an elaborate story about going to MGM to seek the part of Romeo in *Romeo and Juliet,* but no Warner Brothers contract player would have been able to do anything of the kind, and his whole account of his meeting with John Barrymore on the set of that picture is quite imaginary. It is unlikely that he had even met Barrymore at that point, though he continued to idolize and imitate the actor.

In November, Errol flew through storms to New York against studio orders—flying was thought dangerous in those days—to attend the premiere of *Captain Blood*. He checked into a suite at the Ritz Tower.

The same week, the first sneak preview was held in Pomona, with Hal Wallis and Mike Curtiz in the audience. The audience was enthralled. They applauded loudly Errol's speech of defiance to the hanging judge; they cheered when the sails unfurled over Errol's head and he called for his good men and true to avenge themselves against the oppressor; and again when he ran Basil Rathbone through with the sword; and at the rapturous ending, with Errol as governor of Jamaica, winning the hand of the fair Olivia.

The theme of *Captain Blood* was greatly appealing in those Depression times: an underprivileged youth defies the forces of oppression to become a democratic governor of a province. Overnight, Errol Flynn was to become not only the idol of women but the symbol for men of everything they longed to be and could not be.

Errol had acquired a new agent: Minna Wallis, sister of Hal. Minna couldn't wait for a telegram to carry the good news to Errol at the Ritz. She placed a $28.50 telephone call to him instead, and that night he celebrated noisily with some of his New York drinking pals. Minna wasted no time in going to Jack Warner and arranging a new contract, increasing her client's salary to $800 a week, with option renewals to $2,500 a week, and a $750 bonus. Errol rewarded her by dumping her soon afterward for the more powerful Myron Selznick.

The opening in New York was a triumph. The crowd cheered the cast; the reviews were raves; and overnight both Errol and Olivia de Havilland emerged as major stars. In New York, too, Errol became an immediate symbol of everything Depression man wanted to be: happy, free of restrictions, contemptuous of authority (in a time when nobody dared risk defying a boss, as that could mean the breadline), tall—few American men were over five-foot-nine (he had a forty-three-inch chest and a thirty-three-inch waist, with powerful shoulders and biceps). He was animal grace in motion: a hero to match Clark Gable in his revolt against authority in *Mutiny on the Bounty*. Exhibitors rejoiced; money poured in. Warner and Wallis sent cables to Errol urging him to come back at once, and they began casting around for another epic subject. But they still paid Errol forty-five hundred dollars a week less than Basil Rathbone; and he was still furious with them.

In Belfast, where Professor Flynn and Marelle, reconciled, were now living, and the professor, currently a model of moral rectitude, was a distinguished member of the University faculty, there was little rejoicing. Errol told the New York *Herald Tribune* his parents' reaction. The professor was quietly pleased, but didn't bother to send his son a cable of congratulation and spent several weeks dawdling over a lukewarm letter. Marelle was totally unimpressed: she thought being an actor was unfit work for a man, that anybody who became an actor had to be a sissy, and why wasn't Errol a lawyer or a doctor? Not that he would be any good at being either.

Back in Hollywood, Errol splurged his new earnings on a new Auburn, which he fitted up with bull horns on the hood. He would drive the narrow winding roads which led from the house on Appian Way down Lookout Mountain Avenue and to Laurel Canyon and over the hill to the tennis clubs or the studio with a reckless bravado, scattering the dogs, cats, and chickens which ran freely about. He would roar off with a cloud of dust behind him, laughing, his teeth flashing. At home, when not arguing with Lili, he would goose the cheerful cook Rossi di Marcos, and exchange jokes with Jim Fleming. Much of the time he was in uproarious high spirits, but then he would sink unexpectedly into gloom and introspection, ashamed of his image as a screen buccaneer, wishing he could return to the stage.

His clothing was distinctive and expensive. Lili usually had to foot

the bills. He sported blue blazers with large white silk mono-
grammed pocket handkerchiefs spilling out of the top pocket. He
wore ascots and open-necked silk shirts, and white ducks. He hated
to wear BVDs, preferring the tight-fitting Australian swim shorts
which held his genitals tight. Even his tennis clothes were made for
him. He had such a natural athletic ease and elegance in wearing
clothes that even Gable looked lumpish by comparison.

When he rose in the morning with a hangover he would quickly
shake it off by jumping into an ice-cold shower and then doing
calisthenics—bending, stretching, loosening—for twenty minutes,
and digging into an Australian breakfast of steak and eggs and very
strong tea brewed in the pot. Habits like this were hard to break.

Six

Soon after Errol's return to Hollywood from New York, following the premiere of *Captain Blood,* Dr. Hermann Friedrich Erben suddenly arrived in Hollywood. He and Errol had kept in touch sporadically over the years.

According to statements recorded in the reports of United States Government and consular services over a period of six years, Erben had been involved in the atrocious murder of Austrian Chancellor Engelbert Dollfuss on July 25, 1934. Whether he was actually present or simply planned the assassination was never made clear. Hundreds of Gestapo men burst into the Chancellery and cornered the anti-Nazi Chancellor. An SA man, Oskar Planetta, fired into Dollfuss' throat. For hours, the assassins watched Dollfuss suffer an agonizing and protracted death.

In November 1934, following mass arrests of Gestapo men and Planetta's hanging, Erben himself was arrested. Police ransacked his home. They found several guns, obscene photographs, drugs, and an American passport that he claimed he had lost while bicycling in

Vienna. The possession of two American passports was clearly designed to permit him foreign travel if one of the passports was taken up. He was fined for illegal possession of firearms and his extra passport was confiscated by the American Consulate. He was held for twenty-four hours in prison when he refused to pay a fine, but was released for lack of concrete evidence.

After escaping the purge, Erben turned his attentions exclusively to working as a free-lance agent for naval and Gestapo intelligence abroad, with occasional excursions into free-lance agentry for America.

A main purpose of his was to collect photographic and written material on foreign ports, military installations, and ships' gun emplacements, information that would be helpful when Germany declared war in Europe.

As a ship's doctor, Erben was ideally placed to take pictures and make descriptive diary entries. North America, dismissed by Hitler as a Jewish rubbish heap, and South America, a marvelous source of Fascist assistance but still riddled with Hitler's enemies, were his prime targets. It is clear that he was one of the leading figures in photographic espionage—even when he met Errol.

In March 1935, Erben obtained an extremely important assignment overseas. It was clear he was aiming to achieve a major position. Under the cover of joining a widely advertised cross-continental journey by two students to test a new automobile—a journey from Vienna to Shanghai—he could photograph the all important oil pipelines through Iran and Iraq; he could film Palestinian harbor installations and contact Arabic insurgents and Nazi intelligence men in Jerusalem to help foment trouble and lay the ground for possible attack; he could stir up pro-Hitler feelings in India and perform acts of terrorism against the authorities: his military background would prove useful here.

State Department officials and agents were on the alert over this expedition, as the extraordinary succession of very high-level communiqués indicates—but Erben was too skilled a spy now to be stopped or caught. When he was refused a passport renewal by the United States Consul General in Vienna, he tricked that official into supplying a letter of transit. He traveled on this document and a seaman's protection certificate to Trieste, where he picked up drug supplies from a Berlin manufacturer for shipment to Shanghai. He managed to reach Teheran on his documentation and when stopped there and questioned contacted the Austrian consul, an old school friend, and obtained an Austrian passport for the rest of the journey.

Along the way, he boasted to his traveling companions of killing many people for the SA; he said he would have to return, if thwarted by consulates, to Austria and "blow up some people for the Nazis"; he boasted of his involvement in the murder of Dollfuss; he said he was a devoted slave of Hitler.

When Erben arrived in Calcutta, terrorist activities were going on against the governor of Bengal. He contacted members of the subversive groups in Calcutta and Darjeeling. He was most active in Darjeeling, where he addressed a crowd of Indians urging them to rise up against the British and find a leader like Hitler. In Darjeeling, he burst into a church where the governor of Bengal, Sir John Anderson, later Lord Waverley, was administering the holy sacrament and waved a gun at him. Anderson, twice threatened with assassination in the previous year, fled, terrified. Erben was questioned but released and followed to see if his terrorist associates could be found. Pursued by officials everywhere, he lodged a parcel containing his gun at the U. S. Consulate. Staff members opened it. As a result of their report, British police decided to act against Erben.

While he was seated in church one Sunday afternoon, a military policeman slid silently into the seat behind him, pressed a gun into his ribs, and whispered to him to leave the building at once. He was arrested on the church steps and summarily tried and found guilty of illegally using firearms. He charged that the judge was prejudiced. Given the choice of a fine of three hundred rupees or a jail sentence, he flew into a rage and declined to pay any money to the hated British authorities. When told of the conditions of Indian jails, he changed his mind.

Released on payment of the fine, Dr. Erben was deported. He read in a local paper that a dealer from Assam had 1,200 Rhesus monkeys for sale at the equivalent of two cents a monkey. In the era of pre-Salk, experimental Flexner anti-polio vaccine, monkeys were considered indispensable since their reaction to polio virus was the same as man's. He snapped up the whole consignment, knowing that he could sell them at several times their cost to the Monkey House of the Rockefeller Institute in New York. He loaded them in their cages aboard the American Pioneer Lines freighter *City of Rayville*.

For forty-two days at sea, Erben was nursemaid to the tiny creatures. He wore elastic bands on his beard in case they should feel tempted to tear it out by the roots. Stuffed uncomfortably in their cages in the heat, many of the monkeys became sick and began to infect each other. Erben took the bold step of releasing them and letting them run all over the ship. To the combined consternation and amusement of the crew, they jumped onto the bridge and attempted to take the ship's wheel, they crawled up ropes to the crow's nest, they stole the seamen's food and the officers' trousers. About one hundred died on the voyage of pneumonia, dysentery, tetanus, numerous injuries, or brain disease.

When Erben arrived in New York on November 19, 1935, he was carrying enormous glass jars filled with monkey skulls. He had peeled off the flesh and succeeded in preserving the brains. Questioned by customs officers about failing to declare these sinister items of cargo, he announced that he was analyzing neurological brain diseases which had caused the monkeys' deaths.

Errol, learning of Erben's arrival by telegram, sent a friend, the New York society photographer Jerome Zerbe, to take photographs of Erben for the New York *Herald Tribune* showing him glowering through his horn-rimmed spectacles, his beard vast and imposing, two baby monkeys clinging trustingly to his coat.

Erben deposited the monkeys at the Rockefeller Institute and took the train to Hollywood where he moved into the Lookout Mountain house with Errol, Lili, and Jim Fleming. Errol's new valet, Max Carmel, was fascinated by Erben. Carmel had a similar background. He had been the Fascist police chief of Guatemala until deposed in a revolution; he ran guns in China to aid the Japanese; he was a Nazi sympathizer and just before the war he made connections in Vichy.

Jim Fleming vividly recalls Erben's first visit to Hollywood:

> He was obnoxiously anti-semitic, and loud-mouthed about it, which went down very badly in Hollywood. He wore the same clothes every day: a kind of brownshirt uniform, with leather boots. He gave me the impression he was a Communist! He talked about "the revolution," which was supposed to free us all in America. I didn't realize he meant Nazism. Lili was very jealous of his hold over Errol. She felt he was encouraging Errol in his promiscuity. She hated his boorish blustering manner and the fact he didn't bathe.

After Erben left, Errol felt ill with a recurrence of undulant fever. Knowing that this sickness often came back for long periods, the studio panicked. For weeks he lay in bed, sweating profusely and suffering severe headaches, loss of appetite, aching limbs, and sore throat. In the mornings, Errol would rally; but by afternoon the fever had risen again, and in those days before antibiotics, little could be done.

One day in March 1936, he was sitting in bed reading the paper when a small headline in the back pages caught his attention. It read, AMERICAN DOCTOR DIES IN CALCUTTA.

He was amazed to see that the doctor referred to was none other than Hermann Erben. He read on. The story told of a servant finding Erben's dead body in the carriage of a train going from Madras. Police investigations showed that an Indian had flung a garland of flowers around his neck: flowers worn by the corpse of the man's father. This was believed to be a curse. Erben was supposed to have died of a heart attack when he understood the garland's significance.

Errol burst out laughing. He knew perfectly well that Erben was alive and well and living in Vienna. Erben's Nazi activities were continuing there. He planned to go to Ethiopia to aid Mussolini, but the State Department held up his plans. Soon after, Erben returned to New York and strolled into the office of the *Herald Tribune* to announce to the delighted reporters that reports of his death had, in the words of Mark Twain, been "greatly exaggerated." He then proceeded to Hollywood for a longer stay with Errol.

In the early months of 1936, Abraham Jacoby (later known as Michel Jacoby) and Rowland Leigh completed work on a script designed as the basis for Errol's next movie: *The Charge of the Light Brigade*. Flynn was only mildly interested in ideas for the picture. He was busy fending off letters which poured into the house on Appian Way: letters from Australia and New Guinea and England, demanding that he pay his outstanding debts. He ignored them all, instructing Jim Fleming to throw them away.

Flynn found the script of *The Charge of the Light Brigade* a farrago from start to finish. The siege of Cawnpore, which actually took place five years after Balaklava, was shown taking place before it; and the affairs of an imaginary Indian named Surat Khan were woven arbitrarily into the story. Warners, Errol remarked to a friend, cared nothing for history; after all, in *Captain Blood* the Union Jack had flown from Captain Blood's ship before the flag was invented! In *The Charge of the Light Brigade* on the other hand, the Union Jack was flown upside down! Cawnpore was eventually changed to the imaginary "Chukoti" in subsequent script drafts, but the nonsense-history was retained.

The fort of Chukoti was built at the Lasky Mesa, a bare, arid, ugly stretch of land overrun by tarantulas and haunted by tumbleweed. Lone Pine was converted into a surrogate India. Lasky Mesa, Sonora, California, and even Mexico were used for scenes of the final charge. Flynn was horrified to learn that Curtiz would direct the picture, and tried without success to reach Jack Warner to complain.

Dick Carlin drove Errol up to Lone Pine to start shooting at the end of March. The wind was like a saber, and the dust and the cold badly affected Errol's sinuses. In the middle of their third night at Lone Pine Lodge, the lodge's restaurant caught fire. Errol and the rest of the company were forced out into the street.

On March 28, the picture began at Lone Pine, with a scene of the buying of the horses for use in the campaign. Curtiz had them all up at dawn, shouting abuse at everyone as he lined up sepoys and cavalry along a precipitous mountain pass. The wind howled, cutting through the thin uniforms, and Curtiz screamed at the actors, "Okay, *act!*"

Patric Knowles, a handsome young English actor who was playing Errol's brother, had not, it turned out, been astride a horse in years. He dug his spurs in too hard and the horse reared, throwing him from the saddle. He lay miserably in the dust while Curtiz, Errol, and all the other men laughed. Knowles recalls: "Errol laughed the loudest: he didn't give a damn for picture making anyway: he thought it was ridiculous."

Curtiz's typical early-morning address to Errol was, "Get your ass over here. We're behind schedule." Errol flew at him several times, but the other actors managed to restrain him.

Right in the middle of shooting, Errol faced a major threat. He narrowly escaped being deported from the country within twenty-four hours. This came about as the result of a serious setback to Erben's career in Austria. He had been finally pinned down as a Nazi agent and a menace to his government. He was investigated thoroughly and he was deported to Germany on March 16, 1936. The United States consul in Vienna, Francis R. Stewart, reported to Washington the connections between Erben and Errol. Austrian intelligence also made these connections clear.

As a result, the State Department and the FBI decided to seize on a technicality to remove Errol from the United States. His Australian passport, issued in Rabaul on April 21, 1933, was good for five years. In London, he had obtained a visitor's visa at the United States Consulate on November 3, 1934. It was good for a year, but he had neglected to apply for an extension in November, 1935. Worse, he had lied to the studio about his immigration status. He had said that he had come in on a British instead of an Australian quota. So, in fact, he was working illegally. He visited Roy Obringer, the studio legal chief, seven times before leaving for Lone Pine, extremely agitated because Obringer told him he had received letters from Washington demanding that Flynn explain why he had failed to extend his visa.

His excuse was that he had been busy attending the premiere of *Captain Blood* and that he had been ill; but this cut no ice with Obringer, a man worth his weight in iron. Jack Warner panicked: flurries of memoranda went to and fro: here was a new star who could be ignominiously shunted out of the country at any moment! Not that they cared about *his* discomfort or even the national security. Errol represented an investment. Huge sums of money would be lost if shooting of *The Charge of the Light Brigade* had to be interrupted.

The Hays office in Washington, the committee which supposedly watched over the industry's morals, was called into service by Jack Warner.

Will Hays was a man of immense power in the nation. He had been a former Postmaster General and he was very close to the Roosevelts and the heads of every one of the armed forces. Samuel Marx, Hollywood producer and author, says: "Hays could fix anything if a star was in political or moral trouble. He somehow had everyone in Washington hypnotized. And then, one has to understand the unbelievable power of the studios at the time. Jack Warner or Louis B. Mayer could get Roosevelt out of the Oval Office anytime they wanted for a private conversation. If they needed military or naval bases, even secret installations, as locations they could get access immediately." The result was that information was available to saboteurs through the silver screen.

Will Hays's men talked to the State Department officials, who at first were adamant that Flynn must leave within twenty-four hours from March 30. But so great was Hays's pressure that Flynn was allowed to stay on until he could get to Mexicali, just across the Mexican border, and re-enter on a British quota—again quite illegal, since he should have come in on the much more restricted Australian quota.

Jack Warner, William Randolph Hearst—a pro-Fascist new friend of Errol's—and David O. Selznick sent letters to the American consul in Mexico. The production schedule of the picture was rearranged so that the final scene of the charge could be delayed to allow Errol to go to Mexicali.

Production closed down for five days to make his trip possible.

Errol seized the opportunity to take an unauthorized three-day vacation in Mexico City, impudently mingling with Nazis there. He flew on to Guadalajara to bed the local girls—and boys—and enjoy substantial amounts of tequila. Jack Warner and Hal Wallis sent telegrams demanding he return at once, but he ignored them. The executives were terrified he would be caught in a public brawl and disqualified from obtaining his visa in Mexicali and perhaps even prevented from re-entering California.

Errol's luck held out; he returned to Los Angeles with his immigration status assured.

Shooting continued at Lone Pine. Dust storms, lashed by harsh winds, swept across the mesa. Each day the company was up at dawn. The horse-buying scenes were complex and difficult to shoot. A falcon hunt proved problematical when the falcons failed to settle on the actors' wrists on cue.

On April 6, wearied by long hours of shooting—beginning at five or six A.M. and continuing till the last speck of light in the sky—Errol was back at Burbank, shooting scenes of Surat Khan's palace. Two days later, he was at Sherwood Forest near Malibu Canyon, riding in a shaky howdah on top of an elephant, in a leopard hunt scene which was ruined when a howdah containing stuntmen fell apart and crashed to the ground, causing several injuries.

On the tenth, shooting was moved to Lasky Mesa. Errol was again up at 5 A.M. day after day for the scenes of the siege of Chukoti. The white burning light, the tarantulas thick on the ground, the stinging dust, the wind, all frayed his nerves.

Meanwhile, trouble brewed at the studio. Hal Wallis, in charge of production, accused Curtiz of using too many fancy foreground effects, quirky angles, shots in which the actors had their backs to the camera. He threatened daily to have Curtiz removed; this made Curtiz all the more tense and angry, leading him to punish the extras. But the horses suffered the most: they were tortured with infamous "running W's," wires attached to the ground and pulled tight against their legs, making them stumble onto the hard earth of the Mesa. Many were lamed and had to be shot, and the humane societies angrily complained.

The script called for Errol to ride over a cannon and die on camera, falling from the back of his horse. Errol wanted to do the stunt, and Curtiz was more than willing to have him risk his neck, but the prop man, Errol's little British friend Limey Plews, talked Curtiz out of it. "Suppose he should be killed or injured?" Limey said to Curtiz. "Your career as a director would be over." Errol made the jump anyway.

The first shots of the charge were made in front of the British ambassador, who had flown in especially from Washington for the occasion. It was a brilliantly clear and sunny day, and the stuntmen made a gallant sight in their full dress uniforms as they lined up against the harsh brown rocks and a sky filled with dramatic clouds. Limey was allowed to introduce the charge because of his British accent. He took up a megaphone and yelled, "Now are the 27th Lancers ready? Will you please advance into the valley?" The British ambassador was embarrassed. Almost seven hundred men had led the original charge. Warners only supplied two hundred and fifty-nine.

Errol was supposed to lead the charge astride his noble stallion. One of the extras who was envious of him suddenly took a lance with a rubber tip and thrust the lance into the rear end of Errol's horse. It took off at a tremendous speed across the plain, with Errol furiously trying to control the beast. The British ambassador and all of the riders and spectators laughed uproariously at his discomfiture.

It took him a week to locate the offender. He gave him two black eyes and a broken leg.

Back in the studio for the last days of shooting, Errol began a lifelong practice of performing practical jokes. Olivia de Havilland flounced off the set one day in a tantrum only to find that her dressing room door had been nailed shut. He told her that a large wasp had settled on her behind and he took hold of a very large rusty flyswatter and slapped her hard with it. He told her that the wasp had left smears of blood on her dress and fetched an enormous sponge and wiped it off. Needless to say, there had been no wasp in the first place. Her dress was ruined, and she burst into tears.

When she climbed into her long pantaloons one morning she screamed so loudly that several people came running. Errol had put a large green rubber snake with realistic fangs in the underwear. When she was on camera, he would stand behind it thumbing his nose at her or wiggling his hands in his ears. He placed a special rubber cushion in her chair which emitted a loud and definitive raspberry.

He arranged for Limey to put boiling water in the water coolers on the hottest days. On one occasion, the glass cracked from the heat of its contents and the water scalded an extra. He put salt and pepper in the chocolate sundaes in the commissary. One day, he got down on the floor and silently pinned a girl's costume skirt to the floor when she wasn't looking. Then he sounded a fire alarm. As she ran, the skirt ripped off, and she was left standing in her pantaloons.

His pranks were not confined to the studio. He let a raccoon loose into the Brown Derby on Vine Street and in the general melee it ran up Kay Francis' leg. Later, he released a basketful of white mice into Chasen's.

Perhaps Errol's most characteristic joke was when a crowd of fans besieged him for his autograph outside the Beverly Hills Hotel. He signed the autographs but kept the pencils.

He even risked playing a joke on Jack Warner. He sent him a telegram saying he had been in a bad accident. No sooner had Warner flung the telegram down, convinced Errol was playing a gag, than Warner's secretary said, "Mr. Warner, Mr. Flynn is here to see you." Errol hobbled in wearing a bandage around his head and a cast and collapsed into a chair. Warner rose, looking concerned for a moment, and Errol flung off his disguise and roared with laughter.

The practical jokes at Olivia de Havilland's expense boomeranged. They were meant to be signs of friendship, but she didn't appreciate them. Indeed, because of them she never became romantically involved with Errol. She says:

> If only he had been gentle and considerate, if only he had known how to woo and win me! He didn't need to do childish, unfair things to insure his own romantic effectiveness. He disappointed me on more than one level. I had idealistic notions of behavior and his was

hardly the heroic manner he offered the world on the screen. He was attracted to me, psychologically engaged, but he didn't know the right way to go about showing it. He didn't know how close I was to the romantic innocent Victorian girl I was playing. I think we felt a kind of love for each other, but I also know it could never have come to anything.

On wet days, Errol, his pal David Niven, and Knowles would stay in, exchanging tales that were centered on Errol's favorite reading: the English comic papers *Chums* and the *Magnet*. He would send Limey to remote locations to find these magazines and then the group of young expatriates would revel in the latest adventures of the comic-strip heroes.

Out of doors, tennis was their predominant interest. Jack Knie-meyer recalls:

One day, Errol and I went down to Del Mar to play in a tennis tournament there. The day before, he decided on an impulse to go with me and Johnny Meyer to Tiajuana. We stopped off at beaches along the way. I was surprised to see that Errol was self-conscious about his fame and too shy to pick up girls himself. Johnny had to do the dirty work for him. He'd book into motels and make love to the girls and move on. Finally, we got to Tiajuana, and more girls came running. If they heard Errol Flynn's name they'd fling them-selves at him. We got back to Del Mar at 3:04 one morning. The match was to be played four hours later. Lili Damita had arrived ahead of us. When we got to the bedroom door she was standing there with a magnum of French champagne. She was furious that he had been out all night. "You son of a beetch!" She shrieked, and hit Errol over the head with the bottle. She knocked him out cold. He fell bleeding to the floor. Johnny and I fled. Next day he played the tournament with a large white bandage wrapped around his head like a mummy. He still won the match!

During the shooting of *The Charge of the Light Brigade* Errol ex-perienced pains in his chest and attacks of coughing. This was the slow but sinister first indication of emphysema, which was to be the new cross he had to bear in life, hidden from the world and from all except his closest friends. The studio publicity machinery called his condition "athletic heart," because this sounded more romantic and glamorous. But he knew that his breath, his energy, his vitality were slowly but surely being whittled away.

Despite his hatred of Curtiz, Errol liked *The Charge*. And, as it turned out, so did the critics and the public. But Errol felt that the character he played, a young officer in the 27th Lancers, lacked depth and complexity.

The larger theme of the movie, the conquest of Colonial inferiors, is racist and ugly. And the sadistic treatment of the horses makes watching the final charge almost intolerable. Nevertheless, given almost nothing to work with, Errol carried the film. His presence and bearing are always militarily correct, proof of his surprising professional dedication to work.

Physically, the film was realized with an artificial grandeur more typical of Hollywood in 1936 than of the northwest frontier of India in 1856. The sets are ridiculous, the formation of the Lancers inaccurate. Nevertheless, there are striking set pieces: the relief of Chukoti, shot against the burning dusty white light of the Mesa; the escape from the fort by David Niven in moonlight, a masterpiece of direction and photography; and the charge itself, directed with fanatical drive and enthusiasm, its pace mounting from a trot to a gallop in keeping with the horses hoofs, banners waving, lances flashing, the sun glittering on sabers, and the horses pounding horribly to their deaths.

Nervous about being typecast, Errol had requested Hal Wallis as early as November 1935 to find him a vehicle different in character from his first two major films. Wallis came up with Lloyd C. Douglas' novel, *Green Light,* in which Errol would play an idealistic young doctor who fights old-fashioned methods in a hospital.

The shooting of the picture began only two weeks after the completion of *The Charge of the Light Brigade*. Errol's new agent, Noll Gurney, a smooth gentleman working for Myron Selznick, tried to storm into Jack Warner's office to learn why his client was being forbidden a promised eight weeks' leave of absence. Gurney was not allowed an audience, and when Myron Selznick himself arrived at Errol's behest with further complaints about the lost vacation, Warner locked the door in his face. Finally, after innumerable angry phone calls, a deal was made: Errol would be given an increase to $1,250 a week after December 27, and a twelve-week vacation starting in

February 1937. *Green Light* was made under considerable diffi-
culties. Neither Errol nor the director Frank Borzage nor indeed
Hal Wallis himself could endure the empty posturing of the female
lead, Anita Louise. Hal Wallis dubbed her "Anita Adenoidal" and
"as cold as a stepmother's kiss." Borzage was a heavy-handed, sentimental Irishman with crinkly red hair who irritated the executives by
shooting every scene from the same angle. His pulpy, flabby direction exasperated Flynn, who was surprised to find himself missing
the horny hand of Mike Curtiz. Jack Warner screamed that Borzage
was paying more attention to his favorite sport, polo, than to the
picture.

Errol next appeared in a romantic melodrama, *Another Dawn,*
with Kay Francis, shot partly in Yuma and partly on the Lasky
Mesa. The director was William Dieterle, a German so large that he
towered over Flynn. Errol did not like him and proved to be hard to
handle during the production. In a series of memoranda to the studio
heads, the producer indicated that Errol was never on time, it
was impossible to get him out of his chair and in front of the camera,
and that his first remark each morning was, "What do I say here?"
Unless he was carefully told what he would be doing that he would
not do it, and his complaints were constant and nagging. The fact
was Errol was struggling with his sickness, and found it increasingly
difficult to force himself to come to work each morning.

Moreover, Myron Selznick was telling him to go slow because the
promised arrangement for the new contract and agreed vacation had
not yet been confirmed in writing. One afternoon, Errol had to shoot
a crucial scene with Kay Francis. Errol refused to come out of his
dressing room. He had been told not to do so until the letter of
agreement arrived in Selznick's office. The production manager,
Tenny Wright, beat on Errol's door and screamed, "What the fuck
do you think you're doing?" Errol shouted back a stream of abuse.
Tenny Wright called Jack Warner. Warner called Selznick. Selznick
yelled down the line, "Yes, I did tell him to wait there, and he'll go
on waiting there until you send me that letter you promised." The
battle went on all afternoon. Finally, Warner was forced to rush a
telegram to Selznick so that the scene could be shot that night.

Still irritated by the size of his salary and what he felt to be
mediocrity of his parts, Errol continued to pester Jack Warner with
requests that he be allowed to appear in Broadway plays and that he

be allowed to join any group, however amateur, which performed Shakespeare in Los Angeles. He consoled himself for Warner's failure to accede to his demands with the new addition to his life: Arno, a blue-gray Schnauzer given him by a friend, the young producer Robert Lord. Errol loved Arno more than he ever loved any human being; in the years to come, this extraordinarily clever creature would become the star of his private world.

And his obsession with John Barrymore grew. Flynn saw all of Barrymore's movies, collected photographs and stills of him by the score, followed him like a fan, dreamed of owning a yacht like his, flourished an identical ivory cigarette holder, and carried a monkey about with him as Barrymore did.

When the lease was up on the house on Appian Way, Errol dragged Lili off to the pretentious apartment hotel known as the Château Elysée, because he heard (incorrectly as it turned out) that Barrymore kept a mistress there. Errol and Lili were accompanied by Arno, occasional cats and parrots, and the pet monkey.

While there Errol completed a memoir, *Beam Ends,* based on his trip to Queensland on the *Sirocco*. It was published to mixed reviews.

That fall of 1936, Errol became oddly fascinated by police procedures and enjoyed the fact that his fame earned him entree to the Los Angeles Police Department. One night, he contacted Captain Steed of the homicide squad and a man named Pat More, and went out with them in the police car. The three men were dining in Chinatown when Steed received a call that a Chinese had been stabbed to death with a carving knife. The trio sped off into the night. When they arrived at the scene of the murder, a crowd of Orientals was gathered at the entrance. Errol and his friends broke through the mob and climbed the stairs. Later, Errol told a reporter:

> Everything in the room was neat. The body was nattily dressed with shiny, patent leather shoes. There were stills from movies all over the walls. The man had been a movie buff. The head wasn't where it belonged. It was three feet away, looking startled. As well it might. I wasn't surprised to discover that the guy was a movie agent who'd promised too much to a client.

A few moments later, Errol and his companions were off on another call. They arrived at an apartment in Hollywood. The manager came running out and said, "No publicity, please, no publicity!"

"Who do you think we are?" Captain Steed asked. "Advance agents for a circus?"

A woman lay spread over a bed, pills strewn everywhere about her. Dressed in her underwear, she was retching violently. Errol picked up a note from the dresser. It read: "We regret we cannot register your name as we already have over 15,000 people in our books. Jim Carl, Central Casting."

After midnight, Errol found himself with his friends at a mansion in Beverly Hills, where a man had attempted to shoot himself. At about 3 A.M., their car screamed up to a house in Hollywood. There, they found that a well-known character actor had dressed himself up as Pan and chased various girls dressed as wood nymphs around his lawn before swallowing an overdose of pills. When the new arrivals burst open the door, a man screamed out, "Oh boy! It's a gag! It ain't the cops! It's only Errol Flynn!"

Even while he was accompanying the police on their investigation, Errol was indulging in his old habit of lighthearted, Raffles-like theft. It was as though he couldn't see anything valuable without trying to pocket it if it was small enough. He would take wristwatches, pocket watches, earrings, finger rings, and even wedding rings if he felt the urge. No ornament was safe from him. Any woman who spent the night with him usually found herself without some precious article when she got home. He would even secrete items of female underwear. People who came to his house would find drawers filled with an assortment of stolen objects; he was so careless about hiding them that he would even place them in the back of kitchen or bathroom closets. He never sold or pawned them; he simply obeyed the restless instincts of his fingers.

He allowed himself more dangerous pleasures: pleasures which could have destroyed his career had they been discovered. He formed intense brief attachments with both underage girls and young boys. The girls he preferred in the age range from thirteen to sixteen; the boys seventeen to nineteen. He dared not express his homosexual leanings in Hollywood; which explains his frequent visits to Mexico. A prominent director who worked at Warner Brothers says:

William Haynes, the silent star, had been ruined when Louis B. Mayer discovered Haynes had been involved with a sailor. If Jack Warner, who had a soft spot for Errol, chiefly because of Errol's famous success with women, had found out, he would probably have destroyed Errol's career. Errol discovered when he first went to Mexico that at last there was a safe way of indulging his needs: all he had to do was cross the border. He met an Australian millionaire whom he had known before and who lived in a mansion in Cuernevaca and knew how to obtain boys for small amounts of money. Errol would always go to Cuernevaca for these boys. No one got onto it. Not even the most ardent gossips.

I knew a boy, a hustler, who was at one of the Australian millionaire's parties. I asked him about it afterward. He told me that Errol invited him to his room and performed fellatio on him and vice versa. The boy said Errol was so handsome, superbly built and passionate that for the first time in his career as a male prostitute he was genuinely turned on by a client. He was amazed by Errol's staying power, virility, and sheer energy in bed.

For the rest of his life, Errol managed to keep his bisexuality hidden from all except a very small circle. His wives, so far as we know, never suspected it; nor did his very close friend, Jim Fleming. Most of his male friends were—as they are today—so aggressively macho he would never have dared tell them. But there were odd, distorted manifestations of feeling even in his straight relationships: he liked to make love to women while watching other men—often in groups —make love at the same time; the men's bodies evidently excited him as much as the women's; later, he installed a two-way mirror in his house so that he could watch men in a lovemaking derby; and he had a strange habit all his life of exhibiting himself in erection to his supposedly heterosexual friends.

The fact is, Flynn was determined to experience every pleasure to the limit. He wanted to drink deeply of life, and to avoid nothing of what it could offer. He experimented with cocaine, kif, opium, and hashish, not in a spirit of self-destructiveness but in a desire to enhance his senses so intensely that life would seem more brilliantly colorful, less painful and anxiety-inducing than it really was. He lived in a state of acute physical awareness of reality. His nerves tingled with animal vitality. He was aware more than most men of his own physique, his muscles, and the sexual center of his being. Yet,

Errol, aged eighteen months, with his mother, in Hobart.
(Courtesy of Earl Conrad)

Aged six with his dog
"Man Friday" in Hobart.
(Courtesy of Earl Conrad)

Aged six in Hobart.
(Courtesy of Earl Conrad)

Aged nineteen, Sydney. (Courtesy of Earl Conrad)

ERROL FLYNN

Returned from Australia after playing
Lead in "In the Wake of the Bounty"—*Expeditionary Film Co.*
Current Production : "I Adore You"—*Warner Bros.*

Finalist Australasian
Heavyweight Boxing
Championship, 1929.

Olympic Games Trials
(Australasia.)

Expert Horseman and
Swimmer.

(N.S.W. Diving Team
1930.)

Sole Management :
Wieland's Agency,
8, Charing Cross Road,
W.C.2.

TEMple Bar
6788

Photos : Sasha.   Height 6 feet 1 inch.

Advertisement in *Spotlight*,
London, 1934.

Theatre program, 1933. Flynn
is eighth from the bottom.
(Charles Higham collection)

Aged twenty-one, New Guinea.
(Courtesy of Earl Conrad)

WEDNESDAY, THURSDAY, FRIDAY & SATURDAY,
DECEMBER 27th, 28th, 29th and 30th,
WEDNESDAY, THURSDAY, FRIDAY & SATURDAY,
JANUARY 3rd, 4th, 5th and 6th, at 2.30 p.m.

NORTHAMPTON REPERTORY PLAYERS Ltd.
Present—

JACK & THE BEANSTALK

A Fairy Play in Three Acts.
By MARGARET CARTER.

Characters in order of their appearance:

First Weaver	FREDA JACKSON.
Second Weaver	DOROTHY GALBRAITH.
Third Weaver	NORAH GANDY.
Azelle	DORIS LITTELL.
	JULIAN CLAY.
	MARGARET SMITH.
Reapers	PATRICK GOVER.
	ISABEL MICHEL.
Mother Grubble	SHEILA MILLAR.
Peterkins	OSWALD DALE ROBERTS.
Rufus	DONALD GORDON.
	JULIAN CLAY.
Cuckoo (the Cow)	ISABEL MICHEL.
	PETER ROSSER.
Jack	PATRICK GOVER.
King	ZILLAH, GREY.
Lady Flavia	
Prince Donzil	ERROL FLYNN.
Princess Chrystabel	MARJORIE McEWEN.
Dame Gallibantus	DOROTHY GALBRAITH.
Gallibantus	JULIAN CLAY.
Page	ISABEL MICHEL.
	FREDA JACKSON.
Guests	MARGARET SMITH.
	NORAH GANDY.

Toys by Curtis, George Row.
Furniture made in our own Workshop.
Bird Cage by Mence Smith, Mercers' Row.
Basket by Blind Association, St. Giles' Street.

Dr. H. F. Erben after
the monkey voyage,
(Photograph by
Jerome Zerbe) 1935.

Dr. Erben's Nazi Party
membership card.

Errol and Lili Damita, 1935.

Errol and Lili, Hollywood, 1936. (Photograph by Jerome Zerbe)

he remained insecure; he needed the reassurance of his sexuality and the admiration of others both on and off the screen. Popular acclaim meant more to him than he pretended; but even more urgently he needed the intimate approval of the boys and girls he shared his bed with. His sexual compulsion was not merely the result of being aggressively healthy and twenty-six years old; it was the result of wanting to be accepted and admired and proven to be a potent male.

And yet, despite his obsession with sex, he found his deepest satisfactions in the clean life of the sea. Whenever he could, he would drive down to Ensenada, sail with friends to Catalina, fly by amphibian to the same offshore island, and enjoy golden weekends of swimming, fishing, hunting, and sunbathing. He told friends he dreamed of the day when he could afford to buy a yacht and dub her the *Sirocco* after the beloved vessel he had owned in the South Seas. But that day was far off. To console himself, when *Another Dawn* dragged its weary length to a close, he took off with Lili for their first real honeymoon in New York and Cuba and Jamaica. The trip served a double purpose: he could threaten not to come back to the studio unless his salary were to be increased. There is no doubt that his inspiration for this idea was the skillful Myron Selznick.

Errol fell in love with the Caribbean immediately. It became, in fact, his favorite resort area, and he especially liked Cuba and Jamaica. He and Lili hopped islands by amphibian, biplane, monoplane, and even autogiro; they went deep-sea fishing on rented boats. With his shirt off and the sun stinging his skin, with days of straining after marlin or hiking in virgin jungle and romantic green mountains, with the pleasure of good food and grog and Caribbean music and Lili warm beside him at night, the thought of returning to the airless, stifling world of Hollywood sound stages was unendurable. He couldn't face the thought of another costume epic with sweat trickling down his body and stiff period dialogue to speak. And the tension and strain, day after day, and all through Saturday night when all he wanted was to drink and make love and have a good laugh. No, he would never go back. Unless, of course, the studio bosses paid him twenty-five hundred dollars a week.

They did. While in Jamaica, Errol received confirmation that his salary would be increased to the figure he wanted. And Errol would appear immediately in a version of Mark Twain's *The Prince and the Pauper*, to cash in on the current enthusiasm for versions of children's classics and the current interest in royalty stimulated by the death of King George V in England. The story of *The Prince and the Pauper* was essentially, as *Captain Blood* had been, that of a revolt against tyranny: the Depression was still going on, and the theme of the underprivileged against the oppressor was still strongly attractive.

What Errol did not know, and did not find out until later, was that several other actors had been tested for the part in the hope that his attempt to get his increase in salary could be thwarted. Among those tried out in costume were Patric Knowles, Ian Hunter, and George Brent. They all proved to be too reserved for Hal Wallis' taste. Money or no money, Errol Flynn was the only man capable of carrying a picture of this scale on his own.

Rejoicing in his new victory over the studio, Errol flew home with Lili at the end of December 1936. He had forced an agreement that he would return for no more than six weeks and have a guaranteed eight weeks of leave with pay—unheard of at the time—at the end of shooting. But his first day back, he came down with a severe attack of coughing and sinus trouble; he even coughed blood. To make matters worse, the seasonal California rains beat down monotonously on the roof of the Château Elysée. Errol was scarcely able to sleep. And he was not cheered by a visit from his business manager, who bluntly told him he would have to dig into the fifteen-thousand-dollar trust fund set up at the studio from his salary in order to pay his income tax that coming April.

Jack Warner and Hal Wallis were furious that after bringing Flynn back at such great expense, they now had an invalid on their hands. The studio legal chief, Roy Obringer, warned Errol that unless he came to work by February 1, he would be cut off without salary indefinitely. They refused to believe Dr. Frank Nolan's reports on his condition and sent a man on their own to examine him. Even when the studio doctor returned with word that Errol was genuinely sick, they retained their suspicions.

Errol struggled to work on January 25. He collapsed after only an hour on the set and was rushed home suffering from a high fever. Dr. Nolan diagnosed pneumonia. For ten days, he hovered close to the danger list, barely able to take nourishment, and suffering from violent sweating and choking attacks. But by February 2 he was back on the set, weak and drained but still able to joke with the young boys who starred in the picture, the Mauch twins. He took them for hair-raising rides in his Auburn (which earned him two traffic tickets and a near mishap with a truck), and helped them to perform practical jokes, showing them how to drop pins or paperclips down the necks of the extras.

Roy Obringer told him he was still going to be docked his pay for every day he had failed to show up for work because of his illness. Tough as he was, the Hollywood system was tougher.

His illness and his annoyance about the pay loss showed up in his performance. His action scenes lacked the flair he had brought to earlier pictures; he looked tired and pale and drawn in the rushes.

Nevertheless, the picture was ably handled by the sensitive and skillful William Keighley. It turned out to be a pleasant and accomplished historical drama, enlivened by comedy touches. Twain's story of the two boys, one the young Prince Edward, son of Henry VIII, and the other a beggar lad, who changed places with amusing results, was given exactly the right touch of whimsical fairy-tale humor and charm.

In the last days of shooting, Professor and Mrs. Flynn arrived in Hollywood in the course of a tour of America. They were without Rosemary, who was at school in Ireland. Marelle was her usual self, criticizing Errol and everyone else at the studio until he wanted to kill her. But the professor charmed everybody he met in Hollywood, including Lili and Jim Fleming. The visit was brief; although Errol was glad to see his father again, the couple's provincialism proved to be something of an embarrassment to him at the sophisticated parties he gave in their honor at the Château Elysée.

Seven

Soon after *The Prince and the Pauper* was completed, FBI and State Department officials visited Errol and told him an almost incredible story. They said that his friend Dr. Hermann Erben had become involved in a nightmarish incident at sea.

Erben had sailed on the McCormick Lines freighter *West Mahwah* from San Francisco to Buenos Aires in September 1936, as ship's doctor with a handful of passengers and a riotous, undisciplined crew. Passing through the Panama Canal, Erben excited the captain's suspicion by taking numerous photographs of installations and of gun mountings aboard British and American vessels.

In suffocating heat the ship steamed down the coast of Brazil. The captain said he saw Erben hastily thrust a document of German origin into a drawer when he made an unexpected visit to Erben's cabin.

The saloon was hung with American flags for the Christmas holidays. On New Year's Eve, during a party, Erben wiped his dirty hands on the flag. When the officers asked him what he thought he was doing, his reply made him a marked man. He shouted that he was an American only for the material advantages and that when war broke out, as it would, he would immediately enlist in Germany; that Hitler was a supreme being and savior and he would sink his teeth in the throat or crush to a pulp anybody who criticized Hitler in his presence; that his wearing of a Hitler mustache was a proud symbol of his loyalty; and that he had aided in the bloody assassination of Chancellor Dollfuss in Vienna.

Worse was to come. When the vessel sailed to Buenos Aires, a peace conference was in progress attended by President Roosevelt. Erben screamed insults at the American delegation aboard the *Southern Cross*. He rushed to the bridge, gave the Nazi salute and shouted "Heil Hitler!" to a German freighter's crew as the vessel sailed by.

On a stormy night off Rio de Janeiro, Erben took a revolver and a pair of brass knuckles and roamed about, threatening lives. His true Nazi origins were flaring up—ruinous to a secret agent of the Gestapo, who was never supposed to show his political leanings or tendency to violence. By now, passengers and crew had had more than enough. When the ship docked in Rio on January 6, 1937, a delegation of six appeared at the consulate and swore out their horrifying story to Vice Consuls Reginald B. Kazanjian and Emil Sauer. The vice consuls called Erben into the office and demanded an explanation of his behavior. His reply was ingenious but failed to fit the facts.

He was deported to America on the Delta Lines vessel *Delnorte*. On arrival in New Orleans, he was found to have taken the *West Mahwah*'s surgical instruments and drugs.

Errol listened to this horrifying story in amused silence. He pretended that he was unable to cast any political light on it. The instant the officials left, he located Erben in New Orleans and invited him to stay in Hollywood. Members of the FBI tracked Erben to Los Angeles in February. Perhaps because of this, Erben did not join Errol at the Château Elysée but moved into the modest New Rosslyn hotel downtown. The New Rosslyn seemed to be a favorite address for spies. Later, Erben's Nazi associate Hans Adolf Mosberg also stayed there, before sneaking out of America.

The FBI continued to pester Errol and the studio over Erben's presence in Los Angeles, but there seems little doubt that Will Hays and Colonel William Guthrie, a high-ranking army officer on the studio payroll as Jack Warner's troubleshooter in all matters connected with politics, were responsible for the cover-up of Errol at the time. Jack Warner handed over all matters connected with Washington to Hays and Guthrie. Just as Will Hays saved Errol from being deported in 1936, so now Hays and Guthrie managed to smother the numerous inquiries that began seriously to threaten Errol's career.

Guthrie, too, had extraordinary influence in Washington. He, too, had instant access to the White House and was friendly with the heads of the Army and Navy and with the Roosevelts.

Guthrie was not pro-Nazi. He may not have believed that Errol was a spy. Or it may be that he was concerned solely that the loss of Errol would mean a major financial setback to the studio and the shareholders. His suppression of a serious investigation into Errol reflected a Hollywood which cared only for money and had no interest in political or moral principles if an investment was at stake.

As early as the summer of 1936, when Erben briefly visited Los Angeles before taking off on the *West Mahwah,* he and Errol had laid plans for a desperate and dangerous mission: an adventure in the service of Hitler. In an astonishing confession to A. J. Nicholas of the State Department's Passport Division on April 25, 1938, Erben stated that the purpose of the mission was to obtain photographs, names and addresses of all those German soldiers who were fighting for the Loyalists against Franco and his supporter, Hitler, in the Spanish Civil War. These particulars would be taken to Berlin and delivered into the hands of the Gestapo so that the families of those disloyal to Hitler would be punished. In many cases, this punishment would involve concentration camps and murder.

The bulk of the Germans in the Thaelmann Brigade and the other German Loyalist brigades had been decimated in battle. Many lay in field hospitals, severely injured or dying.

Erben, as a doctor, could enlist in these hospitals and tend the wounded. Errol as a world-famous star could visit the stricken men to give them good cheer. It would be a simple matter to obtain from these German veterans the names and addresses of their families in Germany to whom they wanted to send messages. Meanwhile, their own names and addresses could be noted and their photographs taken.

To add to his cover, Errol lied to many people he was taking one and a half million dollars from Loyalist and pro-Communist sympathizers in Hollywood to the Loyalists in Spain. He would hand the money over to the government in Valencia for disposition as it pleased. He said that the purpose would be to finance ambulances and weapon supplies.

Errol also pretended he had commissions from Hearst's *Cosmopolitan* and *Liberty* magazines to write a series of articles on Spain with Erben as his "assigned photographer"(!). As a Britisher, he easily got issued a visa at the Spanish Consulate in Los Angeles. But Erben was faced with a problem. It is clear from her interoffice memoranda of that month, February 1937, that Ruth Shipley of the Passport Division in Washington was exceedingly doubtful about permitting Dr. Erben to travel in Spain.

Erben had been forced to surrender his passport to naval intelligence officers at the American Consulate General in Buenos Aires. The passport had been forwarded to San Francisco, the city of Erben's naturalization. It was still being held and was due to expire the week of Erben's proposed departure for Europe. Errol personally intervened to secure new documents. He telegraphed Ruth Shipley and put so much pressure on her that, impressed by his fame, she unwisely extended Erben's passport to December 7, 1937. By now, Erben had already flown to New York.

Errol cabled San Francisco and Washington to rush the renewed documents to the New York passport office in time for the *Queen Mary* sailing for England on February 24. But, when he checked into the Hotel St. Moritz in New York, the precious document had still not arrived.

On sailing day, Erben rushed over to the passport office on Wall Street. Flustered, his spectacles glistening with sweat from his forehead, he began shouting hysterically at the officials that the *Queen Mary* would be sailing in less than an hour and that if he missed the ship he would also miss his greatest opportunity as a photographer. A. J. Nicholas, the officer in charge, wasn't impressed. He knew Erben only as a doctor and an amateur photographer and felt he could scarcely reach the standard required by *Cosmopolitan* and *Liberty* magazines. He was not impressed, either, by the fact that Dr. Erben had gone out of his way to achieve a resemblance to Adolf Hitler.

In any event, the passport had not arrived, and Nicholas suggested that Erben wait for the next ship. Erben jumped in a cab and sped to the wharf where the *Queen Mary*'s officers were just about to raise the gangway.

Errol was on deck, with fans crowding around. More were gathered on the wharf, screaming their admiration. In the midst of the applause, Erben told Errol that his passport had not arrived. There were only fifteen minutes left before sailing.

Errol dashed to the Chief Officer and explained the situation. While the officer was weighing the matter, Errol and Erben wrote frantic notes to Ruth Shipley on *Queen Mary* stationery and thrust them into the hands of the last passenger going ashore. The letters urged Mrs. Shipley to rush the passport on the next boat. Even in this moment of extremity, Erben characteristically managed to add a postscript: the precise dates and sailing times of the next two ships sailing to England from New York.

By now, the Chief Officer had reached his decision. Overwhelmed by Errol's powers of persuasion, he agreed to let Dr. Erben sail. Errol wrote out a check covering the cost of Erben's passage back to New York on the same vessel, filled out a bond form guaranteeing Erben's proper behavior, and swore that the passport would be arriving in London. He showed the telegrams from the San Francisco passport office and Ruth Shipley indicating that the passport had been renewed. At that exact moment, the *Queen Mary* sailed.

Errol squeezed Erben through immigration at Southampton. He dodged reporters and flew to Paris to avoid awkward questions about his friend. He flew back, pretending that he had disembarked at Cherbourg. On March 6, he and Erben appeared at the United States Consulate General in London the instant it opened. The passport had come in on the next vessel Erben had named. They examined it excitedly. Then they received a stunning shock. It was marked "Not Valid for Travel in Spain"!

Their rage knew no bounds. Nor did their ingenuity. First, Errol got in touch with his old acquaintance the Duke of Alba, and asked for the necessary travel arrangements for Erben. But Alba was indifferent toward the idea of having Erben and Errol attached to Franco's fifth column because of the danger in faking documents.

Errol made contact with his friend Esmond Romilly, a nephew of Winston Churchill, who had just returned from Spain.

Romilly told him of the Spanish Medical Aid Committee, which had been formed in England in mid-1936, under the general direction of Viscount Churchill. Connected to the International Brigade, in which the German regiments fought, the S.M.A.C. had gone to Spain in August. Courageous doctors and nurses had set up five field hospitals in converted monasteries and schools in the line of bombardment.

It was an easy matter to arrange for Erben to join the Spanish Medical Aid Committee. After all, he was a surgeon and experienced in dealing with disease.

The Honorable Christopher Addison was in charge of the Spanish Medical Aid Committee in London. He approved Dr. Erben's credentials and in all innocence agreed to use him, provided Erben could overcome the difficulty of the invalidation for Spain stamped so clearly on his passport. But despite Addison's support, Errol and Erben were unable to shake the consulate in London or the State Department. They traveled to Paris and tried the United States Embassy there, but again their pleas were useless.

Erben went to Berlin to report his problem and to try to arrange American passport and immigration facilities for his two sons, one of whom was on temporary leave from Hitler's Kondor Legion in Spain. Fortunately for American security, his effort failed. Later, Erben tried again—and on the second occasion Errol offered the use of his house in Los Angeles to these boys.

Erben returned to Paris. Both men went to the American Embassy and swore out affidavits asserting that they were under assignment from *Cosmopolitan* and *Liberty*. But the passport restriction was not lifted.

Then suddenly they heard that the Spanish government was so desperate for doctors that safe-conduct documents would be issued to anybody, carrying a passport or not, who was a trained physician or nurse. This was what Errol and Erben were waiting for. They immediately went to the Spanish Embassy and the necessary letter of transit for Erben was issued on March 23.

The normal procedure for famous visitors like Hemingway was by bomber plane to the temporary capital of Valencia. Instead, Errol and Erben proceeded with the aid of a Loyalist named Jorge by train to the border at Portbou and crossed through the tunnel to Barcelona on Easter Sunday.

In a letter written to Erben many years later by Dr. Berger-Voesendorf of the Austrian Foreign Service, Voesendorf said that

Erben's most dangerous activities included his "role in Barcelona." What did this mean?

Barcelona was the headquarters of the Gestapo spy ring known as "The Harbor Service" under Heydrich's appointees Alfred Engling and Hans Hellerman. Since his mission was on behalf of the Gestapo, Erben would have to report to this headquarters—concealed in the offices of an import-export company.

Meanwhile, Errol was received by several senior Loyalist government officials, taken to dinner by a Loyalist local propaganda chief, and entertained by many socialites.

The moment the State Department discovered Errol's and Erben's presence in Barcelona, they wired the local consul to say that Dr. Erben's visit was in contravention of the United States code. He was threatened with immediate deportation but was temporarily saved by presenting the Spanish transit letter.

In Valencia, Errol and Erben met with Constancia de la Mora, the beautiful and brilliant Loyalist chief of press propaganda, who had just been hostess to Hemingway. She was horrified to discover that there was no sign of the money she had been promised Errol would bring from Hollywood. In order to cover her embarrassment, she issued a statement to the local and foreign press quoting Erben and Errol as saying that they brought one and a half million dollars and that nothing was more glorious than the Loyalist cause. She had the awkward task of explaining to her superiors that this entire press announcement was a fake.

Señora de la Mora claimed in her memoirs that Errol and Erben bamboozled officials so successfully that they commandeered gasoline reserved for troop transports in order to undertake their journey. It was a hazardous trip. The roads were pitted with shell bursts and the sky was alive with tracer bullets. The noise of explosions and the stench of smoke accompanied them all the way. At times, ironically, they were in danger from their own side. When they arrived in Madrid, they were lucky to be alive at all. They were greeted by Viscount Churchill, who took them to a Spanish Medical Aid Committee hospital in a monastery, where they interviewed the patients.

Madrid was under siege. It wasn't immediately clear because the front was a mile and a quarter away—puffs of smoke and explosions intermittently punctuating the green vine covered hills and the perfumed orange groves. But shells had begun to burst in the streets themselves, and when Errol and Erben checked into the famous

Gran Via Hotel, parts of the building were already wrecked; they realized they could be blasted apart at any minute. Errol was coldshouldered by most of the Loyalists and foreign correspondents who gathered in the hotel's basement restaurant. Ernest Hemingway, who had dropped over from the Hotel Florida, was not complimentary. He knew at once that Errol was a Fascist. He warned Errol not to spy for the Fascists or to cross to the Fascist lines or his career as a star would be finished.

This spurred Errol on. He and Erben *would* go over to the Fascists—and see what was going on. It was an insane venture that could have destroyed their espionage mission at a blow. Erben was against it; Errol somehow talked him into it.

In a taped interview in 1978, Erben described the journey:

There was adventure in our dark hearts as we crawled into the night. We didn't get very far. The Fascists were shelling. A big shell exploded very close to us and Errol was knocked out by a piece of plaster which fell on his head. And that ended our attempt. I dragged him out; he wasn't badly hurt. I said to him, "Go back to Hollywood, you'll destroy your career if they find out that you weren't really on the Loyalist side but in your main interests wanted to join the Fascist side." Had Errol gone to the Franco side he would have been magnificently treated as the close friend of the Duke of Alba; he would never have been hurt because they would never have allowed their prized publicity image to be injured. The Fascists loved him. It's a pity.

Errol and Erben slunk back to the Gran Via. Erben gave a press conference the next day at the Gran Via saying that Errol had been injured by gunshot. Erben wanted to cast aspersions on the capacity of the Loyalists to defend their famous supporters. The press quickly blew this up out of all proportion and within a few days headlines across the world were stating that Errol was dead.

Erben linked up with Viscount Churchill's Spanish Medical Aid Committee. He traveled to the field hospitals giving blood transfusions, performing operations and obtaining information for the Gestapo under the unwitting aegis of Viscount Churchill. But after some three weeks the State Department made his continued stay in Spain an impossibility. He was forced to return to Paris and thence to Berlin where all further efforts to obtain accreditation for Spain were defeated. But he did succeed in taking a large number of photographs and reports to his superiors.

Errol, with the aid of Sidney Franklin, the famous "bullfighter from Brooklyn," who was a friend of Lili's, made his way to Valencia where State Department officials were waiting for him with instructions to return to America as soon as possible because of his association with Erben. The same day, Warner's Spanish representative flew Errol back to Paris.

As Errol settled into his suite at the Hotel Plaza Athénée, the newspapers arrived. He picked them up and burst into laughter. The front-page headlines said, ERROL FLYNN EST MORT.

He took enormous pleasure in sitting in the lobby of his hotel watching people read the announcement of his death, look at the photograph, and then put the paper down only to confront him sitting there in front of them. In London, Lili was frantic at the news. When she learned that Errol had come to no harm, she was furious at the hoax.

Errol cabled Jack Warner that he would return on the *Queen Mary* on April 12, but sailed on the German *Bremen* a week later instead.

Dr. Erben planned to go from Germany to the Orient, ostensibly for the Red Cross but actually on a Nazi medical mission to Chiang Kai Shek. The State Department was convinced he would be a problem in China because of his spying and narcotics-smuggling activities. His passport was stamped as firmly as it had been for Spain: "Not Valid for Travel in China."

He sailed to Hong Kong in the forlorn hope that he might be able to obtain a revocation of the restriction but his effort was futile. The police arrested him immediately and deported him to Canton. He was thus in the unique position of being deported to a country for which his passport had not been marked valid! Somehow, he managed to proceed to the International Settlement in Shanghai and to Japan and even re-entered Hong Kong before finally making his way back to America the following year.

Errol went to Washington in the spring of 1937. At one of the Roosevelts' very well-attended parties on the White House lawn, he was warned by Frances Perkins, the Secretary of Labor, not to attempt to write articles for the Hearst press about how he and Erben had helped the Fascists as the material was "dynamite" and might upset his career. Instead, Errol wrote a harmless fictitious version of the events under the impudently lying title, "What Really Happened to Me in Spain," for *Photoplay,* a mindless Hollywood fan magazine. But with typical insolence, he included photographs of German soldiers in the article—photographs taken by Erben.

Errol returned to Hollywood to find both Fascists and anti-Fascists ranged against him. The Loyalist sympathizers were disgusted by his Fascist connections. The pro-Franco Knights of Columbus accused him of aiding the Communist Loyalists. The studio emphasized his Loyalist leanings and had him issue public statements denying any Fascist connections. But Lillian Hellman recalls: "We had a screening for pro-Loyalists of the left wing Hemingway-Joris Ivens film, *Spanish Earth,* at the home of Fredric and Florence Eldridge March. Somebody foolishly invited Errol and as soon as the picture began he realized he had come to the wrong house. He fled through a downstairs window to the garden and didn't come back."

Errol found that his next "extremely important" picture was nothing more serious than a silly comedy entitled *The Perfect Specimen* in which he was supposed to play a physically and mentally ideal man who falls in love with a girl reporter.

He was diverted by the spectacle of the studio's futile attempts to cast the part of the girl reporter. Marion Davies, Carole Lombard, Miriam Hopkins, Rosalind Russell, and Olivia de Havilland were each tested, and, by a funny accident, Robert Montgomery was offered the part in a telegram.

Errol's behavior was as extravagantly irresponsible as ever during that period. He walked out of restaurants refusing to pay the bill, and the waiters were too nervous to go after him. He made bonfires of the endless stream of dunning notes from Australia, New Guinea, and England. He gave elaborate dinner parties at Chasen's and then had the bill divided up among all his guests. He bought Lili expensive jewels and furs and had her billed for them.

He still had money invested in a trust fund at the studio but he kept drawing from it to meet the extravagant costs of call girls and drugs. He was still earning twelve hundred and fifty dollars a week when most stars were making between three thousand and five thousand dollars. This drove him nearly mad. There was scarcely a week when he wasn't in Jack Warner's office, demanding he be paid what he was due.

He received the stunning blow that Curtiz would direct *The Perfect Specimen*. He dared not walk off the picture lest he be suspended without salary. Miserable, he went for lessons for a boxing scene with the famous welterweight champion Mushy Callahan, who later became a great friend. He told Mushy, "I'm not going to work at this goddamn picture. It stinks. Why should I bother?" He told Mushy that he had been the Olympics champion in 1928; within ten minutes, Mushy knew the boast was vain. Mushy tried hard to put Errol in shape for the part: he made him do calisthenics to bring his weight down from two hundred pounds to his old one hundred and seventy-five pounds stripped. He brought his waist down from thirty-eight to thirty-four by rigorous sit-ups and dieting on salads and fresh fruit. But Errol refused to cut out drinking and smoking, and when he went into the ring with the stunt double, Jack Loper, he knew he was in trouble. Loper slammed him in the ribs so hard he staggered and fell to the ropes. When Mushy ran up to him, Errol whispered in Mushy's ear, "This is great. I'm going to go to the canvas. It will get me a few days off and the papers will say I've been knocked out. That will make me sympathetic and Loper will be the heavy." With that, in one of the finest moments of his acting career, Errol crashed and lay there, eyes fluttering weakly, apparently unable to rise.

Eight

For months in 1937, Warner Brothers was preparing its most elaborate and expensive production to date. This was the epic romantic drama *The Adventures of Robin Hood*. Even anti-British Errol had to admit that the part of Robin Hood was perfect for him. And the role assured him a permanent place in the history of the screen as no other part ever would.

In the late summer of 1937, Lili returned from Europe and she and Errol were happily reconciled, working together, reading the script of the picture, and going over the costume sketches. The auguries looked good: William Keighley would direct; Olivia de Havilland would play the virginal Maid Marian; Basil Rathbone (still earning almost three thousand dollars a week more than Errol) was to be the villainous Sir Guy of Gisbourne, Ian Hunter the noble King Richard the Lion Heart; and Claude Rains the diabolical regent, John.

In August, Errol formed a new friendship, which was to last until the day of his death. He had been sent by the studio for archery lessons with the leading expert in the field, Howard Hill. Hill was an Errol Flynn without health problems or flaws of personality. He stood at least two inches taller in his bare feet. His shoulders were so broad that Errol could stand behind him and not be seen. His face was startlingly similar to Errol's own, even to the flashing brown eyes and pencil-line mustache. He laughed vigorously and often. His laugh would burst from his mighty chest and shake him to the foundations of his being. He could split an arrow with another at fifty paces. He drank heroically, swam, hunted, and sailed in a manner which had Errol worshiping at his feet. The only important difference between them was that Hill never chased women. He was a family man, utterly devoted to his wife and home.

Errol proved an adept student. He had a quick eye and a sure sense of timing, essentials in shooting with the bow and arrow. Day after day, Hill took him out on the Roving Range, or bowhunting rabbits from a moving car, or shooting wild goats from the deck of a boat off Catalina. Hill taught him how to stand sideways so that a line from his shoulders pointed directly at the target; where to nock the arrow on the string; how to hold the string; and all the other techniques of shooting and aiming. He taught him how, in hunting, he must always wear a neutral color because, although some prey were color blind, they could notice a contrast, especially in motion. He told Errol to wear tennis shoes which would make little sound and an old felt hat because it would help break up the human silhouette. Since human odors were offensive to wild game, Errol learned, a huntsman must mask his own by rubbing himself with crushed pine needles or animal-gland extracts.

Armed with a sharp knife, a length of cord, a deer bag, and rags, as well as the bows, Errol and his friend set off on several expeditions into the wild forests that were still to be found in those days not far from Los Angeles. On one occasion, they hunted mountain lion in the High Sierras. Unable to kill the beast with arrows, they lassoed it, and the furious animal howled and writhed on the rope which Hill wrapped around a tree. "Hold this quick!" Hill snapped. Errol obeyed, but accidentally seized the lion's tail instead of the rope. He narrowly escaped being severely clawed.

On another occasion, he was hunting wild boar with Hill when he slipped over a cliff edge. He hung there, clinging desperately to a tree. Paralyzed by a fear of heights, Errol was unable to pull himself up. He clung there, yelling for help, and closed his eyes as below him, the sea raged over giant, jagged rocks. Only a short distance away, Hill cheerfully opened a picnic hamper, drank leisurely from the thermos flask, and slowly and deliberately ate his way through a hardboiled egg while Errol called to him.

Finally Hill ambled over, and offered Errol a hand. "You goddamned Indian!" Errol shouted, as Hill dragged him to safety. "Doesn't anything upset you?"

Hill was indeed of Indian ancestry, and this gave him a deep, almost primitive response to the wild to which Errol's Australian blood also vibrated. In a preface to one of Hill's books, Errol wrote:

> Although no Indian myself, and laying no claim to being perhaps even an exceptional hunter, yet I do have much in common with Hill. The wailing note of the looh floating across a placid lake, the distant high-pitched cry of the timber wolf, the guttural roar of the jaguar and the blood-curdling cough of the charging wild boar call to some deep inner response within us both that is not acquainted with modern civilization.

By September, 1937, Errol was an accomplished archer and ready for *Robin Hood*. He left for location: Bidwell Park, within the city limits of Chico in northern California. This was a magnificent twenty-four-hundred-acre woodland that ran up into the rugged Chico canyon along Chico Creek. The park was alive with great sycamores and oaks, and grapevines which descended from the tree tops. There were also giant eucalyptuses, which were to give a strange look to some of the scenes on the screen. A large team of artisans working under the guidance of the art director Carl Jules Weyl had turned Bidwell Park into a replica of the legendary Sherwood Forest. Fresh grass had been painted the deep green of English grass; English flowers, bushes, and ferns had been planted; various outdoor ovens, fires, and tents had been set up to create a medieval look. A whole world had been created, even to cottages and blacksmith forges in the great forest. Only the golden sunlight of a still smogless California lancing through the branches of the great oak trees struck an un-English note.

Tents were set up near the gates of the park to accommodate the hairdressers and makeup artists, the wigmakers and costumers; and a field hospital was set up to take care of those who might be injured. One enormous marquee was erected for the electricians and property men and for the arrows, swords, axes, daggers, armor, household articles, and musical instruments, and the medieval coaches, carts, barrows, and wagons. Stables were built for fifty-six horses and kennels for a variety of domestic and hunting dogs.

Shooting was to begin on Monday, September 27, 1937. Errol got out of bed with a hangover and drove to the makeup tent at 4:30 A.M., feeling terrible. The scene was his encounter with Little John (Alan Hale) under a tree, while Will Scarlet (Patric Knowles) played a lute. No sooner had the director, William Keighley, a painstaking craftsman with a passion for unnecessary detail, set up the sequence than a heavy white fog rolled in from the sea, slowing filming. To his great relief, Errol was sent home. Next morning, the scene was elaborately prepared again, and delayed by fog. And the third day, this farcical episode recurred once more, and Hal Wallis, back in Hollywood, sent several complaining telegrams.

The production got fully under way on September 30. But it never became a happy picture for those who made it. It proceeded in an atmosphere of unease and fear that the director might be removed at any time. Wallis felt that the action scenes lacked zip and pace, and the comedy elements were too thin and weak. He sent a long stream of telegrams to Keighley criticizing everything: the focus was too soft in long shots; far too much film was wasted on shots of a single-file caravan riding through the forest, the battle in the river between Robin Hood and Little John took far too long in the shooting, and worst of all, the banquet scene of Robin Hood's men linking hands and dancing in a ring made them look like the patrons of a homosexual bar.

Errol and the other players were painfully aware that a shadow hung over their adored director. To break the tension, Errol became involved with a number of local beauties, spending the evenings drinking, wenching, and playing poker. He took off with Howard Hill on a pheasant-hunting expedition with bow and arrow. Hill warned Errol that the birds were out of season and that killing them at that time of year was strictly against the law. But Flynn insisted that they go. They bagged three. They were still in the forest when late in the afternoon, an irate game warden emerged through the trees with a rifle. He marched them off at gun point to his hut and only released them after collecting an unofficial fine of one hundred and fifty dollars. That night, Hill, who had written the check, went up to Errol, who was playing a poker game with various crew members on the balcony of the hotel and asked him for seventy-five dollars as his share. Errol said, "Why don't I make it double or nothing on the game?" Hill agreed, and lost.

One night, Errol felt an overwhelming urge to take what he was convinced was Olivia de Havilland's virginity. He drove over to her hotel dressed as Robin Hood, charged through the astonished crowd in the lobby and took the elevator to her room. When he banged on the door and loudly announced his intent, her roommate and double, Ann Robinson, told him to go away. He refused, and tried to kick the door down. Olivia and Ann had to summon the help of male neighbors to have Errol removed from the premises.

Patric Knowles asked Errol one weekend if he would like to do some flying. "Christ, sport," Errol replied, "do you think I could?"

Knowles had discovered a tiny airport not far from Chico with one small landing strip. He had managed to obtain the use of a two-seater Piper Cub. Knowles and Errol drove up to the airfield and asked Bill Miller, who ran it, if they could go on a joy flight. Errol of course had no license. Miller said, "If you crack one of these things up you know what will happen to me, don't you?"

Flynn said, "Screw the studio! What the hell! I'll do what I fucking well like! Wallace Beery flies, Jimmy Stewart flies, why shouldn't I?"

Miller looked at him grimly. "Okay," he said. "But don't forget. I wasn't looking when you took the bird up."

They flew off. Knowles managed to teach Errol to solo in just under nine hours. A few days later, the two men took a joy flight to a place called The Willows, where they knew a stunt flyer named Speed Knowlton.

Knowles says:

> We had drunk a great deal and it was beginning to get dark. On the way back to Chico, night fell. I didn't think we'd have a chance. I was sure we would crash. Without a flare path no plane would have a chance to land in that darkness. I looked desperately for landmarks. The only ones I knew of were two big water tanks with the name Chico written in tall white letters on their sides. I knew if I couldn't find them we were goners.
>
> I could see nothing in the darkness. I heard the engine choke. I was almost out of gas. Errol and I realized we had only one cigarette

between us and we had quite an argument about who should have the cigarette and who should try to land the aircraft.

At last, through the murk, I could make out the white letters on the sides of the water tanks. And the welcome site I had longed for: the airport runway itself. My heart turned over when I noticed a long line of automobile headlights. The people looking for us had placed their cars the whole length of the runway so we could see our way in. I handed Flynn the cigarette and said, "Now, Flynn, you let me take this in because I've piloted this thing before and I know what I'm doing." He said, "To hell with you. I'm going to hang on to the controls, too." He threw away the cigarette. We used the dual controls. We bumped our way up and down. It was a very bad landing. We were overcontrolling because we were so damn nervous. We were lucky to make it. As we came in, down that avenue of headlights, I breathed again. Scores of people came rushing up to us. It was a very near thing.

One afternoon, in a break between scenes, Patric Knowles told Errol that his mother- and father-in-law would be arriving from England the following night and would be staying at the local hotel. Knowles asked Errol what could be done to entertain them. Errol conceived the notion of a banquet, with Eugene Pallette, who played Friar Tuck, as master chef. Knowles instantly accepted the idea, and Pallette promised he would do his best to rise to the occasion.

Next morning, Pallette, in brown cassock and robe, told Errol he had decided to have the main course composed of suckling pig roasted on spits in order to give a correct medieval flavor. He required three prize porkers for the feast.

Knowles discovered the name of a pig farmer and a local slaughterhouse. Errol, Knowles, and Howard Hill rode to see the farmer. The astonished man looked up to see three horsemen galloping toward him dressed up as Robin Hood, Will Scarlet, and a period archer. He ran headlong into the farmhouse.

The three men banged loudly on the door. Convinced he had lost his reason, the farmer peeped through the window. Gradually, as Errol removed his cap, recognition dawned. Within a few minutes, the trio had selected the pigs. Carrying the miserably squealing creatures, one under each left arm, the costumed gallants climbed back on their horses and rode off to the slaughterhouse.

It was closed. Howard Hill offered to dispatch the beasts at the base camp. But no sooner had the trio dismounted than the pigs slipped from them and ran off with amazing speed into the woods.

After the company had been on location for nine weeks in Chico, Wallis began secretly to prepare to have Michael Curtiz come in as director, with Jack Sullivan as assistant director. Without the knowledge of either Flynn or Keighley, Curtiz spent three weeks on the preparations for the final action scenes to be shot, a major banqueting scene in which Robin Hood walked in with a deer slung over his shoulders, and a duel scene up and down the stairs of a castle.

The company returned to Hollywood in late November. There was a hearing at the Screen Actors Guild in which Errol was accused of having told his makeup man Ward Hamilton that he intended complaining about his wig, beard, and makeup in order to stall production and obtain an increase in salary. And Knowles was accused of risking money and time by being late on the set and setting off on random joy flights. Both actors were called to order by the Guild.

On November 30, Keighley directed the scene in which Robin Hood climbs up to Maid Marian's castle chamber. Errol had not liked the scene as written, feeling that it was too flowery and heavy, and he had, in effect, edited it himself, down to a cleaner and more modern style. Keighley was delighted with Errol's dialogue, but Wallis was upset that the script had not been adhered to. No star, he felt, should be allowed to tamper with the writing of a major film. While Keighley took enormous trouble with the scene, making Errol and Olivia go through it eleven times, a hasty meeting was held in Hal Wallis' office. It was agreed that Keighley's shooting of an archery tournament completed days earlier was not first class, and would have to be reshot. Wallis made the decision: Keighley must be fired at once.

Hal Wallis told Keighley the news at the end of the day's work. Keighley, shattered, did not have the strength to reply. He rationalized his dismissal to Errol by saying that he had never been "one of the gang," that he was faithful to his wife and did not drink or fool around in bars or get into fist fights. But Errol knew that the real reason for his removal could be summed up in the one word that dominated everything else in Hollywood: money. He had been fired because he was fifteen days behind schedule; hundreds of thousands of dollars over budget, and because the studio's investment was not fully clear in the images to be seen on the screen.

A messenger boy handed Errol a note which read: *Mr. Keighley left the picture today. Mr. Curtiz will begin shooting the banqueting scene at 9 a.m. tomorrow.* Errol stormed into Jack Warner's office, demanding an explanation, only to find that Warner, anticipating his arrival, had gone home.

Errol tossed and turned all night. He dreaded Curtiz more than ever. He was wretched at the prospect of weeks of sadistic treatment ahead.

That night, while Errol lay miserably awake at home, a crew of one hundred craftsmen worked under great pressure, building and furnishing the banqueting hall set. At 9 A.M., completely ignoring Curtiz's "Good morning, Flynn," Errol strolled onto the set and slung the stuffed deer over his back. He played the scene mechanically but efficiently up to the moment at which he had to drink the repulsive blend of soda pop used to give the appearance of wine in the banqueting goblets. He threw back his head in obedience to Curtiz, and immediately spat out the liquid with the words, "Christ! Where did you get this stuff? You know what this is? It's panther piss!"

The expensive scene was ruined; Curtiz shouted at Errol; and Errol responded by tossing the contents of the goblet in the angry director's face.

The archery tournament was partly reshot at the Midwick Country Club near Los Angeles. The movie was completed at the end of January.

The Adventures of Robin Hood, like *Captain Blood* before it, was concerned chiefly with the oppression of the masses by the rich, and the essential energy and decency of underprivileged people. Shot in primary colors like the vivid tints to be found in illustrations to children's books, the movie seemed centered less on the subdued atmosphere of an imagined England than on a heightened and fanciful storybook world which could have been anywhere, and was drenched in light and alive with brilliant action.

Released in the spring of 1938, the picture was rapturously received and became a deserved hit. At twenty-eight, Errol was established as one of the leading box-office stars of the world. His performance was electrifying. It could not be dismissed as the work of a handsome amateur who had become lucky. He *was* Robin Hood: he remains immortal because of the part. Impish, mischievous, wickedly self-assured, alive with youthful vitality, he conveyed the insolent contempt of the natural rebel for all authority with an intensity of feeling perhaps only an Irish-Australian can have felt. Actor and part were so closely enmeshed that they were inseparable. He never looked better before or since. His body was still perfect, despite his increasing abuse of it. He was sinewy, lithe, muscular, and arrogantly sexual. He laughed; his eyes sparkled; his cheeks flushed. He seemed more alive than anyone else.

He knew his success and relished it, no matter what he said in later years. But he was still earning two thousand dollars a week less than Basil Rathbone!

Characteristically, instead of giving him a rest, and preparing an equally worthy vehicle for his talents, the studio insisted on rushing him into a worthless comedy entitled *Four's a Crowd*. He finished *Robin Hood* on January 15, 1938, and began shooting the new picture only fifteen days later. The reason for his being rushed into it was that Joel McCrea had just turned down the part of the leading romantic actor in the movie. It went through twenty-five titles before it was made, and several writer, director, and cast changes.

While at North Linden Drive waiting to start work, Errol and Lili had Patric Knowles and his wife, Enid, to dinner. In the midst of the meal, the doorbell rang. The maid went to the door to discover two policemen standing there, asking to see Patric Knowles.

The maid announced to Knowles that the cops wanted to see him. Shocked, wondering what he had done, he rose and went out.

He was handed a summons stating that he was accused of alienating the affections of Carole Landis from her lover, Busby Berkeley. He protested loudly that he scarcely knew Miss Landis. Angrily, he thrust the warrant in his coat pocket and began walking back to the dining room. The policeman shouted, "You can't go there. You have to come back with me to the station."

Knowles was pushed into the police car and driven to a building in downtown Los Angeles. He was interrogated by police and was too bemused to ask for his attorney. Just as he was being trundled off to a cell, the policemen burst out laughing. They revealed to the exasperated actor that they were on Errol Flynn's payroll.

That winter, Bud Ernst, the flyer who had taken Errol and Lili to their wedding in Arizona three years earlier, told Errol he had found gold in Alaska. Gold was an obsession of Flynn's; he immediately sank several thousand dollars of his savings into the expedition up north. Ernst left with a team of men by private plane for Nome. It was not until later that Errol discovered all the men were bit players and that they had gotten no closer to Nome than the bars in Vancouver. They spent all of his money.

Although Errol owned an extensive wardrobe, he refused to wear his own clothes in *Four's a Crowd*. He pretended to the producers that he had nothing suitable to wear. He was hoping to obtain the clothes from the wardrobe department, clothes he would keep when the picture was over, but Jack Warner insisted he go and buy his suitings. Errol refused. At the very last minute before shooting began, he still had nothing to wear. The associate producer, David Lewis, took him to wardrobe. Lewis describes an odd thing that happened:

> He was very proud of his body. He insisted I go with him to the dressing room. He stripped very slowly, teasingly in front of me. He was playing with me, to see what I'd do. He got down to his shorts and kept pulling them off his hips inch by inch to tantalize me. Finally he was naked—and I did nothing at all.

Supposed to be a fashion plate in the picture, Errol teased Warner by putting on a moth-eaten cardigan, saved from his school days, under his well-cut studio suits. To irritate Warner further, he kept lacing his speeches with "old chap," "old boy," or, most aggravatingly, "old cock," when he was supposed to be an American. He had to remove the offending cardigan and reshoot the scene.

But no amount of reshooting could make up for the fact that this picture wasn't worth making in the first place.

On March 28, 1938, during the last week of shooting of *Four's a Crowd,* Erben returned from his disastrous trip to the Orient and disembarked in San Pedro. When immigration inspectors threatened to arrest Erben, Errol lied that he didn't know Erben's whereabouts. They grilled Errol relentlessly, but he didn't crack. Erben dodged them and sailed to Mexico and the Panama Canal in safety on the S.S. *Triton.*

Erben traveled to New York in April. His activities intensified. He insinuated himself into meetings of the Lincoln Brigade, composed of American supporters of the Loyalist cause in Spain and reported them to the Nazi spy group at the German Consulate in New York. He attended a Blackshirt Nazi dinner in Yonkers. On April 21, he was present at a Hitler's birthday celebration in an Eighty-fifth Street meeting hall of the German-American Bund that was broken up in a famous riot.

Four days later, Erben was at the Passport Division in New York, where officials questioned him on his activities and examined his Nazi documents. He was astonishingly bold in his responses. He spelled out the nature of the mission to Spain; he boasted of his Nazi sons, and showed them in their uniforms, despite the fact that he had recently stated that they had been in a concentration camp where his elder son had been sterilized.

While he was gone, Austria had been annexed by Hitler. Erben was issued a Nazi Party card dated May 1, 1938, which was held for him in Munich. Sending it to New York could have blown his cover.

Nine

In the spring of 1938, Errol rented a house on North Linden Drive in Beverly Hills, and sailed to the Bahamas. He enjoyed swimming underwater with a spear gun, catching dangerous sting rays and dragging them up in nets to the surprise of the local populace. He even managed to shoot sharks with a bow and arrow, the arrow supplemented with explosive devices. The studio panicked when he failed to return for additional shots of *Four's a Crowd*. They sent troubleshooters to follow him along his complicated trail through the various islands, but he was hard to reach and refused to listen to reason. He was having far too good a time; Lili had stayed at home on this trip, leaving him to pleasure himself with both sexes in the remoter islands where gossips did not penetrate.

It was during this period that he saw in *Yachting* magazine a picture of a boat which had just been built in Boston. Eighty feet long and twenty-two feet abeam, she was a beauty—sleek, shiny, and made for adventure. Errol's pulse raced. He had to have her.

But he needed money. Although it nearly killed him to yield to studio pressure, he flew to New York and then to Hollywood to try to put his finances in order. His business managers told him he was in trouble. His equities were stretched finer than ever thanks to his real estate speculation. He owed money everywhere. They advised him not to buy the yacht, for which the Boston owner, John Alden, was asking $17,500 in cash.

He decided to withdraw every penny of his trust fund at Warner Brothers and borrow on his expected earnings for the rest of 1938. He rushed the money to Alden and wrangled for hours with friends about whether to have the vessel sailed by an eastern crew or a western one to California. He settled on a western crew. He felt that a western crew would have more incentive to bring the vessel home fast, whereas an eastern crew might use the voyage as an excuse for an extended vacation.

Flynn and C. J. Wood, one of his business managers, spent several days in San Pedro, hand-picking a professional crew which was flown to Boston. But the crew reneged on their promises to sail quickly westward. They spent days drinking and wenching in Balboa, Cristobal, Panama City, Acapulco, Ensenada, Cabo San Lucas, and Tijuana.

Just when Errol's patience was exhausted, he got word that friends of his in the Navy had spotted the boat about eighty miles off the coast near San Diego. Immediately, Errol and Wood made berthing arrangements at San Pedro and drove down to greet the vessel.

Straining his eyes through a pair of binoculars, Errol stood on the dock all day long, waiting for the boat to appear. At last, as sun set, he could make her out, scudding in a fine breeze against a blue horizon. Then he saw something that made him drop the binoculars in dismay. *"Good Christ!"* he exclaimed to Wood. *"She's flying a quarantine flag!"*

Convinced the crew had contracted smallpox, which was raging in the Panama basin, Errol feared the yacht would be impounded and stripped down for inspection. He paced up and down. Finally, a quarantine team went aboard. They re-emerged and walked down to the wharf, laughing mightily.

"What the hell's going on?" Errol asked.

"You know what's the matter with them?" the officer said.

"Smallpox?" Errol asked, looking pale.

"No. The other kind of pox," the man replied. "They've all got the clap."

Errol laughed with relief. The crew was driven in station wagons to the San Diego Naval Hospital for treatment.

Errol renamed the yacht the *Sirocco,* after the boat he had sailed between Sydney and New Guinea. As a yacht owner, Errol's social standing in Southern California was greatly increased. He luxuriated in long, leisurely, golden spring voyages down the coves and bays from Santa Cruz island to the Todos Santos group and Ensenada: a few days' sailing. There he met people who had become his peers: John Ford, famous director and fierce-tempered Irish American, in his 110-foot ketch, the *Araner,* James Cagney on the *Martha;* Harry Cohn, the Atilla the Hun of Columbia Pictures, aboard his *Gem of the Breakwater.* He picked up yachting lore: Preston Foster shooting a whale off Catalina and then turning around and running before the wind in his boat when the furious creature set upon revenge; Gary Cooper's manager tumbling into the water when a yellowtail snapped at his bait; Jack Oakie appearing on Richard Arlen's *The Joby R* dressed in a rear admiral's uniform only to find himself thrown unceremoniously overboard.

Actor George Brent recalled a curious episode of 1938:

> Errol's yacht and mine were often in sight of each other in those days. We both liked to sail to Mexico on Sundays. One weekend I saw him signalling to Japanese fishing boats. I became suspicious. I reported the matter to the Coast Guard. As a result, the Maritime Board made moves toward having Errol's yacht withdrawn permanently on the ancient law that said foreign citizens could not sail yachts of more than a certain number of feet, though other foreigners sailed all the time in bigger boats. For some time Errol's *Sirocco* hung in the balance. But he pulled strings in Washington. Nothing ever happened. I hated him the rest of my life.

Most weekends, Errol and Lili set sail with Dolores Del Rio and Cedric Gibbons. They would catch yellowtail and berth in a cove on Santa Magdalana Island to cook it. After dinner, they swam in the coves or took a speedboat to the Mexican coast to pick up bottles of wine.

That summer of 1938, Errol had to make *The Sisters* to meet his thousand-dollar-a-weekend costs of running the *Sirocco.* Fredric March had been offered the part of the drunken, self-pitying reporter who marries a Montana girl and drags her down to a life of poverty in San Francisco, but March had refused the part, writing to Jack Warner, "It is not a particularly interesting character, principally because he is so frightfully weak and sorry for himself throughout." John Garfield tested briefly with Bette Davis, who was to play the reporter's wife; Franchot Tone, George Brent, and Jeffrey Lynn were all considered before Wallis decided to try Errol for the part.

The childish misery of the character went quite against his grain, and he felt little in common with the character, aside from a fondness for drinking.

Still, under the direction of Anatole Litvak, he gave a convincing performance, and received some of the best reviews of his career. But, his pleasure in these was undermined by the news that he would have to start another movie immediately: a remake of the early talkie hit, *The Dawn Patrol*.

This story of heroism in the Royal Flying Corps in World War I was clearly designed to cash in on the current feeling that war in Europe was imminent. Errol begged the studio to give him a break, because his sinuses were causing him trouble, and he was exhausted after the strenuous work on *The Sisters*. But Wallis was adamant.

Under the direction of the English Edmund Goulding, and with many fine British actors around him, Errol was at his best, even tolerating Basil Rathbone, who as usual played the villain of the piece. He enjoyed working with David Niven, who had become an intimate friend. Niven actually lived for a year and a half as a paying guest in the Flynn home. Lighthearted, full of mischief and fun, Niven was a man after Errol's own heart. They chased girls together and sailed together on weekends, Niven holding his breath while Errol took the *Sirocco* at astonishing speeds through the crowded yacht basins, almost scraping the paint off the hulls.

Errol worked hard on *The Dawn Patrol*. He gave one of his best performances as the cheerfully ruthless flyer. Goulding told him to play the scene in which he receives news of his best friend's death with tears in his eyes, but Errol refused, saying that a man like that would hide his grief in bold, seemingly heartless laughter. Goulding agreed, and the sequence worked well. It was a good picture.

In late September 1938, Errol set off on the *Sirocco* with a business associate, Wally Heinze; a cameraman, Al Wetzel; the ship's skipper, Douglas Dawson; three crewmen; the Chinese cook; his dog

Arno; and the archer Howard Hill, on a voyage to Cabo San Lucas, on the western coast of Mexico. Lili stayed at home. By this time, because of his suspected spying activities, *Sirocco* had been banned from every port on the coast except Wilmington.

The voyage began beautifully; the sea was as flat as a washboard, the sky a blazing clear blue, and the fishing good; Errol caught marlin. The *Sirocco* was nearing Turtle Bay when a man o' war bird suddenly appeared, followed by an albatross, a squawking black merganser, kites, swallows, hawks, all hurtling in fear toward the land. Without warning, the wind died completely. The sails slackened and drooped. The booms swung uselessly.

Howard Hill wrote in his memoirs:

The *Sirocco* lay dead in the water. We were experiencing the calm before the storm, and we knew that the storm was about to strike. Hurriedly we dropped the main sheet and made it fast. While some of the fellows hauled down the foresail and jib, others were busy battening down the hatches.

Lightning zigzagged through an enormous cloud the color of a bruise; thunder split the air. A nor'easter swooped down. The *Sirocco* was tough to handle in a heavy sea; she was top-heavy and rolled terribly. Errol shouted, "We'll have to ride her out! It's too late to head for land!"

Howard Hill continued:

The waves rapidly grew higher and the troughs between became so narrow and deep that the ship did not have enough running room. She would glide down the steep side of a huge wave and plunge her bow into the one ahead.

Freak waves slashed across the boat's decks. Her spreader sail was ripped from the crossarm. Howard Hill and Flynn were knocked several times to the deck. A sailor injured his shoulder falling down a companionway.

There were two days of relentless buffeting. It was impossible to cook any food. Nobody ate for thirty-six hours and nobody could obtain a wink of sleep.

At last, the storm blew itself out. Displaying first-class seamanship, Errol and Skipper Dawson saved the boat, but the yacht had been blown two hundred miles off course. By the time Errol managed to berth the *Sirocco* at Cabo San Lucas, he and his crew were totally exhausted. They were wet and cold and hungry, barely able to cheer the sight of land.

The next few days were spent in repairing the damage to the *Sirocco* and sampling the local girls and the local wine. The gang went out shark spearing and skin diving, and hauled in manta rays and rock bass. They could find no marlin, but Al Wetzel did pull in a magnificent five-hundred-pound hammerhead. They caught barracuda and dolphin, yellowtail and skipjack and fin tuna: enough to eat for days and days.

Errol could have stayed aboard forever. He loved stretching naked on the deck, the sun boring into his flesh; or exchanging yarns on the watch very late at night, with the boards creaking softly, the sails plump with wind, the water slapping against the hull, a big yellow moon in a fleece of silver cloud, and the stars as big as Christmas-tree spangles in the inky sky. He told many versions of his life to the other men: tall tales of gold and buried treasure and sexual escapades. And then, with Arno at his side, he went down to his bunk at dawn and dropped into the only uninterrupted slumber he knew in his life.

But for all of his love of the sea, the strenuous voyage, the struggle with the great tropical storm, had weakened him. When he flew by Beechcraft from Mazatlan to Mexico City to return to Hollywood for costume tests for his next picture—a western called *Dodge City* —he did not feel well. By September 19, he was in Cedars of Lebanon Hospital with a recurrence of his old problem of undulant fever. He sweated, suffered from headache, aching limbs, and sore throat; his temperature rose to 103 degrees and a rash spread over his body.

While he was sick, he was offered forty-five thousand dollars to appear on the Woodbury Program, a radio series. The studio refused to let him do it, until he countered by threatening not to make *Dodge City*. As a result, he was allowed not only to do the radio show but to take a vacation to Honolulu in October to recover from his illness.

He sailed alone on the Matson liner *Lurline* on October 18, arriving in Honolulu six days later. He immediately decided to invest in cattle properties on Oahu. When he cabled Wally Heinze to send over some money, it turned out he didn't have the necessary fifty thousand dollars down payment in cash. He was fretting over this late one night at the Royal Hawaiian Hotel when he fell into a fitful sleep and was plunged into a nightmare. He found himself standing on a promontory overlooking Pearl Harbor. It was a brilliantly clear day. Clouds scudded overhead. The great warships rode at anchor. Suddenly he heard a roar. A squadron of fighter planes and bombers appeared. There was a loud explosion; screams; white figures of navy men scattered against steel-gray decks. Errol woke with a scream of horror. It was just before dawn. He drove over to Pearl Harbor. Nothing had happened: everything was calm, undisturbed.

He called Jim Fleming in California to tell him of his bizarre dream. Jim Fleming said, "Don't buy that land. Something's going to happen." He canceled the deal at once. Soon he would help make that dream come true.

Errol returned from his trip on November 15 with photographs of Pearl Harbor. He was told he had been suspended for two weeks for failing to fly back as promised. One week later, he left for San Francisco and Modesto to start work on *Dodge City*.

While in San Francisco, he ran into Johnny Meyer, the nightclub owner who had hunted for available girls for him years before. He had Johnny put on his payroll as a pimp and Johnny stayed with Errol for years until he left to join the personal staff of Howard Hughes.

Johnny Meyer's death in 1978 was sudden and shocking. While he was working on his car, on a hillside in Florida, close to his home, the car mysteriously backed over him, crushing him to death. During an interview shortly before this, he had admitted to me that he had helped Errol with his Nazi connections in 1938, when, even though Jewish, Meyer, like most Americans, was naïve about Nazis and iso-lationist in politics. He introduced Errol to Fritz Wiedemann, the Nazi consul general in San Francisco and a prominent social figure, at a party on Nob Hill. Errol and Wiedemann got to know each other very well during 1939.

Johnny Meyer told me: "I believe Errol was not merely in touch with the Nazis in San Francisco but was actively aiding and abetting them. Exactly in what capacity, I can't be sure, but I know that they counted him useful as a contact in the film industry. Also, you must remember that he was—thanks to his constant moving around on lo-cations and his sailing in and out of every port with his yacht— familiar with every naval installation in California and filmed them

•

all. He knew all about the layout of the harbors, the movements of the ships, the fleets. Indeed no one could have been more valuable in the event of a possible attack by ship from the mainland of California.

"When Errol and I went to Latin America in 1940, we met many Nazis. Errol was friendly with them in Rio, Buenos Aires, Valparaiso.

"I blame myself to a great extent for having encouraged Errol in that direction. I dropped my own connections with the Nazis—I turned to hate them after Pearl Harbor—but Errol did not. Right up to the end of the war, I am sure he was working for them."

Meyer also revealed another side of Errol's nature when he disclosed that Errol had become involved with the famous and handsome motion picture star Tyrone Power for a few months in 1939. Tyrone Power had recently married the French actress Annabella. She was in Europe. He was moving toward the peak of his career; and he had been a great success in *In Old Chicago, Marie Antoinette,* and *Alexander's Ragtime Band.* His dark hair and eyes and sunburned skin were very attractive to Errol, who of course liked Mexican types. Power was twenty-four; Errol thirty. Annabella never knew about the relationship. It was by no means sustained; the two men were not friends, had met each other socially only at the parties of Jean Howard, the brilliant and charming Hollywood hostess.

Their affair was conducted in secret, not because of fear of public exposure—newspapers and magazines would never have reported the story (the subject is still taboo in the press today)—but because of fear of studio reaction. The well-known MGM star William Haines was discovered in the downtown YMCA with a sailor, and the studio dropped him immediately, though the matter was never made public.

Errol and Ty met at obscure motels, at the private home of a trusted homosexual director friend, at the West Coast home of a prominent New York orchestra conductor. The meetings were extremely sporadic and scattered and known only to a tiny handful of friends.

Ty had been intensely bisexual from his early teens. At the time Errol met him, he had had several affairs, all with famous stars. He was fascinated by people of his own rank, character, and fame. Errol, by contrast, was interested in obscure people with little or no intelligence, so that his interest in Ty was unusual for him; perhaps he enjoyed the excitement and danger involved.

In any event, both Errol and Ty had other partners while going to bed with each other.

Johnny Meyer says:

> I never had any prejudices against homosexuals. I knew that Errol and Tyrone were both concerned to keep their images as macho as possible in the public eye. But the attraction was obvious from the start, and I saw no reason to discourage it. Errol in fact had asked me if it was possible that any of the male teenage stars he met at parties were homosexuals. He was tired of the furtive desperate flights across the border into Mexico to indulge his appetite.
>
> He was fascinated by Tyrone. In a sense, the relationship should have worked, because of the attraction of opposites. After all, Errol was very much the male in the relationship, Tyrone, very much the female.
>
> Tyrone Power was certainly in love with Errol. Errol was incapable of loving anyone. Even himself. Indeed his attitude to life was one of contemptuous hostility, trying to grab as much out of it as he could before the dark night came and swallowed him up at the end. Ty had a better attitude to life. He enjoyed people, things, events, with an almost puppyish charm.
>
> They had to meet in complete secrecy. I set up meetings at the home of a director I knew who had homosexual leanings, Edmund Goulding. He had a very sophisticated and sharp sense of humor and was vastly entertained by the idea of two great stars fornicating under his roof. He used to give male orgies to them both, but Ty would not join in. He was too shy and sincere. Errol, who was incapable of being faithful to anyone, whether it was Lili, Tyrone, or anybody else, would enter into the spirit of those orgies with great intensity. Sometimes, the director would even stage bisexual orgies and Errol entered into the scene with a will.
>
> I think this hurt Ty, who reacted to Errol's ruthlessness, and as a result they drifted apart. They saw each other for only a few months. In fact, they did not meet again until after the war.
>
> I will tell you something I have never discussed with anyone before. Howard Hughes, whom I worked for later, was in my opinion, and I was as close to him as anyone, definitely bisexual. That whole image of his, of having women stashed away in apartments that were

set up for him was a lot of baloney. In fact, I deliberately set up these women as a disguise for him. In most cases, he never even went to bed with them. He would go by and discuss the latest events and disappear, in the confident knowledge that the press was following him to the front door and would report on the period he had spent there, imagining all kinds of macho events going on inside. The fact of the matter is that I doubt if Howard went to bed with these girls more than once or twice, and then only for a quick fuck and departure. I don't think he could satisfy women and I very much doubt if he ever had an orgasm with one. On the other hand, he was fascinated by men. In complete secrecy, I would arrange assignations for him with boy hustlers. And at one time, in a spirit of outrageousness, I actually set him up on a date with Errol.

Neither one would ever tell me what took place. The meeting was arranged in Santa Barbara. It was very late at night. Errol arrived in his Packard, looking very drunk. Howard arrived in his battered car, much less grand than Errol's, although he could have bought Errol a hundred times over, winding up the windows of his Chevrolet, looking to right and left with terror in case he be seen and creeping into the house under a heavy felt hat, wearing a Humphrey Bogart raincoat. They disappeared into the house. I drove off like a bat out of hell, terrified that the Feds would follow them and the whole thing would be blown. I have no idea whether they went to bed or not. But I think it is likely.

Ten

Errol's next picture, *Dodge City,* was little more than a flatly conventional Western with the usual elements: the young, spunky Wyatt Earp-like hero who becomes the sheriff and brings law and order to a cattle town; the competition between the railroad and the stagecoach; the depredation of cattle by a villainous thief and murderer.

Errol felt he was unsuited to a Western, and the writers added a scene explaining that he came from an Irish background. He walked through the part; even in a scene in which a child is dragged to its death on the reins of a runaway horse, he looks puzzled rather than horrified. Bruce Cabot, as the villain, stole the movie from him. It is strange to reflect that Cabot later became a destructive agent in Flynn's life. Brutal, physically massive, with harsh, crude features and supermasculine bearing, Cabot was a man to reckon with, as Errol, who became friends with him, discovered to his cost.

On location, Errol once again pursued Olivia de Havilland, who played the demure frightened heroine, and once again failed to make

an impression. He had twisted his ankle in San Francisco, making a
rapid exit from some girl's room when her husband came home, and
scarcely presented a romantic figure as he appeared in Modesto for
work the first day, hobbling up to Olivia for a love scene. She says:

> I think I was still in love with him, and perhaps he with me, and
> soon after that, when we went to the premiere of the picture in
> Dodge City by train together, we talked for a long time about many
> things, and were closer than ever before. I saw that he was a poetic,
> gentle creature behind all the braggadoccio and wildness, and I felt
> great tenderness for this lovely man. But he still had no idea how to
> woo me.
>
> A little later, I had to go to Canada, to Banff, Alberta, for a pic-
> ture, and he was at the airport. I walked over towards him—he
> didn't see me—with incredible feeling in my heart. But then I real-
> ized why he was there. Lili came in an airplane looking wonderful in
> a lovely polka-dot costume and he took her by the arm and kissed
> her tenderly and they went off together. And I thought: that's where
> his heart is. And he never saw me at all.

What she didn't know was that Errol still longed for her and was
furious at her refusal to go to bed. Indeed, a year later, he wrote to
Jack Warner: "Please make sure Olivia de Havilland is not in my
next picture."

Dodge City went on shooting all through Christmas, winding up
on January 14. Immediately, Errol, Howard Hill, and the rest of the
gang left on another voyage to Mexico.

Meanwhile, the studio had begun preparations for *The Knight and
the Lady,* later called *The Private Lives of Elizabeth and Essex.*
Shortly before he reported for costume tests, Errol, who had been
hungering for a more spacious house than the Tudor home he was
sharing with Lili at 601 North Linden Drive, bought, for thirty-five
thousand dollars, a lot on Mulholland Drive, amounting to some
eleven and a half acres overlooking the San Fernando Valley. In
order to obtain the land, he had to sell off some minor properties.
He also invested in land on Huntington Drive in Pasadena, apartments on Selma Avenue in Hollywood, and land on Sunset Plaza
Drive in West Hollywood near Beverly Hills, all of which tied up his
salary, now about four thousand dollars a week, for months ahead.

This suited the studio bosses, who wanted him bound to them for life.

In April 1939, Errol started work, again for Curtiz, on *Elizabeth and Essex*. Bette Davis was cast as the Queen and Olivia as a lady-in-waiting: a sad demotion for so important a leading lady. Bette had quarreled with his being cast as Essex—she wanted Laurence Olivier—for she felt Errol was totally inadequate. She had even given up a chance to play Scarlett O'Hara in *Gone With the Wind* because Warner would only lend her to David O. Selznick if Errol were Rhett, and Errol, who had longed to be in the Selznick classic, had never forgiven her. He reacted now by giving one of the worst performances of his life. And she showed how she felt about him. In a scene in which she was supposed to smack his face she came so close he felt the rings brush his ears.

In the midst of shooting, in mid-June, Errol and Lili were driving down a street off Sunset Boulevard when they swerved suddenly to avoid a truck and crashed into a wall. Errol was carried out, bleeding badly; Lili was only scratched; and both were driven to the hospital in an ambulance. The episode was hushed up; the driver of the truck paid off to say nothing. The assistant director, Sherry Shourds, went up to North Linden Drive when Errol and Lili were taken home after treatment, reporting that Errol had a bad cut in his head, and that "perhaps the injury was caused not by a car crash but by Lili hitting him with a champagne bottle." Errol received a ticket and a warning for drunken driving: his third in a month.

Elizabeth and Essex turned out to be a heavy-handed historical pageant, distinguished only by Bette Davis' ferocious performance as the Queen.

On September 3, when war broke out between Germany and Britain, Winston Churchill asked all able-bodied Englishmen who had not become naturalized Americans to report to Washington or their local consulate for instructions by diplomatic officials. Of the Hollywood contingent, Errol was the only British star who flatly refused to answer Churchill's orders.

When he gave a five-minute short wave broadcast to his native

Australia in early October, Errol failed to express any patriotism but said instead that if he were enlisted for service in Sydney or New Guinea he would not pay any overdue bills. The Australian people were infuriated; fortunately for Errol the broadcast was not heard anywhere else.

He did not volunteer for service either in Britain or Canada, as his friends David Niven and Patric Knowles did, and when Edward Ashley formed a local counterintelligence unit to flush out Nazism in Hollywood, he refused to join it.

Why did Jack Warner protect Errol to the end? One answer is given by Errol's agent, Arthur Park, referring to an event of some years later:

> One day, I received a frantic telephone call from Jack. He was screaming, literally screaming with terror. He said I had to come to the studio at once. He had fled there from his house. He had called the guard out in force.
>
> "What's happening?" I asked. "What can be so dangerous to you?"
>
> "I can't speak now. I'm desperate. Just come here at once."
>
> I tore down the streets of Beverly Hills, almost out of my mind with worry. When I got to the studio, I didn't wait for the elevator but ran three steps at a time up the stairs. I was stopped by a patrol of guards, armed to the teeth. They let me through. When I reached his office, one of the guards said that Jack was in the bathroom. I found him being violently sick in the toilet.
>
> When Warner saw me, he stood up, white as a sheet, and tottered into the office where he sank into his chair.
>
> "He's going to kill me," he said, in a whisper.
>
> "Who's going to kill you?"
>
> "Errol."
>
> At that moment, a guard walked in and announced that Errol was fighting his way up the stairs and would have to be shot if he continued. I went out and saw Errol. He was frenzied, his clothes in disarray. I guided him into the office. Warner cowered against the wall.
>
> "Errol, what's this all about?" I asked.
>
> Errol replied, "He's been spying on me with all those other guys. I'm going to kill you, Jack, unless you lay off immediately."
>
> Warner put his head in his hands. Shaking with fear, he promised he would never let the truth about Errol be known.
>
> I never found out what the truth was.

Afraid of Errol, Jack Warner passed any political inquiries about Errol to other members of his staff.

But there was more than fear to deter Jack Warner from acknowledging Errol's guilt. Equally powerful was the fact that Errol was a big money earner. Besides, Mrs. Roosevelt invited Errol to her parties. Why should Jack Warner worry about what the FBI said?

That fall of 1939, while *Virginia City* was being scripted, Errol became involved in a dangerous new occupation: running guns along with contraband gold and drugs to and from Mexico. The *Sirocco* became a traveling arsenal: the guns were stuffed behind the convertible sofa in the master's cabin—powerful rifles including .220 Swifts with tremendous shells. These were resold in Wilmington, smuggled ashore wrapped in spare canvas.

The gold was for Errol's private hoard. He often used it deliberately to shock friends by showing them small gold ingots taken from his pockets—when possession of gold was strictly illegal.

He also came close to a kidnap charge that fall. Tourists would take water-taxi rides to circle the various ships at anchorage in Wilmington. Errol delighted in stripping down to his shorts and displaying his body to the various men or women who would come out for the tour. One day, a young woman asked her water-taxi helmsman to circle the *Sirocco* six times so she could feast her eyes on Errol's body.

He stood up, stretching his muscles, and gave her her money's worth. He hailed her and invited her to come aboard for lunch. She climbed up the Jacob's ladder. He took her to his cabin for a bout of lovemaking. When the taxi went back without her, her husband demanded to know what had become of her. The helmsman explained. The husband took the water taxi to the *Sirocco* and yelled out to the sailors on deck, "Where's my wife?" A moment later, the young woman dove in and started to swim over to the water taxi, but the husband ordered it back to Wilmington. Meanwhile, the *Sirocco* sailed off, leaving the wife to swim two miles to shore.

Such episodes were frequent. Women would flock to the boat and offer themselves: Errol dubbed them the SQQ, or San Quentin Quails. He awarded his favorite stud crewmen or friends, men who could guarantee to satisfy the Quails sexually, the insignia of FFF, or Flynn's Flying Fuckers. He gave the men a badge of honor, made up of a metal image of an erect penis and testicles to put in their lapels. He kept track of their daily or nightly intercourse in a score book on board; Errol himself was invariably the victor.

With nothing more than a few pages of script, *Virginia City* was rushed prematurely into production in November. Errol was unable to dislodge Curtiz from the job of director, but he did succeed in removing Olivia de Havilland. Miriam Hopkins was cast as the hero's dance-hall girl friend. The unit took off by train from Pasadena on November 1, on the way to Flagstaff, Arizona, for three weeks of location work.

Cast and crew made an uncomfortable journey overnight from Pasadena only to be faced with torrential rain on location. Errol's hatred of rain assumed an alarming new intensity: Miriam Hopkins recalled that when the rain began to beat heavily and monotonously on the windows of the hotel, Errol screamed and fell to his bed in the grip of a blinding headache. He lay and moaned for hours as the thunder broke and the lightning fitfully lit his room.

He hated this concocted Western even more than its predecessor. There was no full script, and on November 10 he cabled Hal Wallis in Hollywood that it was impossible to proceed with the picture without the middle portion of it in his hands. There followed an ironical and weird exchange in which Errol obliquely referred to his political activities. He said in the telegram, "Do you think I belong to the Gestapo?" referring to a statement director Curtiz had made (presumably with unconscious humor) that Errol was acting like a storm trooper on the set. Wallis replied—not realizing what he was saying—"Dear Heinrich Himmler Flynn: Will show you copy just as soon as ready. Thanks old fellow, keep up the good work. Regards. Hal."

The rain did not stop for two weeks, and Errol was barely able to make his way onto the location for work each morning.

Back in Hollywood, a long delayed production of the epic historical movie, Michael Curtiz's *The Sea Hawk,* was finally getting under way. Errol went into costume tests in January 1940. He was still unwell, and after only a few days' work he collapsed once more and lay in bed with a high fever. Every day hours of work were lost because of him.

In a scene in the Spanish galleys a man was seen whipping the slaves as they toiled at the oars. He actually lashed the bare backs of the men as Curtiz laughed sadistically. Though weak and running a high temperature, Errol jumped to his feet, cast off his shackles, and thrashed the slave master until he bled. Curtiz fled from the set.

While his troubles with Curtiz continued, he developed a friendship with Flora Robson. Fortunately, this patriotic actress and friend of the Queen Mother of England guessed nothing of Errol's Nazism. Dame Flora recalls:

> We hit it off from the beginning. He was naughty about his homework. I told him that because he couldn't remember his lines it would hold up the picture and I would be delayed going to New York to do a play. When I told him this, he was very kind and learned his lines to help me: the work went so fast we were finished by four in the afternoon on some days. I remember Mike Curtiz saying to him, "What's the matter with you? You know all your words."

The two of them worked together on some of the script problems. They both felt that Flynn's part called for him to be too deferential toward Queen Elizabeth. They changed the emphasis so that he treated the Queen like another man. They believed the Queen would have liked an adventurous man: a horse that was difficult to ride.

Flora Robson continues:

> Errol used to play the most terrible practical jokes on Mike Curtiz. There was a scene in which he had to fight his way back into the palace to see me with some important news. As we finished the scene, Mike realized we had changed the script completely and Mike screamed for his lady secretary. We all stood and watched. A door flew open and an old man appeared in a long flowing white beard and hair. Curtiz screamed again, "Where's my secretary?" The "old man" said, "Don't you recognize me? You must be blind. This is the way I really am." It *was* the lady secretary. Mike burst into tears.

Errol used to tell Flora stories of his dog, Arno. She says:

> He told me Arno was very well brought up and wouldn't go to the bathroom on his yacht. But at first he would mistake the anchor for a lamppost. Every time he would raise his leg to it Errol would fling the chain over and drop the anchor and Arno would fall over sideways. That's how he got him house trained.
>
> One time, they sailed to an island. Errol went overboard and jumped in for a swim and lay on the beach and sunned himself. Out

of the corner of his eye, he saw the cook give Arno a bone. Arno jumped overboard, swam ashore and dug a deep hole, burying the bone in the sand. With a silent look of "X marks the spot" Arno ran off. Errol dug up the bone when Arno wasn't looking and put a hard boiled egg in its place. When Arno came back, the dog sniffed around and found the spot and started digging. When he saw the egg, he did a double take. He ran round and round the hole bewildered until Errol finally threw him the bone. Errol loved the dog so: it used to sit and watch the shooting, so quietly, and only bark when a scene was over.

Errol told the very proper Miss Robson about the goings on in a famous bordello downtown, and drove her by it one night so she could see the madam, covered with jewels; he showed her a photograph of himself with George Sanders flanked by the brothel girls, symbolically holding up a cricket bat.

During the picture, Errol arranged yet another of his complicated jokes. He announced that a native princess from South Africa who owned several diamond mines would be coming on the set and would give a diamond to the crew member whose looks she liked best.

The princess arrived, wearing a rich silk dress. Her face was dusky —because of makeup—and her figure attractive. All the crew men made eyes at her and walked up and down showing off their physiques and flexing their biceps. At the end of shooting that day, everyone waited anxiously to see who she had chosen. She selected the head electrician and gave him the diamond. Everyone cheered. Broke at the time, he rushed off eagerly to the nearest jeweler, only to be told the jewel was made of glass.

Another joke occurred at the end of shooting. Errol gave out bank notes as tips for the crew. He told them the notes were very large and they must not look at them until they got home. They expected one hundred dollar bills. But instead, the notes turned out to be Monopoly money.

After the picture was finished, Errol was seated with Flora on the set, waiting for publicity photographers. She says: "I asked Errol if he would sign a picture for my nephew with the words, 'To a fellow adventurer.' Errol looked at me and said, 'To another phony you mean?'"

In New York shortly afterward, Flora Robson and Errol appeared in a radio version of *The Lady Vanishes* for the "Philip Morris Playhouse," a spy story based on a film of Alfred Hitchcock's. The code in the story was worked out to the tune of "Country Gardens" by Percy Grainger. Errol had to whistle the tune to the officials at the Foreign Office. Flora Robson remembers:

> I was afraid he would forget what he was supposed to do and I was right. Instead of whistling "Country Gardens" he whistled "The Wedding March." In the rehearsal, I told him he had made a mistake and he said, "What shall I do?" He was afraid he would forget it again. I said, "Let me do the whistling. No one will know the difference." He was delighted with the idea and when it came to the cue I took care of the whistling. He flung his arms around me in gratitude.

Errol was worried that Flora Robson was returning to England in time of war and he insisted she telegraph him at every stage of the journey. They corresponded for years afterward.

In October 1940 Errol attended a party at the home of the Brazilian ambassador. It was full of Nazis. Among them were George Gyssling, consul general in Los Angeles, and Fritz Wiedemann, consul general in San Francisco. Federal agents watched Errol very closely at the party. Accompanied by Johnny Meyer, he was seen talking cheerfully with Wiedemann, dancing with two Heil Hitlering Nazi actresses and a Nazi nightclub singer. He was seen in close discussion with Wiedemann and a member of the Brazilian film industry who was a Nazi sympathizer.

The federal agents reported the matter to the studio, but no action was taken.

During this period, Errol was almost constantly in the company of Fritz Wiedemann. In vain, a local member of the FBI who wishes to be anonymous pointed out to his superiors that Errol would not consort with Wiedemann after 1939 if he were a loyal British subject. Errol also began an intense love affair with a Nazi singer named Gertrude Anderson. She was dark-haired, slender, attractive, and very young. She was also on the American government's list of wanted Nazi agents and had connections at the highest level of the Nazi Party in Berlin. But every effort to pin her down on specific charges failed.

Errol's affair with Gertrude caused the most drastic consternation in the Warner publicity offices. Every effort was made—

successfully—to keep it out of the press. Even when federal agents combed Los Angeles and Beverly Hills, obtaining countless depositions by famous actors and actresses about this woman and Errol's association with her, not a word leaked out.

Errol extracted no pleasure from the making of *Santa Fe Trail*. He knew the script falsely presented the facts of the antebellum period, and that the portraits of John Brown, played by Raymond Massey, and of Colonel Jeb Stuart, his role, were feebly and superficially written.

He underwent a strange experience on location in October which, following as it did his prophetic dream of the attack on Pearl Harbor, awakened an interest in the supernatural that he never lost.

As Colonel Stuart, he had to witness the public hanging of John Brown. The hanging scene was staged on a windy, overcast day, with brooding, crow-black clouds. As Raymond Massey was led to the gallows, Errol felt an ancient, ancestral memory stirring. He cried out in agony at the spectacle of execution, burst into tears, and buried his face in his hands.

Over the artificial, theatrical, pure "Hollywood" scene he saw, like an oil painting covering another in impasto, a scene of someone who looked like himself being hanged long ago. A suggestion of olive-colored eucalyptus trees and low, breast-shaped, ancient hills swallowed up the bare landscape of the Providencia Ranch. He knew with a sudden sense of terror that some Australian ancestor had been killed by the noose. The fear of it leaped through his nerves and he became weak and dizzy and sank into a chair.

At thirty-one, Errol should have been the most confident man in the world. He was the greatest male star at Warner Brothers, earning six thousand dollars a week. He was at the peak of his physical beauty: the odd, disconcerting softness in his face had disappeared; the long years of sailing had weathered it, giving it interesting lines and strength of character. His bodily proportions hadn't changed a great deal since his twentieth year. With war in Europe and the threat of war in the Americas, he still offered an apparently free, cheerful, mindless image of a man as a heroic animal to the world.

But he longed for the life he had known in Australia and New Guinea, when executives were not harassing him. His knowledge of his poor health, the crumbling constitution behind the physically perfect façade, was a constant challenge to his pride, the more so because he constantly had to give the illusion of health. He hated giving interviews in case his condition might be exposed, and handed the job of seeing reporters to Jim Fleming. He was depressed by the social life of Hollywood: the flattery, the parties, the pathetic snobbery. His marriage was breaking up at last. Lili's jealousy of other women, his own need for freshness in sexual relationships, his restless promiscuity, had destroyed the relationship.

By now, he had abandoned all hope of marrying Olivia de Havilland. He had grudgingly allowed Warners to cast her in *Santa Fe Trail,* where she had continued to resist him, supported by her double, the charming Ann Robinson, who hated Flynn. Soon after, Olivia's involvement with the well-known director John Huston destroyed all chance of a relationship.

Errol was disappointed because his efforts as a writer had come to nothing. His memoir, *Beam Ends,* had flopped. He had published a series of articles on his life in *Photoplay* that were sheer fiction and begun work on a novel about Hollywood that was never completed. As early as 1936, he had sold the studio a script of his own, *The White Rajah,* but it had not been made into a film; his efforts to develop a comedy, *Jupiter Laughs,* with himself as producer, had also failed to bear fruit.

He slept very badly, and by the end of 1940 he could not sleep at all without a sexual release or a mixture of drink and drugs. His mind racing, he would rise in the night and wander about the new house he and Lili had taken next door to his friend columnist Hedda Hopper, in Beverly Hills while the house on Mulholland was being built.

One night, Hedda told me in 1965, she annoyed him by yelling out a complaint about his and Lili's quarrels. In retaliation, he went to her front door, masturbated vigorously, splattering his semen over it. She saw him through the window and laughed. He asked, "Will you invite me to *come* here again?"

He returned to a habit that had been latent since boyhood: of reading deeply in many fields. Those who associated him solely with physical activity and outrageous behavior would have been astonished had they come to his house on several nights of any given week. They would have found him wearing horn-rimmed spectacles, poring over such works as Darwin's *Voyage of the Beagle,* Hakluyt's *Voyages,* diaries of eighteenth-century writers, and poems by Browning, Shelley, and Keats. He rediscovered an earlier fascination with Robert Louis Stevenson's *Dr. Jekyll and Mr. Hyde* and with Conrad's *Heart of Darkness*. He was especially fond of Herman Melville's *Typee*. He delved into Dickens and rejoiced in Scott. His many letters throughout his life reflect his precision of expression and his feeling for the language.

Yet there was always his restless, intensely sexual nature, driving him away from study into the jungles of experience.

His interest in women, mostly young prostitutes of fifteen or sixteen, his trips to Mexico to enjoy young boys, two further visits to Hawaii in 1940 to sail and contact Nazis and film Pearl Harbor, the cost of drugs, and his lavish expenditures in every direction, drained his income of over $300,000 a year. What little he had left over, he plunged into land in Utah.

In the late fall of 1940, Errol became involved in an independent film-making venture with Skipper Douglas Dawson, Howard Hill, cameraman Al Wetzel, special effects man George Senaja, and several others who had had a good background in documentary work. Errol sold the footage as background material to Warner Brothers for later incorporation into a full-scale record of his numerous oceanic adventures that was not finally made.

Some of the films were shot aboard the *Sirocco* on high seas, and on installations along the coast of California and Mexico. These features showed Errol and his friends shooting wild boar on Catalina Island. Lili, Mrs. Wetzel, and Buster Wiles and even Dr. Erben came along for voyages. The men were equipped with bows and arrows. They also carried rifles for use against snakes or other reptiles.

Hill and Al Wetzel handled the direction. There was no script because of the unpredictable movements of the wild animals. The boar were very dangerous. Their ancestors had been swept ashore in the seventeenth century when the Spanish ships had been wrecked in storms off the Isthmus. They had never become fully domesticated, but in some cases had mated with pigs on the local farms. They averaged about one hundred pounds and were about two feet tall. On one occasion, a boar charged the game warden, who was on horseback, with such violence that it frightened the horse and unseated the rider.

In order to stage certain shots, the boar had to be provoked into rushing the cameras. They disliked the sun intensely and hid in dark, damp caves during the daylight hours. If they did emerge, they liked to keep in the shadows and dig surreptitiously for roots or mushrooms.

It became necessary to flush the boar from their lairs. On one trip, Errol, Hill, Wetzel, and the team set out from the hunting lodge with Errol's favorite African lion hound, Bill, named after William Keighley, and his less favored campanion, Mike, named after Michael Curtiz. The problem with Bill, who easily led the field, was that he was slightly overweight. He had to sniff after boar through narrow corridors of cactus plants, and because of his girth got several spines stuck in his fur. This irritated him, and he started to whine, but he still kept to the chase. The boar slipped easily through the cacti, using the thorny masses as protection against the new arrivals. Bill and Mike slid smoothly across a puzzle of tracks, sniffed the boar's spoor, and found ways to worry the creatures from the rear. They snapped at the beasts, biting into their testicles. The boar became maddened, but were too cumbersome to twist around and avenge themselves.

Finally, the boar were forced to charge forward into the cameras. Hill and Errol picked them off with bow and arrow. They made excellent eating that night, roasted on a spit at the hunting lodge. Lili pronounced the liver the most delicious she had ever eaten.

The gang sat up late exchanging tales of various adventures. Mrs. Wetzel finally retired. She had scarcely been in bed for more than a few minutes when a boar suddenly appeared in her cabin and snapped at her. Screaming, she fled into the night. The boar chased her all the way to the lodge and she was barely able to get the door shut.

Manfully, Howard and Errol decided to take revenge on the discourteous animal. With a couple of carefully aimed arrows, they killed the beast.

The next day, Buster Wiles almost had an arrow through his heart when, with incorrigible humor, he got on all fours behind Errol and made a sound exactly like a boar snorting. There was another antic episode when a boar with an arrow in its flank charged Al Wetzel and he ran headlong to the nearest cliff. He held onto a tree. The tree was hanging over the precipice, top down, so that Wetzel became one of the few human beings to have climbed a tree upside down.

On December 17, the team set off for Honolulu while Errol was in New York on business. He was to fly to Hawaii after them. He had been in Hawaii dating a Nazi agent named Erna Bauer, and the FBI had been intercepting her telegrams to him—which mentioned the sinking of Allied ships—and to Fritz Wiedemann in San Francisco. The team added to their normal contingent an actor named Joe Hartman and an assistant director named Bill Kiel. The master of the vessel was the blond and handsome Viking-like Hayward Kingsley, who had taken over from Douglas Dawson.

No sooner was the yacht past Catalina than she ran into a series of violent storms. The decks were completely awash and the engine and auxiliary were both rendered inactive. The sails were taken down but the mast was splintered. Some of the waves were sixty or seventy feet high, and the southerly wind reached a velocity of eighty miles per hour. The radio went out of action and no further communication with the mainland was possible. *Sirocco* was blown two hundred and fifty miles off course.

One of the problems was *Sirocco* herself. She had very little freeboard and indeed had never met the specifications of the Yachting Association and therefore had never been permitted to enter cup races. In rough water she performed unevenly, and high seas caused the crew to be drenched to the skin. She would dip heavily into the troughs and the water would swamp her main deck. Even the cockpit would be swamped.

The lifeboat was smashed in that December storm. Finally, on Christmas Eve, the ship's master had no alternative but to scud back before the gale to the leeward side of the Isthmus. At last, the seas calmed down. Two days later, Bill Kiel managed to repair the radio. They moored at Avalon on December 28. Al Wetzel says:

> I thought we would never get back. I was convinced *Sirocco* was a goner. The engine was virtually useless. Not a scrap of food was unspoiled. We all thanked God we were alive.

Errol was at the Ritz Tower in New York when he received word that the *Sirocco* was almost lost at sea. Within an hour, the news was on coast-to-coast radio. In considerable anguish, he flew to Los Angeles and then took a flying boat to Catalina. When he arrived, Al Wetzel recalls saying to him, "Next time the *Sirocco* goes to Honolulu, she'll be carried aboard a Matson Line ship." Errol was unable to argue.

On another voyage, an ordinary seaman fell ill with appendicitis. Errol contacted the Coast Guard vessel by ship-to-ship radio and the Coast Guard ordered the boy's stomach packed in ice to subdue the inflammation. When the boat came into San Diego Harbor the Merchant Marine put the boy into a plane and flew him to a Navy hospital in Burbank. But after the operation, Errol coldly refused to pay the expenses.

Another version of the story saw print. In this, Errol and Buster Wiles made their way through heavy fog in defiance of regulations to fly to the boy's rescue. Working in relays, with an improvised stretcher, they struggled across marshy territory to fly the patient back to Los Angeles. C. J. Wood describes that story as a masterpiece of public relations.

An exciting episode took place on the same journey. Off the headland of Cabo San Lucas, Howard Hill attempted to shoot a shark between the eyes at thirty paces. He stood in the dinghy with the arrow nocked and ready. He saw a sickle-shaped fin break the surface about thirty yards away. A fifteen-foot black shark emerged as Errol shouted a warning. Hill pulled the bow and the barbed arrow found its target in one of the shark's eyes. Twisting in pain, the shark dived and charged the dinghy, hurling Hill and Errol to the deck. Errol raised his bow and shot twice into the shark's flank. In its furious thrashing, the shark upset the boat and pitched the two men into the water. They beat at the shark with their bows and shouted loudly. The shark spun around. On a screamed instruction, the cook aboard the *Sirocco* flung raw meat into the water, temporarily distracting the creature. Errol and Hill managed to scramble back into the dinghy before it capsized and dispatched the shark as it fed on the bleeding meat.

Marlin fishing offered similar high adventure. Hill would send barbs, white-painted arrows into the mouths of the marlin, the arrow attached to a powerful rod and reel. Teasers—red, white, and blue plugs that floated and jiggled in the water—were trailed behind the stern to attract the fish. Flying fish were also used as bait. A marlin would leap out of the water to snap at them, and at that exact moment Hill would shoot the arrow into a high curve, piercing the fish's mouth. Al Wetzel photographed the action. Fifteen foot steel leaders had been attached to the arrowheads to prevent the thrashing fish from cutting the line. The leaders were attached in their turn to special reels of six-hundred-yard capacity. The line could take a strain of two hundred pounds or more. The double barbs on the arrows could not be pulled loose even with the most violent thrashing of the victim. One marlin taken on the trip weighed two hundred and eighty pounds. They brought in sixteen marlin and eight sharks (one of them four hundred and eighty pounds)—four of the sharks with bow and arrow.

Eleven

In the late summer and early fall of 1939, Dr. Erben was almost consistently in the service of German ships. In July, while in Hamburg, he was issued the German Nazi Party card authorized in May of the previous year. He sailed from Hamburg to South Africa aboard the German freighter *Ussukuma* as ship's surgeon. En route down the African west coast, he went aboard another German vessel, the *Weigon,* where he met a mysterious passenger, traveling in disguise, whose real name was Louis Siefken. Siefken later was in charge of the espionage ring in Shanghai of which Erben was to become a prominent member.

The vessel sailed to Lourenço Marques, home of spies and center of operations for the famous "Hamlet," the Nazi agent who guided U-boats against British and American ships. When war broke out on September 3, Hitler sent special orders that the *Ussukuma* must immediately proceed to South America to act as decoy and supply ship for the famous pocket battleship *Admiral Graf Spee.*

Erben knew a fellow American on board: the ship's pianist and piano accordionist, Hellmut Schuetze. Schuetze, now living in New York, recalls the journey vividly. He remembers that the vessel traveled without lights at night in order not to be detected by British warships. He remembers also that Erben was afraid of being arrested when they docked in South America and charged with being in violation of Section Five of the Neutrality Act as an American serving as a ship's officer for a belligerent nation.

Unable to make contact with the *Graf Spee, Ussukuma* proceeded up the coast of Argentina and berthed in Bahia Blanca on October 11. Erben acted characteristically. He spoke to the American consul and explained that since the war had started while he was on the voyage, he was unable to refuse service. The explanation was accepted but the Argentinian authorities were unwilling to grant him free transit. Gestapo headquarters at the German Consulate provided him with a Codula Argentina, or transit document, forged by a Nazi code specialist, Heinz Peerschke, who later became a member of the Siefken spy ring in the Orient. He obtained a German passport along with a German seaman's identification book to add to his credentials: his Nazi Party card, his 1938 Aryan Certificate (required for and exclusive to all SS or Gestapo officers, and showing pure Aryan descent back to 1750) and his membership in the National Socialist Colonial Bund.

He traveled to Montevideo, Uruguay. There, he filmed the *Graf Spee* as well as British vessels and their gun installations. He met the *Graf Spee*'s commander Captain Langsdorf and other officers, and when the *Graf Spee* was scuttled, he filmed her smoking hulk. He gave an interview the following year to the San Francisco *Examiner* stating that he issued cyanide pellets to the crew of the *Graf Spee* in case orders should come from Hitler that there should be a mass suicide when he boarded the supply ship *Tacoma.*

On his return to Argentina, Erben was arrested by local authorities because he had been traveling on the forged documents. He arranged his release with great ingenuity. He offered the United States Consulate in Buenos Aires films of the *Graf Spee* which could have been obtained by any tourist, pretending to the officials that this photographic material constituted major intelligence. As a result, the grateful consul arranged for his release. He then proceeded to take his actual intelligence on British vessels of war to the Gestapo chief who issued him the funds to proceed to the Panama Canal and to

California to obtain intelligence on the Canal and on California coastal installations and shipping movements.

He traveled by train across the Andes to Chile, arriving in Valparaiso in January 1940. By now, Ruth Shipley was telegraphing warnings to American consulates not to trust him, warnings which unfortunately were ignored in some cases.

He obtained the support of the American consul in Valparaiso by supplying intelligence on the German seaman's home which he described as a clearinghouse of information. He also said that the Gestapo had an operative there under orders from Buenos Aires. This fact was already known, but nevertheless, his device worked and the consul allowed Erben to sail, at America's expense, on the *Heiyo Maru,* a Japanese vessel bound for Los Angeles via Mexico and Panama.

Erben became terrified while aboard because there were twenty-three German employees of the Standard Oil Company who were returning to Germany. He knew the British patrols were looking for them because British intelligence wanted to learn the connection between Standard Oil and the Nazis. He knew that if the British spies boarded the *Heiyo Maru,* they would identify him and seize him as a major Nazi. They had boarded other ships that week.

On her way north to Callao, *Heiyo Maru* docked in the copper port of Antofagasta. There, Erben immediately went to the German Consulate, contacted the Nazi Gestapo chief and arranged for his precious Nazi documents and authorizations as a Gestapo member to be sent by surface mail to his friend Dr. Rudolph Scharf, of Park Avenue, a society physician in New York. They never arrived. The mail was intercepted by British agents and the Nazi Party card reproduced in this book was among the contents of the seized package.

Erben then proceeded to the American vice consul and begged him for a job on another ship of American registry. American Nazis could only be seized by British intelligence if they were found on non-American neutral vessels. As an American citizen on an American ship, he would be safe from the British patrols.

The vice consul proved to be very useful. He told Erben of a vacancy for the job of dishwasher on the Grace Lines vessel *Nightingale,* bound for New York, and helped Erben get the job. After he had made the arrangements, the vice consul visited the British consul. The Englishman said, "I appreciate the information and find it amusing. Dr. Erben is number one on the British wanted list of German agents and will, most certainly, be taken prisoner if found on a neutral ship or anywhere else by British authorities, naval or otherwise."

As soon as Erben went aboard, he began his spying activities. He filmed the *Nightingale* from stem to stern. The ship sailed south to Valparaiso before proceeding north. On arrival in that port, an astonishing episode took place. This obscure dishwasher was greeted on the wharf by a delegation of the entire crew of an important German training vessel, the *Priwall.* The crew lined up and gave him the Nazi salute, thus indicating his importance in naval intelligence. The effect of this reception on the other dishwashers can only be imagined.

Despite this blowing of Erben's cover, he was still permitted to sail on the *Nightingale.* He worked fiendishly hard in Valparaiso. He filmed every inch of the naval and military installations of the harbor; he photographed the Chilean battleship *Latorre;* he took pictures of strategic copper being loaded on the *Nightingale* for use by the allies in Europe; he tried desperately to film the cargo in the hold and to obtain entry into the engine room to photograph the *Nightingale*'s revolutionary apparatus.

With all this, he was allowed to continue on the *Nightingale.* When the vessel reached the Panama Canal, he made frantic efforts to disembark, in order to photograph the Canal. When United States agents questioned him in Panama City, he said he merely wanted to reach his "close friends, Errol Flynn and Ernest Hemingway(!) in Hollywood." He was allowed to continue to take photographs on board of every visible installation, military or naval, in the Canal.

He continued to New York. On his arrival, naval intelligence men seized all of his films and developed them. A few days later, he boldly entered FBI headquarters and told Federal Agent Langille that he had aided naval intelligence by presenting it with all of his important information on South America! He was counting on the lack of communication between naval intelligence and the FBI.

He traveled to Washington, and tried to obtain a renewal on his passport, but Ruth Shipley told him that he would never be given a passport again. He was hysterically protesting his loyalty to America when he was ejected from her office.

Mrs. Shipley sent a further memorandum to all foreign consulates specifying that Erben was a Nazi agent and that no further courtesies would be extended to him. By 1940, security in America had tightened enormously and Nazi agents were being watched, reported, or imprisoned.

A time-honored method of disposing of undesirable aliens was to revoke their citizenship on the grounds of false procurement. Erben had lied on numerous passport renewal forms between 1926 and 1930 (the year of his citizenship), saying that he had been almost continuously present in America, whereas in fact he had been frequently absent. The Secretary of Labor, Frances Perkins, ordered Revocation of Citizenship proceedings in San Francisco.

At that moment, Errol stepped in with perhaps the most diabolical action of his career. He used Eleanor Roosevelt, of all people, to protect Erben and—by extension—himself.

Errol had met Mrs. Roosevelt through his work for the March of Dimes, at parties at the White House, in New York and in Hollywood. He was a friend of Franklin D. Roosevelt, Jr., who recalls, "Errol used to join me and the Whitneys in fox hunting in Virginia. Knowing how he hated Jews, we used to call him 'Flynnberg' to annoy him."

Nineteen forty was election year and Mrs. Roosevelt was on a nationwide tour on her husband's behalf in the early spring. At the beginning of March she met Errol in Miami. It was easy to get to her by mentioning his fondness for her son.

He asked her to have the revocation case against Erben's citizenship called off. The exact details of the conversation will probably never be known. But the thrust of the plea must have been to Mrs. Roosevelt's legendary concern for the underdog. Erben had often used the conventional Nazi spy's technique of claiming that his family in Europe would be murdered by the Nazis if he did not seem to be a Nazi himself. (This was an ingenious inversion of the truth. Members of Gestapo agents' families *were* often held hostage but not for the reasons given. By holding them, the Gestapo could make sure it was not betrayed.)

Whatever approach Errol took, it worked. Mrs. Roosevelt promised to do what she could.

Records show that she contacted J. Edgar Hoover, the Attorney General, the Secretary of Labor, and the Secretaries of the Navy and Army. In March 1940, the grueling investigation of Erben and Errol was suddenly suspended. For six months, while Mrs. Roosevelt's attentions were taken up with aiding her husband's campaign for reelection (a campaign severely threatened by Nazi-controlled political interests), Erben and Errol were able to operate freely as continuance after continuance was granted on the revocation case.

Errol was questioned about Erben on March 15, 1940, when he was in the midst of a difficult action sequence of *The Sea Hawk*. Special FBI agent Richard Hood conducted the interview.

Hood asked Errol, "Do you know Dr. Erben?"

Errol replied, "I am *acquainted* with him. I regard him highly."

"How long have you known him?" Hood asked.

"For about ten years. We have traveled extensively together all over the world."

"Where did you first meet?"

"In New Guinea. Erben was there as the head of an expedition for the Rockefeller Institute! And I saw him work twenty-four hours at a stretch entirely without compensation. He was amazing."

Hood went on, "What do you think of Erben?"

"He has a very brilliant mind and is an excellent physician. He is the type of person who would do everything in his power to make it appear that in fact he was an espionage agent. He has a propensity for getting into trouble."

"What are his politics?"

"He's very much opposed to Nazism and Communism and from what I know of his background I don't believe he would *now* be a devout Nazi. I have letters from him which I'll turn over to you for examination. I can show you that I have communicated with Mrs. Roosevelt in an effort to have her do anything possible for Erben."

In subsequent weeks, Hood did everything in his power to obtain the letters from Errol. But he soon realized he would never get them.

It is appalling to note that on April 3, 1940, with full government approval, Erben sailed on the Panama Lines vessel, S.S. *Panama* as ship's surgeon, bound for the Panama Canal. On board, he openly expressed his Nazism. He filmed the Panama Canal installations again and obtained entree to military installations by attending a Militia Day ceremony. And all this without interference by anyone. He returned to New York and his pictures were not impounded.

For months, Warners had been wanting Errol to undertake a Latin American tour to promote his pictures. The State Department had been blocking the applications, but suddenly he received permission to go ahead.

He was accompanied on the trip by Johnny Meyer. Meyer

confirmed that he and Errol constantly met Nazis at the highest level of the Gestapo—in Buenos Aires, Rio, Valparaiso, Chile, and every other major city. Errol visited American ambassadors, toured the military and naval installations, and even boarded American ships. No doubt he obtained a great deal of intelligence. In Mexico, when Carl Schaefer of Warner's publicity staff met with him, Schaefer was warned by his head office in New York to make sure Errol laid off his Nazi connections.

In Buenos Aires on July 1, the American ambassador, Norman Armour, asked him point blank what his connection with Erben was. He again replied that he knew him as an acquaintance—and then proceeded to defend him in almost exactly the same words that he had used to Richard Hood of the FBI. But he slightly overdid his protestations. Armour became alarmed and sent copies of his report on Errol to the offices of military and naval intelligence, the Department of Justice, J. Edgar Hoover, the Attorney General, and even the White House. He felt that even if Errol was not a collaborator, he was flying in the face of information about Erben that was already appearing in newspapers from Alaska to Patagonia. It seemed Errol was the only individual on earth who did not know Erben was a Nazi, and this gave rise to the gravest suspicions of collusion in Armour's eyes.

Errol said, in brief, that Erben hated the Nazis with all his soul; that Erben would make a very bad Nazi spy because he was wanted in every port in the world; that Erben was his own worst enemy— but was a loyal American.

It was quite clear to every Latin American consul that Errol was defending Erben in order to protect himself. However, Mrs. Roosevelt's umbrella of protection held good. And by now, the formidable Hollywood machinery designed to protect its own was working well.

It is hard to realize the extent of the studios' political influence at the time. One Hollywood executive said to me recently, "We were constantly reminding Congress that they were working for us—we weren't working for them. We represented the public and big business. Stars were idols of the public and they *were* our business. We didn't want our nest invaded. We didn't welcome the FBI or anybody else who tried to expose our stars. If the devil himself—or Hitler's brother—had worked for Jack Warner, if he was making millions he would have been protected."

Errol returned from Latin America flat on his back on a stretcher from a recurrence of undulant fever—murmuring about "the Nazi threat."

Meantime, during Errol's long absence through the spring and summer, Erben was extremely active. Exhilarated by the protection of Mrs. Roosevelt and by his friendship with the great Errol Flynn, he had the audacity to write directly to the Attorney General and to J. Edgar Hoover asking, in effect, whether the heat was off. They reassured him that he would be able to obtain employment wherever he chose. In fact, the most appalling episode of that year occurred at the end of March.

Strict security surrounded the Civilian Conservation Corps camps, also known as CCC camps. In these, private citizens, mostly young men of close to military age were trained to be ready for soldiering in time of national emergency.

The camps were run strictly under government control, yet Erben was invited to be the camp doctor at the CCC center in Fort Moultrie, South Carolina. Fortunately, his outrageous expressions of Gestapo philosophy and extravagant praise for Adolf Hitler resulted in his being asked to leave. As he departed, he remarked to someone in the camp that "there is so little to spy on here it isn't worth staying."

He then proceeded to another CCC assignment in Sebring, Florida.

In Sebring, his behavior reached an extreme. He took numerous photographs of the CCC training methods, installations, guns and other weapons, the layout of the huts and headquarters offices. He obtained lists of the young volunteers, especially those of German parentage, in the camp. He discussed his Nazism openly and, when Hitler marched into Paris, expressed his delight and said that he wished he were there. He made efforts to drag out and whip the boys working for him in the dispensary.

A very important businessman sent a telegram to Florida's Senator Claude Pepper complaining of Erben's behavior and demanding a full senatorial inquiry. How, the telegram asked, was it possible for a civilian training camp to engage a known Nazi agent who could endanger military security and to permit him to take photographs of top secret installations with a microscopic lens? Pepper forwarded the telegram to the army authorities who tabled it. He also sent it to the FBI.

J. Edgar Hoover showed some mild response. In a memorandum to several of his agents he said that in time of national emergency it might be necessary to consider interning Erben. And that was as far as he went.

But by midsummer, the effort to revoke Erben's citizenship began to be reactivated. War was getting nearer to America. Every month brought news of Americans going down on torpedoed vessels or being interned in Europe. Erben's protections had worn thin.

After endless postponements, the revocation hearings began in San Francisco in August.

Erben acted up a storm on the witness stand, grumbling that he and Errol Flynn had been hounded, that his luggage had been seized and searched, that his pictures had been impounded, that his life was miserable. "My citizenship," he said, "has brought me nothing but misery from the beginning." He asserted he was a loyal American, that all this mass of evidence against him was fabricated.

But by September, it became clear to Erben that he had little hope of winning the case. While the hearing was still going on, he decided to try to escape to the Orient or South America, where he could link up with Nazi intelligence nets. But because his name and face were in all the papers as a Nazi spy he dared not attempt to leave in the normal way. San Francisco District Attorney Louis Mercado held the passport canceled by Ruth Shipley; Erben had surrendered his naturalization certificate long before.

All he had left was his invaluable seaman's protection certificate. With Errol's help he applied to various union officials and managed to enlist as an ordinary seaman on the Japan-bound Dollar liner *President Garfield*—the selfsame vessel on which he had served eight years earlier as ship's surgeon.

But despite his newly regrown beard and rough longshoreman's outfit, he was quickly identified from newspaper photographs, and deposited ashore.

Undaunted, he enlisted once more as an ordinary seaman, this time aboard the freighter *Admiral Nulton* sailing from Seattle to Russia and Japan. The freighter was intercepted by a British vessel off the coast and intelligence men came aboard. Although they had no power to arrest Erben since he was still an American citizen, they induced the captain to dump him ashore in San Francisco.

Erben traveled north to Tacoma, Washington, in October and

signed on the *Staghound,* bound for Mexico and Argentina. Detected for a third time, he was placed ashore once again in San Francisco.

When U. S. District Attorney Mercado reprimanded Erben, the doctor announced that he intended to enlist in one of the armed services. This he said would prove his loyalty to the country. Obviously, he was hoping to be given travel documents by whichever service was foolish enough to accept him.

Word went out and he was not recruited. Furthermore, a federal warrant was put out for Erben's arrest on the ground of his having attempted to leave the country illegally while on trial over his citizenship.

Errol immediately sprang to action. He hid Erben aboard the *Sirocco* through the late fall of 1940 and into the early winter. Noticing the attention Erben's case had received, Fritz Wiedemann, German consul general in San Francisco, and George Gyssling, German consul in Los Angeles, got in touch with Erben and proposed a remarkable scheme. They wanted him to join the Abwehr—German military intelligence command in Mexico City—for training in microdots and microfilm techniques. Then he would be transferred to the Orient where he would become a founding member of a Nazi spy ring to be set up in Shanghai. His American contact in the Abwehr would be a well-known New York journalist named Hans Adolf Mosberg, whom he would later join in China. The Jewish Mosberg had been granted the special title "Honorary Aryan" in return for his services and for arranging the free movement of Nazi agents.

But there was a problem. How could Erben make his way across the border into Mexico? He was a wanted man. How could he get a transit card?

Errol knew there might be just a chance of getting such a card through his business manager, C. J. Wood. Wood recalls what happened next: "Errol called me at my office in Los Angeles and told me he had a friend, Dr. Erben, who urgently needed papers to get out of the country. I was dubious about what could be done but agreed to see the man. Soon after, there was a commotion in my outer office. A huge, burly, rough man burst in in a longshoreman's outfit, needing a shave. He talked to me in an aggressive, loud German voice that instantly antagonized me. He said, 'I don't give a damn for America or American passports but documents like this are very helpful if you want to get to the Orient.' I immediately rose from my chair and told him to leave at once and never come back."

With astonishing boldness, risking his career, Errol went ahead and took Erben to Mexico. In 1944, while in a prison camp in Shanghai, Erben said to a fellow inmate that Errol had gone on hiding him on the *Sirocco* and that from there he had gone ashore in Mexico direct. This certainly was the easiest way of aiding a spy to escape from America.

In 1978, Erben said that Errol drove him to the border, got him through immigration and customs with a Mexican transit card and embraced him in friendly farewell. Whichever of these versions is true, Errol committed an act of treason by giving aid and comfort to an enemy at a time when he was still a British subject. If caught by British intelligence agents, he could have been extradited and tried in England as a traitor. The world-famous star could have ended his life on the hangman's noose.

The FBI's failure to follow Erben and Errol and determine the nature of their plan was unhappily typical of the Bureau's handling of the case from the beginning. Chauncey Tramutolo, Johnny Meyer, Max Carmel, and many others who knew of the Flynn-Erben connection were never subjected to questioning. Worse, the border control wasn't even checked once it had been determined that Erben had left for Mexico. When FBI agents reported his presence in Mexico City the following month, local agents were forced to admit they had no idea how he had gotten there. Errol was questioned about Erben's whereabouts but pretended he had no idea of them.

The FBI was not an intelligence organization, and their agents were not trained in intelligence techniques. They failed to coordinate their investigations with those of the State Department, and even when they tried, they often found their complaints blocked. They also failed to correlate with military and naval intelligence. The fact is that thirteen months before Pearl Harbor, America had no central intelligence organization. The absence of the OSS—precursor of the CIA—until 1942 proved to be fortunate for Erben and Errol.

According to Colonel W. E. Williamson, one of the leading figures in military intelligence in Asia under General MacArthur, military intelligence was aware of Errol's connection with Erben from the beginning. Why then did it not strike? Because, Williamson implied, of Errol's close association with the Roosevelts and with Sumner

Welles. Intelligence made detailed checks on several of Errol's associates until the end of the war, including two of his mistresses and his friend Freddy McEvoy. But the war ended before any of these could be pinned down.

It is most unfortunate that British intelligence was not working in harmony with American intelligence at the time. Neutral America, with its overpowering isolationist elements, was uneasy about admitting Britain into its secret files and private investigations. Furthermore, both Cordell Hull, Secretary of State, and Lord Halifax, British Foreign Minister, were following an ambiguous, uncertain course, despite Winston Churchill's and President Roosevelt's adamant stand that the war must be fought to its conclusion.

. Had British intelligence been in charge of the Flynn matter, there is no question that they would have succeeded in arresting him. They had enough to ask him: why he went to Spain with Erben to help him spy on the anti-Fascist Germans there. They would have asked among other things, why he paid Erben's legal fees, gave him succor and shelter when Flynn's country was at war with Germany, why he aided and abetted Erben by helping him get aboard vessels, why he invited Erben's Nazi sons to stay at his home, why he hid Erben on his yacht—in short, why he traitorously assisted Britain's enemy.

But because this was neutral America, Errol went on, smiling his flashing smile, to make a series of anti-Nazi propaganda pictures: the supreme irony of his career.

In Mexico City, Erben reported to Consul General von Wallenberg at Gestapo headquarters, located, strangely enough, in a former convent. Erben also connected with the Abwehr where he was given intensive training at spy school in Microdot.

Then, with a forged German passport under the alias of Alois Ecker, ship's musician, he sailed to Los Angeles in February. Ecker was the name of a friend of his in Vienna. Errol was in Honolulu as a guest of Captain James Robb of the Pearl Harbor Naval Base, taking films, photographs, and notes.

Erben was in transit in Los Angeles when Tramutolo called him to say his citizenship had been revoked. It was in the papers on January 29.

For years, he claimed he did not know this until 1943. The reason was that when he reached Shanghai he had to pose as an American for espionage purposes.

While Errol was in Honolulu, Jack Warner cabled him that he wanted him to appear in a picture called *Dive Bomber* to illustrate the problems of Naval Air Corps fliers during their intensive training.

By this time, naval intelligence records show, Erben's activities in South America had been carefully followed by that service and Errol's links with Erben were known. Naval authorities were most reluctant to have either Errol Flynn or Warner Brothers have access to the San Diego Naval Base and the aircraft carrier *Enterprise* for the picture.

Jack Warner sent his personal troubleshooter, Colonel William Guthrie, to Washington to sort the matter out. Blocked at every turn, Guthrie went all the way to the Secretary of the Navy. So great was the power of Hollywood studios at the time that the Secretary of the Navy overruled the others and ordered the San Diego Naval Base staff to put the base at Warners' disposal.

As a result, *Dive Bomber,* with all of its graphic portrayal of secret installations and aircraft carrier decks, was shipped, as Errol undoubtedly hoped, direct to Japan.

When Curtiz, Flynn, and the rest of the cast and crew went aboard the *Enterprise* on the first day of shooting, they were greeted with silence and hostile stares. Curtiz's foreign accent made many men aboard feel that he was a German—and certainly so did his behavior. He would scream out to the crew: "Hey, you bums, get back in line!" or "Stand back there, you bums, you're blocking the plane!" When the admiral appeared, he yelled, "Hey, you gold braid bum, get back there! Get out of the shot! We need you in the next shot! And look, look! That smoke from your chimney is going in the wrong direction!"

His face red with rage, his fists clenched, the admiral muttered, "And how may I ask do you suggest I change the direction of the smoke, sir?"

"Turn the ship around!" Curtiz shouted.

To make matters worse, Curtiz, Errol, and the film crew occupied officers' quarters, which meant that the officers had to double up. But the admiral and the captain of the *Enterprise* had their revenge. No sooner had the movie makers settled in their bunks than a loud bugle was sounded, depth charges went off, guns were discharged, and lights exploded outside the portholes. The deafening noise went on all night. As a result, nobody slept a wink; in the morning, Errol and his companions were visibly exhausted and barely able to work. The vengeful barrage continued every night until the end of the shooting.

Errol contrived his own vengeance. While the officers and men were lined up for a film shot, he arranged for Limey Plews to arrive with a fake bomb which had buzzers going and green and red lights flashing. Limey put it on the deck and said to the admiral on Errol's orders, "Here is the stuff you asked for, Herr Hitler. The secret weapon you were waiting for!"

On the last day of shooting, the captain asked, "Are you on the final lap?" And when Curtiz said, "Yes," the captain ordered the *Enterprise* so rapidly out to sea that the cameras fell to the deck. Navy boats came alongside, and the captain said, "Drop all your equipment overboard or it will be thrown in the sea." The movie people obeyed quickly. Everyone, even Curtiz, had to scramble down the Jacob's ladders to the boats, dangerous at the *Enterprise*'s speed. Errol lived up to his screen image by stripping to his shorts and diving heroically from the flight deck.

Curtiz's eccentric behavior continued ashore. He told the Air Corps pilots, "See you fly low, you winged bums. Ten feet off the ground. And stay up in the sky in flight pattern till I let off the firework and tell you you can move." The men would walk off, scratching their heads, convinced the "Nazi" director was not only a spy but a crazy one.

Dive Bomber had a curious aftermath. The producer of the film, the late Robert Lord, said, many years later:

I do not want this statement published until after I'm dead. In our advance prints of the picture, before it was released, we used most of Errol's land and air shots of Pearl Harbor at his suggestion in a special, semi-documentary presentation of America's power in the Pacific.

An advance print was sent to our representative in Japan in the normal course of events in the late summer of 1941. Needless to say, it was examined with great interest by the Japanese Chiefs of Staff. It proved to be most valuable to them in their plans for an attack on Pearl Harbor.

It's also shocking to think in retrospect that again at Errol's suggestion, we showed every detail of the San Diego Naval Base and the entire structure of the *Enterprise*. I believe that the Japanese kept the film under study for years in case of a possible assault on California.

Early in February 1941, Erben somehow managed to give the FBI the slip at San Pedro, Port of Los Angeles, and sail by a Japanese freighter as ship's musician under orders from Hans Adolf Mosberg, who left only two weeks later, also aboard a Japanese ship and also avoiding the FBI men. Inconveniently for American security, the vessel stopped at Pearl Harbor for refueling, before proceeding to Japan, where Gestapo and naval intelligence men eagerly waited Erben's extraordinary collection of photographs of naval installations.

Erben planned always to return to Errol, and, in 1944, two underground OSS agents in Shanghai were to make an extraordinary statement. It was as follows—as reported to the FBI in Los Angeles and San Francisco in a report dated May 15 of that year:

Erben tried recently to return to the United States as a repatriate. We believe that if he had been successful in so doing, he would have been acting in the United States as an agent of the German government. Erben's only contact in the United States was Errol Flynn. We know of absolutely no other contact with Dr. Erben there.

And even after this astonishing revelation of Errol's Nazism, nothing whatsoever was done about it.

Twelve

Lili had become pregnant in September 1940. Errol was indifferent. He returned from a visit to his Nazi mistress in Hawaii only briefly after Lili's baby was born on May 31, 1941. He told her quite bluntly he had come to drive her home from the hospital for publicity reasons.

The child was a healthy boy of seven pounds two ounces, whom Errol and Lili called Sean. Fair-haired, blue-eyed, he was a knockout. Errol was proud of Sean but resented him because he provided a tie to a woman whose presence he could no longer endure. The rift was so severe after Sean's birth that Lili swore Errol would never have custody of the boy. Errol spent very little time with Sean during the first twelve years of his life. When Sean was ten, Errol taught him to smoke a cigar, and when he was twelve, Errol took him to his first whorehouse. Lili complained bitterly when Errol attempted to take the boy from school at sixteen, offering him a chance to undertake a world voyage on his yacht.

For the previous two years, Errol had been part of the circle surrounding the famous and eccentric artist John Decker and Decker's
even more eccentric friend, John Barrymore. Flynn had finally gotten his wish: to meet his idol. Unfortunately, this was at the end of
Barrymore's life; but at least, for a time, they became good friends
and drinking partners.

John Decker's real name was Leopold von der Decken. He looked
like John Barrymore in a distorting mirror. He enjoyed a vogue as a
painter in the 1940s partly because of his clever caricatures of the famous, including W. C. Fields as Queen Victoria, a work which still
hangs in the lobby of Chasen's Restaurant in Beverly Hills. Decker
had a colorful background. He was born in Germany, the son of a
baron. His mother was an English opera singer. His father worked as
a correspondent for the London *Times*. Decker was interned as an
alien on the Isle of Man during World War I. He had been commis-
sioned by a German to do some paintings that were used to cover espionage messages. The German was executed, but Decker escaped.
He was probably innocent.

Decker had a lasting dread of sunsets because he had watched so
many through the barbed-wire fence in the internment camp, wondering if he would see another dawn. "We always had to pull the
drapes when the sun was setting," his widow, Phyllis, recalls.

He got to America in the 1920s without a passport, having stowed
away on board ship. Asked by authorities on arrival in New York
why he didn't have papers, he said that he had been unable to obtain
them because his birth records had been destroyed in the San
Francisco earthquake. He got away with it.

In the late 1930s, his raffish, vivid caricatures became the rage in
Hollywood. John Barrymore was crazy about him and they used to
get drunk together, telling complicated jokes far into the night.

A rift between Errol and Decker started when Errol began stealing
things from Decker's cottage: silver matchbox covers, a cigarette
box and a cigar box, small clocks. Phyllis Decker recalls:

> He took one of my rings and his butler returned it the next day.
> We had two very pretty little Chinese brass horses sitting together
> on a windowsill. After a party, one of the horses disappeared. I said
> to Errol one day, not knowing his kleptomanic habits, "What a pity
> the thief just took one horse. He should have taken two, so the

second one wouldn't be lonely." That evening I noticed the other horse was missing.

In the summer of 1941, Errol received the welcome news that his next picture, *They Died with Their Boots On,* would be handled by Raoul Walsh, considered one of the finest action directors in Hollywood. A rugged, forthright giant, he had lost one eye when a buck rabbit had jumped through the windshield of his car several years before. With his massive head and body, his black eye patch, his ten-gallon hats and habit of carrying a stockwhip to work, he was a magnifico after Errol's own heart, and Errol affectionately dubbed him "Uncle." In turn, Raoul Walsh called Errol "The Baron," a recognition of rank which soon became generally used for Flynn in Hollywood circles.

Errol gave his best in *They Died with Their Boots On.* The theme was the relationship of the officer and the regiment as shown through the life of George Armstrong Custer, who was at first self-serving and undisciplined, but who at last learned that service meant more than the individual quest for glory. Custer, with his long hair, his handsomely designed uniform, his gaudy social manners, his obsession with action and glory and fame, his tremendous ego and his extravagant style, was ideally suited to Flynn, and reflective of him. He acted the part with a commitment, a passion, a degree of color and grandeur he seldom equaled in any other picture.

In its sweep, its sense of leather and stirrup, proud men and powerful horses, dust and sunlight, *They Died with Their Boots On* was masterfully achieved. Yet this fine picture was not made without suffering and misadventure. Many of the extras had never ridden a horse before and did not know how to put the animals through the various attacks and counterattacks. As a result, they fell, breaking legs, arms, and, in some cases, necks: three died in the sequence of the Battle of Bull Run. Worst of all, a handsome young polo player named Ralph ("Jack") Budlong died in a sequence shot on the Warner Ranch. His horse swerved and as he was falling off, he flung down his sword. It fell blade up, glancing against the rock; as he plunged from the horse, he was impaled upon the weapon. It pierced his side and emerged from his back. Had it been left in, he might have been saved, but he insisted that one of the other men draw it out. He bled so profusely he was already dying when he reached the hospital.

If ever proof could be given that Errol did not fake his successive illnesses (as the studio still maintained) that proof lay in this film. Here was a part that fitted him like a scabbard; a director he admired; a script that for once he could respect. Yet he was hospitalized for more than ten days of shooting, and sick for many more.

The smoke from the cannon and the gunpowder from the lighter weapons, caused him to have a violent sinus attack, with headaches so terrible that he cried loudly in agony, and had to be rushed to the Good Samaritan Hospital in Los Angeles.

Recovering slowly, Errol took off on the *Sirocco* to Mexico in June 1941, with a small crew, headed by his new skipper, Hayward Kingsley, and his cook, a Filipino named Pio Espiritu. Arno, as usual, went along for the voyage. The dog had developed an odd, disconcerting habit of snapping after flying fish. At night, Arno was normally locked up in the galley, where he had a spacious kennel and a variety of large, juicy bones. But on the night voyage from San Pedro to Balboa, Arno apparently slipped his leash and made his way up a companionway to the deck while the watch was sleeping on duty. Spying a fish, Arno had jumped up to snap, and had fallen into the sea.

Errol woke at dawn and walked about, checking the vessel as usual. When he looked in the kennel, he was shocked to find Arno missing. He began whistling and calling but there was no merry, responsive bark. He began to panic. He woke the crew and searched the cabins.

But there was no sign of his beloved Schnauzer. Realizing what must have happened, he broke into tears.

Docking in Balboa, Errol went to the harbor master. The whole available fleet was put out at sea to search for the missing dog but by nightfall, Arno had not been found. Errol went out on the *Sirocco*, pacing the deck, training binoculars on the sea.

Three days later, Arno's remains were washed ashore a few miles down the coast. Errol took the collar, and buried it solemnly in the tiny animal graveyard under the walls of the house on Mulholland Drive. Members of the Coast Guard staged a replica of a naval burial, shipping the dog out to sea in a tiny coffin and slipping it off the deck under the Stars and Stripes by moonlight.

It was a fateful period. On August 1, the day of Arno's burial, Lili Damita Flynn walked out of Errol's life with young Sean. She immediately started divorce proceedings. Recovered quickly from Arno's loss, the next day Errol asked Jim Fleming to contact the Warner Brothers publicity department for available girls to pose for him in a photographic layout for *Life* magazine. The layout was to show him skin-diving and sailing off Catalina. Fleming discovered that all of the available starlets were booked up for the weekend, so he called an occasional date of his, Peggy Satterlee, asking if she would be willing to undertake the trip and pose for the pictures.

An ambitious hopeful from an obscure whistle-stop named Applegate, California, Peggy Satterlee was delighted with the opportunity. She had been introduced to Errol by her sister at a nightclub in Balboa on the night of Arno's disappearance at sea: they were at the club with Buster Wiles. Errol had invited the three of them to go aboard the yacht and do a tour of inspection.

Errol was pleased with the arrangement. Peggy was exceptionally pretty, charming, and very friendly. Jim Fleming arranged for photographer Peter Stackpole to fly to the Catalina Isthmus on Sunday morning to join the sailing party. At 6:30 A.M. on Saturday, August 2, the *Sirocco* left San Pedro for the voyage. Shortly before midnight on August 1, Buster Wiles, Errol's stunt double and equally mischievous friend, and Buster's girl, a carhop named Elaine Patterson, had arrived with Peggy Satterlee, whom they had picked up at Chasen's. Errol joined them at the California Yacht Club at 11 P.M. and preceded them aboard to confer with Captain Hayward Kingsley.

Sirocco berthed in Fourth of July Cove on Catalina at 10 A.M. There was little wind, the sea was flat, and *Sirocco* towed a speedboat.

Most of Saturday was spent swimming and sunbathing. On Saturday evening, Errol, Buster, Peggy, and Elaine went ashore and danced until late at the Hawaiian Hut, a local restaurant-nightclub. They all came back by water taxi at 2 A.M. on Sunday. Errol told Jim Fleming later:

"I went to Peggy's cabin. At first, she said 'No.' Then she said 'Yes.' We went happily to bed."

Captain Kingsley, who slept on deck, heard nothing. Early next morning, Buster Wiles took the outboard motorboat to Avalon and returned with Peter Stackpole. The party lunched on board. In the afternoon Stackpole took pictures of Errol plunging vigorously off the deck in swimming trunks, skin-diving and spearing fish, and surfacing with his latest catch. Errol was photographed seated on the deck, his arm around Peggy while Buster had his arm around Elaine. There were shots of Errol, Peggy, Buster, and Elaine riding in the speedboat around the *Sirocco,* and of the party enjoying drinks at sunset. Peggy took the wheel, her hair blowing free under Kingsley's skipper's cap, Errol standing behind her, helping her to guide the vessel.

During the first spear dives, Peggy had accidentally kicked Errol in the nose. This, combined with the water pressure, caused his sinuses to act up.

After dinner, the party sailed from Fourth of July Cove, leaving at 7 P.M. Errol took the wheel. The boat docked at 10:30 P.M. Later that night, Buster Wiles drove Peggy and Elaine to their homes. Whether Errol slept with Peggy that Sunday night at sea is open to some doubt. And it is hard to believe that after docking there would have been an opportunity to make love to her, let alone rape her, as she later charged.

Aside from the time factor, neither Errol nor Peggy was well. Peggy was depressed and a little seasick, and Errol was still in the grip of the sinus headache. As she came up on deck and leaned over the rail, he asked, "Are you all right?" She sobbed that she hated the idea of going home, that she had no money, and jobs were few and far between, and that life seemed black and full of despair, with nothing in the world to look forward to. Errol promised to help her.

Next morning, Errol felt so ill when he woke that he had to send for an ambulance. Then he called the studio and advised them that he could not work on *They Died with Their Boots On* that day.

Peggy Satterlee was still feeling unwell and depressed when she went home. She may have been slightly injured because of the intensity of Errol's sexual attack on her on Saturday night, and it is just possible that she had still been a virgin at the time. No doubt her mother dragged the truth from her and, since her daughter was underage, decided to do something about it.

Errol spoke to Peggy from his hospital bed late that afternoon. Peggy said, "I told mother what you did."

Errol replied, "Did you tell her it was on the decent side?" She hung up.

Mrs. Satterlee took Peggy to the District Attorney's office where she was examined and there seemed to be evidence of forcible entry into her vagina. Errol called Jim Fleming and asked him to find out what Peggy was up to. He would soon find out.

From *Charge of the Light Brigade* (*Charge of the Light Brigade,* Copyright ©, 1936, Warner Bros. Pictures, Inc. & The Vitaphone Corp., Renewal ©, 1964, United Artists Associated, Inc./Released by United Artists
Television, Inc., all rights reserved)

On location of *Charge of the Light Brigade* with Arno, 1936 (*Charge of the Light Brigade,* Copyright ©, 1936, Warner Bros. Pictures, Inc., & The Vitaphone Corp., Renewal ©, 1964, United Artists Associated, Inc./Released by United Artists Television, Inc., all rights reserved)

L. to R.: Lili Damita, Errol, and Howard Hill in a rare photo on the yacht *Sirocco* (Courtesy of Al Wetzel)

The Duke of Alba, 1937. (Alfred Eisenstaedt)

With his favorite pet, Chico. (Photograph by Jerome Zerbe)

With Paul McWilliams, Sr., 1938. (Courtesy of Paul McWilliams, Jr.)

The only picture taken with Jack Warner (on right), Los Angeles, 1938. (Courtesy of Solly Baiano)

With Gilbert Roland (second from left), Mervyn Le Roy (fourth from left), Charlie Ruggles (extreme right) at Los Angeles Tennis Club finals, 1938. (Courtesy of Solly Baiano)

Max Carmel, 1938.

"Rise, Sir Robin of Locksley" from *The Adventures of Robin Hood,* 1938.
(*The Adventures of Robin Hood,* Copyright ©, 1938, Warner Bros. Pictures, Inc., Renewal ©, United Artists Television, Inc., all rights reserved)

According to Jim Fleming, Errol arranged for money to be paid to a certain member of the District Attorney's department in order for the case to be dropped. Nothing more was heard of it for fifteen months.

Errol's attorney, Jerry Giesler, warned him to be extremely careful for the next few months. Errol told Giesler Peggy had lied about her age, that she looked much older than fifteen. "You better look at their birth certificates next time," Giesler advised.

Errol cheerfully ignored Giesler's warning. As soon as *They Died with Their Boots On* was finished, he flew to New York with Buster Wiles, checked into the Ritz Towers Hotel, and used the money from some radio program appearances to pay for a series of wild sessions with girls of every age and description.

In the period following *They Died with Their Boots On,* Errol was very frequently in Mexico. FBI agents trailed him everywhere, and by so doing uncovered an enormous list of agents. He mingled with an extraordinary group of expatriates, including the heads of the Gestapo and Abwehr. By that period, seven hundred Nazi agents had poured into Mexico from the United States, Japan, Central America, and Spain. In her brilliant book, *Covering the Mexican Front,* Washington *Post* correspondent Betty Kirk wrote: "These agents were preparing for the Axis conquest of Mexico. German was heard on streets, in cafes, bars, and nightclubs. German drinking songs rang out at the cocktail bars, followed by blustering shouts of 'Death to the Jew Roosevelt!' Germany's coming victory was shouted to the skies."

Errol's most frequent visits were to the apartments of George Nicolaus, of the Nazi Party, and his associate Hans Hellerman, Errol's and Erben's Gestapo contact in Barcelona. Every effort to bug these homes failed; they were guarded day and night by Mexican and German police approved by a certain high-ranking general who was very close to the President of Mexico.

From Mexico, Errol flew to the Bahamas in early October. There, he was the guest of Axel Wenner-Gren, the Swedish creator of the Electrolux industries, whose personal fortune was estimated at one billion dollars by the United States Treasury that August. He was almost certainly the richest man in the world. Part of his fabulous wealth came from his sale of munitions and other strategic materials to Hitler. Although Sweden was neutral, he made the deal through his intimate friend Goering; and he also arranged for Hitler to ship arms through Sweden during the invasion of Norway.

This supremely evil man was one of Errol's closest friends. Tall, magnificently built, he looked like a Viking, but had the soul of a rattlesnake. His home, Shangri La, on Hog Island (later Paradise Island) not far from Nassau, was stuffed with rare furnishings and paintings: the loot of Occupied Europe. His glittering swimming pool was lined with marble. Wenner-Gren was so rich he regarded himself above international law.

When Errol arrived by Wenner-Gren's private flying boat he was greeted by his host, who walked up the ramp with good news: Errol would be joining him immediately for a voyage on the *Southern Cross*. The most elaborate yacht afloat, bought from Howard Hughes for one million dollars, she could take parties of thirty and more and was fully staffed with white-tuxedoed waiters and the finest chefs available. The crew were hand-picked Nazis. The yacht was equipped with a radio signaling station and a searchlight that, in contravention of existing regulations, swept the waters, circling and circling, while the radio system guided the U-boats to British shipping.

Back in Nassau later on, Wenner-Gren introduced Errol to the multimillionaire Canadian Sir Harry Oakes and the Duke and Duchess of Windsor. Since they shared his admiration for Hitler, Errol was in ideal company. He returned to Mexico after two weeks and traveled to Cuernavaca where he became the guest of a British homosexual and Nazi spy called Harry Carstairs. Carstairs was the wealthy heir to a bakery fortune. He was a handsome, black-haired, dashing Apollo of a man in his late thirties whose whole life was filled with male prostitutes who were supposed to be available to any guest who wanted them. People like Errol who came to stay could simply walk to the pool any afternoon or evening and select one of the many superbly built boys who lay around it naked.

Cuernavaca was a hotbed of vice and perversion. There was a place where men could go—Errol loved it—and watch women make love through peepholes in a wall. In another place, for a price a woman or man could be seen having sexual intercourse with animals. There was a nightclub where sex acts were performed on the stage.

Back in Mexico City, Errol became involved with a beauty named Tara Marsh. She was an American Nazi who had formerly been involved with Goebbels and even boasted she had been to bed with Hitler. She told Errol that Hitler, so far from being impotent as many people claimed, was a normal male despite the loss of a testicle in World War I; that Hitler had stored one hundred million in gold bars in the basement of Berchtesgaden, and that he was building a plane, even at that early stage, which could fly him without refueling to South America if Germany lost the war.

Frequently in Mexico, Errol saw his friend Freddy McEvoy, whom he had known as a small child in Sydney and whom he had run into in London and Paris when he was there with Erben in 1937. Born in Melbourne, Australia, in 1907, Freddy was one of the most legendary playboys in Europe. Six feet tall and one hundred and seventy-eight pounds, with light brown hair, sharp green eyes, and an Errol Flynn profile, he earned the attention of women everywhere. He was a famous stud whose staying power in bed made him much prized among wealthy women. He was supposed to have been the only man who could bring the Woolworth heiress Barbara Hutton to orgasm, and in later years he literally sold that other superstud Porfirio Rubirosa to her in marriage for a fee of $100,000. He ran a stud farm of good-looking males whose potency could satisfy even the most demanding.

Educated at the exclusive Jesuit school of Stonyhurst in Britain, he, like many of its graduates, was an expert in spying and intrigue. He mixed with Nazis when he was in the South of France in 1935, making his more serious connections in Berlin during the Olympic Games of 1936 when he was captain of the British bobsled team. A year later, he captained another team to win the World Championship Bobsled Run at St. Moritz. He was a champion racing car driver, backgammon player, and deep-sea diver.

His special virtue for the Nazis was that he could bring socialites into Hitler's orbit. He was undoubtedly helpful to Vichy in convincing many French aristocrats that they should be loyal to Hitler and Laval. He moved along the French Riviera, checking everybody out for their loyalties. His problem was explaining why, when the Germans occupied Paris and Vichy took over in the South of France, he was not immediately interned, along with all other British nationals. His explanation was ingenious: his friend Prince Umberto di Poliolo says: "Freddy told all of us who were working for the Free French that he was feeding false information to the Nazis to keep out of prison when any other British subjects of military age were being arrested. We believed him."

In 1940, Freddy set out to capture the attention of the sixty-two-year-old American heiress, Beatrice Cartwright, who could be a "beard" for his pro-Nazi activities. He was having an affair with the mistress of a high-ranking Gestapo official in Paris.

Beatrice was not an easy catch. She was a clever, sophisticated woman who had been married twice and knew the score. A keen backgammon player and bridge expert, she ruled her house with great skill from a wheelchair: she had been crippled for some years. Her major weakness was a lust for virile young men. Thirty-year-old Freddy, tough and thin as a whip, was just her dish.

McEvoy knew only a direct approach would succeed. A friend of his arranged an introduction, graphically describing Freddy's skills as a sexual athlete. Mrs. Cartwright was intrigued. She invited Freddy to an elaborate dinner party. During the course of conversation, he gently took Mrs. Cartwright's hand and led it to a significant position under his napkin. Impressed by what she found there, she made it clear she would like to investigate further. Freddy informed her that would indeed be possible—provided, of course, that he emerged with a cash gift and a parcel of shares in Standard Oil, in which she had an interest.

He stayed that night, and the crippled woman was not disappointed. They were married in 1940. It was scarcely a romance. Beatrice gave Freddy an allowance and one day a week to make love to other women. To his surprise, he found Beatrice strenuously demanding in bed.

She became restless in Occupied Paris with its many stringencies and asked Freddy to accompany her home to America. Freddy had Gestapo orders to go there and contact Errol. But there was a problem of getting him into the United States. British intelligence, working with the French underground, was trying to kidnap him. Terrified, Freddy went to Nazi headquarters and obtained travel documents which would enable him to travel to Mexico. He and Beatrice went to Nice and flew to Lisbon. They took a clipper from Lisbon to New York, where, like Erben, McEvoy made connections with the Gestapo headquarters in the German Consulate. Freddy met with a group of oil executives with Nazi leanings at the Hotel Pierre and at the Waldorf, where he and Beatrice took the royal suite. Errol was frequently the McEvoys' guest for dinner.

The FBI was on their trail. Agents followed them all literally around the clock. Every waiter, maid, bellboy, member of the managerial staff was conscripted into government service. When the group went to El Morocco, the staff was alerted to keep an eye on them.

The McEvoys and Errol left for California in the late fall. Porters on the train, the conductor and brakeman were delegated by the FBI to monitor the travelers' conversations in the private car.

They were met at Pasadena by a fleet of Cadillacs. While Errol returned to his home on North Linden Drive, the McEvoys checked into the Beverly Hills Hotel.

The FBI warned the hotel staff that the guests must be watched. Each of these staff members was sworn to secrecy in the matter, and they kept their pledges so completely that not a word leaked in Hollywood. Part of the reason was that several of these employees were Nazis themselves.

Several local British actors and actresses, and members of the British nobility, were asked to keep checking on Errol and the McEvoys as they moved about Los Angeles together. Special agents were planted everywhere. There was a dinner party at the home of the well-known Hollywood society hostess Countess Dorothy Dentice di Frasso. The countess was herself a pro-Nazi operator under intensive FBI investigation. In 1938, she had visited Mussolini in Rome. Together with her friend Buggsy Siegel, the famous gangster, she had offered to finance an elaborate explosive device for use by the Axis. But arrangements fell through. And Goering and Goebbels had been guests of honor at her rented villa in Rome.

During the dinner party, an FBI plant heard McEvoy declare himself a proud draft dodger. He said that under no circumstances would he fight the Nazis, whom he admired unreservedly. At a later party at Ciro's, McEvoy made further outrageous pro-Nazi statements. On both occasions, Errol listened without objection, apparently indifferent to his friend's opinions.

What was the purpose of McEvoy's visit to Hollywood? It was to stir up pro-German, anti-British feeling there. The English director Victor Saville remembers: "There was a strong element in Hollywood that was trying to stop the making of anti-Nazi films. I made a picture called *Keeper of the Flame*. It was about someone like Errol:

a national hero, the adored idol of the boys' clubs who is at heart a Fascist. Every effort was made to stop this picture. It was bitterly criticized in Hollywood."

Keeper of the Flame was based on a novel by the Australian I. A. R. Wylie, who knew Errol only too well.

Errol, the McEvoys, Gertrude Anderson, the Countess di Frasso, and several other Nazis made their way into Mexico again just before Pearl Harbor. There, Freddy became involved in an extraordinary activity. Through codes and secret-ink contacts with German diplomat and secret agent Theodore Herstlet, who had been living in Mexico, and the Nazi sympathizer oil millionaire William Rhodes Davis, Freddy arranged to set up U-boat refueling bases on the Atlantic coast of Mexico and Central America. Despite the fact that State Department officials, and even J. Edgar Hoover, consistently denied the existence of such bases until the end of the war, Herstlet, now living in East Germany, told the historian Ladislas Farago that Freddy, while in league with Errol, did begin to set up these bases—before he was stopped by naval intelligence.

When Beatrice became disgusted by Freddy's activities, he was rude enough to remind her that a large part of her income came from Standard Oil deals with the Nazis. They moved to Miami, where Freddy traveled frequently to the Caribbean islands on the U-boat refueling mission. She bugged his hotel room. One morning, the results were brought to her. First, she sat stunned with horror at the sounds of Freddy making vigorous love to a prominent New York socialite. After the cries of an orgasm, the unhappy Beatrice heard him say, "Compared to making love to Bee, this is the difference between a vacation in the Bahamas and drilling a road."

Mrs. McEvoy had a stroke soon after she heard these words. Her recovery was slow. Soon after, in an exceptionally messy divorce case, she cut Freddy off with a very modest income.

Thirteen

In November 1941, Errol became involved in a new interest: building his dream house on the eleven-and-a-half-acre lot on Mulholland Highway which he had bought two years earlier. He supervised the construction himself. He built a hexagonal hallway, a glass-enclosed dining room overlooking the pool, and a Chinese puzzle of upstairs bedrooms, with room opening into room opening into room.

The house bristled with sexual jokes. On Flynn's instructions, John Decker designed an obscene mural for the fish tanks which ran high along the walls of the first floor den: the painted fish behind the real ones boasted enormous pendulous testicles. The cocktail bar was decorated with the scene of a bullfight. In order to open the cabinet, the bartender had to press a pair of testicles on the bull. Trick chairs released large, quivering penises at the press of a cushion; a cigarette lighter became a penis when a guest tried to operate it. The bookshelves were crowded with pornographic literature placed strategically among the volumes of Dickens, W. H. Hudson, and Kipling.

The living room was handsome and sprawling, running the entire length of the front of the house, with a record player under the windows next to a table covered with picture books. Ships' models stood in glass cases, alongside rows of guns. There were big open fireplaces in both living room and den.

Characteristically, Errol cheated on his expenses where he could, while never giving up his personal comfort. He persuaded an engineering student at USC to undertake the wiring and plumbing of the house as a master's thesis; he paid the student only the cost of the actual materials. And it was years before he paid the architects.

His bedroom was impressive: it had a huge bed covered entirely in Russian sable, and surrounded by black silk drapes covered with golden question marks; the same question marks appeared on Errol's handkerchiefs. He had a sauna and a bathroom with his and her toilets side by side: he later changed the second toilet to a bidet.

The stables, designed in part by Jim Fleming, were circular, similar to the Lipizzaner stables in Vienna. There, he housed his favorite black stallion, Onyx, and a polo pony, Beaumont. Kennels housed a brace of African lion hounds, with bristling hair which stood up like the quills of a porcupine when prowlers were heard or a hunt was on. He had imported the hounds from Lady Bailey's kennels in England.

The stable contained a highly illegal cockfight arena with seats set around a sawdust ring. At night, Errol and his friends would sit around the ring cheering lustily while the game birds tore each other to shreds with the razors attached to their claws. The betting was fierce but the contestants were usually named in a jocular fashion: Jack Warner would fight Roy Obringer or Michael Curtiz would fight Jim Fleming.

Errol also raised various forms of livestock, including ducks, for their meat; and he would walk around with a pet fox tucked under his arm.

In those years, there was a woman who was to become a close friend. The friendship was buoyed by the fact that they never went to bed together. Ida Lupino first met Errol in Palm Springs in 1936, when she was married to Errol's good friend Louis Hayward. They liked each other at once. Errol saw her on and off after that, and loved her performance in a very good melodrama, *Ladies in Retirement*—she was noted for the intensity of her playing—but they did not become close until they began to see each other frequently, thanks to their mutual friendship with Raoul Walsh.

Knowing of Errol's heroic struggle against a variety of sicknesses, his effort to give the best of himself in his playing, she became his staunchest defendant against studio charges of laziness, incompetence, and irresponsibility. Her mother, the English actress Connie Emerald, loved Errol like a son. So now added to Errol as the Baron and Raoul Walsh as the Uncle were Connie as the Duchess and Ida as the Little Scout.

Often, Errol would call up Ida and say, "Is the Duchess cooking boiled chicken tonight?" If the answer was in the affirmative, he would ask, "Can I come by and grab some?" He would drive over and dig into the dinner like a child. After dinner, on cold winter evenings, he would lie on his stomach on the living-room floor and gaze into the fire, talking about life and death. Ida Lupino remembers:

> He had a very strong feeling that dying was only dying on this earth; that one went beyond death into another life. As he gazed into the fire one night, he said, "It's only dying in this rotten place." And there was a terrible bitterness in his voice as he added, "And a rotten, lousy place it is, too."
>
> He told us: "When I pass on I want my body to be cremated and my ashes placed in a little container and when the boat is out to sea I want my ashes tossed over the bowsprit." And then, bitter and unhappy again, he added: "I can tell you I know my wishes will not be carried out." He told us he had had a recurring dream that he was standing looking at his own grave in Forest Lawn, and that there was no marker on it. He despised Forest Lawn.
>
> But he also said: "If I have to go to that lousy place, I want you, Connie, Duchess, to be next to me, dear. And in my dream I saw that you were next to me." And he added, "When you're ready to pass on, I'll hold out my hand to help you cross over. We'll laugh like hell together but ain't goin' to hell, darlin, we're going to heaven. And we'll laugh over Forest Lawn at all those fools down there."
>
> He had a power to see the future. He was buried in Forest Lawn against his wishes and without a marker. And when we buried Mother there was a place right next to him.

Often, Ida and Errol would visit with John Decker. Ida recalls:

> The Baron would go with John to the city morgue. They seemed to be fascinated by the dead. One day, it was my birthday, Errol had a

large wooden crate delivered to my house. Connie and I struggled
and finally managed to pry it open. I said to Connie, "What the hell
is in here?" I found another box inside, and in that another box, and
another still inside that one. It was like a Chinese puzzle. We worked
on and on, becoming more and more impatient and intrigued, finding
box inside box inside box. At last we reached a very small box indeed. On it was a note reading, "Happy Birthday, and don't let this
happen to you. John Decker." We opened it up, and there was a perfectly wonderful painting of a young Mexican girl from the shoulder
blades up. There was only one strange thing about it. Her throat was
cut.

When the phone would ring at some strange hour of the very early
morning, Ida would always know it was the Baron. But at least once
it was urgent:

One night he called, waking me up, and said, "Oh, Little Scout,
come up here, will you, darling, I don't think I'm going to make it. I
think I'm dying." I looked up at the window and rain was beating
hard against it. I knew this was the time Errol was afraid: when it
rained. I drove up to the house at once and the door was ajar. I
looked all around the living room and the hall. There was no one
there. And then I had an instinct he might be in the den.

The fire was roaring in the grate, lighting up the room eerily, and
I could see it flickering across the tropical fish swimming in the green
water of the tank. I saw a shape in front of the fire. It was Errol.

He was lying face down. He was completely motionless. Heavy
and still. I hooked his head on my arm and I said, "Oh, God, oh,
Baron, what is it?" He opened his eyes, and he said, "Can you get
your Doctor Bernstein up to help me? I can't breathe." I called
Maurice Bernstein—he had been Orson Welles' guardian—and he
came up and gave Errol an intravenous. At last the Baron pulled
around and we managed to get him upstairs and into bed.

After Doctor Bernstein left, the Baron whispered to me, "I'm not
asking you to do anything indecent, but would you lie on top of the
far side of the double bed? And keep an eye on me. If anything happens to me I want you to be around." I said, "Sure I will." I gathered
some pillows from the chair and put them behind me and stayed on
top of the bed and watched out for him all night. He was better in
the morning.

With Ida, Errol could indulge his frustrated desire to act those major Shakespearean roles that Jack Warner refused to allow him to play. He would spend evening after evening in her living room reading *Hamlet* or *The Tempest* or *The Merchant of Venice,* speaking the central parts while Ida acted opposite him. He was especially good as Henry V and as Macbeth. Monty Woolley had taught Ida a new interpretation of Lady Macbeth and Errol was deeply impressed with it. On other occasions, Errol would weave marvelous stories of the South Seas and the Spanish Main in which Ida and Connie would be cast. Ida recalls:

> Errol used to say, "I believe in reincarnation. I was a pirate in another life." Connie, her eyes gleaming, would say, "Oh, yes, Baron, I'm sure you were!" Errol would say, "I can see you now, Duchess, as a captive, and you, Ida, in an evening gown with black velvet and white ermine tails, coming up the gangplank with my men holding you at sword point. And a black flag with skull and crossbones flying from the mast."
>
> He planned to use the *Sirocco* for offshore gambling. Connie and I would be in charge of the roulette wheel and Errol would be the croupier. He'd say, "We'll take all the silly asses' money from them because I'll have the wheel fixed." And I said, "Oh, naturally!" And he said he would take solid gold out of Mexico and ship it all the way to France. And Connie said, "You're going to get us all in jail!" She was obviously delighted by the idea.

There was another night when the phone rang very late in Ida's house. It was raining hard again and she had been tossing and turning, wondering if Errol was all right. He said, "Oh God, Little Scout, it's raining. It always brings me bad luck. Now listen carefully. Put on your raincoat and drive as fast as you can to the house. And bring with you the largest and sharpest carving knife you can find in your kitchen."

Ida listened intently. Errol went on: "I'll leave the front door slightly ajar. You'll hear loud Wagnerian music as you drive up. I want you to walk in very quietly. Don't make a sound. And I want you to put on that look you had in *They Drive by Night,* when you went mad in the courtroom. As though you could easily kill somebody."

Ida said, "Baron, is some dirty guy up there trying to murder you?" Errol answered, "Yes. He's outside the door now. A nasty German beast. He's trying to kill me. With one of my own rapiers. I've told him I have a mad friend who has a special habit of using knives, very dangerously. And that you're coming up to the house immediately to do a little carving up."

With a spunky, "I've got it, Baron!" Ida jumped in her car with the knife in hand and drove furiously through the storm up the crumbling cliffs of Mulholland Highway. There only one light on in the house as she drove up the drive: a table lamp in the window of the den. Drenched to the skin, she pushed open the heavy front door. By the dim light filtering from beneath the door of the den, she made out the hulking figure of a man threatening Errol with a rapier, while Errol fought gamely back.

Errol looked over the man's shoulder and saw Ida standing in the doorway, the rain streaming off her carving knife. He said, "She's come. I told you she'd come." The German swung around to face her, so startled that he dropped the sword. Ida put on her best *They Drive by Night* face and said, "You see this knife, you filthy German pig? I'm going to cut your throat from ear to ear! Baron, get out of this room! I don't want you to see this man die a bleeding death!" The man rushed past her and down the lawn, jumping headlong into the swimming pool to escape her. Errol walked out ahead of Ida and looked at the man floundering about in the rainswept water. He said, "All right, you German bum! Drown!" He and Ida went into the house, and he said to her, "What a performance! Uncle (Raoul Walsh) should have seen it! It's the best thing you've ever done!"

They went to various windows and laughed together as they saw the man struggling out of the pool in the storm. Errol picked up a flashlight and went back to the garden, carrying his rapier, Ida following with her knife. The man started to run toward his car. Ida said, "We're both going to kill you now." The German jumped into his car and drove off wildly into the night.

The German was a character actor Errol had hired. Ida never suspected.

From the moment Dr. Erben had left Los Angeles, Errol had been writing to him. In February 1941, Erben had traveled to Tokyo under instructions from the Mexican Abwehr and by ship to Shanghai where he linked up with his American mentor Hans Adolf Mosberg, the Jewish Nazi journalist, who had given the FBI the slip at San Pedro. In Shanghai, where he met Mosberg at night in a church, he was brought under the direct command of the sophisticated and elegant Louis Siefken, who also had come from America to become the local bureau chief of the Abwehr and break the U. S. Coast Guard code.

This group of intelligence agents collected information through radio codes spreading as far as the East Indies, the Philippines and Australia. Erben was specifically relegated to studying ship movements because of his maritime background.

Erben wormed his way into the American Consulate and American businesses in Shanghai. Under orders from Bureau Siefken member Bodo Habenicht, he, in his own words, tried to find people "who were stigmatized by their habits, men who had something to fear; men who were addicts, drug addicts; men who were homosexuals, who would be easier for me to detect as a physician. These were the type of men who could be bought more easily than others; and if not bought, scared; and if not scared, framed, to do the bidding of our mission."

He also had to investigate British or other nationals at war with Germany, to see if they were dangerous to the Nazi cause. If so, they would be trapped and hanged. He was to contact recently naturalized Americans aboard ship, officers, sailors, and passengers, to try to make them commit sabotage, steal a code, or work in intelligence on the American mainland.

Erben also became closely involved with the amazing Abbot Chao Kung, formerly Trebitsch Lincoln, with whom Errol had been so greatly impressed in Hong Kong in 1933. Trebitsch Lincoln had the idea of going with Erben to India to whip up pro-Hitler enthusiasm among the masses of people, but Trebitsch Lincoln's declining health made the venture impossible. In another scheme, Erben was to return to Lourenço Marques on the repatriation vessel *Conte Verde* to link up with "Hamlet" and guide the U-boats from a radio station. This idea was abandoned because of the risks involved.

And in yet a third unused scheme, Erben was to return to America under an assumed name and forged documents to contact Errol and other reliable friends in Hollywood and set up a secret printing press as well as a vigorous intelligence network on the Pacific coast.

In October 1941, Errol was called to the offices of Lili's lawyers, Loeb and Loeb, to discuss a proposed property settlement running to some thirty-five closely packed pages of type. His net worth was given as approximately a hundred and fifty thousand dollars: surprisingly low in view of his earnings of three hundred thousand dol-

lars a year at a time when taxes were low. Lili would receive all of
the household furniture formerly at 601 North Linden Drive; Errol's
Cadillac; one-half of all interest in Crude Oil, Inc., a California corporation jointly owned by Thomson, Inc., Flynn's tax-shelter corporation; half of all shares in Flynn and Thomson, Inc.; some of
his property in South Pasadena. Errol would pay fifteen hundred
dollars a month, plus one hundred dollars a month for Sean's education. This was a very reasonable amount, since it was barely 5 per
cent of his total income at the time. But in return for this leniency it
was agreed that Errol would pay Lili's income tax on her alimony in
perpetuity, the tax to be used as a tax deduction on his own income.
As it turned out, he neglected to pay Lili's tax but continued to make
the deductions from his. This illegal action caused him constant
trouble with the government for over twenty years.

After a year of struggling with Errol to obtain her alimony payments, Lili offered an agreement whereby Errol would pay a total
sum of ninety thousand dollars and be rendered free and clear of any
further obligations to her or her son.

Errol refused. For more than fifteen harrowing years, he fought
Lili every inch of the way. She had him served with no less than seventeen summonses to appear in court and explain why he had
neglected to meet his obligations and to pay for Sean's education. At
intervals of five years, they would stand together before a judge and
argue every particular of the alimony. Errol constantly applied for
relief; and he was promptly denied. When the bills for back alimony
came, he was seldom in a position to meet them.

Further problems lay ahead after the United States was attacked at
Pearl Harbor. Most of the stars enlisted immediately. Hollywood
began to devote itself to propaganda pictures and band tours. Although Errol told columnists that he very much wanted to join the
Canadian Air Force, the fact was that he was desperately trying to
avoid the draft. The studio files show that he was always taking off
whenever the draft board called. He had no interest whatever in
serving in Canada or anywhere else against the Nazis. Nevertheless
the reports continued to appear with Errol as fighting—even begging
—to be admitted to Canada for service. Roy Obringer helped Errol
by applying for a deferment, since Errol was needed for a movie

called *Desperate Journey*. Ironically, this would be the story of an Australian army in Europe fighting the Nazis.

Errol took off for a vacation to Norden Hot Springs, Nevada, in January 1942, before his deferment had been approved. On January 20, Tenny Wright sent a memorandum to the assistant director schedule for *Desperate Journey* reading:

> Max Carmel, Flynn's man, called me this morning to ask what would happen to Flynn for disregarding a notice from the Selective Service Act. Max informed me that Flynn was ordered to report yesterday but was in Nevada. This is none of my business but for your information the FBI could pick him up and put him in jail.

Fortunately for Flynn, the deferment came through. But he went before the Selective Service Board on February 16. The medical examination took up most of the morning.

He wasn't ready for what he heard. He knew about the sinusitis; the emphysema; the gonorrhea; the chronic irritation of the urethra, which so often caused painful erections; and the heart murmur. But the bombshell was saved for the end: he had tuberculosis in his right lung. The sergeant in charge, Gene Jasin, recalls:

> My wife, who was the nurse in charge of the X rays, and I went to lunch with him at a restaurant across the street. His face was gray and he was trembling. He scarcely ate anything. He kept saying, "It can't be true, it can't be true," over and over again. He ran out the moment lunch was over and drove home without saying another word.

Errol arrived back at Mulholland Farm in a daze. Twice on the way home he almost crashed the car. He rushed to a medical encyclopedia on his shelves. Now he understood why he was prone to nervous irritability, sudden attacks of fatigue, lack of energy over long periods, night sweats.

He dared not tell the studio. He was afraid they would lay him off for eight months without salary so that he could rest in a hospital. With his property and capital slashed in half, following the divorce settlement, and with the alimony he had to pay, not to mention the costs of sustaining Mulholland Farm, the *Sirocco,* and his women, he needed every cent Warners could pay him in order to live. He knew he must lie to everyone. He did.

Like most liars, he made mistakes. He told Jim Fleming and Buster Wiles he had spots on his lungs; he told the producer Robert Lord he had syphilis. Everyone was given a different story; and everyone was sworn to secrecy. Yet, inevitably, the truth leaked out. But the FBI didn't believe it—they thought he had bribed the medical board. It was certainly an irony that this medical reason should keep him from the draft he dreaded.

Errol's agony of mind can only be imagined. Knowing that untreated tuberculosis could mean a death sentence, he still felt he had to go on and make *Desperate Journey*. It was a tough picture, handled by Raoul Walsh with his customary vigor. Walsh shot fast, without fuss or frills; unlike Curtiz, he was always on schedule and could obtain results in not more than three takes. He hated fancy angles, and liked to tell a story simply and sharply. This extreme swiftness proved wearing to Errol, despite the fact that Walsh was considerate of his condition.

Eating little, drinking too much, and suffering from sleepless, headache-ridden nights, Errol had to be made up very heavily and have his uniform refitted because he was losing weight. In some scenes, his body had to be padded because he was down to one hundred and sixty-five pounds. He was late on the set every day he was in; some days he left early, others he came not at all. Over and over again, Raoul Walsh had to dismiss the company. On March 28, Errol reported for work and went home minutes later, telling the assistant director, Claude Archer, that he was feeling weak and ill and groggy and had to go to bed. It turned out that he was scarcely able to walk by March 29, and hadn't helped his condition by taking three sleeping pills mixed with vodka the night before in a desperate attempt to obtain a night's rest.

Jack Warner sent a typically icy memorandum: "Be sure that Errol Flynn is not paid for the days he doesn't show up." Errol began to panic that Alan Hale and Ronald Reagan, who played other members of the aircraft crew, were stealing scenes from him. Knowing how bad he looked, he was well aware that these healthy, vigorous men might be a threat to his prominence. Ronald Reagan recalls:

> When I made *Santa Fe Trail* with Errol, I had not been very well known. But in between that picture and *Desperate Journey* I had be-

come a star in *Kings Row*. So I had several big scenes in *Journey* in which I had a chance to shine. In one of these, I was interrogated by a Gestapo chief and I gave him double talk. He became completely bamboozled and I clubbed him on the chin. Errol was furious that I had been given the scene. He felt it was perfect for him, since it called for his special kind of impish comedy. He insisted it be completely rewritten for him. I was very angry, and Hal Wallis got wind of it. He went into a dressing room with Walsh and we all could hear the terrible quarrel that went on. Finally, I heard Wallis say, "The script will not be changed by one single word. Reagan will play the scene." I've always been grateful to Hal for that.

The company was on location in Sherwood Forest one afternoon when studio manager Tenny Wright said to Flynn: "Did you tell the company that if you had an eight o'clock call you would not work past five P.M.?"

"I did. Yes, that's exactly what I told them."

"There's nothing in your contract which says you can quit at five P.M."

"Then it becomes a legal matter. What are you going to do, sue me?"

"We're on location," Wright screamed. "Is it any fucking hardship to work till after the light fades—say six P.M.?"

Flynn flared back, "I won't work beyond eight hours of working time. I'm a sick man. Don't you believe me? Look up the Army record. Goddammit, can't you see I'm exhausted?—But I still keep on . . . nobody does me any favors—I do the favors, working nine to five."

Tenny Wright said: "But I've agreed to give you five days' salary when you are on suspension if you cooperate."

"If you think you are doing me a favor giving me that five days' salary you can stick it."

"Will you work until six P.M.?"

"No, I will not. No. And you can repeat for me, I will not work beyond five P.M. for an eight A.M. call."

Errol's reason for refusing to work at night was clear: he had read during the course of his medical research that tubercular patients must not undertake any serious activity after dark. But he couldn't tell anyone that. So his studio reputation grew worse. By the time *Desperate Journey* was finished, he was very unpopular with Jack Warner.

Fourteen

It seems almost incredible that, given his state of health, Errol managed to make the most taxing picture of his career, that summer of 1942: *Gentleman Jim*. It called for serious boxing against a real boxer, the stand-in for Ward Bond, Ed ("Strangler") Lewis. Only the most difficult movements would be matched by his own double, the champion Freddie Steele.

Gentleman Jim was based vaguely on the career of James J. Corbett, culminating in the classic Corbett-Sullivan fight in which Corbett won the heavyweight championship of the world.

In late May 1942, Errol went into hard training at the Warner Brothers studio gymnasium with welterweight champion Mushy Callahan, who had worked with him on *The Perfect Specimen*. Callahan worked with Errol now for six weeks, work which was interrupted twice when Errol collapsed and had to be taken home. He was impressed with Errol's courage and devotion. He says:

> Sullivan, Corbett's rival, was slam-bang. He had no footwork; he
> was a powerhouse who would smash into his rivals in the ring like a

ramrod. Corbett used to drive him crazy because he'd dance around
so fast that Sullivan could never hit him. Corbett would prance about
the ring, irritating Sullivan, tormenting him like a gadfly tormenting
a bull. Corbett would dance his way in and duck under Sullivan's
fists and jab, jab, jab into the big guy's solar plexus and then come in
with one brilliant uppercut that would stun him. He used his left fist
brilliantly.

Errol tended to use his right fist. I had to teach him to use his left
and to move very fast on his feet. I had to turn him into Corbett.
Luckily he had excellent footwork, he was dodgy, he could duck
faster than anybody I saw. And by the time I was through with him,
he'd jab, jab, jab, with his left like a veteran.

He cut out his drinking, but we still had to shoot all the boxing
scenes in the last week in case he folded up or got a black eye. And
we could only work one minute at a time. After that he was
exhausted. Errol would box for a minute, and then Jim Fleming, who
was acting as the stand-in, would scream, "Cut! Cut!" That was the
director's privilege. Raoul Walsh, who was directing, would go crazy.
The first time Jim did it Walsh screamed, "Who yelled cut?" And
Flynn replied, "I asked Jim to do that. I can't work for more than a
minute at a time." Walsh went black in the face but there was nothing he could do.

Ward Bond, as Sullivan, hated just standing there like a big bull
while Errol dodged about and he hated stopping the scene over and
over again after just one minute of action. It drove him mad.

Errol's illness continued into June and July 1942. On June 22, he
was too sick to come to the studio. By the following day, he could
work for only two hours in the afternoon. He struggled downtown
for an interview with the immigration authorities on his prospective
citizenship on June 24 but did not show up to work. On June 25, he
went home at lunchtime. On the twenty-sixth, after only half an hour
on the set, he was too tired to go on. By June 29, Errol was so
seriously ill that his temperature rose to 103 degrees.

He struggled back to work early in July. On the morning of July
15, at eight forty-five, he appeared at the makeup department in
fairly good spirits in company with Buster Wiles. He was joined a
few minutes later by Mushy Callahan and Ward Hamilton, the
makeup man. Errol's friend musical star Dennis Morgan, came by
and exchanged a few words with Errol; suddenly, Errol stood up,

looking gray. He walked a few steps, only to fall headlong into the arms of Dennis Morgan.

Errol was rushed to Good Samaritan; the doctor said he would not be able to do any strenuous fighting for two weeks. But X rays were not taken and the doctor reported to Roy Obringer: "There's nothing wrong with Flynn that cannot be corrected by proper diet and proper hours of sleep." Errol could only smile.

In very poor shape, Errol went into his citizenship ceremony in August. He had lied on his application that he had first entered America from Mexico in 1936 and about much else. Most movie stars by now were at war: his ex-lover Tyrone Power, James Stewart, and Clark Gable among them. The women stars, led by Bette Davis and Marlene Dietrich, were giving enormous amounts of time and effort to war bond tours and to running service canteens. Warners could explain that Errol had a "heart murmur" that kept him out of the Army (tuberculosis sounded less glamorous) but how could they explain that he failed to sell war bonds? That he didn't volunteer for ambulance service or other hospital service, like the pacifist Lew Ayres? They had to say, in press release after press release, that he was too busy making propaganda pictures against the Nazis to have time to help the war effort any other way.

Errol recovered from his sickness with surprising speed only to become the victim of a particularly macabre prank. He was in New Orleans on a promotional trip when, late one night at a bar, he fell asleep from a combination of drinks and hashish. A group of friends carried him into a car and drove him to the morgue where they bribed the morgue attendant to allow them to place him on a slab. He awoke horrified, convinced he was dead. He lay there for hours, unable to move. Finally, he realized he had been the victim of the kind of practical joke at which he himself was such an expert. He ran out, found the culprits, and thrashed them to within an inch of their lives.

Shortly after that, he was at the Hearst ranch at San Simeon. Hearst forbade drinking on the premises. Guests at his table were served water with their dinner. Annoyed, Errol invited a girl to a gardener's shed which he had already equipped with several bottles of vodka. It was pitch dark in the hut, and as he embraced her, he stepped on a garden hoe. The handle flew up, hit him in the head, and knocked him out.

Gentleman Jim turned out to be a first-rate motion picture, a commercial and critical success. Vigorous and full of action, laced with salty Irish humor, it vividly evoked the golden days of boxing. Despite all his problems, Errol's fancy footwork looked splendid on the screen.

The movie was finished in August 1942. Errol flew back to the tried-and-true delights of Mexico City. He was looking for a new romantic involvement with a woman; in spite of himself, he missed Lili's presence at the house. When he checked into the Hotel Reforma in Mexico City, it was for the specific purpose of finding a Mexican beauty.

Divorced now from Beatrice Cartwright, Freddy McEvoy had been living in Mexico for a year on the Abwehr's business. He had helped Errol in the running of gold, guns, and drugs from California to Mexico. He also staged illegal cock fights on the *Sirocco,* and on various millionaire yachts off Balboa and Newport.

McEvoy was in Mexico City when Errol arrived. Since Freddy knew everyone, Errol asked him to select a girl for him. McEvoy came up trumps: he found an enchanting and lovable beauty called Blanca Rosa Welter, later to become famous as Linda Christian. She was the eighteen-year-old daughter of a Dutch oilman who had been raised in Mexico and Venezuela. She had chestnut hair, slightly slanting green eyes, a perfectly shaped mouth, and high, firm, exquisitely formed breasts. Errol, who was accustomed to an extraordinary variety of beautiful women, was overwhelmed by this one.

They met in the bar of the Ritz Hotel. Errol thought he held the passkey to any girl's heart: skillful flattery of herself and, more important, her mother, followed by the offer of a lucrative Hollywood contract. When that didn't win her, he gave Blanca a topaz, ruby, and diamond ring of great price. He flew with her to Acapulco, hoping that the combination of sun and sand and a warm tropical sea would prove seductive. She remained uninfluenced by his fame and his reputation as a lady-killer. He resorted to a frontal attack, a full-scale romantic scene worthy of *Robin Hood* or *The Sea Hawk*. She described it in her memoir, *Linda*.

He and Freddy McEvoy obtained guitars and practiced for hours. A local singer taught them how to perform a Mexican love song. Trained for their adventure, the two men appeared under the balcony of Rosa's suite at the hotel. They began to sing and to twang the guitar strings. It was 3 A.M. Rosa woke up and walked to the window in her nightgown. Freddy McEvoy disappeared while Errol climbed the drainpipe and made his way Tarzan-like across a complicated trellis to the balcony. Rosa was so amused by his athletic prowess and enterprise she couldn't resist when he embraced her.

Errol and his new girl flew back to Mexico City where they saw the fabulous Manolete perform in the bull ring. She described a tremendous moment, straight from the pages of *Blood and Sand*, when Manolete flung his scarlet cloak at Blanca Rosa Welter's feet, and she, in turn, tossed him a yellow rose. That evening, Manolete, delicate and bonily handsome as an El Greco saint, joined Errol and Rosa at their table. This extraordinary honor dazzled the young girl.

During August, Warner Brothers had completed plans for a film entitled *Edge of Darkness* in which Errol would play a leading figure in the Norwegian Resistance movement(!). It was based on the theme of speeches by Roosevelt and Churchill exhorting the Norwegian populace to rise up against the oppressor.

Errol ignored successive cables from Roy Obringer to return to Hollywood for wardrobe tests by August 17. On August 18, a representative of the studio from Mexico City ran down the beach brandishing a telegram at Errol, who was gamboling in the waves with Rosa. Errol cheerfully invited the man to come in and hand the wire to him. The man, rolling his trousers above his knees, struggled out. A sandbank gave beneath him and Errol dragged him to the surface, taking the sodden telegram from his hand. It was a demand that he go to work at once or be instantly suspended.

Errol pulled the man ashore and filled him up with drink. By nightfall, he was facing the fact that he would either return home or lose his new salary of seven thousand dollars a week for every week he failed to appear. He broke the news to Rosa late that night and promised to arrange a screen test to be directed by Raoul Walsh. She said she would follow him to Hollywood.

He flew back to Hollywood on August 21 and from there drove north to the Monterey Peninsula, where shooting had begun the previous week. But now weather conditions were making filming impossible. The notorious Monterey fogs had rolled in from the ocean, blanketing the cliffs and reducing visibility to almost zero. Errol found himself stranded at the Del Monte Hotel. He spent his nights with his co-star, Ann Sheridan. Her husband, George Brent, caught them in bed together; Errol beat Brent up.

The fog seriously affected Errol's sinuses and he took miserably to his bed, gazing out at the blank sheet of gray beyond the windows. But once shooting began, he worked hard at his role, looking convincingly haggard and unshaven, responding vibrantly to director Lewis "Millie" Milestone's careful and considerate guidance.

Yet, back in Hollywood, Errol's devilish alter ego surfaced once more. Saturday was always the most important day of shooting in any given week, and frequently work would continue throughout the night into Sunday morning. Without warning, on Saturday, September 26, 1942, he announced that he would not be coming to work. He decided to have an early night so that he would be in good shape for a tennis match with Bill Tilden to be held the following day, during a party at the Bel Air home jointly rented by Freddy McEvoy (who had come back to live in Hollywood), Bruce Cabot, and a wealthy young Englishman named Stephen Raphael. It would turn out to be a major event of his life.

Fifteen

At about 1:30 P.M. on September 27, Errol climbed into his new, specially made Packard Darin convertible to drive to the party in Bel Air. The car boasted a great bachelor's trap: a front passenger seat which, at the press of a secret button, lowered and tilted back to form a comfortable bed, trapping the victim.

Errol arrived at the house on St. Pierre Road shortly after 2 P.M. A crowd of guests milled on the lawn, splashed noisily in the pool. Errol with Freddy McEvoy as partner beat Bill Tilden and Bruce Cabot in the second and third sets. Toward sundown, Errol grew tired and wandered into the house to enjoy a martini at the bar. As he walked into the living room, a car raced up the drive. It contained three good-looking studio messenger boys, a blond girl of seventeen named Betty Hansen, who was looking for a chance to be in the movies, and two other girls.

One of the studio messenger boys, Armand Knapp, had been dating Betty for some time. The two teen-agers, ambitious, feisty, with little or no money, were typical of the countless young people who occupied a Nathanael West world of cheap apartments, hamburger joints, doughnut stands, and late-night sex in the hills above the Hollywood Bowl. Theirs was the artificial black-and-silver world of the movies. They collected cigarette cards and movie-star photographs and talked about their crushes on the latest idols of the screen. Their life was relieved by fantasies of achievement and fame.

Armand Knapp had been told by Buster Wiles, Errol's stunt double, that Errol would be coming to the tennis party. Knapp introduced Betty to Errol. She perched on the edge of Errol's chair as he told tales of New Guinea, the details becoming more and more colorful after his third martini. He smiled indifferently as she passed an arm around his shoulders and squeezed his biceps. Then, apparently carried away by drink herself, she suddenly slid into his lap.

Testimony shows that he continued the conversation coolly right over her head. She grew dizzier, flopping down into his arms while the other guests smiled understandingly. The call for dinner came at about 8 P.M. Errol rose, dropping her unceremoniously to the floor. She trailed in after the other guests, and later rushed from the room and threw up as a result of too many drinks during the main course.

After dinner, Errol felt a twinge of compassion and went into the living room to see how she was. He found her lying on a sofa and suggested she should come up to his bathroom (attached to Freddy McEvoy's room, which had been lent to him for the day) and wipe her face. Silently, still feeling ill, she nodded. They went to the bedroom together. Errol later told Jim Fleming that, without much hesitation, Betty Hansen lay on the bed, waiting for his inevitable pass. She denied this, saying she had struggled. He said he obliged her by pulling off her clothes and stripping to the waist, dropping his trousers to his feet. He made love to her for half an hour before climaxing. He claimed she enjoyed it; she denied under oath that she did.

The girls who had come with Betty in Armand's car—a nightclub singer named Lynn Boyer and a dancer named Chi-Chi Toupes—became worried about her absence from the party. Lynn Boyer went upstairs and began banging on the doors. At last she reached Freddy McEvoy's room. When she asked, "Betty, are you there?" and rattled the locked door, Betty, half asleep, giggled. Errol was just about to climb into the shower. He cheerfully suggested that Lynn should come in if she wanted to. Summing up the situation quickly, Lynn returned to the living room and told Chi-Chi what had happened upstairs.

The following day, Betty told her sister Errol had seduced her. She was taken into protective custody in Juvenile Hall.

Not realizing the forces that were moving against him, Errol went back to work on *Edge of Darkness*. He so quickly dismissed the episode at the Bel Air house that he even forgot Betty Hansen's name.

The district attorney thought of a way of closing in on Errol. He recalled that a girl named Peggy Satterlee had lodged a complaint almost fourteen months earlier with the sheriff of Los Angeles County about an episode aboard Errol Flynn's yacht. That charge had been dropped, but when he called the sheriff, and Miss Satterlee's parents, they reluctantly agreed to cooperate. Within a week, Peggy Satterlee's affidavit was in the files along with Betty Hansen's. The pincers were ready. It was only a question of time before the D.A. would close them on the unsuspecting star.

On the morning of October 11, Errol awoke with a hangover and a stiff neck from sleeping awkwardly on a large pillow. His eyes were smarting and he felt sick at the stomach. He drank a prairie oyster and had Alex Pavlenko, his new manservant, call Warners to say he would be unable to come to work until three o'clock. After about two and a half hours on the set, Errol returned home and lay down with an Alka-Seltzer. He forced himself to eat a meager dinner, feeling slightly better after black coffee as the grandfather clock struck ten.

Exactly half an hour later, Police Lieutenant R. W. Bowling and Sergeant Edward Walker of the Los Angeles Juvenile Control Division drove up to the house with a nervous Armand Knapp and another messenger boy, Morrie Black. Leaving Black in the car, they knocked at the door. Alex opened it, and reported their arrival to Errol, who was sitting in the living room. The two policemen and the trembling Mr. Knapp walked in. Bowling said without any preliminaries, "Mr. Flynn, you have been accused of the felony of having intercourse with a minor child. You have the right to engage the services of an attorney. But we ask you to come with us."

Errol played the scene suavely, and without appearing to be disturbed, offered his visitors a drink. They declined. He asked the name of his accuser. Told it, he pretended that he'd forgotten her. The policeman turned to Knapp, who told the star that Betty had confessed everything. Errol remained outwardly cool as Bowling

said: "Please come with us to Juvenile Hall. Miss Hansen will identify you. She will accuse you in person."

Errol crossed to the telephone and called his attorney, Robert E.
Ford. Ford asked him, "Is there anything in it?" And Errol replied,
"Good God, no." Ford said: "Go with them anyway. It's wiser. I'll
drive down there. Don't say a word until I meet with you. Okay?"

Chain-smoking through his John Barrymore holder, Errol walked
with the men to the waiting police car. Errol's feelings on this dark
journey to Juvenile Hall can easily be imagined. For a major star to
be arrested at the height of his career was unheard of. It was horrifying to think that a casually enjoyed act of sex on a hot summer afternoon might lead to the destruction of his future. Yet, given his peculiar nature, there was a challenge to the occasion: if he could get
out of this, he could get out of anything.

He was led into the dismal, gray-painted rooms of Juvenile Hall,
where his attorney, Ford, was already waiting. A prison matron
stood beside Betty Hansen, who was slumped in a chair crying miserably, flushed by a high fever caused by an allergic reaction to vitamin shots. She looked weak and pale, her skin blotchy and her hair
bedraggled. Lieutenant Bowling said, "Miss Hansen, is this the
man?" She looked up through tears, "Yes, it sure is, it sure is."

"Did this man have an act of sexual intercourse with you?"

"Sure," she answered, and began to cry again.

Bowling told Flynn and Ford: "You'll be advised when the hearing is before the grand jury. Don't leave town."

Ford nudged Errol to remain silent. But Errol said angrily, "This
is all a mistake. I scarcely touched the girl." The look on the detec-
tive's face told him he had practically sunk himself with that one
statement. Very pale, he left with Ford for an all-night conference at
his house.

He was fortunate that Ford had become a partner of Jerry Giesler,
for Giesler, the most famous trial lawyer in the country, was the one
man in Los Angeles capable of saving his career.

Giesler was not physically prepossessing. He was a short, squat,
round-shouldered man with a pot belly and a pale face. He talked in
a quick, nervous, high-pitched voice. He wore rumpled dark suits
which fitted him badly and had permanent rings under his eyes from
nights of sleeplessness. He was also a genius of sorts.

Giesler's ruthlessness had quickly earned him a reputation in the cutthroat atmosphere of the Los Angeles courts. He became famous through the Pantages case of 1927. The theatre mogul Alexander Pantages had been accused of raping the seventeen-year-old Eunice Pringle in the mezzanine lounge of his own flagship theatre in Los Angeles during a performance. Giesler drew up a list of the girl's various supposed misbehaviors and tried to disrupt her testimony by showing that she had aroused Pantages with her seductive behavior and bright red dress. He failed to achieve his purpose: the district attorney admonished the jury that no matter what the provocation may have been, the law was still the law: the girl was a minor, and statutory rape was statutory rape. Giesler was not satisfied. He took the case to the appeal court and got the judgment reversed by proving that the district attorney had sought to frame Pantages for political reasons and that the girl had falsified her age and encouraged the seduction to further her own career.

Giesler's specialty was smearing dubious witnesses. He would draw them out with honeyed phrases, flattery, and relaxing humor, and then, when they revealed themselves as not as pure as they pretended to be, he would pounce for the kill. He had a photographic memory and a posse of sleuths who infiltrated apartment buildings, newspaper morgues, libraries, and even (with inside help) police files in order to dig up every scrap of dirt on the people he wanted to destroy on the witness stand.

Giesler and Flynn hit it off at once. Neither was overburdened with moral considerations and both were as cunning as foxes. Nevertheless, they were both worried when, only four days after the meeting at Juvenile Hall, Lieutenant Bowling turned up on the set of *Edge of Darkness* and told Flynn that he would have to answer a second charge of statutory rape brought against him by Peggy Satterlee and her parents.

Betty Hansen and Peggy Satterlee were so terrified of the stone faces of the grand jury that they gave muddled and inaccurate accounts of what had taken place. As a result, the grand jury failed to bring in a true bill.

But the district attorney and his assistants held a conference and decided that the accused star wasn't going to get away so easily with statutory rape. Chief of Police C. W. Horrall discussed the matter with Lieutenant Bowling. The police and the district attorney held a hurried late night meeting and reexamined the complaints. The grand jury's decision was overturned. Errol was formally charged on October 16, and ordered to appear the following day before Municipal Judge Oda Faulconer.

On October 17, the judge coldly told attorney and client that it was obvious the grand jury had been swayed by Flynn's fame and had failed to examine the evidence in the case. Errol was in the midst of filming some of the most difficult scenes in *Edge of Darkness*. He had to continue with them for another six days while waiting to be arraigned on two counts of raping Peggy Satterlee by force on the *Sirocco* on the nights of August 2 and 3, 1941. When he appeared before Municipal Judge Byron Walters, Errol said, ignoring Ford's suggestion he not speak:

> I am not guilty in this matter and of course will be exonerated. In the meantime, all I can say is I hope my friends will withhold judgment in this matter and not censure me on the basis of false accusations.

It was a difficult beginning to an ordeal that was to last for over four months. First of all, there was the problem of the studio. Jack Warner had tended to dismiss the matter at first as a typical attempt to frame a star. But he was quickly disabused of this attitude when he talked with the district attorney. Afraid of public censure and a boycott of Warner pictures, he rushed *Gentleman Jim* prematurely into release, instead of holding it back to cash in on the subsequent publicity of a trial. As a result, the first wave of reaction kept many people away from the picture.

Warner had promised Errol support, but the atmosphere at the studio became even more charged and anti-Flynn than usual. Flynn's enemies Roy Obringer and Tenny Wright rejoiced in his downfall, though Raoul Walsh, Hal Wallis, and Lewis Milestone rushed to his defense. Alexis Smith and Ida Lupino refused to believe he had raped any woman. Ann Sheridan dismissed the whole matter as "a load of crap." In Palm Beach, Florida, where she was raising two-year-old Sean as far away from his father as possible, Lili Damita was scarcely surprised.

Errol did not bear up well. More vulnerable and sensitive than he seemed to those who did not know him, he spent the nights pacing up and down and smoking, while friends like Raoul Walsh did their best to set his mind at ease. He slept restlessly, seized by nightmares of his death and destruction. Night after night, Giesler, Ford, and their associates would arrive for dinner; Alex Pavlenko recalls them arguing and drinking, discussing ways and means of blackening the witnesses' names.

Released on one thousand dollars' bail, Errol reported for the preliminary hearing on November 3. He was fortunate in having made a friend of both Hedda Hopper (whose column he had sometimes written when she was on vacation) and Louella Parsons. These two gossip columnists who could be powerful enemies hovered over him like protective angels, remembering his many favors to them. Both the Los Angeles *Times* and the right-wing *Examiner* proved sympathetic. Reporters and photographers regarded Errol as one of their own kind because of his photography and journalism and the fact that he always remembered their names at press conferences. He had, to put it succinctly, the press in his pocket.

Nevertheless, despite this support, Errol knew he might well lose the case. He devised a plan of escape in case he was found guilty, a plan which he confided to only a tiny handful of friends, including Jim Fleming, Buster Wiles, his boyhood pal Charles Pilleau who had come to live in Hollywood, and Freddy McEvoy. He would be rushed by a circle of specially chosen bodyguards to a car before the police could put handcuffs on him and driven at high speed to Burbank Airport, where the famous stunt pilot Paul Mantz was waiting to fly him to Mexico. From there he would fly by easy stages to Argentina, which did not have an extradition treaty with the United States, and where Nazi elements were paramount.

The sensation seekers had a wonderful time. They gathered about Mulholland Farm day and night and had to be chased off by the African lion hounds. They crawled through the underbrush on the mountainside and used binoculars to try to spy out the dirty doings in the house. They intercepted Errol's Packard wherever it went. They wrote him hundreds of letters of support or condemnation and one eager fan even sent him a message of condolence and an offer of marriage by carrier pigeon. He had to hire detectives to keep off prowlers. Every time he left for the studio, people would rush screaming and blowing kisses at him from the cliffs and bushes of Mulholland Highway.

Public hysteria reached a peak when the preliminary hearing began. Crowds swarmed about the courthouse, mobbing him as he made his way up the steps accompanied by Bob Ford, Jerry Giesler,

Raoul Walsh, and Buster Wiles. They grabbed at him, trying to pull off his buttons as souvenirs; one woman flung herself to the floor of the corridor and tried to drag free one of his shoes. He kept up a good front, smiling firmly but not too boldly at his fans and enemies thronging the entrance to the courtroom.

The proceedings went swiftly. Betty Hansen nervously described the events of the party in Bel Air. Peggy Satterlee talked about the nights on the *Sirocco,* causing him to look annoyed when, with a landlubber's ignorance, she talked about "upstairs" and "down-stairs" on the yacht Aside from scowling at these distinctly non-nautical terms, he stared deadpan at the witness, almost daring her to continue.

Giesler said little, saving his big guns for the trial itself. Judge Byron Walters bound Errol over for trial in superior court on November 23. Bail was continued.

Errol finished work on *Edge of Darkness* thirty days behind schedule because of the director's slowness and his own legal conferences. Meanwhile, he and Giesler and Ford dealt with their problems one by one.

First of all, they had to decide which witnesses they dared use in Errol's favor. After sifting through the list, they realized that very few of these could survive expert cross-examination. Buster Wiles had shared the cabin with Errol. He had been present at the party in Bel Air. He still maintains loyally that Errol played tennis all the time in Bel Air and never went upstairs with Betty Hansen, and that Errol's sinus condition would have prevented him from having any sex drive on the yacht voyage Yet the evidence overwhelmingly showed that Errol did go upstairs with Betty without Wiles's knowledge and that the sinus trouble only affected Errol seriously on the *second* night of the voyage. Evidently, Giesler feared that Wiles would crack under cross-examination. Jim Fleming confirms this.

The second witness to be considered was Jim Fleming. Fleming had not been present at either the yachting party or the house party. But he knew by Errol's own confession that Errol had slept with both girls. If Fleming were to be called in defense all he could say was that he had virtually set up Errol with Peggy Satterlee, a statement which would not have helped Errol's case. And under cross-examination, in order to avoid perjury, he would have been compelled to tell the truth of Errol's confession.

The third witness who would be problematical was Captain Hayward Kingsley, master of the *Sirocco*. In theory, Kingsley, a strait-laced pillar of the yachting establishment with social connections, would be helpful: his evidence would weigh more heavily than that of a double and a stand-in. But in fact Kingsley could neither prove nor disprove that intercourse had taken place on the yacht, and indeed his evidence could easily be taken apart. He had stated to Giesler that on the night of August 2, he had been unaware of any sounds of struggle, and on August 3, on the journey back to San Pedro, he had seen Errol at the wheel until 10:30 P.M. Unfortunately, Peggy had not claimed that she had struggled on the first of these nights, and on the second she had described intercourse as taking place after 11 P.M.

Giesler sent Jim Fleming to Mexico for the whole length of the trial. There was always the danger he might be called as a prosecution witness. Buster Wiles was to be absent for part of the trial, visiting his sick mother. Hayward Kingsley was conveniently enlisted in the Navy. He made out an affidavit at the San Diego Naval Base before leaving for service as boatswain's mate on a PT boat located in Pearl Harbor. His deposition could be used as evidence without the cross-examination which would considerably reduce its effectiveness.

Giesler used Kingsley's absence to obtain a continuance of the trial from November to January because Kingsley was not immediately available to give evidence. Presumably, a telegram to Honolulu could have had him released and flown back at once, but Giesler never sent any such invitation. Giesler was playing for time so that he could amass more evidence against the two girls.

He also needed time to rehearse Errol thoroughly for his appearance on the witness stand. Whether Giesler believed in Errol's innocence or not, he knew his client's talents well. Errol would satisfy the jury by merely talking to them. He would be composed, "sincere," and organized. Who were these trashy girls anyway?

Giesler took a terrific gamble in this decision. But he took a greater one in his selection of the jury. He relied on the fact that women by the million adored Errol Flynn, that he was their dream of male beauty and virility, and that a jury largely composed of women might be so impressed by his bearing and physique that they might overrule their better judgment. And yet many of these women might be mothers of young daughters and therefore want to make an example of a famous and ruthless seducer of the innocent.

He decided to take a chance and go with nine women, few of whom had children, and three men; and this decision was accepted with surprising swiftness by the district attorney. He chose more or less ordinary jurors who seemed to have little or no prejudice on either side. But as it turned out, the initial selection proved to have its problems.

On the afternoon of November 13, shortly after 2 P.M., Errol was at Mulholland Farm when a letter arrived in his mailbox. Although it was stamped, the stamp hadn't been canceled, so it was unclear whether it was put through the mail or put into the box by hand. The envelope was white and of poor quality. Errol's name and address were written in blue-black ink.

Errol tore open the end of the envelope and removed a large sheet of cheap yellow stationery. The letter so upset him that he sank into a chair and read it again, scarcely able to believe its contents:

Dear Mr. Flynn:

If you value your life and career send ten thousand dollars in cash wrapped in a small package addressed to Phil Owens, Gathos Malt Shop, San Bernardino or your phone will be tapped and you will be followed so make no attempt to tell police.

A hint—this concerns Betty Hansen and Peggy Satterlee—have it there by November 18, or something will happen.

Errol called Jerry Giesler. Giesler and Ford reported it to the police who in turn informed the Federal Bureau of Investigation since J. Edgar Hoover had insisted on being personally informed of everything connected with Errol at the time.

The police wrapped a box of candy in a package and a plainclothesman took it to a malt shop addressed to Phil Owens on November 18. FBI agents and the local police surrounded the store.

They waited most of the day, expecting a man or woman to claim the package. To their astonishment a slender thirteen-year-old boy appeared and asked for the parcel. The agent let him walk to the door and then seized him.

The boy tried to squirm free but he was quickly surrounded by plainclothesmen and driven to the local precinct. He broke down at once. He admitted he was a fan of Errol's and that he wanted the extortion note to "test" Errol to see if the star was guilty.

He gave his name as Jack Harding and said he was in the eighth grade in public school in San Bernardino. He declared that he had written the note at school, bringing it home with him and rewriting it there without his parents' knowledge. He had told his elder brother, age sixteen, what he was doing; his brother had told him he was "crazy" if he mailed it. Jack said he had hoped Errol would come to the malt shop in person so that he could obtain his autograph. His fingerprints were taken, but in view of his age he was not booked and the entire matter was dropped.

Errol was unsettled by the incident. The idea of a thirteen-year-old boy threatening his life was really frightening. Suppose a youth (or other young girls) should threaten him on a sexual matter now —when he was most vulnerable?

Right in the midst of this period, Blanca Rosa Welter arrived from Mexico. Because of her friendship with Errol, she had been followed from Mexico by the FBI, and all of her phone calls to Errol were intercepted and recorded by the authorities. As it turned out, her conversations with Errol were innocent and harmless. Errol signed her to a movie contract at fifty dollars a week.

When she arrived, FBI agents lurked in the grounds of Mulholland Farm. Their field glasses flashed from the surrounding hills. Alexandre Pavlenko recalls that Errol in a fury literally rode down on these men on horseback and sent them fleeing far and wide.

Despite the worry and strain of those weeks, Errol arranged a screen test for Rosa. She breezed through the test effectively, Errol playing a love scene with her. He said to her, "We'll save L'Aiglon for your next role! But for the moment, if you come across as a gypsy, you've got a part in my next film."

Errol, remembering his ancestor Fletcher Christian, called her Linda Christian. Or so he claimed; she maintained that she invented her own name. Linda was her nickname at school and among friends.

While Linda was at Mulholland Farm, Errol was dating the glamorous Gertrude Anderson, the Swedish Nazi singer he had known earlier. She was pursued by FBI agents. Carl Schaefer, head of foreign publicity at Warners, remembers that he ran into Errol and Gertrude at a Los Angeles restaurant. Knowing Gertrude's Nazi background, he was uncomfortable about joining them for a drink. As he was hesitating, a telephone call came from New York. It was from the Warner Brothers publicity chief, Charles Einfeld. Einfeld said, "Errol is mixing with that Anderson dame. We've had word from the FBI. She's an out-and-out Nazi. Keep Errol away from her at all costs, or it's going to get out about him dating an agent." Schaefer was unable to respond satisfactorily at the bar telephone because Gertrude was within earshot. He simply said he would do what he could and hung up.

Later that day, he managed to draw Errol aside. He said, "For God's sake, Errol. That woman is a Nazi. Keep away from her." Errol laughed at his suggestion.

During December 1942, Giesler began to build a damning case against Betty Hansen and Peggy Satterlee. The fact that Betty Hansen was under investigation on a charge of oral intercourse with Armand Knapp was, of course, more than helpful. It showed that she was far from being the innocent she claimed; and Giesler believed she had also had oral intercourse with Knapp's fellow messenger boys.

As for Peggy Satterlee, he had to delve deeper. He found that she had been romantically interested in a well-known flyer named Owen Cathcart-Jones. Cathcart-Jones was an Englishman who had made a pioneer flight to Australia and who had acted as technical advisor in Hollywood on the scenes involving the crashed RAF bomber in *Desperate Journey*.

Cathcart-Jones had gone to Canada in 1941 to work on a James Cagney film, *Captains of the Clouds*. During his absence, Peggy Satterlee had used his apartment in Hollywood. It was suggested that she had shared the apartment with Cathcart-Jones, who was thirteen years older than she.

A curious episode came to light as a result of Giesler's investigations. He discovered—and it was later confirmed in court testimony—that Peggy Satterlee and Cathcart-Jones had together visited a mortuary in downtown Los Angeles where they had played hide-and-seek among the dead. Peggy Satterlee had lifted a cloth from the face of a Filipino and shown Cathcart-Jones the man's fatal wounds. She had pressed her face against that of another male cadaver and had darted in and out of the still, sheeted figures on the tables. Although this was a fairly harmless if peculiar prank, Giesler felt that he could hint at the horrible perversion of necrophilia: sexual attraction to the dead. Giesler could afford to overlook nothing which would ruin Miss Satterlee's reputation.

Giesler also found out that Peggy Satterlee had been sharing an apartment at another address during 1942 with an actor named John Dale who was helping her obtain work in the movies. And in July 1942, while she was living with Dale, Peggy had had an illegal operation.

Giesler knew that all of this information, though most helpful, was insufficient to disprove the charge of statutory rape. Even if Peggy had been a whore on Main Street the fact that she was under eighteen would still have made Flynn's a punishable offense. Yet he hoped that these revelations would shape the jury's reaction to the girls' testimony.

Giesler next had to destroy the actual evidence of the girls. To this end, he managed to obtain access to the house in Bel Air where he carefully examined the lock on the door of the bedroom in which the alleged rape took place. Then he went over Peggy Satterlee's testimony at the preliminary hearing referring to the moon and its position in relation to the yacht on the night of her alleged rape. He also noted that in one statement she had said that intercourse took place on only one night while in another statement she had said it took place on two nights. But he was still up against it: he knew that a respected physician named Etta Gray had examined Peggy's hymen after the voyage and had found it to be forcibly ruptured, and that the entrance to her vagina had been slightly torn.

Giesler went over the yacht with a fine-tooth comb. He discovered that the cabin in which Peggy claimed she had been raped had a bunk raised two feet from the deck. He decided that her description of a bunk that was level with the floor was not correct.

It now came to the question of rounding up the other people on the yacht, beginning with Buster Wiles's girl friend, Elaine Patterson. A sailor on the *Sirocco,* Hubert Oliver, was subpoenaed while in army training in Texas. So were two other members of the crew, also in the armed services.

In December, Errol was to appear in an elaborate musical revue entitled *Thank Your Lucky Stars* in which virtually all of the Warner Brothers contract players would star. (Errol refused to appear in the later *Hollywood Canteen,* the proceeds of which went to that patriotic institution.)

In view of the fact that he could neither sing nor dance, Errol had at first been excluded from this musical, but he had told Jack

Warner he would "kill" if he were not in the picture. As a result, a special number was put together for him to star in, under the direction of LeRoy Prinz: "That's What You Jolly Well Get," with lyrics by Frank Loesser with help from Errol and music by Arthur Schwarz. Errol played a cockney in a London pub who told false tales of his war heroism only to be shouldered around the bar by his mates to a chorus of, "Urrah! 'E won the war!" to which he replied with equally heavy-handed irony, "And oi won the one before!" He managed to have Buster Wiles and Freddy McEvoy included among the "cockneys" who made fun of him.

It was typical of Flynn that he would seek to disarm British accusations that he was a draft dodger by making a joke of them. Unfortunately the idea backfired: many people on both sides of the Atlantic believed he was making fun of patriotism, and many British people called him a Nazi sympathizer.

He worked very hard on the number, rehearsing for five days under the dance director LeRoy Prinz, and another five under the direction of David Butler. He sang and danced with animal high spirits if little skill. This elaborate example of hi-jinks was put together on the very verge of his trial, and completed only two days before the trial itself began.

Sixteen

On January 11, 1943, Errol was driven to the courthouse downtown. He looked drawn and red-eyed, and seemed to be about to collapse. Despite his enjoyment of the black humor of his "That's What You Jolly Well Get" number, he was exhausted by the days of drilling by choreographer and director and the late afternoon and evening sessions with his attorneys. When the car swung into the Hall of Justice parking lot, an immense and feverish crowd swept forward, completely blocking the way, so that the driver had to honk loudly and the police had to clear a path.

Ashen, Errol refused to speak or sign autographs as he strode to an elevator. The corridor outside the courtroom was filled with photographers, reporters, and sightseers. He ignored everyone, seemingly cut off on an island of his own.

He twice put his hand to his eyes when bulbs popped so sharply they almost succeeded in temporarily blinding him. At last he managed to find his way to the seat, where Jerry Giesler was waiting.

The Warner Brothers executives were nowhere to be seen. Not one had appeared to give him moral support. He resented their stand bitterly.

At the start of the hearings, the prosecuting Deputy District Attorney Thomas W. Cochran made his opening statement, reminding the court that Betty was seventeen on September 21, 1942, six days before the party in Bel Air, and that he had a birth certificate showing that Peggy Satterlee was born in Dallas, Texas, on September 7, 1926.

Giesler then summed up the defense contentions, saying that he intended to prove that there was a conspiracy between Knapp and Betty Hansen to play up to Flynn, that Flynn never had an improper relation with her and that her motives were bad. He also drew the court's attention to Peggy Satterlee's residence in Owen Cathcart-Jones' apartment and to the fact that there was no evidence of rape on the yacht. He made special play of the fact that Peggy Satterlee had waited thirteen months to make her accusation, and that during that time she had worked as a movie usherette, a dance-hall hostess, and a singer in a nightclub. She had admitted these occupations under oath and witnesses had confirmed them.

On January 14, Betty Hansen gave her testimony. She was dressed in a tight gray sweater and a red and green cotton skirt. A poodle was stitched into the sweater over her breasts, and its movements during her evidence caused ripples of laughter in the courtroom.

Cochran urged Betty to describe the events of the afternoon in Bel Air. She admitted she had sat on the arm of Errol's chair, slid onto his lap, and then had lain on the divan in the living room. She talked of going to the bedroom and of lying down. Cochran asked, "How was it furnished?"

"It had two beds," Betty replied.

"Then what happened?"

"The next thing he done [sic] was to sit me down on the first bed closest to the door."

"What did you say?"

"I said I did not want to stay up there. I was feeling all right and wanted to go down and stay with the others. And then he said to me, 'You don't think I would really let you go downstairs, do you?' and I said, 'Yes, I do.' I was still sitting there and the next thing he did was to walk to the door, the main door, and I heard a click and I didn't know whether he was locking the door or what."

Betty went on to describe Errol undressing her. She hesitated, on the verge of tears. "Go ahead," Cochran urged her. "Tell everything in detail, the way it occurred."

"Well, the only reason I thought he was undressing me was because before I went to the room he said he was going to put me to bed. And he said he would come right downstairs afterward and all, and so I thought that was the idea of undressing me and putting me to bed."

"So," Cochran asked, "he undressed you, removed all of your clothing?"

"Yes, sir. Everything except my shoes."

She went on to describe Errol stripping off his own clothes.

"What clothing did he remove?"

Her reply brought a burst of laughter. "He removed everything but his shoes."

Several reporters rushed to the telephones. *They Died with Their Boots On* was still in circulation.

Cochran obtained a complete description of the witness's clothing. When he asked her what Flynn had actually done, she blushed deeply. "He had an act of intercourse with me."

"You mean by that, Miss Hansen, that the private parts of Mr. Flynn were inserted in your private parts?"

"Yes."

There was a din in the courtroom. Cochran pressed on. He determined that the intercourse took at least half an hour; that Betty Hansen went to the bathroom after the intercourse to use a douche bag; that they discussed the hair oil Errol favored; and that Errol took her address and phone number. She also confirmed Lynn Boyer's knocking on the door.

But here her testimony varied slightly from preceding ones. This time she said Lynn Boyer was looking for a telephone.

Giesler stood up. He behaved considerately and warmly toward the witness, lulling her into a sense of false security. He asked her, "With reference to the alleged sex act, you were dressed in slacks and a sport shirt, were you not?"

She agreed that this was correct.

Giesler began to close in. "And those were very tight-fitting slacks, were they not?"

Betty Hansen was ready. "No, sir."

Giesler tried to be patient. "They were not?"

"No, sir."

Giesler was not fazed. He said, quietly, "I beg your pardon, Miss Hansen, but in your testimony before the grand jury, on page 88 of the transcript, you stated that the slacks were tight-fitting. Do you recall saying that?"

Betty Hansen was sunk. "Yes, I guess I did."

Giesler had gained a victory in round one. He had shown that Betty had dressed provocatively and that she had lied on the witness stand about a simple matter of her clothing. Might she not be lying about everything else?

He made her describe Flynn's removing her slacks and was pleased to hear her say that she did not object to this, until he realized that she was going to pretend she had no idea what Errol intended to do.

"He said he was going to put me to bed," she said.

Giesler almost laughed with contempt. "You mean," he said, biting his black spectacles and staring sharply at the jury instead of at the witness, "you thought he was going to *tuck you in?*"

"That's right," Betty snapped.

Giesler went on to question Betty on Errol's removal of her panties. He asked her, "Even then, Miss Hansen, you did not think he intended sexual intercourse?"

Her answer was firm. "No, sir, I did not."

"When did you first think about sexual intercourse?"

Betty's reply brought the house down. "When I had sexual intercourse with him."

Giesler ridiculed this answer. He said, "You mean you thought, 'This nice, considerate man is helping me to undress and take my things off so I can lie down because I was sick at my stomach?'"

Betty said, "That's right."

Giesler looked at the courtroom with blank astonishment. Even some of the jury had to laugh.

"Miss Hansen," he said sarcastically, "when Mr. Errol Flynn started to have intercourse with you, then you knew what he was trying to do?"

She could not deny it. She did.

"Did you object then?"

"Yes."

"Hmmm. A moment ago you said you did *not* object."

This was, of course, a cynical ploy. Cochran objected, and Giesler was forced to admit that she had objected to the intercourse but not to the preparations for it, the intentions of which she had misunderstood. Nevertheless, astonishingly, he made her supply a *reverse* of this. He made her say that she had objected to the undressing and foreplay, but not to the intercourse itself. By now, she had become hopelessly confused.

He did not succeed in making her admit that she had wanted to meet Errol Flynn to obtain movie work, but he did force her to say that Armand Knapp had encouraged her to play up to Flynn. Against Cochran's objections, which Judge Still overruled, Giesler asked Betty if she had had intercourse with Armand Knapp. She emphatically said that she had not. On that note, the court was adjourned.

Errol returned home to Blanca Welter, shortly to be known as Linda Christian. Alex, the butler, recalls that he was silent and moody at dinner. He could sleep only with the aid of pills. He awoke feeling groggy the next morning. He was so depressed that Alex remembered he even took a gun from a closet and looked at it, contemplating suicide. He felt he could not face the long ordeal ahead.

Next morning, Giesler tried to tear Betty Hansen apart. He questioned her on the fact that she was being held in Juvenile Hall on a possible felony charge of oral intercourse. Cochran tried desperately to stop this fact being admitted in evidence. Judge Still knew how crucial it was, and firmly overruled Cochran's objection. When Giesler said, loudly and sharply, "Did you not admit, Miss Hansen, under oath before the grand jury that you have performed two acts of sexual perversion with a man?" the court was thrown into a frenzy. Judge Still banged his gavel and called for silence. In tears, sobbing helplessly, Betty Hansen under oath admitted having oral sex with Armand Knapp. Giesler rested his case. He saw the expressions on the faces of the jury. He knew that several of them were disgusted. It was what he wanted. Once he had established that Betty Hansen was capable of sexual perversion and that her account of the intercourse at the house in Bel Air was confused and dishonest, her case was virtually ruined.

Errol must have felt very satisfied at that moment. But Peggy Satterlee still had to give evidence.

Lynn Boyer, the singer who had rattled the door at the house, was due next on the stand. She appeared to be hysterical as she made her way through the throngs of reporters, a black wig her attempt at a disguise. When the cameras flashed, she screamed and covered her face, announcing that if this continued, she would throw herself from a window. Weeping, she struggled through the crowd into the courtroom and began to give her memories of the events in Bel Air.

But no sooner had she begun her testimony than, after a hasty conference, the district attorney suddenly stood up. While Giesler, Ford and, most of all, Errol looked at him in astonishment, Cochran called for a mistrial.

A mistrial? It would mean a new judge would have to take over, and a new jury would be chosen. Betty Hansen would have to tell her whole story again. Errol leaned over and asked Giesler, "What does this mean?"

It seemed that there was a problem with a woman member of the jury, Mrs. Elaine Forbes. A Mrs. Harriet Ponder, who had been in the pool of prospective jury women had reported to District Attorney Cochran in an affidavit under oath as well as in person that Elaine Forbes had told her just before Christmas 1942, "I must get on the jury for the Flynn trial no matter what happens," and that Mrs. Forbes had said to her, "If we get on the Flynn jury, we will take care of Mr. Flynn, won't we?" Mrs. Ponder had replied that if she were to be selected as juror, she would be governed solely by the evidence and did not think that anyone should serve who had a fixed opinion beforehand as to the guilt or innocence of the defendant.

The D.A. told the court that Mrs. Ponder had also reported on another juror, Lorene Boehm. Mrs. Boehm had asked Mrs. Ponder to accompany her to the seventh floor of the Hall of Justice to "get a good look at Errol Flynn." Harriet Ponder said she had complied and that Lorene Boehm looked Flynn over with considerable interest and said, "I am for him in a big way."

Amid a general commotion in court, Cochran continued. He said that a Mrs. Gussie Alliet Rowe, another prospective juror, had sworn out an affidavit saying that on January 5 when she was in the jury room waiting to be examined, she had heard Elaine Forbes saying, "I just must get on that jury; I don't know what I will do if I don't get on Flynn's jury." So far Mrs. Rowe's statement tallied with that of Mrs. Ponder. But from that moment, it diverged. She said that Elaine Forbes would, if she got on the jury, not convict Flynn, a most confusing matter for the district attorney to consider. As a result, still another prospective juror, Mrs. Emily Blue, was asked to give an affidavit. She too confirmed that Elaine Forbes had made a statement but again contradicted Mrs. Ponder. She also said that

Elaine Forbes wanted to make sure Errol Flynn was declared not guilty.

Yet another affidavit had been prepared by a Mrs. Beckman confirming that Elaine Forbes was a fan who would prevent Errol from being brought to justice.

After an agonizing wait in which Errol's attorneys argued the matter before Judge Still, it was decided to proceed with the trial and simply replace Mrs. Forbes. For reasons that remain obscure, the other prejudiced jury woman, Lorene Boehm, was permitted to remain on the jury, and proved influential in obtaining a verdict later on.

Lynn Boyer was allowed to complete her evidence, which was of little consequence one way or the other. There was laughter in court when Judge Still asked Miss Boyer to repeat something she had mumbled inaudibly. "Oh, it was nothing," she said. "Never mind, Judge."

"Well, whether it was nothing or something, keep your voice up," Judge Still said.

The two policemen who had apprehended Errol gave a brief resume of what had taken place. Chi-Chi Toupes spoke briefly about the events of the party.

The courtroom snapped awake when Peggy Satterlee was called to give evidence. She looked stunning, her pale skin and green eyes and piled dark hair making a striking impression. She seemed nervous, trembling and clutching her hands tightly together, but she quickly composed herself and smiled directly at the jury as she answered Cochran's questions. It was clear she had been very carefully rehearsed.

She went over the description of her first meeting with Errol at the nightclub after Arno's death off Balboa, about the arrangements made to have her go on the yacht, and about Buster Wiles driving her and his girl friend Elaine Patterson to the California Yacht Club for the voyage to Catalina aboard the *Sirocco*. She said that Errol had called her by the nickname J.B., short for jail bait and SQQ, short for San Quentin quail. Cochran had made his point. By using these terms to Peggy, Errol had revealed that he knew she was underage; he could not use as an excuse the belief that she was over eighteen.

She stated that on the first night of the voyage she was not disturbed in her cabin. She told of the trip ashore to the Isthmus with

Errol, Buster, and Elaine, and that they had danced at the Hawaiian Hut. She said she had a rum and coke and then a glass of milk with rum in it which Errol had arranged, spiking the milk without her knowledge.

She said that the party returned to the yacht at 2 A.M. on Sunday. She described preparing for bed.

"What," the district attorney asked her, "was the next thing that happened?"

"Mr. Flynn came into the room."

"How was he dressed?"

"He had on pajamas."

"What was said?"

"I asked him what he wanted and he just said he wanted to talk to me. I asked what he was doing in a lady's bedroom . . . he asked if he could get in bed. He said he would not hurt me, but would just get in bed with me."

After some hesitation, she continued: "He got into bed with me. And he completed an act of sexual intercourse."

"What, if anything, did he do to your clothing?"

"He pulled it down. He pulled my underwear down and pushed my underskirt up as far as my navel."

"Did you resist him?"

"I'm not sure. I was very upset."

"Just tell us what you did, Miss Satterlee. And what Mr. Flynn did."

"Well, I resisted at first. I mean I did not fight or anything. I just told him that he should not do that."

"Did you struggle with him at all?"

"No, sir. Not at that time."

"Did you strike him in the face?"

"I can't remember."

"What was the next thing that occurred after he completed this act?"

"Well, he went out and got a robe and brought it to me."

"And what did you do while he was gone?"

"I pulled my panties up and my underskirt down."

"Then what did you do?"

"I went up on the upper deck with him and he brought me a glass of milk."

Once again, the courtroom dissolved in laughter. Peggy went on to describe the Sunday swim she had taken with Errol for the *Life* magazine photographs. Then she proceeded to the events of the Sunday voyage home. She said: "We had a conversation about the moon and I mentioned how pretty it was."

"What did he reply?"

"He said it would look prettier through the porthole."

"What else did he say?"

"I can't remember exactly, but he said to come downstairs and look through the porthole."

"So you did?"

"Yes."

"Where did you go?"

"To Mr. Flynn's stateroom. The one he and Mr. Wiles used."

"And what happened?"

"Well, I wanted to look at the moon, so I got up on the bed, the one on the right side, and I looked out through the porthole."

"Did you see the moon?"

"I think so. Yes, sir."

"Then what happened?"

"After I looked at the moon, I started to get off the bed and he pushed me back on."

"Mr. Flynn did?"

"Yes. And he said that as long as he had once had possession of me—" She broke off, then continued, "I guess those were not his exact words, but he insisted that he could not see why I would not let him do it again. And he began pushing me down hard on the bed and at the same time that he was doing that he was taking his pants off. And I—"

"How were you dressed?"

"I had on blue denim slacks with one of those big belts that you can slip easily and a blue denim windbreaker with a zipper down the front."

"What did Mr. Flynn do next? How much of his clothing did he remove?"

"Just his pants."

"Then what did he do?"

"He kept pushing down my pants and then he got up on the bed with me."

She went on to describe the actual intercourse, and insisted she had struggled. She said she had fought so hard she had kicked the drapes down that were hanging by the berth. Cochran had made another telling point. He had shown that actual rape as well as statutory rape had taken place, and he proceeded to show that even after she forced Flynn's penis from her body he once more attacked her.

"Did he again insert his private parts into yours?"

"Yes, sir."

"Did you suffer pain as the result of this act?"

"Yes, I did."

"Did you say anything to Mr. Flynn?"

"Yes, I told him to leave me alone!"

"Did he say anything to you?"

"Yes, he kept saying that since he'd done it once he couldn't see why he couldn't again."

Errol looked grim. He could not pretend that this evidence, delivered in a near whisper and obviously under agonizing strain, was not extremely damaging to his defense. Yet a moment later he must have remembered: "No, she got it wrong; this couldn't have happened on the way back to San Pedro; there was rough weather and she was seasick and I was suffering from a blinding sinus headache. She got her nights mixed up. That is going to help me."

That night, Errol sat down and wrote out detailed notes which would be helpful to Giesler's cross-examination of Peggy Satterlee the following day. Unable to sleep, he shot himself full of morphine. Next morning, he looked notably pale in court. And he had a cut and bruise on his nose: he had tripped and fallen in the shower while under the influence of the drug.

Peggy Satterlee also looked ill and her eyes were bloodshot. Giesler began by drawing her out on her background in Applegate, California, and Whiskey Gulch, Montana: her leaving high school after her second year, and her jobs as usherette, dance-hall camera girl, and nightclub showgirl. He also established that she frequently lied about her age. He linked her easily to Owen Cathcart-Jones, making her admit that Jones had asked her to marry him and had given her gifts of clothing and the use of his apartment. Giesler tried to bring in the matter of her abortion and implied that she had made a deal with the district attorney to give evidence in the Flynn case if the district attorney would excuse her lover and herself from abortion charges. Cochran objected, yet the information stuck in the minds of the jury.

Asking Peggy what happened in the cabin of the yacht, Giesler took her through the discussion of the moon once again. She repeated her description of the sexual act.

"How far down did he pull your panties?"

"To my ankles or completely off."

"Did he tear your slip in any way?"

"No."

"Did he tear your panties?"

"No."

"Did you on that first occasion attempt to scratch him?"

"No."

"Did you make any noise, Miss Satterlee? Did you try to attract the attention of anyone?"

"No. I was too frightened and embarrassed to do anything."

"I see." Disbelieving, Giesler looked around the court.

"I thought about it," Peggy added. "But I didn't think it would be worth it because the people on the boat were all his friends."

"I see." Giesler added: "Miss Satterlee, when you decided to look at the moon through the porthole, did Mr. Flynn carry you down the stairs?"

"No, sir."

"He didn't pull you or drag you down the stairs?"

"No, sir."

"You say that when you tried to get down from the bed Mr. Flynn pushed you back on?"

"Yes."

"You were pretty mad then, were you not?"

"Yes."

"You had in mind that what had happened before might happen again?"

"Yes."

"You were angry?"

"Yes, I was very angry."

"When you get that mad you can fight pretty hard?"

"Yes, I was fighting pretty hard."

"As hard as you could?"

"No, not as hard as I could because I was trying to fight and trying to think at the same time."

"I see. Now, Miss Satterlee, *did you cross your legs?*"

Peggy was shocked by the question. Clearly, it was intended to establish that she was lying. "I don't remember," she said.

Giesler looked contemptuously around the court over his spectacles. "You mean to tell us, you remember everything else, but *you don't recall crossing your legs?*"

"No, I don't!" Peggy snapped.

"Were you on your back?"

"Yes, I was. But part of the time I was lying on my side."

"Were you trying to prevent him from accomplishing the act? Do you recall uncrossing your legs at any time?"

Peggy was furious. "I did *not* say I crossed them!" she shouted.

Giesler changed course. "All right. Did *Mr. Flynn* uncross your legs?"

Peggy was not fazed. Her voice was icy. "I told you. I can't remember everything."

Giesler had tried to trip her up in her testimony, but failed. Later, he tried to imply that after her mother had taken her to the district attorney's office where Peggy made out a statement against Flynn, a bribe had been given to her mother, who had suddenly bought her a wardrobe of new clothes.

Despite frequent objections by Cochran, and violent arguments before the judge, Giesler succeeded in leaving in the minds of the jury the strong possibility of a payoff. But this was a double-edged weapon: though he intended it to mean that the district attorney had paid Mrs. Satterlee to insure a case against Errol, many people felt that Errol had bribed the district attorney and Mrs. Satterlee to drop the case. It was dangerous territory, and it is surprising that Giesler entered it. Furthermore, it made little sense, since, if the district attorney had in fact wanted to start proceedings against Errol for political or other reasons and was prepared to pay for the opportunity, he would surely not have waited thirteen months to do so!

Nevertheless, Giesler had succeeded in making Peggy Satterlee admit extramarital relations with another man and an illegal operation. This effectively reduced the picture of innocence the district attorney had built up. But Giesler overlooked an equally important matter. He failed to have Peggy admit that the sailing conditions on the way back to San Pedro were rough, and that Errol was stricken with a sinus attack. And it is surprising that he did not reconfirm Hayward Kingsley's statement in his affidavit that Errol was at the wheel of the boat during almost all of the homeward voyage.

Next to give evidence was the photographer Peter Stackpole, followed by Peggy's mother, her sister, and a police department physician named Etta Gray. Mrs. Satterlee talked of Peggy's crying when she returned home after the voyage and of taking Peggy to the police precinct. Mickey June Satterlee confirmed details of Peggy's testimony. Dr. Gray testified: "I found a slight break in the hymen tissue on the left lower side. It was a recent rupture and the tissue bled readily. The hymen tissue was swollen." She went on to explain that the rupture was very recent indeed, and that the examination had taken place on the Monday after the voyage. She said the tissues were black and blue. Cochran tried to have Dr. Gray testify that the breaking of the hymen was caused by a penis in erection but Giesler objected and the objection was sustained. However, she finally was allowed to say that this in fact had been the cause.

Giesler tried desperately to wreck Dr. Gray's testimony, but failed. The jury clearly noted that a police doctor who was unlikely to perjure herself had proven enforced intercourse.

Next day, Freddy McEvoy perjured himself, pretending Errol never had intercourse with Betty. Owen Cathcart-Jones confirmed the hide-and-seek games in the mortuary. Giesler asked: "And did she take you back where they inject the corpses, and pull the sheet from the body of an elderly man, and place her face next to his?"

"Yes."

Even the jurors looked shocked by this extraordinary statement.

Errol's appearance on the witness stand was, of course, what virtually everyone in the courtroom had really come to see. The opportunity to observe a leading box office star giving evidence in his trial for statutory rape was irresistible. As he stood up, in a dark brown suit and gray tie, pale under his tan, several women stood up saying, "Oh, I just want to get a good look at him!" and "What a dreamboat!" Judge Still ordered silence. But throughout his testimony, their cries went on.

Errol gave his testimony smoothly until the lunchtime recess, looking directly at the jury as Jerry Giesler had told him to. When the recess came, one of Giesler's assistants, Robert Neeb, took Errol to lunch in Chinatown. Giesler had told Neeb to watch Errol at lunchtime in case he misbehaved or disappeared entirely on a drunk. On this day of all days, it was essential that Errol should be sober.

Neeb recalls:

We arrived at the Chinese restaurant. I suggested he have some food. He said he didn't feel like anything to eat. I told him he should try. I said, "Don't drink." He smiled and ordered a large glass of milk. The Chinese waitress took the order and I could see that sparks were flying between them. Their eyes met significantly. Then, to my horror, Errol asked her to put five jiggers of vodka in the milk. My heart sank. I knew if Errol got drunk now he'd blow the whole case and it would be my head for having let him. I begged him not to. He said, "Let me do it. I know myself. If I've had the five jiggers I'll be as smooth as silk. If I haven't had a drink I'll be a bundle of nerves on the stand." I had no alternative but to let him go ahead. I sweated all through lunch and all the way back to the courthouse. Well, he went back on the stand. And he was perfect, one of the best witnesses Giesler and I ever had, just terrific.

That afternoon Giesler took Errol quietly through point after point. Errol denied he had called Peggy jail bait or San Quentin quail; that he had laced her milk or her Coca-Cola with rum; that he had been to bed with her or even entered her cabin; that he had asked her into his stateroom the following night to look at the moon; that he had had intercourse with her again.

Giesler moved on to the Bel Air party. Errol admitted Betty had sat on his chair but denied she slid onto his lap. He said he had not gone into the upstairs bedroom with her and that he had not had sexual intercourse with her. By the time he finished his statement, there was a riot in court. The bailiff threw out two men who had been calling obscenities and a hysterical woman who had repeatedly banged her lunch pail on the seat beside her. He promised to clear the court if there were any further disturbances.

Surprisingly, Cochran did not cross-examine. Instead, it was the assistant prosecutor, John Hopkins, who closed in on the witness. He was a much more ruthless figure than Cochran. Hopkins started well. He asked Buster Wiles's whereabouts. He forced Errol to lie that Buster was visiting his mother. He made it clear to the court that Wiles was too dangerous a witness to be called by the defense, that he might have cracked under cross-examination. Surprisingly, Hopkins did not also refer to Jim Fleming's absence from the courtroom, which, of course, was even more significant.

Hopkins dragged Errol through every moment of the Bel Air party and the voyage on the *Sirocco* but failed to shake his testimony. Errol continued to respond as politely as he had to Giesler. It was the performance of his lifetime. He miscalculated only when he pretended that he might be able to enter military service if acquitted and when he tried to milk sympathy by referring to the death of Arno.

When Errol stepped down from the witness stand, there was a burst of applause. He smiled faintly and sat down and began doodling on a pad. It looked as though the case was in the bag. But the district attorney had a surprise in store. Two policemen carried in an unusual exhibit: the door to Freddy McEvoy's bedroom at the house in Bel Air.

Errol conferred with Giesler and Ford. What did this mean? They shrugged. The door was propped up below the judge's bench.

Prosecutor John Hopkins called Sergeant Leland Jones, forensic chemist for the Police Department, to the stand. Jones revealed that someone had tampered with the lock, using a file to render it useless. He had discovered long scratch marks on it and tiny fragments of metal in the carpet. The purpose was obvious. One of Giesler's men had been trying to prove that in fact the door was not locked as Betty had claimed and that Lynn Boyer had also been lying when she said she had struggled to open the door.

Giesler was not fazed. He forced Sergeant Jones to admit that the scratches and filings could have taken place at any time *before* the night of the intercourse, September 27. But Prosecutor Hopkins also was not to be outdone. In re-examination he determined that the carpet had been regularly vacuumed before and during September 27, but not, for reasons of police inspection, *after* that night. Giesler was sunk.

Prosecutor Hopkins now brought out another piece of evidence. He summoned a well-known astronomer, Dr. C. H. Cleminshaw, to the stand. His purpose was to prove that Peggy Satterlee was telling the truth when she said that the moon was shining at an angle to the boat. This pleased Giesler. He had a trick up his sleeve.

While the court watched fascinated, Cleminshaw produced an enormous map of the sun, moon, and stars. It was pinned to a blackboard. Painstakingly, the bespectacled scientist explained that on the night of August 3, 1941, the moon had been at thirty-seven degrees from the zenith, or a fraction more than one third above the horizon.

Giesler zeroed in with all guns blazing. He asked, "Dr. Cleminshaw, if a boat was sailing from the Isthmus of Catalina toward Point Firmin, where would the moon be on the night of August 3, 1941, in relation to the boat, assuming that the direction from the Isthmus to Point Firmin is approximately nor'nor'east?"

•

Dr. Cleminshaw clucked and consulted his maps. Finally he said, "The moon was in the southern sky and if the boat were going nor'nor'east the moon would appear at the right of the boat."

"Then," Giesler said triumphantly, "it would not be visible through a porthole on the left side of the boat?"

Once again, Errol winced at these non-nautical terms. Giesler pressed on. "I ask you," he said, "to look at this map of the *Sirocco*."

Cleminshaw obliged. "That is where Mr. Flynn's cabin was, and that is where Miss Satterlee's cabin was. As you can see, they are both on the left of the boat."

Hopkins objected. He pointed out that the court only had Giesler's word for it that that was where the cabins were situated. Giesler promised to take the jury, prosecutors, and judge en masse for a personal tour of the *Sirocco* at Balboa. Judge Still cheerfully declined. He said that Giesler could proceed with his cross-examination.

Giesler had made his effect on the jury. He had shown them it was quite possible Peggy Satterlee had been embroidering her story when she said she had seen the moon through the porthole.

With one loss and one victory that day, Giesler and Errol went back to the house on Mulholland, and Errol had a shock.

Linda Christian had disappeared from his house. The reason she had fled was that, sensitive and sweet, she had become offended by Errol's indifferent treatment of her.

Her hairdresser had arranged an apartment for her, and she was hiding there. Errol was very upset. By 2 A.M., he still hadn't found her. At last he had an inspiration and called the hairdresser.

He reached her apartment at 3 A.M. She described the scene in her memoirs. He banged drunkenly on her door. She refused to let him in. He begged her. He pretended to cry. He told her he loved her. She still would not come out.

Finally, the manager emerged and told him to leave at once. He drove home recklessly, picking up a speeding ticket on the way. The cop held him, questioning him on the case.

Still very upset, Errol sat numbly through Giesler's and Hopkins' closing arguments—Giesler's that the girls were lying to avoid being charged with the felonies of, respectively, abortion and oral intercourse; Hopkins' that Errol was lying and committing perjury from beginning to end and had taken advantage of innocent underage girls.

Judge Still's summing up was careful and fair. He made the point that whether the girls had been of low moral character or not, statutory rape was still statutory rape. But he also pointed out that when there was evidence on both sides, Errol must not be condemned unless every possible doubt of guilt had been removed. If there was any question in the jury's mind that the girls had been lying, then he must be given his freedom. In law, a man was innocent until *proven* guilty.

The jury retired. Errol was able to breathe a little.

Hour after hour went by without a decision. Errol paced the corridors of the Hall of Justice or sat playing solitaire, trying to keep his nerves steady. He checked out his escape plans with his friends.

Meanwhile, in the jury room, a bitter argument went on. The nine women on the jury and one of the men were adamant from the outset that two girls were common tramps whose evidence was worthless. They refused to believe them against the word of a famous movie star. Two of the male jurists were equally convinced that Errol was guilty. They felt that the women were swayed by Errol's looks and fame.

Mrs. Ruby Anderson, the jury foreman, pointed out that the men had to be satisfied the girls were telling nothing but the truth and that, as Judge Still had said, if there was the slightest hint of a lie Flynn must be acquitted. Mrs. Mildred Leahy said, "The girls' case is weak. We must form our opinions solely on the evidence." Mrs. Theresa Woods said, "The girls' evidence is not conclusive enough." Mrs. Jennie Larson said, "Rape in that narrow bunk four feet off the ground would have been impossible. Besides, it was a rough journey home. Flynn was sick. And why didn't she cross her legs?"

By 10 P.M., the argument was still going on, and the two men were unshaken. The jury was locked up in a hotel for the night. Errol had to sweat it out until morning.

He was unable to eat his dinner with Raoul Walsh. He drove home to sink onto his bed with a combination of morphine and vodka.

Next morning, when he appeared in court, there was no sign of the jury's having reached a decision. The two holdouts for a guilty verdict, Charles Boyd and Homer Jacobsmeyer, were still adamant that Errol was guilty. But after a day the men began to crack. Seizing the opportunity, nine ladies closed in on them. At eleven-eighteen, they gave up the unequal struggle.

As they left the jury room, their decision unanimously agreed upon, the jury saw Errol striding up and down the corridor more nervously than any father waiting for a baby. Several lady members just managed to resist an impulse to throw their arms around him and tell him the good news. Meanwhile, Bailiff Fred Moxom told Jerry Giesler, Robert Ford, and Errol to "get their asses into court," conveying to them that the verdict was definitely favorable. As Errol, still not convinced, walked into the courtroom, a hysterical woman rushed up to him and planted a kiss on his mouth.

As he sat down, Errol said to Giesler, "Does it look all right?" It did. Several jury women looked directly at him and smiled. The court filled up in seconds.

Judge Still asked Foreman Anderson if the verdict had been reached. Mrs. Anderson cheerfully announced that it had. It was "not guilty" on each charge. The crowd screamed; Errol jumped from his chair and ran in one long sweeping movement up to Mrs. Anderson and shook her hand. Then he shook the other jurors' hands one by one.

Several of the lady jurors were in tears. Mrs. Nellie Minear, aged seventy-one, said to him: "I have three boys of my own. I thought of them, and I know I shouldn't want any of them to go to prison."

Juror Warren Curtis, who had been on Errol's side from the beginning, had forgotten that Errol was 4-F in the draft when he said, "My boy, you got the verdict you deserved, and now I'd like to hear something of you in the army."

A little girl ran up and pressed flowers into Errol's hand. Nobody had any intention of leaving the courtroom. Every attempt of Judge Still to clear it proved futile. Errol turned to the crowd and gave an elegant little speech: "My confidence in American justice is completely justified. I am happy and I am sincerely grateful to all those whose confidence in me encouraged me to go through this ordeal." It had lasted three months from the day of his arrest.

Trembling when he finished the speech, Errol was too nervous to light the cigarette he had fixed in the holder. Buster Wiles, who had returned from his convenient absence to hear the verdict, lit the cigarette for him. Then Buster and Raoul Walsh guided Errol to an anteroom, where he relaxed on a sofa feeling suddenly dizzy, as reporters and photographers banged furiously on the door.

District Attorney Cochran cornered Mrs. Anderson and asked her irritably: "How did you reconcile your verdict with Dr. Etta Gray's testimony of Peggy Satterlee's ruptured hymen?"

Mrs. Anderson looked him in the eye and replied coldly: "We felt there had been other men in the girls' lives. We were married women, and we discussed all medical aspects of the testimony. Frankly, the cards were on the table and we couldn't believe the two girls' stories."

Later, she told a reporter that she had especially disbelieved Peggy Satterlee's account of the rape on the second night, refusing to credit that it would have been possible to have achieved intercourse against the occupant's will on so narrow a bunk high above the floor.

Peggy Satterlee returned to her mother in Applegate, California, saying to reporters at the depot, "I think it's horrible. I didn't want it to come out this way. But maybe it will be for the best so far as I'm concerned."

Betty Hansen returned without comment to her parents in Lincoln, Nebraska.

Errol enjoyed a quiet luncheon at Perino's with Raoul Walsh. He returned home to tell Alex the good news. Alex recalls his jumping up and down and rubbing his hands in the living room.

His only sadness was that Linda Christian was no longer a part of his life.

In the wake of the trial, Errol's popularity soared more dramatically than ever. *Gentleman Jim* and *Desperate Journey* suddenly became enormous box office hits. The testimony of the two girls on the witness stand enhanced, if that were possible, Errol's reputation as a stud; the feeling that he had been maliciously damaged by two tramps made the public feel an even stronger sympathy with him. Warner Brothers increased his salary to nine thousand dollars a week and made an announcement that it would generously meet Jerry Giesler's bills. Actually, Jack Warner merely advanced fifty thousand dollars from Errol's anticipated earnings at his request, so that he could avoid selling off any of his real estate.

During the weeks of the trial, Errol had noticed a very pretty half-Mexican girl with red hair and fascinating light green eyes who was filling in for a friend of hers at the tobacco stand in the lobby of the Hall of Justice. He sent Buster Wiles to find out her name. Buster reported she was Nora Eddington, daughter of Jack Eddington, who was a secretary to the Los Angeles County sheriff.

Photographs of Nora at the time reveal a striking resemblance to Errol's mother when Marelle was in her late teens. (Marelle herself had lost her looks, and with them her early bent toward promiscuity. She and her husband were still happy in Belfast.)

Nora Eddington began her interesting memoir, *Errol and Me,* with the bitter words: "I should never have been conceived." She was writing soon after Errol's death: heartbroken over their shattered relationship. But in 1943, when she worked the tobacco stand in the Hall of Justice, she was a warm, strong, good-natured, unsophisticated girl. Her main interest in life was leaving the swing shift where she normally worked for an evening of jitterbugging with a handsome young Marine. She was self-conscious about her skinniness but attractively proportioned. With her piled-high forties' hair and bobby-soxer's charm, she resembled any one of the countless switchboard operators, stenographers, doughgirls, or factory girls who stare back at us out of the gray and silver images or bright-hued Technicolor of Hollywood movies of the time.

After Lili, Errol wanted nothing further to do with sophisticated, worldly, well-traveled women. He wanted a simple, down-to-earth sex partner and chum; a bright, sassy, tough, all-American girl. He needed someone who would never be sharp enough to guess that he was an enemy of America; who knew nothing of espionage or politics. It is deeply significant that she has never *heard* of Dr. Erben, that she knows nothing of, and is horrified by any reference to, Errol's bisexuality. She loved him blindly, physically, emotionally, as Lili did. And like Lili, she got from him only the pretense of love: romantic Barrymorean manners, the elaborate silent-movie-title love speeches, all of a surpassing phoniness, are recorded in *Errol and Me.*

Nora in 1943 knew little of movies, and was not particularly impressed by the idea of dating a movie star. Yet Buster Wiles managed to intrigue her. He recalls, "Nora laughed at my jokes. It helped. Soon after that, I arranged for them to meet at a party. They were attracted right away."

In his fatal ignorance of the female psyche, Errol assumed that he could enter casually into a physical relationship and as casually leave it when it no longer became convenient. He didn't understand that Nora was not like the string of carhops or cocktail waitresses whom Buster or Jim Fleming had fixed him up with in the past. She was proud, volatile, and sensitive.

She told me, "I was a virgin. And I already had a beau. Errol was charming, but I didn't want to be involved."

At first, they had a pleasant and surprisingly (for Errol) platonic relationship. Nora says she would come to Mulholland Farm after a day's work on the swing shift. She would go from the deafening clangor and heat of the factory to the cool beauty of the house on the hill, with its glowing Gauguin and Van Gogh, its bearskin rugs and hardwood floors, its high ceilings and beautifully appointed glass-tabled dining room. Alex, the major domo, recalls Nora's appreciation of the house, her exploration of the stables and the servants' quarters in the grounds. Certainly, the house was a far cry from the apartment where she lived with Jack Eddington and Marge, her step-mother. She was stepping up in the world.

Errol assumed the role of Professor Higgins to her Eliza Doolittle. His own taste in music was comfortably middlebrow: Wagner's *Siegfried Idyll,* Rimsky-Korsakov's *Scheherezade* and Rach-maninoff's Second Piano Concerto were his favorites. He also had a weakness for Grieg. She listened dutifully, but the dreamy and exotic music Errol loved grated against her even less cultivated spirit. She preferred Tommy Dorsey. And Alex remembers how Errol used to be infuriated by her playing noisy swing records as soon as he left the room.

Errol had begun to work, during the trial, on a novel called *Showdown* which would in many ways be a companion piece to *Beam Ends.* It began more or less on the same territory: the fabulous New Guinea of his imagination, a romantic tropical island far removed from the place it really was. It was an ice cream sundae of rich, overcolored emotion. The central figure was modeled narcissistically on Errol himself. He was described as sensationally handsome and beautifully built, slender and muscular at the same time. In New Guinea, Sean O'Flagherty (the name was changed to Shamus O'Thames) meets a beautiful blond girl, Cleo, a Hollywood movie star on location. Cleo rejects Shamus from her bosom: "As will sometimes happen in moments of stress, (Shamus') gaze focused . . . upon a . . . tiny mole, high up on her left breast. 'Scram!' she cried, dashing a bucket of water over him."

Cleo is "an exotic and beautiful wild creature . . . trampling the quiet loveliness of the well-tended tropical garden . . . her breasts strained, aggressively pointed and challenging. . . ." Suddenly we are in Peggy Satterlee land: " 'The bunk's so comfortable and so roomy and all,' cooed Cleo to Shamus one evening, '—but, well, Captain, it's sometimes so lonesome . . .' " One of the yachting party warns Shamus, " 'These days . . . there is a lawyer hidden behind every girdle.' "

At last, Cleo gives her all. Shamus and Cleo transcend the "barriers that separate one human from another."

The whole second half of the novel was dropped for legal reasons when it appeared some four years later. In the original, the story moves from New Guinea and Australia to Hollywood, where the hero and Cleo have a tangled love-hate relationship and the character of Cleo is transformed from Nora into an unmistakable Lili Damita.

The novel is brutal in its portrait of Hollywood: there is a merciless caricature of Michael Curtiz and his assistant Irving Rapper. Jack Warner becomes the monstrous J. T. Wertzer who despises the public and the stars equally. There is a telling scene in Wertzer's screening room:

> The lights went out and there flashed upon the screen an emotional passage between Miss Bette Davis and another, but lesser, satellite. Wertzer watched morosely for a moment. "She's getting hammier than ever," he said. "Like they all do. And tough to handle," he added. "They're all the same—actors. Soon as we give them a break, they get tough."

The dashing hero sums up Errol's opinion of acting:

> There was no secret to the mastery of this art, or profession. Unlike other callings, seamanship for instance, it requires a mere modicum of common sense plus, if you have it handy, a little Vitamin B-1 whiskey (short snort).

The uncut manuscript makes fascinating reading. In its passion for the South Seas, its fierce love of sailing, and its evocation of a cruel, despotic studio, it is pure Flynn. The writing is generally bad, modeled very largely on the Australian novelist Norman Lindsay, a favorite of Errol's young manhood. Large chunks are lifted bodily from Lindsay's semi-erotic novels, given a heavier top dressing of description.

Whenever she had time off, Nora would listen, respond to, and write down the story in shorthand, often making suggestions as she typed it.

There is no question that Errol hoped to establish a reputation as a writer with this book. He worked hard and doggedly on it for almost three years. Its complete critical and commercial failure upset him tremendously. And he was furious at the lawyers who made him drop the Hollywood portions.

In April 1943, Errol began work on a new picture, *To the Last Man*, later renamed *Northern Pursuit*. After the second unit returned from Ketchum, Idaho, on April 15, Errol began work at the studio. He had temporarily been in Mexico, staying at the Flamingo Hotel in Acapulco and Zihuatanejo, seen mingling with high-ranking Nazis by FBI agents.

Working on *Northern Pursuit* proved to be problematical. It was a very hot spring. He had to wear heavy furs and fur caps for the scenes of crossing an icy wasteland. Studios in those days were not air-conditioned. The heat was almost unendurable. Cornflakes dipped in gypsum swirled about him as imitation snowflakes, driven by the wind machine. One small flake caught in his nostrils and started an infection which kept him home for two days. At lunch one day, nauseous from the suffocating atmosphere of the sound stage, he ate corned-beef hash. It made him sick, and he had to go home in the middle of the afternoon. Next day, foolishly, he ate the hash again, to see whether the previous day's serving had been poisoned due to deterioration: he hoped to start a lawsuit against the studio. But the joke was on him: there was nothing wrong with the meat, and he was seriously ill once more.

He was in bed for over a week. His old problem of dysentery recurred. Groggy, he made his way back onto the set at the beginning of May, swearing loudly at the discomfort of shooting a blizzard sequence in a temperature of over 110 degrees.

During these weeks, he was faced with a worse problem than his sickness: he received another extortion letter, even more harrowing than the one sent by the thirteen-year-old schoolboy from San Bernardino. The letter was handed to him on the set on April 23. The envelope was postmarked Quincy, Massachusetts, April 23, 1943, 8

P.M., and was addressed to the old North Linden Drive house. On the face of the envelope were printed the words, DO NOT IG-NORE. On the flap was written the one word, BEWARE.

The letter read:

MR. FLYNN!!!!

If you know what is good for you you will pay attention to them girls you raped. I know you did it. You cannot fool me so you better fork over some dough.

Put your answer in the BOSTON DAILY RECORD. Put it near WINCHELL *column* and just say anything but give a hint you received this and in a week if you don't want trouble. Get what I mean chum. Be hearing from you don't forget a week from today. That will be April 29 and then I will send you your instructions on where and when to leave the money and how much. Do not worry it will not be over $15000 for that's all I need to skip town.

The message, unsigned, was printed in very large letters. Errol handed it to Buster Wiles and then called Robert Ford. The Los Angeles field division of the FBI contacted Washington. Hoover advised that precautions be taken to avoid premature publicity and that the Bureau be told of any pertinent developments by telephone.

The FBI in Boston placed an advertisement in the *Boston Daily Record* next to Winchell's column on May 1. It read: "Received your letter, Mr. Flynn."

Meanwhile, police in Quincy, Massachusetts, obtained names of people known to have written similar letters. Fingerprints were taken from the note and compared with others. Everyone waited for a response to Errol's reply in the paper. It was not forthcoming. Then, somebody in Quincy said they had reason to believe that two "neighborhood screwballs" had a tendency to indulge in this kind of extortion practice.

As a result of the information, a man called Robert Street was taken into headquarters in Boston and questioned. He admitted he was on parole from Medfield State Hospital, a mental institution, and was employed as a laborer at a company in South Braintree, Massachusetts. After four hours of grilling he became more and more excitable and hostile, saying that people hated him, that he was an underdog, and that individuals were always trying to "pin things on him" or "bag him." He finally agreed to submit samples of his handwriting and hand printing.

Street admitted later he hated Errol Flynn. He said he was convinced Errol had bribed his way out of the charges against him, that Errol was undoubtedly guilty, and that he hoped to influence Walter Winchell against Errol. But he refused to admit he had penned the note. The note was examined and re-examined alongside the many words written by the suspected man. The two handwritings did not match. Months went by and the case was dropped. Then suddenly there was a break.

In August, the estranged wife of the accused man confessed that she had hand-printed the extortion letter under threat of severe bodily harm from her husband. She told an extraordinary story, evoking a strange world of mentally distorted movie fans, obsessed with and half-hating and envying the stars. She said that Street had come into her room and picked up a movie magazine containing pictures of Errol and said he was sure of Errol's guilt. Mrs. Street argued with him, saying that she was convinced Errol was innocent. They had a furious quarrel.

Street said he needed money and knew a way to get it. He asked his wife if she would write the letter for him. "Who to?" she asked. "To Flynn," he replied. "I'm going to give him my viewpoint of what happened and get dough from him. If you don't write the letter it will be too bad for you."

Street was never prosecuted. The FBI, which had so diligently pursued Errol, let this case of attempted extortion drop. It was as though Hoover wanted Errol but not his enemies.

Throughout the spring of 1943, Errol was frustrated by Nora's continuing refusal to sleep with him. One night, after a party, drugged with cocaine and filled with drink, he was determined to take her virginity.

He managed to negotiate her into the bedroom and stripped off her clothes before she could stop him. He flung off his own. Nora told me in 1978 what happened next:

> I didn't know what was happening. I was terrified. Suddenly he was thrusting into me. It was like a knife. I felt I was being killed. I screamed and screamed. He went on and on. I couldn't push him out. There was blood everywhere. It was on the sheets, on the *wall* . . . Alex came rushing in, convinced there was a killing going on. He was *horrified*. At last, Errol got off me. Later, when he realized

what he had done, he wept and begged forgiveness. He told me, "I didn't know what I was doing. . . ."

Despite this brutal act of rape, Errol won Nora back with his charm, and they began an affair. But he still continued to have relationships with other women. Nora wrote in *Errol and Me:* "I wanted to love Errol to death and then alternately to kill him each time I learned about those other girls."

She and Errol planned a trip to Mexico together, for which Nora had written permission from her parents.

The FBI got wind of the trip. Hoover, evidently smarting because of his failure to pin espionage on Flynn, was determined to entrap him on this occasion. He sent a personal memorandum to the local office saying, "It is desired that all effort be made to ascertain from bank records or otherwise any information which might reflect that subject Flynn pays for his victim's passage to and from Mexico City." The FBI files make clear that Hoover wanted to prosecute Errol on charges of white slave traffic: paying for the passage of a woman for purposes of immoral intercourse across a state border.

The incredible story of Hoover's pursuit of this matter in the middle of a war when his attentions should have been fully occupied elsewhere emerges from well over one hundred documents declassified by the FBI. Agents checked every airline company as soon as Errol told his friends that he was going to Mexico. He flew from Los Angeles with Freddy McEvoy and his new wife, Irene. Agents followed the three of them to Mexico City. Nora followed on August 7, her reservation made by the same travel service. She, too, was followed on the plane, the FBI man sitting behind her.

Errol was seen arriving at Acapulco airport on July 26 and going to Cottage 7 in the Hotel La Riviera. On August 9, Nora arrived in Acapulco and was traced to the hotel. She was assigned Cottage 14.

The entire staff of the hotel was conscripted by the FBI to watch both Errol and Nora. Each of the few guests in the hotel was brought into police headquarters in Acapulco, told of the FBI's purpose, and asked to help watch the lovers.

From that day on, neither Errol nor Nora made a move without being observed. They appear to have been quite unaware of this remarkable fact—and there is even a twist in the story. According to the late actress Mari Blanchard, Errol was having an affair at the same time with a handsome and well-to-do beach boy, Apollonio (named after Apollo) Díaz. The FBI completely neglected to follow Errol to Apollonio Díaz's quarters.

Nora knew nothing of Errol's interest in Apollonio: the idea would have appalled her. To this day she denies that Errol ever slept with a man, and says that homosexuality disgusted him. It is typical of Errol's cynicism and black sense of humor that, as reported in the many FBI reports, Errol, Nora, and Apollonio were seen together constantly. They traveled in Errol's motor launch, known as *Little Sirocco,* fishing and swimming, while Apollonio tended the anchor and performed menial tasks aboard, and spent time at the Acapulco Yacht Club, Los Hornos Beach, and Caletilla Beach.

Errol used a small harpoon propelled by air for fishing underwater and wore a makeshift diving helmet. He used water skis, which were illegal at the time because they were considered dangerous, and the police harassed him over it. This fairly innocent vacation, with its harmless diversions of snorkeling and sunbathing and bar-hopping, was put under such a microscope that even breakfast, lunch, and dinner conversations were recorded by waiters, maids, and busboys who lingered at the tables unnecessarily as they put down dishes or picked up glassware.

Yet despite Hoover's most desperate efforts, nothing immoral could be proven. Every friend Errol had in Mexico was investigated, including those people whom the FBI most wanted to entrap for spying. The astonishing use of time, money, and effort, all to ruin Errol under the provisions of the Mann Act went on relentlessly.

Even when Errol and Nora returned to Hollywood the investigation proceeded. Letters to Errol from a girl in Pennsylvania signed Lois were supposed to be proof of his malfeasance simply because Lois expressed sympathy with him in his fights with the law!

Since nobody had been able to peek through the drapes of either Errol's or Nora's hotel room, and since Apollonio Díaz announced that Errol had not been to bed with Nora, Errol was let off the hook. Or rather, Hoover was unable to fish him on it. Even so, incredibly, the FBI took the entire report to a district court judge in Los Angeles and tried to make the matter stick. They failed and Hoover was forced to abandon the "white slave traffic" charges for good.

In Shanghai in December 1942, Louis Siefken was summarily dismissed by Abwehr and was replaced by the dangerous and powerful Nazi spy Ludwig Ehrhardt. Ehrhardt gave Erben an exceptionally menial and unpleasant task: he planted him in the newly formed Pootung Civil Assembly Center, a filthy and verminous Japanese concentration camp where he was disguised as a Communist German-American garbage collector. Under the pretense of being a special camp employee, he was able to keep in touch with both the Japanese guards and the British and American prisoners, hiding messages in the garbage cans. Whenever he learned of a prisoner's plan to escape, he reported it to his superiors, and the *kempeitei,* the dreaded Japanese police, sent the victim to the bridge house for torturing. He proved so adept at getting information that a plan was hatched to have him pretend to escape with another prisoner to the free-Chinese city of Chungking. The idea was to determine which other escaped prisoners were in that city and what was going on there. But Ehrhardt was worried that Erben might report secrets to the free Chinese instead. So he kept him in Pootung until the end of the war.

In 1978, Erben revealed that Errol wrote to him continually through the war years, that Errol's letters were a great and sustaining joy to him in that period.

The question is, how did those letters reach him? Censorship intercepted every letter mailed from America to enemy or enemy-occupied countries, including those which were sent through the Red Cross. But there was another way he also used, for more important correspondence: through Switzerland, and the Swiss Consul in Shanghai. He sent some letters from Mexico, where they would not be censored. Did they contain intelligence? We may never know—but it is likely. That they very probably did so can be judged by the fact that after the war, Erben risked his life to retrieve them.

Seventeen

In the late summer of 1943, Errol was busy preparing a new picture, *Uncertain Glory,* for his independent outfit, Thomson Productions, named after his father's mother's family.

Based on a real-life incident, it was an intriguing, Simenon-like story of guilt and retribution. A French criminal escapes the guillotine. He is pursued by a dogged Sûreté officer who finally succeeds in capturing him. The convict makes a deal: he will surrender himself to the Nazis, pretending to be a saboteur, in order to save the lives of one hundred hostages. His motive is not unselfish: he has an obsessive dread of decapitation, and prefers the thought of a cleaner death —by a firing squad.

Errol was fascinated by the part, seeing in it a chance to give a performance different from his stereotype. Besides, the criminal Jean Picard was a man he could identify with: a thief and spy, hard, cynical, and contemptuous of authority, especially organized religion, who thinks of any woman as fair bait, and delights in manufacturing tall tales. There is an intriguing self description in Errol's notes. He describes Jean Picard as: "About thirty-six, his features hard, determined, and his body like a tiger's, perpetually poised for flight—or attack if cornered." Errol loved the idea of the deal made by Picard, but decided to add an even more skillful twist to the plot: Picard would renege on his agreement and escape both forms of punishment.

Errol was intrigued by the curious relationship between Picard and his captor, the correct and ruthless officer of the Sûreté, Marcel Bonet. Picard is hard and disillusioned; Bonet is guided by the law and only by the law. Handcuffed together, caught in a struggle of wills, the men discover a curious blend of affection and hatred.

Errol contributed both good and bad ideas to the script. Among his excellent concepts was the opening. Jean is discovered in jail, about to be taken to the guillotine. In the original draft, he was resigned and cynical, ready to lose his head without struggle or rancor; Flynn had Jean be bitter and angry, refusing to have his neck shaved by the prison barber, dismissing the priest and his mumbled prayers with an icy, "Save it for the next one." Errol wanted Bonet, the captor, to be present at the guillotine to make sure his mortal enemy is dead: a marvelously tough idea which the producer, Robert Buckner, rejected.

But Errol's vanity caused him to wreck the last half of the script. Having ingeniously helped to build up the character of Jean, he throws it away in an absurd sentimental resolution in which Jean gives up his life for the sake of an innocent girl. In this, he was influenced by his friend Charlie Chaplin, whose tennis parties he frequently attended and to whom he showed the screenplay.

With Raoul Walsh as director, Errol began shooting the picture in late August. He started it several days late because of sinus trouble, and during the movie itself, he often felt ill, but he managed to be on the set for every day of the shooting, virtually a record for him and fuel to the fire of those who said he was faking when other people were producing.

Deeply admired by François Truffaut, *Uncertain Glory* remains the most fascinating of Flynn's pictures: in its effortlessly realized French milieu, in its extraordinary first half, in which both Flynn and Paul Lukas as his captor are especially fine; and in the intelligent, bitter writing, with its subtle comments on human duplicity, much of which Errol can be said to be responsible for.

But the public didn't like this new "serious" Errol. The picture flopped.

At the same time, Errol was charged by a young girl with being the father of her child, and he narrowly escaped a paternity suit.

All through the statutory rape trial, District Attorney Cochran had kept another rabbit firmly concealed in his hat: a girl named Shirley Evans Hassau who claimed that Errol had made her pregnant in the spring of 1940, had promised to support her daughter, and had failed to do so. Cochran had thought of adding Miss Hassau as a possible third plaintiff in the rape trial itself, but had omitted her because of some weaknesses in her story.

When charged with her statement that he had had intercourse with her in the front of his car, Errol had dismissed the idea with a laugh, saying that there "wasn't sufficient room." He had neglected to mention that the front passenger seat of his automobile lowered into a bed.

Shirley's daughter, Marilyn, had lived with her grandmother and aunt in San Francisco since her birth, traveling to see her mother once a month. On one occasion, Shirley managed to induce Errol to see the child, which he instantly said was "too unattractive to be his own." Nevertheless, since he was afraid of her public statement, he paid Shirley the two thousand dollars she demanded for expenses and five hundred dollars for the cost of the baby's birth.

There, it seemed, the matter was at an end. But early in October 1943, Shirley Hassau's determined mother and aunt tried to attach all Errol's property, and warned that unless he surrendered his home, savings, and real estate holdings, they would make a public spectacle of him.

Errol and Giesler went into a lengthy conference. They had an ace in the hole: the fact that Shirley had no access to her baby except once a month suggested that her mother and aunt did not consider her a fit mother for the child and had virtually adopted it. Giesler's sleuths discovered that Shirley and her relatives had been fighting violently. Shirley had virtually abandoned her baby to her aunt, who had been so disgusted with her behavior she had locked Shirley out of the residential hotel apartment where the aunt lived. In return, Shirley had accused her mother and aunt of mistreating Marilyn.

Errol refused to pay off the mother and aunt. As a result, the district attorney moved against him, and on October 17, he was brought before Superior Court Judge William S. Baird to show cause why he should not pay the Hassau family $17,000 in legal and medical expenses and $1,750 a month for Marilyn. Errol answered boldly, "This is a lie. I will fight this charge to the bitter end." Judge Baird ordered him to go to San Francisco for a blood test.

Errol made the journey, only to discover that his blood type was the same as that of Shirley and the child so that there was no proof either way. The case was temporarily dropped, but only after Errol had handed several people substantial checks. It was not finally let go until 1953, when it was withdrawn "for lack of sufficient prosecution."

Late in 1943, Errol had a different kind of an escapade. He was at a party in honor of Gloria Vanderbilt in Manhattan, with Freddy McEvoy and Johnny Meyer. During the swirl of conversation, he noticed a pretty, eighteen-year-old boy with a cherubic face and a slender, well-made figure. He was deeply attracted. He went over and talked to the boy, asking him what he did for a living. "My name is Truman Capote," the boy replied. "I'm trying to be a writer and I'm living on Gramercy Park."

Around midnight, Errol invited Truman to El Morocco, where Errol's friend John Perona was having a late-night party for friends.

Truman accepted, but the two men had barely reached the lobby when Errol took a deep breath and said, "Let's forget about El Morocco. Why don't we go to your place?"

Truman explained he lived in a tiny walkup. Errol didn't care. So long as there was a bed, it would be all right.

They spent an enjoyable night; Errol didn't leave until noon the next day.

Years later, Marilyn Monroe asked Truman whether he enjoyed it. He shrugged. "If it hadn't been Errol Flynn, I wouldn't even have remembered it," he said.

Partly to escape yet another summons from Lili for failure to meet his alimony payments, and partly to bury his image as a draft dodger (many would not believe his studio's "heart murmur" story), Errol in late October accepted an offer to tour Alaskan army bases as part of a vaudeville show in which he appeared with Martha O'Driscoll, Harry Mendoza, Ruth Carroll, and Jimmy Dodd. He enjoyed being in front of a live audience again, some eleven years after the Northampton Repertory Company, and brought the house down each time with his standard opening: "There were thousands of people waiting to see me off at the airport. (Pause) Most of them were lawyers!" He was usually followed onto the stage by comedian Harry Mendoza dressed as Jerry Giesler, with well-chewed glasses and rumpled, dark suit, and delivering Errol a writ charging him with having had sexual intercourse with a girl at the airport just before the plane left. "Oh yes, I remember her," Errol would say. "She was the one I visited with behind the tail of the plane when the engine started up." The audience of GIs screamed with laughter.

In May 1944, just before Errol's new picture, *Objective, Burma!*, was due to start shooting, Nora had missed another period. She recalls in her memoirs that she was terrified to tell Errol the truth; and when she did, he coolly suggested that she should make arrangements to have an abortion. She flatly refused.

Nora returned to Mexico in the summer of 1944 so that Errol would not have to be present during the pregnancy. Meanwhile, her father and stepmother were in the peculiar position of not knowing whether their own daughter was married or not. Eight months after the supposed marriage took place, Jack Eddington, who had left the sheriff's office to become a petty officer in the Navy, was calling Jim Fleming constantly at Mulholland Farm, and even visiting with him, nagging him to find out about the marriage arrangements. But Jim Fleming had not been told, and his reply to the Eddingtons and the columnists was that even though Nora was pregnant, the question of her marriage had not yet been resolved. The marriage, according to *Errol and Me*, took place by proxy in Mexico in September 1944.

While Nora was conveniently out of the way in Mexico, *Objective, Burma!*—the story of American paratroopers landing in Burma for an operation against the Japanese—went into production. It was a studio, not a Thomson production. Errol was alternating studio pictures with his own. Errol enjoyed a dark laugh or two at the interferences of the Breen office with the script: even the word "lousy" was forbidden, none of the soldiers was allowed to talk about a "helluva" betting, or have the "bejesus" beaten out of them. The result was that hard-bitten paratroopers were made to talk like choirboys. It was laughable, but Errol became exhausted with the struggle of trying to make the story work.

He suggested two ideas, both of which were acted on. He wanted the introduction of a journalist, played by Henry Hull, attached to the parachute troop to obtain a story for his newspapers. Errol also wanted the central figure he played, the major, to have had a background of fighting in New Guinea. This nostalgic touch helped him to give the part more conviction. But he made a serious mistake. Instead of taking vocal lessons to master the convincing American accent he needed, he resorted for no discernible reason to a horrible Australian drawl which wrecked the authenticity of his playing.

He had cause to regret *Objective, Burma!* The scenes of the parachutists wading through a Burmese swamp were shot in marshy ground near the Santa Anita racetrack near Los Angeles. Errol and the other players spent many days in the brackish water with their heavy gear—an ugly experience in the sticky heat, with mosquitoes and flies whirling about their heads. Errol's tennis playing had caused him sacroiliac problems, and the damp affected his sinuses. When the company shifted to an imitation jungle in Whittier Park, conditions were even more fetid, humid, and insufferable than they had been in Santa Anita.

On June 19, after seven solid weeks of swamp and jungle, something snapped. Because of his own experience in New Guinea, Errol could endure the physical problems but he couldn't cope with the fact that the script still wasn't finished and that the pages supplied from day to day gave him no characterization to work with, just a series of snapped commands and grim marches. He refused to report for work unless his part was improved. He told production manager Frank Mattison: "Mattie, I'm just walking through this goddamn picture. Or *wading,* if you like. Not a bloody thing has happened since this picture started except routine dialogue and walking, walking, walking." He went home on June 20, his birthday, and stayed in bed until June 26, when Raoul Walsh finally persuaded him to return to work. But the next day, he came down with a severe case of pleurisy and undulant fever.

By June 29, he was very sick. His back was agonizing, his bladder malfunctioned, and he was in the grip of high fever. Raoul Walsh shot around him, achieving miracles with Buster Wiles as his double and Jim Fleming as his stand-in.

Then, on July 9, Errol noticed bleeding when he defecated; he panicked that he might have cancer, and Dr. Frank Nolan arranged for him to have a barium test. There was a grueling wait for the results. Once again, Alex recalls, he contemplated suicide, looking into the muzzle of a gun in his bedroom for hours. Finally, he decided to face up to whatever problems lay ahead.

It was a lucky decision. Dr. Nolan called to tell him that all he had was a bad case of internal piles aggravated by the heat and the humidity. He was consoled by a fallacy he believed in: after all, hadn't piles been the irritant that produced Napoleon's victories?

He struggled back to the strictly un-Napoleonic campaign in Whittier Park. The trees were so dense the day he returned that light could not penetrate and nothing could be shot. Groaning at the futility of picture-making, he sat down on a tree stump and lit a cigarette. "I'd like to burn up the whole fucking studio with this," he said, looking at the match until it charred his fingers.

One consolation of the shooting was that he made a new friend in the warm and outgoing young Paul McWilliams, a stuntman who was the son of the studio's beloved First Aid boss, "Doc" McWilliams. Paul McWilliams says:

> We'd all catch crawdads for Raoul Walsh the many days Errol was sick. Sometimes we'd sit for hours waiting for Errol to turn up. We didn't mind. We'd much rather fish for crawdads than work on the picture.

On August 6, Errol was bedridden again. The shooting of the tortuous picture had gone on for almost fifteen weeks. It was twenty-six days behind schedule because of Errol's sickness and because of fog and rain, both of which were entirely out of season. Sinus trouble caused Errol's face to swell in many of the shots. Buster Wiles and Jim Fleming rebelled against the terrible conditions and refused to work for several days.

On August 17, the company had to move to a mountain location. Errol insisted they use the mountain near his home on Mulholland Drive to make his movements easier. A doctor gave him Vitamin B-1 shots to help him pull through. Dr. Nolan painfully lanced the hemorrhoids when they refused to respond to ice-shrinkage treatments.

In great pain, Errol struggled along for several more weeks, but *Objective, Burma!* wasn't finally finished until October. It had taken six months to shoot, an insufferable ordeal. And it turned out to be the greatest embarrassment of Errol's career.

When the picture opened in London in mid-September 1945, it

Errol (left) with crew at sea on *Sirocco*, 1940. (Courtesy of Al Wetzel)

Two Nazi spies: Hermann Erben and Ignatius Trebitsch Lincoln (Abbot Chao Kung). Photograph by the late Albert von Miorini (murdered 1944) Shanghai, 1942 (Charles Higham Collection)

Jerry Giesler, Peggy Satterlee, and Errol at the rape trial, 1943. (Courtesy of Larry Horn)

With Nora Flynn on the yacht *Zaca*, 1946. (Wide World Photos)

Errol in his home with portrait by John Decker. (Photo by Bert Six)

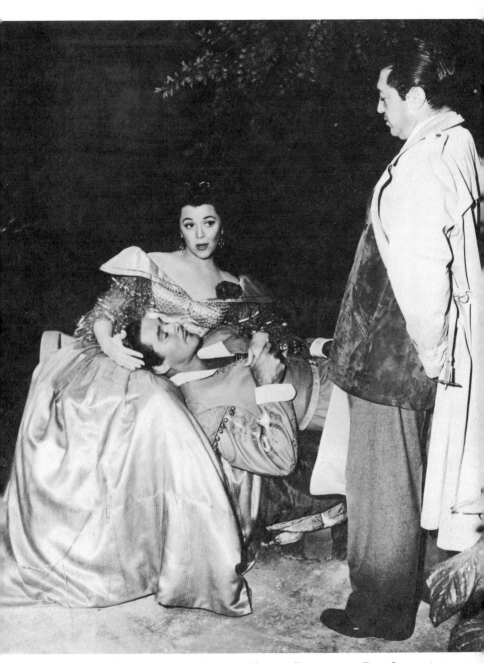

With Ann Rutherford and director Vincent Sherman on *Don Juan* set,
1948. (*Adventures of Don Juan,* Copyright ©, 1949, Warner Bros. Pictures, Inc., Renewal ©, 1976, United Artists Television, Inc., all rights
reserved)

Jim Fleming, Errol's devoted friend and stand-in, and Errol, 1948.

With his second wife, Nora Flynn, 1948. (Wide World Photos)

In *That Forsyte Woman*, 1949. (From the MGM release *That Forsyte Woman* © 1949. Copyright renewed 1976 by Metro-Goldwyn-Mayer, Inc.)

was subjected to a harsh attack by the British press, furious that the script omitted anything except a token opening reference to the achievements of the British Fourteenth Army in Burma. The influential C. A. Lejeune of the London *Observer* and Campbell Dixon of the London *Daily Telegraph* both denounced the film. Dixon wrote that it was "well made, well acted . . . and well nigh intolerable." Other reviews were equally damaging: "ERROL FLYNN WINS WAR IN BURMA" one headline read. Asked by the British Broadcasting Corporation to make a public statement when Warner Brothers protested against its treatment, United States Army Air Force Lieutenant Colonel William H. Taylor said, "As one of the Americans who, contrary to the film, were in the minority in these particular operations, privileged to fight alongside our Allies in Burma, I am embarrassed by the implications of this film."

Angry crowds gathered outsided the Warner Theatre in Leicester Square in the West End of London urging prospective patrons not to go in.

Max Milder, managing executive of Warners in Great Britain, almost immediately withdrew the picture.

In Hollywood, Errol did not know whether to laugh or cry over the incident. He had already written the picture off in his mind.

In the fall of 1944, Errol traveled to Mexico to see Nora, who was in the company of Freddy McEvoy and his second wife, Irene ("Puppy") Wrightsman. According to Nora's book, she and Errol had a brief romantic idyll in Acapulco which oddly echoes his previous dalliance with Linda Christian under almost identical circumstances with the McEvoys.

He had previously used morphine largely as an experiment when it became available through the doctor he knew at the San Diego Naval Base, and its effect on him was chiefly to subdue the genteel surface, the cultivated mask of his nature, and unleash the more primitive forces within. Now he took morphine more regularly, the pain in his back and the hemorrhoids, despite the lancing, causing him to need the drug on a daily basis. Former bandleader Teddy Stauffer, who often escorted Nora and entertained her in his nightclub in Mexico City, remembers that after morphine injections, Errol became a terrifying monster, a Hyde peeping out frighteningly from the smooth Dr. Jekyll face. He also took more cocaine and marijuana, fancying that they helped his sinus trouble; in fact, the co-caine ate away at the mucous membrane of his nose.

Friends of Errol in Mexico testify that Nora's account of a sublime "honeymoon" on the Mexican shore was inspired more by love and loyalty than by accuracy. However warmly Nora may have tried to portray it, their relationship suffered profoundly from Errol's failure to commit himself to her.

But she kept her suffering to herself. When interviewers called from Hollywood or New York to ask Nora about Errol, she invaria-bly said that he must not be "trapped," that he was a free spirit who "mustn't be restrained." She told Louella Parsons for *Photoplay* magazine: "A wife who demanded a conventional life would become like an iron chain to him. I couldn't bear that. I cannot think of any other man. I can't believe I will love like this again. Don't make Errol a heavy or blame him. There aren't any heavies in our story." But he still was the heavy in his attitude toward her.

Errol returned to Hollywood to work on a new Western, *San Antonio,* at the beginning of September 1944. Errol continued to detest the idea of making Westerns, convinced that he was far too "British" and cultivated for the genre, and his only interest in the picture was that he learned to play the guitar for it, in a number called "Put Your Little Foot Out."

Errol's friend and co-star, Alexis Smith, was absent during most of the shooting, first because she had a mysterious virus ailment that dragged on for weeks, second because she had to shoot sequences for another picture, *The Horn Blows at Midnight.* Errol tried to help Butler by knowing his lines ("We'd better not slap him on the back," read a chilly report by production manager Frank Mattison, "because it may not happen again") and by managing to be present on the set every day. But after two months of monotonous work, he caught a severe cold, followed by influenza, on the damp, miserable location of the Warner ranch. He was ill through part of November, and refused to take the risk of coming out in the icy rain and chilly dark days; he did struggle to a party on December 8 for Colonel Roosevelt and Roosevelt's bride, but collapsed, gray and trembling, before the party was over, and had to be driven home. The big cli-max of the picture, a free-for-all fight, had to be delayed until De-cember 18, almost four months after shooting began. Errol was so sick during the shooting of the fight that most of his shots had to be doubled by Buster Wiles; the scene took twelve days to shoot, and much of it had to be redone before the picture could be released.

Errol suffered from another vexation at the time. Early in 1944, producer Jerry Wald had dreamed up a scheme to make a picture about Don Juan, with Errol playing the lead. Errol was only moderately interested in the idea and refused to commit himself to the project until a satisfactory screenplay was worked out. During Errol's bout of illness on *San Antonio,* Wald drove over to Mulholland Farm to confer with him. They agreed that of the three scripts Wald had, Harold Goldman's was the most workable, and Errol suggested some witty lines and situations.

After Wald left, Errol sat up late at night with a pencil and note pad and several books on Don Juan, trying to note down new plot twists and surprises. He became convinced that the subject was too loose and unfocused to make a good movie and decided to call Jerry the next day to let him know his reaction. Next morning, he was horrified when he picked up the trade papers and saw announced *Adventures of Don Juan,* starring Errol Flynn, to be produced by Jerry Wald, and directed by Robert Florey, would begin production on the first of the new year. Errol was unable to reach either Wald or Jack Warner.

He telephoned Tenny Wright, the studio manager: "I haven't said yes to this project yet. I should have been given official word from Trilling [Steve Trilling, head of production at Warners] or Jack Warner. And then there's the director. Florey isn't right for this picture. And I don't want Fred Cavens to teach me to fence. He's too old-fashioned. I want Aldo Naldi, the Italian champ."

"Naldi," Tenny replied, "is an arrogant son-of-a-bitch. He created nothing but trouble when he was at Paramount."

"If I'm going to do this goddamn picture, I want Raoul Walsh to direct it and Naldi to work on the fencing with me." Errol paused a moment. "If you give me Walsh and Naldi, when do you want me?"

"The first of the year," Tenny Wright said.

Errol snapped back: "I won't be available. Nora's having her baby in Mexico. I won't be here between January 15 and February 1. So don't get any ideas I will be!" Errol slammed the receiver down.

Later that night, Tenny Wright reached Jerry Wald at home and told him what Errol had said. Jerry called Errol close to midnight and said, "Okay, we'll give you Raoul and try for Naldi. We start fencing rehearsals in three weeks." Errol grumblingly agreed to report for work but only on condition Naldi was hired. He also insisted upon script approval.

Errol left for a Caribbean vacation the next day. Although he flew through Miami, he made no attempt to see his son Sean in Palm Beach. He arrived in Jamaica on New Year's Eve. He read the script, found it unsatisfactory, and spent most of his time skin diving for sunken treasure near Port Royal.

He was shocked to find most of the island devastated by the hurricane of August 20. He seized the occasion to buy real estate, including the tiny Navy Island, in partnership with Stephen Raphael. Many white settlers had left following the hurricane and were disposing of land at very reasonable prices.

He had loved Jamaica in 1937, and now he loved it again. He delighted in his stay at a wonderful old Somerset Maugham hotel, the Titchfield, a relic of Empire days. Wooden ceiling fans revolved slowly, barely disturbing the air of the wooden-walled, fern-and-aspidistra-filled rooms.

Most of the people in the hotel were old colonels and their dowager wives: faded ghosts of the past. In their midst, Errol was delighted to find a marvelous old empress of a prostitute, with dyed red hair, garish makeup, and green and red beads tumbling over her ample bosom. She would sail like a galleon through the public rooms, fixing everyone balefully with her monocled eye.

The hurricane had battered the hotel, ripping off many of the rattan blinds and making a hole in the roof. He snapped it up for very little four years later.

Errol was fascinated by many things in Jamaica. He loved the emerald mountains, with jungle growth crowding up their sides; the winding dirt roads with their dazzling views of the Caribbean; the sapphire-colored moon which sometimes occurred just before twilight after a burst of rain; hunting wild hogs in the highlands; chasing the Pedro seal; shooting alligators; or simply listening, rum drink in hand, to the song of the nightingale or the faint murmuring of the Mountain Witch dove. The rivers were stocked with mullet; there was fine deep-sea fishing for marlin; there were romantic cotton trees, bamboo and coconut palm; the blaze of poinciana and bougainvillea, and the taste of fresh breadfruit, guava, mango, and avocado. Jamaica was everything Errol's beloved New Guinea should have been and was not: a paradise. All he wanted was to move there eventually and to build an estate high up overlooking the ocean.

Eighteen

Errol felt that it was painful, after this glorious trip, to face up to the reality of flying to Mexico City to be with Nora for the birth of their child on January 10, 1945. From the glamour and exoticism of Jamaica he had to enter the sterile, heartless world of the hospital where Nora's screams of pain were so terrible he was unable to endure them. He demanded the doctors give her something to ease her agony, and when they refused, he punched one of them in the nose. Two powerful orderlies flung him almost literally into the street.

Nora's severe pains were caused by the fact that she was small-framed and thin and that the baby was an enormous twelve pounds. At last the ordeal ended at 10:50 P.M. on the tenth. It was a girl. She was not only plump but very pretty, with her mother's red hair. Errol and Nora had agreed she would be called Deirdre.

Something in Deirdre awakened Errol's feeling of being a father. In spite of himself, he was thrilled by the sight of his daughter. Yet he was still as frighteningly heartless as always toward Nora. When a reporter called him from Los Angeles the same day asking if he was married, he said, "No comment, except to observe that this makes the third or fourth time I've been 'married' in the last couple of years. At this rate I don't see how I could fail to cop the bigamy award of 1945."

Nora was horrified when she read this in print. While breast-feeding Deirdre, she announced that not only was she married to Errol but would very soon be divorcing him.

Nora arrived in Hollywood with Deirdre in the middle of March. Errol was ill with a recurrence of undulant fever at the time and so was not present to greet her. Instead of inviting her to Mulholland Farm, he seemed coolly satisfied to have her go instead to the apartment rented by her father and stepmother, and contented himself with talking to her on the telephone.

On March 24, he suddenly experienced an impulse to see his child. He asked Alex to pick up Nora and Deirdre and drive them over to Mulholland Farm. He managed to struggle into a sitting position and inspected the baby with fascination. Nora and Deirdre stayed an hour, until Errol lapsed into a restless sleep.

Later that night, he called Nora to tell her he had decided not to go ahead with the divorce on which they had agreed. His motive, probably, was a desire to keep Deirdre. Would Nora come back to him?

Nora gave a confusing series of interviews in the next few days. Sometimes she said she would divorce Errol, sometimes she said she would not. On April 9, she told the Los Angeles *Times,* "All love is gone. Whatever I felt for him has vanished completely. What I want now is a job. I'll file for a divorce, right here in Hollywood."

He persuaded her once again to change her mind. Eleven days later, he flung a surprise luncheon at the farm to introduce his "new bride" to his friends. Surprisingly, she came. Yet the next day, Nora told a reporter, "The marriage with Flynn was the result of a girlish infatuation which cooled soon after we were married. I now feel a divorce would be best for all concerned."

She seemed not to know her own mind, any more than Errol knew his.

One week later, David O. Selznick threw a party at his house in the San Fernando Valley for Errol and Nora to meet more of the great figures of Hollywood. Among the guests was John Huston, the

famous director of *The Maltese Falcon,* who was a major in the
United States Signal Corps. Huston made a slighting remark about
Errol's previous fascination with Olivia de Havilland. Flynn asked
him to step outside.

The two men fought violently in the back yard. Errol was easily
the victor. He beat Huston so thoroughly that a doctor had to be
called, his lacerations so severe they required two stitches in an eye-
brow and two in a lip. Errol nursed a black eye but was otherwise
unscathed.

Not long afterward, Nora and Errol were seeing each other again.
Errol held a "mouse derby" at Mulholland Farm. He and Marge Eddington sat up for several nights working out the scratch sheet. One
mouse had the name El Nora, who was described as "slow to get
started, but excellent in the final stretches." Another mouse was
called Tiger Lil, after Lili Damita. Errol described her as "running
best with money on the nose. Especially mine." Various other mice
were named after women he had known. They all had tiny saddles
with colors illustrative of Errol's humor. El Nora's was green for jealousy, Tiger Lil's was scarlet for rage, and Linda Christian's known
as El Linda, was white with red spots. Errol refused to explain why.
A program was prepared covering the entire race. Errol's favorite
was El Nora. To make sure she came in first, he placed a thin copper
strip the whole length of her run, and attached a tiny electrical device which at the imperceptible pressure of a finger caused an electric shock to run along the copper. Inevitably, El Nora was the
champion of every contest.

That year, Errol started alterations to Mulholland Farm that cost
more than the house itself. He designed an elaborate guest bedroom,
which he sometimes used himself, with an adjoining screening room.
The screening room was used for Warner Brothers pictures "borrowed" from the studio, cartoons for Deirdre—and for pornographic
films. Errol told Jim Fleming he wanted a two-way mirror running
up the wall beside the bed so that guests could watch selected couples making love. Fleming pointed out that the arrangement of the
room did not allow for this. Instead, Jim suggested a two-way mirror
over the bed. A special room was constructed above this device, so
that guests could watch the sexual acrobatics below.

The first to volunteer was Bruce Cabot, who was proud of his powerful physique and sexual staying power. Errol and Jim Fleming and others peered through the glass as Cabot climbed onto a selected woman. They clapped loudly at the moment of orgasm. Sometimes, Jim Fleming would call the famous Los Angeles madam, Lee Francis, and have groups of whores shipped up to the house at great expense. Each man in Errol's circle would have to perform with the whores in turn, with a prize for the man who climaxed last.

Then Errol would perform. Despite (or perhaps because of) his constant drug taking, he was remarkably virile in his thirties. His male friends recall that he enjoyed showing off exceedingly hard and sustained erections and could hold back from an orgasm for over an hour. He was a practiced master of oral sex.

In view of these activities, Errol installed Nora at a separate address. She moved into a house on Cordell Drive above the Sunset Strip, a modest residence which she shared with her parents. Sometimes, she would go up to Mulholland Farm and spend blissful evenings with Errol. Once again, he strove to teach her subtle points of art, music, and literature. But these evenings were rare. Jim Fleming recalls that Errol "beat the bejesus out of Nora" on several occasions. He couldn't change.

In view of his nocturnal activities it isn't surprising that Errol looked tired and pale in *Don Juan* fencing rehearsals with Fred Cavens, whom he had been unable to dislodge in favor of Aldo Naldi. For six weeks, he half-heartedly went ahead with this training, and then, much to his relief, Jack Warner postponed the entire production. Warner felt that with no satisfactory script and the dissatisfaction of his star, the massive costs of such a production would not be justified. Moreover, there was dissension in the craft unions and a sudden strike. It had become an inopportune moment for the studio's biggest historical epic since *Robin Hood*.

With *Don Juan* tabled, it was unclear what Errol would do next. He had been offered another Western, *Cheyenne,* for his own Thomson Productions, but, disliking Westerns as always, had refused even to read it. By the terms of his deal with Warners, the second script sent by the studio to Thomson Productions could not be refused by him. With an impish sense of humor that matched Errol's own, Jack Warner had no sooner received *Cheyenne* back by messenger than he sent the same messenger off again to Mulholland Farm with another Western: *The Frontiersman,* about the early riverboat gamblers. To add insult to injury, this was a property Errol had turned down the previous year.

Warner insisted he begin work on the picture within five days of receiving the script: on May 14, 1945.

Errol decided to outwit Warner. The script called for the use of two riverboats. He discovered that only two such boats existed in California. One of them had sunk in an accident and lay at the bottom of the Sacramento River. (Warner told a friend he was convinced Errol had sabotaged it by fixing up a bomb in the engine.) The other was on the San Joaquin River. He suggested to a friend at Republic Pictures that they snap up the boat for a gambling story they were preparing before Warners could get hold of it. As a result, Warners had nothing to work with and the picture was canceled.

Because it would not involve hard work, Errol arranged to star in a comedy for Thomson Productions entitled *Never Say Goodbye.* Once again, Errol's sense of humor asserted itself. Not only did the title ironically summarize his marriage to Nora, the story itself dealt with a married couple unhappy and at odds with each other, who are brought together and have their marriage saved by the love of their little daughter. Errol walked through the picture in seeming high spirits, lacing it with impromptu lines referring to his relationship with Nora.

That summer, he sold the *Sirocco,* which had lain inactive since the trial, to a gas-station owner. He began plans to buy another yacht, the 118-foot *Zaca,* originally sailed on scientific expeditions in the 1930s by its owner, the banker Templeton Crocker. Ironically, in the war, *Zaca* had been used by the navy as a listening post, to pick up signals that might indicate a Japanese submarine attack on the mainland. The boat was so run down that she was available for a mere thirty thousand dollars after V-E Day. Errol and Hayward Kingsley made a thorough inspection of the hull to make sure she was seaworthy. She was, but Errol made such a fuss about imaginary problems below the waterline that the San Francisco naval authorities let him have the boat for twenty thousand dollars.

Kingsley and a scratch crew sailed *Zaca* south to Newport, where Kingsley grounded the handsome craft on a mud bank. She lay there until the tide finally loosened her. Furiously calling Kingsley a "dry land skipper" Errol handed the vessel over to Jim Fleming and told him to make *Zaca* one of the finest vessels on the coast.

It cost eighty thousand dollars to refurbish her. Fleming worked tirelessly with the decorators. The master cabin had a king-sized bed with a mirror facing it to reflect lovemaking, and rich drapes and carpets. The saloon was furnished with handsome sofas, tables, and lamps, and the bulkheads were lined with mahogany. There were mirrors and paintings everywhere. The bathroom had a glass-enclosed tub. The forecastle slept a crew of twelve. There was a magnificent galley with pinewood closets, sinks, stove, and a deep-freeze unit. The radio room over the engine room was cleverly redesigned. Unlike *Sirocco,* the *Zaca* had a fine freeboard; she drew about sixteen feet loaded. She flew a flag embellished with a large scarlet cockerel and the name *Zaca* underneath. Those who said "cock" and the name of the vessel very fast to Errol's instructions invariably wound up looking embarrassed.

The war was over and along with it Errol's profits from McEvoy's U-boat refueling scheme and from his own high-level Nazi contacts in America and Mexico.

The returning heroes among the stars accepted his "heart condition" as a genuine reason for his not serving, but many of them were more than a little wary of his lack of evident patriotism.

In 1944, Erben's old friend, Albert von Miorini, was poisoned to death with bamboo shoots by the Nazis at a dinner party in Shanghai. After he was released from Pootung Camp, Erben was put to work in a United States Government malarial control unit as a poison-spray man. At the end of 1945, he was arrested for treason and placed in Ward Road Jail. Captain Frank Farrell, former *World-Telegram* columnist, war hero, and OSS Counterintelligence Chief, was told by his friend Baron von Reichenau that Erben would make an ideal informer, that he "had the survival instincts of a cockroach" and would do anything to save himself from being hanged as a traitor. Farrell arranged for Erben's release and granted him immunity from further prosecution in return for his help in flushing out every member of the Shanghai spy ring.

Farrell met Erben in his lodgings. He was astonished when Erben boasted of being Errol Flynn's close friend. Erben, pale now, with iron-gray hair, wearing smoked glasses, turned to a typewriter and tapped out a list of names to prove he was telling the truth: Jim Fleming. Max Carmel. Buster Wiles. Robert Ford. Johnny Meyer. Mulholland Farm.

Farrell didn't know it, but Erben had made a slip. Buster Wiles didn't join Errol until *They Died with Their Boots On* in September 1941. Robert Ford didn't become Errol's attorney until December 1942. Mulholland Farm was neither named nor finished until after Pearl Harbor. Thus, it was easy to see that Erben had been receiving mail from Errol after March 1940 when he arrived in China.

On April 20, 1946, Freddy McEvoy was arrested in Miami and charged with extorting two hundred thousand dollars from Beatrice Cartwright four years after their divorce. And Errol was named in the charge.

The trouble began when, on April 15, Henry Rogers Benjamin, Beatrice's brother, wealthy socialite and Standard Oil executive and heir, made a detailed report to J. Edgar Hoover in person. He charged that since the divorce, Freddy and Errol, along with a Nazi count in New York and a New York attorney, had put Beatrice on drugs and played on her sympathies to get her to change her will in favor of Freddy, leaving him her villa on the Mediterranean, her yacht, and two hundred thousand dollars.

Errol flew to Miami and bribes in the right places resulted in Freddy's release and his and Freddy's exoneration. It was a very close call.

With the war over, Freddy McEvoy began to run short of money. He had squandered his wartime profits at the gambling tables in Las Vegas and Reno. As a result, he shifted his base semi-permanently to Miami, where, separated from his second wife, Irene, he ran drugs for Errol through the islands to Bermuda and Europe.

Nineteen

Early in 1946, Errol was closely in touch with his father in Ireland. Professor Flynn wanted to organize an expedition together with Professor Carl Hubbs of the Scripps Oceanographic Institution of La Jolla to collect marine specimens off the coast of Baja California and Mexico. Errol needed a tax write-off on the *Zaca* for 1946, and the expedition would justify this. Moreover, he wanted to get away from the studio for several months. He decided to extend the expedition to include the Galapagos Islands and the Panama Canal, the Caribbean, his beloved Jamaica, and Europe—make it a trip of at least six to seven months. He was hoping that the sunken riverboat on the Sacramento River would not be salvaged for use in *The Frontiersman* and that the second boat would be kept in use by film crews from other studios. He got his wish.

From February through May 1946, with Nora living on Cordell and Lili in Beverly Hills, Errol saw little of either. He was working out the itinerary for the voyage, corresponding with his father in Ireland and conferring with Professor Hubbs and Professor Edward Zobell at Scripps.

In order to obtain money for the expedition, he borrowed heavily on future earnings from the studio, and hastily agreed to do his third Thomson Production: *Cry Wolf* directed by Peter Godfrey. The character he played was very similar to that of his own father: a professor of chemistry who enjoyed a pipe and wore horn-rims and had an oddly eccentric surface concealing a more amorous nature underneath.

He made the picture in the summer of 1946.

On July 29, Professor Flynn arrived in Los Angeles. He was alone. At Errol's request, Marelle had been excluded from the trip and had gone instead to visit with her sister in Maine. Looking very much like Leslie Howard in his fifties, the handsome professor smiled faintly at the large crowd of reporters at the depot as Errol posed with him for the photographs.

That night, Professor Flynn met Nora, and his granddaughter Deirdre. He hit it off with Nora immediately, telling Errol she was "lovely, and you should take care of her." He was shocked to find Nora was living at a separate address, and upbraided Errol for his indifference. There was some tension between father and son over the situation, and the professor was not amused when Errol reminded him of the days in Hobart when he had been "a married bachelor."

In the first two weeks of August, Errol assembled his crew. Hayward Kingsley was about to retire and did not want to go on the voyage. His place as captain was taken by a man of Scandinavian extraction, Toivo Wicklund. Unfortunately, Errol did not support Wicklund with a particularly good crew. He was more interested in cutting costs than in finding experienced sailors. However, under great pressure from Professor Hubbs, he agreed to add a young man named Robert P. Vincent, as ship's carpenter, first class, and as a diver after specimens.

Errol engaged a director of documentaries, Chuck Gross, and a very good photographer, Jerry Courneya, to make a film of the expedition. He planned to use some of it as background for a movie entitled *Treasure in Yucatan* in which he would co-star with Nora.

He asked John Decker to accompany him on the voyage to paint marine specimens. Teddy Stauffer arrived from Mexico to act as as-

sociate cameraman and to write an illustrated article for fan magazines in Hollywood and Mexico. Howard Hill was brought along to
assist in hunting animals and fish. Nora was the only woman aboard
—she would help supervise the cooking. It was brave of her to go—
she was pregnant with her second child.

The famous screenwriter and wit Nunnally Johnson heard about
the expedition. He was in the middle of scripting a movie called *Mr.
Peabody and the Mermaid.* Nunnally sent a telegram to Errol in care
of the *Zaca,* Newport Harbor: DEAR ERROL: AM LOOKING FOR A
MERMAID FOR MY NEXT PICTURE. KEEP YOUR EYES OPEN. IF YOU SEE
ONE PLEASE SHIP HER COLLECT TO ME. And he also sent a telegram
to Professor Flynn at the same address reading: IF YOU FIND A
MERMAID ON YOUR EXPEDITION PLEASE KEEP AN EYE ON ERROL.

To provide entertainment at night, Errol obtained prints of his favorite films from the Warner 16mm library. Among these were *Now,
Voyager; Kings Row; Jezebel; The Man Who Came to Dinner; Yankee Doodle Dandy; Action in the North Atlantic;* and the movie of
his own he liked best, *Gentleman Jim.* He also added several shorts,
including *All-Star Melody Master Bands; Borrah Minevitch and His
Harmonica Rascals;* and *Fight Fish Fight;* as well as a Howard Hill
archery short done as a Pete Smith Specialty for MGM in 1938. He
"borrowed" these prints; needless to say, they were never returned.
He also "borrowed" clothes from wardrobe for the trip, and these
met the same fate. They were part of a steadily growing collection of
suits, shirts, ties, and even shoes that he had made off with over the
years.

Professor Hubbs obtained a large and a small dredge with mesh
bag and protective chains; a 135-foot beach seine; two long-handle
dip nets; a submarine lamp; two lobster traps; lobster buoys; a metal
and wood water glass for the skiff; a small photographic aquarium;
and a 1,300-pound scale. Jim Fleming prepared the food and liquor,
and large amounts of ice for the ice chest. Courneya and Gross provided microscopic lenses for the underwater cameras, and Errol installed lighted tanks where the behavior of marine specimens could
be studied. He obtained 26,000 feet of 16mm film for scientific
study, and 10,000 feet of 35mm black and white film for *Treasure in
Yucatan.* He also made sure through his contacts in Mexico that

when the *Zaca* arrived in Acapulco, contraband gold and cigarettes and drugs would be stored in a number of hiding places including a special closet under his bed.

On August 10, Jim Fleming completed his work on insuring that everything aboard was comfortable for the passengers. That same day, Fleming recalls, Nora appeared on board and began giving Flynn's detailed instructions. "The crew was furious at a woman telling them what to do," Fleming says. "They wanted Errol to tell them. They all walked off." Actually, one member did stay on board: Robert P. Vincent. And the captain also decided to continue with the voyage.

Errol was furious when he heard what had happened. He instantly obtained a new crew, but a totally inexperienced and undisciplined one, some of whose members were persona non grata on the California coast. He had no alternative, since the *Zaca* was to sail on August 12, and the smuggling aboard of contraband in Acapulco had been timed to the split second. He was also carrying drugs for Acapulco, as he had done previously on the *Sirocco*. Unfortunately, Besnovitch, the ship's cat, showed an alarming propensity for sniffing out these drugs during the voyage.

There was a large press party on board on August 11, at which most of the reporters got happily drunk.

The next day, *Zaca* sailed for the Guadalupe Islands. The weather was rough, and Nora and John Decker were seasick. Professor Flynn complained of John Decker's revolting body odor—the two men shared a cabin—and Decker, a major practitioner of the art, grumbled about Professor Flynn's drinking. Errol began sampling the morphine he was supposed to bring intact to Acapulco. As a result, he lost control of the crew, which became increasingly disobedient.

Since Nora was pregnant, Decker painted a portrait of her on a bulkhead with a protuberant stomach that grew larger with every successive day of the voyage. She was furious about this, but Errol simply laughed at her discomfiture.

On Guadalupe, the scientists picked up specimens of fish which they called, among other things, *gibbonsia errolae* and *gibbonsia norae*. Unfortunately, Professor Flynn gave little or no aid to Professor Hubbs. Hubbs wrote to his wife, "The Professor is in great pain from a lame leg. He is helpless and hopeless as a naturalist. He is a sweet old devil at that, and never loses, rather exaggerates, his British haughtiness when under the influence. Yesterday, he was really 'out.' "

The party continued to the San Benito Islands. The team explored mainly at night by flashlight, and caught some flying fish. They observed endemic disease among the fish and collected some fifty unusual specimens. There were sea elephants and a large pride of sea lions on the island. Howard Hill picked off a couple of seals with bow and arrow but was prevented from continuing by Errol, who hated to see the creatures destroyed, and almost plunged into a fist fight with his old friend because of his ecological conscience. Errol was very much interested in seal, knowing them to be harmless, gentle creatures. He diverted Hill's attention to seining lobster and collecting some more small fish.

The *Zaca* sailed to Cedros Island and Socorro Island through somewhat choppy seas. By this stage of the voyage, everyone on board was disgusted by Decker's smell. A hasty conference was held and Errol decided to have him keelhauled: thrown overboard in a net and dragged behind the vessel until he was thoroughly washed, a variation of a technique used by Captain Bligh of the *Bounty*. Swearing and screaming and throwing his arms about, the unfortunate artist was picked up by his arms and legs and with three hefty swings tossed into the sea. When he was dragged out several minutes later a long brown puddle at his feet indicated how long it had been since he last took a bath.

On Socorro Island, an unfortunate event took place. Wallace Berry, a young, inexperienced sailor dived into the ocean to attack a shark with a harpoon gun. When he saw the shark's mouth snapping at him, he clambered up the Jacob's ladder to the deck and in his haste stumbled and drove the double-pronged harpoon right through his left foot, pinning the foot to the deck. His agonized screams attracted the attention of the various members of the expedition who had gone ashore dredging for specimens. Errol and Hubbs and Teddy Stauffer ran over to the boy and discovered that the hook had completely disappeared in the foot and there was blood in abundance on the deck. Errol decided that to avoid the possibility of gangrene, an operation would have to be performed on the spot. The hook was sandwiched between a bone and a tendon. Errol gave the boy ether and he and his companions extracted the harpoon. The boy felt little or no pain. But he became delirious after the operation, and Errol decided, despite Professor Hubb's annoyance, to cut short the expedition and sail directly for Acapulco ahead of schedule. It would no longer be possible to visit the Clipperton Islands.

The last part of the voyage had a nightmarish, bizarre quality. Wallace Berry lay tossing and groaning in pain in his bunk. A sudden wind blew up, followed by a lashing storm. The boat pitched and tossed wildly and the *Zaca*'s engineer was caught off balance and fell against the bulkhead, fracturing two ribs. The rest of the crew mutinied and decided to do no work. One angry member, furious with Nora, actually sealed off the water supply with a metal plate which could not be pried loose. Errol told Nora to lock up the ice chest so that at least ice could be melted if the vessel were blown off course and water was not available. Unfortunately, John Decker's insulin needles and shots were kept in the ice chest for hygienic reasons. He became panic-stricken at the lack of medication and of ice for his liquor and he attacked Nora and broke into the chest. Errol was so heavily doped that Nora begged Professor Flynn to help. When Errol found out she had spoken against his dear friend to his father, he struck her violently and kneed her in the stomach. When Professor Flynn tried to intercede, Errol, a monster under the influence of the drug, flung his father down a steep companionway, injuring his already lame leg still further. Professor Flynn was barely able to walk for the rest of the voyage.

As if all this were not enough, the engine went out twice and the storm increased in intensity. Many of the marine specimens were lost, and the floating aquarium was damaged. When Errol returned to sanity and discovered what he had done, according to Professor Hubbs he "tried to kill himself. He wanted to throw himself into the wild sea." His friends restrained him.

At last the storm blew out and the boat limped toward Acapulco. But Captain Wicklund almost ran her onto a reef.

Nora, who had narrowly escaped a miscarriage, left the ship and flew to Los Angeles to her father and stepmother. As soon as he discovered that contraband was being smuggled aboard, Captain Wicklund resigned and went home. The crew disappeared into the bars and bordellos of Acapulco. When they did not return, Errol had to hire a scratch Mexican crew.

Professor Hubbs obtained substantial specimens in the Acapulco region. He remained in Acapulco until September 21, making very important collections of fish and other marine life and recording his observations of the flight of flying fish. In all, he analyzed and classified some three hundred important specimens, and so the terrible voyage had been scientifically important.

Because of Nora's departure, Errol had to cancel all plans for *Treasure in Yucatan*. Professor Flynn, in excruciating pain from his doubly injured leg, made a journey back to Los Angeles with John Decker in a cockpit plane; Decker insisted on peeing into the wind as they crossed the border of Mexico.

Professor Flynn, furious with his son for his behavior, continued on to New York.

Errol might have sailed on directly to the Caribbean had he not heard that Orson Welles was in Acapulco needing a yacht for use in *The Lady from Shanghai,* a melodrama starring Orson's wife, Rita Hayworth. Errol rented him the boat—at an exorbitant price.

For the five weeks of the shooting, Errol acted as captain and technical adviser on the ship's simulated voyage to the Caribbean. Welles seemed to be making up the story as he went along, and the actors, among them Everett Sloan and Glenn Anders, proved notably eccentric. In many scenes, insects were so numerous they blotted out the arc lights, and in one river sequence, sharks swarmed in from the sea, endangering the lives of the crew.

Many scenes shot by Errol, including a startling view of the whole boat taken from the top of the mast, found their way into the jumbled footage that Welles shipped back to Hollywood.

In Acapulco, Errol, drinking and drugging heavily, began to behave erratically. The ship's engineer, recovered from his broken ribs, became sexually attracted to a beautiful nightclub head waitress known as Choo-Choo. With her perfect figure, exquisite breasts and legs, Choo-Choo was the talk of town. Errol was fascinated by her himself. Yet he always suspected there was something strange about her, because no man he knew had actually been to bed with her. One night, there was a big party at the nightclub. The engineer announced drunkenly that he would marry Choo-Choo, and he dragged her onto the stage to make this declaration.

Errol was waiting in the wings. Without warning, he ran out and stripped Choo-Choo. The beautiful girl turned out to be a man. The engineer cried out in horror and fled. Errol doubled up with laughter, and the crowd cheered.

It was during this period that Errol renewed his earlier sexual affair with Tyrone Power, who was equally fond of Mexico. Power was just breaking up with a famous Latin lover of the screen. Errol was still seeing Apollonio Díaz. Díaz had money of his own, and his life as a beach boy—he used to dive with a flaming torch from the balcony of an Acapulco hotel—was one of choice. The actress Mari Blanchard fought with Errol over Apollonio and lost. Later, Lana Turner discovered Apollonio and dated him frequently.

Errol talked openly about his relationship with Tyrone with his secretary, Jane Chesis, and his agent, Dick Irving Hyland.

Tyrone seems to have been fascinated by Errol because of his tremendous masculinity. They slept together on a number of occasions in 1946, at the Hotel Reforma in Acapulco, but the affair did not last. Tyrone wanted things done to him Errol found repellent, for Errol preferred oral sex with men.

They broke up in 1947, but remained friends. In 1948, Ty married Linda Christian. Errol always laughed with Johnny Meyer about that.

In September 1946, while he was in Mexico, Errol had word from Erben in Shanghai. Once the members of the Nazi spy ring were rounded up, Erben and Louis Siefken had become the chief prosecution witnesses at the trial of the espionage agents held in Ward Road Jail. In the stuffy, airless courtroom, with a civil war exploding beyond the dust-grimed windows, Erben gave an amazing performance, reported in the papers which friends of his shipped to Errol in Hollywood. He hid the fact that he had been working for the Gestapo since the early 1930s, and pretended that his whole mission for Abwehr was a freelance venture on behalf of America. When asked by the associate defense counsel, Lieutenant Colonel Bodine whether he realized he was a traitor to his country, he even got away with the response, "The explanation for that is restricted information. And I'm not at liberty to explain 'restricted.'"

As a result of Erben's and Siefken's testimonies, the twenty-six members of the spy bureau were sentenced to prison terms ranging from fifteen years to life in Landsberg Prison in Germany. But most

of them were out of prison within five years, and some of them remained unrepentant Nazis.

After the trial was over, Erben left Captain Frank Farrell's investigative team and joined Colonel Amos Moscrip of OSS. Moscrip took
Erben to Japan on a very dangerous mission. Erben was to make
contacts leading to the uncovering of anti-American Soviet spies in
Tokyo. As a result, several important Soviet agents were located and
killed. Erben returned to Shanghai. By now, China was in the grip of
Civil War. The remarkable Louis Siefken had made a deal with the
Chinese and had become head of Chiang Kai-shek's military intelligence. Siefken was convinced Erben was working as a double agent
for the Russians, despite the fact that Erben had just caused the
deaths of certain Russians. The Chinese in Shanghai had never forgiven Erben for betraying certain Chinese agents to the kempeitai.

Acting on instructions from Siefken and certain other members of
Chiang Kai Shek's government, Captain Chow of the Chinese Militia
decided to deport Erben to Germany. The American consul approved. Erben had spent several months preparing dossiers for Farrell on all of the Nazis who were to be shipped back to Germany for
imprisonment on the U. S. Army transport vessel *General William
Black*. Ironically he was now on that deportation list, being shipped
off with all those he had named. This was totally illegal. He had not
been tried or sentenced. All his property was taken from him.

He was considered so violent and dangerous that he was locked up
in the brig with the chief of the Gestapo of Peiping.

The journey to Bremerhaven was under the command of Major
(later Colonel) William E. Williamson, who tried to help Erben by
allowing him a quick, guarded walk around the deck in the afternoons. Erben was grateful, and for years wrote to Williamson, pouring out his troubles and begging Williamson to help him return to
America. Williamson, who knew all about Erben and Errol, was not
interested in assisting him at all.

The voyage was a nightmare. Unbeknownst to Williamson, corrupt
officers had stuffed $5 million worth of heroin behind the bulkheads
and were experimenting with it. There were sudden outbreaks of
murderous violence. Erben spent the voyage writing, in his angular
Germanic hand, many letters and autobiographical statements: to
his landlady, to Errol, to Farrell, and to Moscrip. Only Errol responded; and it is significant that his were the only letters that were

not censored or intercepted and have vanished from the files. He offered to pay for Erben's defense should he be tried for treason, to send ten thousand dollars to get Erben established in America and to do everything in his power to get Erben restored to citizenship.

Erben's deepest fear was that he would be returned to the Russian zone in Vienna where his home was situated, and that he would be killed instantly for his anti-Soviet activities in Japan. He was terrified also of undergoing denazification proceedings which would bring to light his record with the Gestapo. He begged Errol to help bring about a voluntary trial for treason in America which, he gambled, would result in his acquittal on the grounds of his having supplied information on the Shanghai spy ring. Besides, since his citizenship had been revoked before the war, he felt no treason charge could hold against him.

Errol tried to arrange for this trial—even using Mrs. Roosevelt's help. But after the death of her husband, Mrs. Roosevelt's political influence had waned. President Truman was suspicious of Errol. For the rest of Errol's life, his passport was restricted and he was kept under strict political surveillance.

Erben was placed in Ludwigsburg Repatriation Prison in Germany, where he protested his punishment by going around naked except for a U. S. Army regulation blanket. He finally obtained his release in 1948 on compassionate grounds; his mother was desperately ill in Linz. He never returned to the Russian zone and, incredibly, turned up on the medical staff of the U. S. Army headquarters in Vienna instead.

Errol, his cameraman, and a Mexican crew sailed from Acapulco to the Caribbean in late October 1947. After leaving the east coast of Mexico, *Zaca* ran into a tremendous storm. She was driven into harbor at Kingston.

Despite the attentions of Jamaican customs, or perhaps as a result of a bribe, Errol managed to smuggle his gold and other contraband ashore and sell it for good prices in the British colony. He then proceeded to Haiti, where he had an introduction to the Premier from the Jamaican branch of Warner Brothers. As soon as he arrived there, he proceeded to investigate a subject which had fascinated him ever since he had left New Guinea—voodoo.

He contacted a relative of a mambo or priestess, who made arrangements for him to go to her house, where in a special shrine, she kept fetishes dangling from the ceiling, and pale green bottles that contained the souls of the dead. Driven by an acolyte in a red shirt, he would travel up the winding roads that traversed the hills overlooking Port-au-Prince, surrounded by men and women running with torches and accompanied by the sinister slow rolling of drums. He would enter the special enclosure where wild dancing took place around the pole of Damballah-Uedo, the serpent god. Painted with the figures of writhing serpents, the pole was believed to be the conductor down which the serpent god would come to penetrate his female acolytes through their vaginas and possess them so completely they would turn into snakes. They would writhe in orgasm below the pole and then, wriggling in serpentine formation, crawl out into the darkness on their stomachs.

Haitians recall that Errol attended ceremonies in honor of Lola Criminel, the God of Fire, which involved girls dancing with live coals in the palms of their hands and under the soles of their feet. Often, during these ceremonies, chickens would be decapitated and the blood squirted in the faces of the worshipers, Errol's among them. High on drugs, he apparently obtained an almost sexual pleasure from the experience.

His taste for the exotic and the romantic was never more deeply satisfied than in Haiti. He dreaded the thought of returning to Hollywood. But how else could he afford the free life of the West Indies?

During this period, the *Zaca* ran aground in the Panama Canal Zone and had to be salvaged. Errol refused to pay the bill and the law case dragged on for years.

Soon after, he sailed the *Zaca* to Venezuela and the Argentine, where he met Eva Peron and she fell for him. Fascinated as much as ever by Fascism, he was greatly intrigued by her. Theirs was an affair that would last until her death in 1951—as they met from time to time in different parts of the world. Errol confided to Charles Pilleau, the friend of his teens who had moved to Hollywood, "Eva and I were lovers for a very long time. At one time, when I was in Buenos Aires, Peron found out about it. He told me if I didn't get out of the country in twenty-four hours I would be found dead in my room."

Errol went on to the Cocos Islands to look for the treasures the Peruvians had buried there long ago—treasures rumored to amount to a hundred million dollars in gold. He found nothing, not even a rusted nickel or peseta in the undergrowth. Or did he?

There is a mystery here. For years, he confided to a German friend, he carried deep in tar in the hold of the *Zaca* three hundred and fifty thousand dollars' worth of gold bars. Where did he get so much gold? America was off the gold standard. He never could save that much money, excepting for the funds tied up in investments in England for him by his friend Stephen Raphael. Did he find the treasure and have it converted into solid ingots in Mexico? Was it all a lie? We will probably never know.

Twenty

Errol went back to Hollywood in March 1947, and immediately made plans to sponsor another voyage of the *Zaca* in 1947 or 1948 to seek out the mating habits of the whale.

On March 12, Errol's and Nora's second daughter, Rory, was born in Hollywood. Like Deirdre, Rory was a very pretty baby. And unlike Deirdre, she was of moderate size: under nine pounds. Errol was delighted with her, and despite his mixed feelings about Nora, adored both his daughters. He even began to take an interest in six-year-old Sean, and gave him a handsome birthday party in April. To Errol's credit, despite his differences with his wives, he always made sure that Sean, Deirdre, and Rory were close, and grew up as normal children. "But," Rory says, "mother's misery at Errol's indifference to her and his absence during the late stages of both her pregnancies and the events of the voyage to Mexico, seemed to affect her attitude toward me. I felt she never really liked me. Later, when there was a divorce settlement, she seemed to want Errol to have me while she kept Deirdre. We were never close. Mother and I—we couldn't get along. It's very sad."

Bizarrely, Errol agreed to have Nora's stepmother, Marge, work for him as a housekeeper, while Nora was kept at her separate address on Cordell Drive. Marge took care of him like a baby, running the household with meticulous care. This was fortunate, because Alex, Errol's beloved major domo, had decided to go east and perhaps return to Europe now that the war was over. And Jim Fleming had become increasingly irritated by Errol's drug taking and erratic behavior. Within three years, this loyal and devoted friend, perhaps the best friend Errol ever had, also drifted away.

In May 1947, Errol agreed to make a western, *Silver River*. The surprising fact resulted from the powers of persuasion of the genial producer, Owen Crump, and the writers, Stephen Longstreet and Harriet Frank, Jr. Owen Crump wrote to Steve Trilling, Hal Wallis' successor as head of production, "[Errol] approved—even liked [the pages], surprisingly . . . God is love!"

Shooting began with Errol in a euphoric mood over a picture for the first time in years. His health had improved in the months of sunshine and swimming in the Caribbean, and he had even kept a promise to Nora, and cut down on the drug taking. But *Silver River*, begun in high spirits, proved to be a problem. Raoul Walsh was extremely strict about Errol's drinking, and he resented this. He felt he had the right to do what he wanted at night so long as he was punctual on the set every day. Moreover, Errol was furious because Jack Warner kept sending spies down to the location sites to see that he was behaving and not shooting up with morphine in his dressing room.

In June 1947, the company was shooting *Silver River*. Flynn was late on the set several times. Owen Crump complained to Warner who, on the telephone, asked Flynn why he was so tardy. Flynn said that he had not been able to get a driver to bring him to the location on time and he began to swear at Jack. Warner stated that Flynn would be held responsible for every hour he held the company up.

Another telephone conversation between Flynn and Warner took place on January 20. Flynn called Jack and demanded a private conversation with him. When Warner refused, Flynn said, "I'm trying to be humble and kind but I'd like to be asked to *please* go to work. I'm not going to stand here and be bawled out publicly and listen to a lot of shit. My record is absolutely clear. Nobody's ready to work yet. You and I can always work together but I can't do any business with any in-between man. . . . I will not work until the set is cleared of any stool pigeons. You should come down to the set to see what's going on. The sooner you come the happier I will be. You have too many stool pigeons around."

The quarrel continued, with Flynn demanding that the agents and lawyers of both sides meet and sort the problems out. Warner threatened to close the picture and hold him responsible if he didn't want to work. Flynn said that he would send for his doctor. "What do you want a doctor for?" Warner asked. "You're making me nervous. Ann Sheridan [his co-star in the picture] is so nervous she can't hold a paper."

On June 19, Flynn failed to turn up after lunch. It was clear he had been drinking. On July 3, Flynn again failed to turn up for work, announcing that he refused to shoot the picture in anything other than chronological order. This was, of course, impossible.

Foolishly, Errol did not tell Owen Crump or Raoul Walsh the reason he was drinking so heavily on the picture. Only two days before production began, his beloved John Decker had become seriously ill. He had had cirrhosis of the liver even during the *Zaca* voyage and now, disobeying his doctor's orders about drinking, he had radically declined. He was admitted to Cedars of Lebanon Hospital at the end of May, and Errol visited him night after night after the shooting. Nora hated Decker, and had no interest in going along with Errol.

Paradoxically, although Errol could see the ravages that alcohol had caused in his old friend, he went home from these visits to Cedars and drank more heavily himself. He had to blot out the thought of Decker's downfall, even if he himself risked sharing it.

On June 7, Decker had thirty-six blood transfusions and an emergency liver operation. But he could not be saved.

The body, by Decker's request, was taken to a crematorium to be burned. Errol led the crowd of friends who laughed and drank as Decker would have wished. Just after they arrived, an attendant said, looking at the body, "Is that John Decker?" And Errol answered, "Yes, and he hasn't been feeling well all day." The attendant said they could watch the cremation and they did, through an aperture in the wall. The intense heat made the body sit up. Errol said, "Oh my

God, Uncle John's still alive. Let's get him out!" And the whole
drunken gang tried futilely to pull their friend back from the flames.

Next day, the still inebriated crowd had another party in the form
of a wake in Decker's studio. They propped up his painting of John
Barrymore on an easel and toasted it. Errol gave a speech that ended
with the words, "And now Uncle John has gone to join our other
dear friend of Bundy Drive, John Barrymore!" At that moment, the
painting tilted seemingly of its own accord, leaned forward a moment, and then crashed to the floor. There was a shocked silence.
"Well done, Uncle John!" Errol whispered, pale and shaking.

One of the pleasures of making *Silver River* was the company of
Errol's co-star, Ann Sheridan. She could outdo him in her outrageously raunchy use of language and even in her drinking of vodka.
As soon as she arose in the morning, she would arrange an unusual
cure for her inevitable hangover: a small Mexican band would appear on her patio and play Mexican tunes while she took her prairie
oyster. Between scenes at the studio or on location, the Mexican
combo was present at all times, thrumming softly romantic tunes on
the guitars and singing in gentle voices, while she cried into her liquor. If for any reason the band was not available, or reduced by
sickness, her acting was very poor that day.

She and Errol delighted in shocking everyone who visited the set.
In scenes when their backs were to the camera, they would talk dirty
with great expertise. Raoul Walsh would scream for proper dialogue.
Errol would say something like, "The moon is shining in your hair
. . . just like piss," and she would say, "Your eyes are a deep brown
. . . just like shit." Production was called to a halt while the stars
were called to order.

Silver River was completed in August, and turned out to be of no
particular consequence. Nora, Rory, and Deirdre moved into the
house on Mulholland. A friend, director Alan Crosland, Jr., says:

> Nora wanted the best for Flynn. She tried to have a normal life
> with him, to be a housewife to him. But that wasn't possible; she
> couldn't seem to grasp that his whole way of life wasn't normal, that
> a pipe-and-slippers existence was totally unacceptable to him. From
> this came a great bitterness. And she resented his "pack," his tough,
> hard-drinking male friends. And the two-way mirror, the orgies he
> would have when he sent her away with the children. It wasn't the
> kind of life she wanted at all.

Fencing rehearsals began on a reactivated *Adventures of Don Juan* in September 1947. Errol was frequently absent from these and his double, Don Turner, had to do most of the work for him. There was still trouble with the script. George Oppenheimer, a witty homosexual writer and alumnus of the Algonquin Round Table, had written a new draft. It was civilized and clever, but Jack Warner hated it. Vincent Sherman, director of *Don Juan,* tried to defend it with: "It's like a piece of Venetian lace." Warner replied, "Yes, and the writer's wearing the lace. To hell with it. There's not enough action. With Flynn there has to be fuckin' and fightin'. One or the other. That's all the public pays to see him in. Have the script done by a man."

Harry Kurnitz, who apparently met Jack Warner's sexual and professional requirements, wrote a new draft that had enough "fuckin' and fightin'" even for Jack Warner's tastes.

Errol liked the Kurnitz script well enough. It had some amusing lines, including, "There's a little bit of Don Juan in every man. But since I *am* Don Juan, there must be more of it in me." The story was largely Don Juan's adventures in England and at the Court of King Philip III and Margaret of Spain, in the period around 1600.

Warners set about fashioning a luxurious production, with rich costumes and sets, and hordes of extras. Errol personally made sure his jerkins were cut higher than they would have been in 1600, so that they would display a heroic crotch. Cameraman Woody Bredell complained to Vincent Sherman after the first costume test, "For God's sake, Vince, I can't photograph that. Especially if he stands sideways. The Breen office would never stand for it." Errol overheard this and said, "I'm the one who'll be doing the standing."

Irritable with the weeks of fencing practice and in excruciating pain because his hemorrhoids were acting up again, Errol started to drink heavily again in October. He began with vodka on the rocks at nine in the morning, believing that the vodka was odorless and would not be detected by fencing master Fred Cavens. Between the hemorrhoids, the alcohol, and the drugs, lay the blame for a disaster: at a mere thirty-eight years of age, he had noticed for the first time that he was losing his potency.

Even with Nora in and out of the house, he began hiring prostitutes at upward of one hundred dollars a time to help him regain his virility. Alan Crosland describes a curious incident at a party:

> He introduced a very reserved, pretty girl to us. She seemed subdued and well brought up and he gave the impression she was a Bos-

tonian. Errol got drunk and passed out and I arranged to take the girl home. I was astonished when I found out she was a whore. He had hired her for the night and hadn't even used her. What a waste of money! None of the other guests ever suspected. During this period, Errol picked up a young male hitchhiker and installed him in a cottage in the grounds; but it seems unlikely that the dark intent behind this ever came to anything, and the boy finally left.

He seems to have had other, fleeting homosexual experiences during the period but only when he was drunk or drugged.

Alan Crosland says:

You take people from nothing and rocket them to fame and fortune and they become satiated. They've tried everything and then they go out looking for different kicks. They get involved in homosexuality—they're not strictly homosexuals—but they have had everything else so why not try this? It means nothing; and then they start to feel the guilt well up. And we live in Peyton Place in Hollywood: a tiny world. Sooner or later, somebody starts to talk. And then the real trouble starts. A label is put on. Errol suffered terribly from this.

But Nora never even heard the rumors.

Errol gave a party to which he invited his old tennis-playing companion, Jack Kniemeyer, who asked if he could bring a friend of his, a British lawyer named Giles Hernshaw. Errol asked if Hernshaw would come to the phone. Hernshaw did so.

"What do you look like?" Errol asked.

Hernshaw was surprised by the question. "I'm tall and dark."

"How old are you?"

"I'm thirty-eight," Hernshaw replied.

"Good-looking?"

"I suppose so." There was a pause. Then Errol said, "How would you like to suck my cock?" Hernshaw was horrified. He went to the party with great reluctance. But he had made it clear he was not interested, and Errol made no further suggestion.

Errol told director Vincent Sherman just before *Don Juan* production began in the late fall, "I'll be on time, Uncle Vince, I'll know my lines, and you'll see I'll behave. Forget all the stuff you've heard about me. This is a good script and a good story and I'll give it my best."

Sherman was delighted with Flynn. The first week went beautifully. Errol was on time every day and he looked superb in the period costumes—as though he were born to wear them. He still moved with the grace of an animal. Sherman remembers:

For the first few days we improvised happily, without a script. Everything was fine. Then something happened. Flynn had a picture open in New York. It was the remake of *Escape Me Never*. I came into his room one morning to say hello to him. It was about nine o'clock and he seemed a little over-jovial. Full of fun. He said, "Did you see the reviews in New York of *Escape Me Never?*" I had seen one or two which were not very good for him. In essence what they said was as long as he was in costume on a horse he was all right but when you put him in a straight role he was terrible. I pretended I hadn't seen any reviews and he said take a look at them.

I glanced through them and they were very unkind. He just laughed but I could sense that he was hurt by them. He wouldn't show you that he was hurt. Believe it or not, the next day was the first day that he drank on the picture. This was after ten days of shooting. The bad reviews triggered that response, in my opinion.

My own feeling is that Errol really wanted to be a good actor. He pretended it didn't mean a thing to him—he would laugh at the whole thing. I once said to him, "Errol for God's sake, man, there are very few people who can do what you do." And his reply was, "It's nothing to wear a costume, ride a horse and flourish a sword, it's no accomplishment at all."

Errol would come in every morning, his eyes bleary and red and half-open, and would say, "What are my lines today? What do I do?" And when Sherman would reply, "It's this particular scene," he would show little or no interest. At eight-thirty Dr. Nolan would give him Vitamin B-1 shots. Only with these would he be capable of going on the set.

He was forbidden drugs. Jack Warner made a firm rule that if any drugs were found in his dressing room he would be instantly suspended. But he obtained permission to have cocaine mixed with water inoculated into his hemorrhoids. Actually, he would take the mixture and put it in an eye dropper instead and use it in his sinuses. When he felt like vodka (also forbidden), Jim Fleming brought it in a soup bowl for lunch.

Errol found Viveca Lindfors, the beautiful Swedish actress who played Queen Margaret, extremely attractive. But she was in love with director Don Siegel and had no wish to be involved with Flynn. He would say things deliberately to annoy her. One day, during a break in an important scene, he said loudly to Robert Douglas, who was the villainous Duke de Lorca, "Are you fucking her, Bob?"

Douglas said, "Unfortunately, no."

Errol told him, "All right, I will."

Viveca Lindfors observed, "No you won't!" Errol tried to make her change her mind, but she succeeded in freezing him out.

Errol played practical jokes all during the picture. One day, the assistant director, Dick Mayberry, went over to Vincent Sherman and said, "Errol wants to talk with you." Vincent went to the dressing room. To his surprise, Errol was stark naked except for a towel over his crotch. Errol asked Sherman some questions about a scene. Sherman continues the story:

> As we were talking, he sort of surreptitiously withdrew the towel and a giant imitation penis jumped up at me. He roared with laughter when I looked at it in horror. He said, "Let's get Alan Hale in." He wrapped himself up in the towel as Alan walked in and then suddenly whipped the towel off and the dildo rose up. Without turning a hair, Alan Hale said, "I'll take a pound and a half."

Robert Douglas recalls a similar episode:

> There was a big scene in the picture in which numerous ladies-in-waiting would watch Errol approach a throne room. He needless to say auditioned them all in person. Now all these girls were lined up and it was lunch time and Errol hadn't been on the set all morning. Finally even Vincent Sherman lost his temper. He banged on Errol's dressing room door. No answer. Vince said to Limey, Errol's prop man, "Do you have a key that opens this door?" Limey produced it but warned, "I don't think you should go in there, sir." Vince opened the door. All of us in the cast and crew stood back and watched to see what was going on inside. Well, you couldn't believe it. Errol was sitting there stark naked reading the trades while a girl was going down on him in a mantilla. She was all dressed in court finery. Errol wasn't fazed in the least. "I'll be 'coming' in a minute, Uncle Vince!" he exclaimed. And he was as good as his word.

One night, Errol was shooting a prison scene with Alan Hale when Jack Warner came visiting. "Welcome to the torture chamber!"

Errol said. "I'm sure you'll feel right at home here!" A few minutes later, Errol said, "There's something wrong with this scene, Uncle Vince." Sherman asked what that might be.

Alan Hale said, "I know what's wrong. We need a rat for realism."

Errol said, "Well, there's always Jack."

In some scenes, Errol and Alan Hale were so drunk they had to be propped up by crew men on their horses. Errol quarreled with Jack Warner on the telephone or in person throughout the entire picture. One day, he said to Warner, "Just come down here and I'll take care of you, you son-of-a-bitch." Jack Warner appeared on the set wearing boxing gloves and Errol said, "We don't allow any Jews on the set."

On weekends, Errol informed Jack Warner, he "needed to rest." Actually, he would leave on Saturday morning at the crack of dawn by helicopter piloted by Paul Mantz and fly to the Scripps Institution at La Jolla. There, he would be greeted by Professor Carl Hubbs and Professor Flynn, who had returned from Ireland, and taken up a teaching job in Los Angeles. With them were Alan Crosland and photographer Jerry Courneya. The group would sail out at great risk into the ocean to photograph the wild thrashing and beating against the water of the migratory mating whales that had come down from the north to spawn in Baja California. At any moment, Jack Warner could have lost his most famous male star. Errol insisted on taking the whale boat in and out of the creamy wake of the great beasts, as Courneya daringly filmed their movements. Often, the boat almost capsized. Errol was completely fearless, defying the sea to drown him. The studio insurance people luckily never found out. Later, he would show films of the escapade to his friends at home, entitling the show Those Fucking Whales.

His constitution held up incredibly to his taxing demands upon it. Each night, while Professors Hubbs and Flynn made notes of the day's observations, Errol and his friends Crosland and Courneya would visit the various bars and bordellos along the coast, drinking and wenching until dawn. Then they would set off for another day of rough and dangerous sailing.

Some scenes were added off the coast of California near Point Magoo, where Alan Crosland had contacts in the Coast Guard station. Errol wanted a trick shot in which he would be gamboling in the water in the wake of the whales. Since even he had to admit this was too dangerous to perform in actuality, he went into heavy waves off Point Magoo and fooled around, the footage to be matched in later with the whales that had been separately photographed.

By January 1948, his health cracked again. The undulant fever returned as always in the heavy rain of winter, and the hemorrhoids became excruciatingly painful. He was off work for several days in January. He struggled into the studio in agony on January 8. The doctor told him that unless he obtained relief from the use of suppositories, he would have to be operated upon immediately. He refused an operation.

On January 12, Flynn was taken to the Montesano Hospital. His temperature was 102 by the following night, and he was vomiting. Apparently, in addition to the hemorrhoids, he was suffering from a recurrence of malaria, and the doctors did not feel it was advisable to operate on him right away.

It was later determined that Flynn had still another ailment: the so-called Virus X, a dangerous form of pneumococcus then virulent. By January 14, his temperature had gone up to 103 degrees. By January 15, he was in the grip of pneumonia. His pain and his stress were increased by the badly protruding hemorrhoids. The studio worried whether, if he were operated on for piles, he would be able to leap around in the duel scenes.

Dr. Nolan pointed out that if the operation was performed successfully and Flynn recovered from pneumonia, he would still be away from work for thirty days.

His temperature went to 104 the following day. Chest specialists were called in. Flynn was delirious. Frank Nolan told Tenny Wright, "He won't be available till February. When you get out of bed after a thing like this you're not about to whip anybody, you know."

C. D. Dickey, the studio doctor, had a violent row with Frank Nolan on the telephone, accusing him of lying about the severity of Flynn's condition with "a lot of double talk." Nolan was so disgusted he called Flynn's attorney, Bob Ford, who sent Dickey an angry letter threatening a suit for slander unless he apologized. The illness dragged on for two more weeks, scarcely alleviated by Dr. Dickey's tacit apology.

Flynn struggled into makeup on January 28. The makeup artist, Perc Westmore, noticed that his face was streaming with perspiration. It was impossible to work on him. Sherman and Tenny Wright went to the makeup room and, horrified by Errol's condition, called Dr. Frank Nolan and asked him to come to the studio at once. Nolan ordered Flynn to go home. He said it would now be February 2 before Flynn could return to work.

By February 4, Errol was still in bed, running a subnormal temperature, suffering from chest congestion and being shot full of penicillin. He was ordered to take an immediate vacation, but studio memos told him that for every day he was sick he would be suspended and the time added to his contract. By February 4, now suffering an acute ear infection, he went to Phoenix to rest.

On March 6, Flynn sent a telegram to Warner from Phoenix: "Dear Jack, I thought you might like to know I have lost none of my cunning. I have just made a solitary entrance into the main dining room, looking wan and rather wistful, with a yellow-jacketed copy of Sex Behavior in the Human Man (sic) under my right arm. Errol."

Warner replied on March 7, 1948: "Very happy to hear from you, especially your vivid description of Don Juan off and on. I just made the same entrance in the Lone Palm at Palm Springs but without a book. So pleased to hear you are back on one and a half feet, with the good old sun beating down on your vivid kisser, you will soon have that other twelve inches back. Be seeing you soon. Every good wish for a speedy return to your normal self. Jack." Jack sent another telegram to Errol which read, "There was a typographical error in the fifth line of my wire. Delete the word twelve and insert six. Yours. Jack."

In March 1948, Flynn was back in Hollywood, but his inner ear infection had not responded to sulfa drugs. He was off work for over a week. Jack Warner telegraphed from Palm Springs telling him not to return to work before he was completely well; the doctors had advised Warner that Flynn might be stricken with mastoiditis if he attempted to continue with the shooting.

During his sickness, Errol received several visits from Vincent Sherman. One afternoon, Errol told Sherman he would be leaving the house for treatments at the hospital. Sherman asked, "When are you going out?"

Suddenly, with rage in his face, Errol said, "You want to know the exact time, don't you? You want to come back and bang my wife, don't you?"

Sherman was horrified. He says, " 'God Almighty, I thought, does he think that every time you look at a girl, you have to have her whether she's married or not?'" Sherman walked out.

Two days later, Errol was back on the set. It was time for the elaborate scene in which Don Juan dueled with the Duke de Lorca on the grand staircase of the palace in Madrid. During a preliminary scene, Errol was so drunk he was unable to stand up. He couldn't remember his lines. Sherman had to drag them out of him. Sherman himself broke down from the strain, suffering a raging temperature and sinusitis. He struggled into work after one day out to find that Errol was not on the set. Ready to kill, he drove home. When Errol received word of this, he called Mrs. Sherman and said, "Oh my God. I wouldn't do anything to hurt Vince in this world. Please, I didn't know he was so sick or I'd have made a special effort to come in. I'm so sorry."

At last both director and star were present on the set for the duel scene. But it was miserably slow in shooting. Errol complained that his legs ached, and after only thirty seconds of dueling he was black in the face and sank into a chair. He went home early each day and could barely bring himself to return in the mornings. A further problem was that his opponent, Robert Douglas, was suffering from a lame leg. As a result, a great deal of the duel had to be performed by doubles. Alan Crosland, the editor of the picture, says, "I had to cut from Errol every time his eyes crossed. Which was often."

At the climax of the duel, Don Juan had to leap down an entire flight of steps and fling the Duke de Lorca to the floor. Needless to say, it was impossible for Errol to make the leap, or for Robert Douglas to be on the receiving end of it. Errol's regular doubles, Don Turner and Sol Gorss, refused to perform the stunt. Finally one man agreed to perform the death-defying leap: Jock Mahoney, who later became a famous Tarzan. For a price of three hundred and fifty dollars he leaped from the seventeenth step, and succeeded in smashing into and injuring the other double's testicles.

Adventures of Don Juan turned out to be Flynn's best picture in years. It may have lacked the joyous, youthful spirit of *Robin Hood,* but it was sophisticated in its mocking humor, and Errol's performance, lighthearted and adept despite the misery of his illnesses, is permanent testimony to his professionalism. It is hard to believe that any other actor, stricken with disease, testing his body to the limit in weekend battles with the sea, could have carried off the part with equal grace and wit. He even added a "tag" scene in which

Nora appeared as a lady in a carriage inquiring the way to Barcelona. Don Juan cannot resist her, and the ending shows Errol and Alan Hale intending to catch up with her. Much to Nora's embarrassment, the sequence was shown after she and Errol were divorced.

Errol's chief consolation during the six months it took to make *Don Juan* was a pet gibbon, Chico, he obtained during the making of *Silver River*. He found it a delightful pet; he laughed like a child as he watched the animal sliding down ropes that he had strung from one eave of Mulholland Farm's roof to another. Chico would tease Errol's dogs and pull their tails; when they turned around snapping, the creature would dart with amazing speed up the ropes, and sit on the roof chittering with laughter.

Errol's fascination with Chico was shared by few others. Nevertheless, he persisted in introducing Chico at fashionable events. Called upon to shake hands, the beast would scratch famous palms. Celebrities would leave bleeding and muttering about catching tetanus. Lawsuits were threatened. Important friendships were broken. And worst of all, Chico would suddenly urinate over anyone he took a fancy to.

Twenty-one

Errol's relationship with Nora ranged from periods of affection and warmth—when Sean came by to play with his young half-sisters—to those marked by violent arguments.

In late summer of 1948, he took her to Jamaica in a desperate last move to save the marriage, leaving the children in the care of Marge Eddington. In *Errol and Me,* Nora describes a ghastly stopover in Chicago when Errol returned from a monumental bar crawl to humiliate her so cruelly that she settled into a bathtub with an overdose of sleeping pills. She was saved by a house doctor.

In Jamaica, the unhappy couple lived aboard the *Zaca,* moored off Navy Island, where Errol was building a marine biological observatory for his father, who planned to settle there with Marelle on his retirement in 1950. Errol continued shooting *The Cruise of the Zaca,* attempting to pick up the continuity from the voyage of almost two years before. While days were spent acting out the movie fantasy on screen, nights were vicious and ugly. Nora wrote that after hours of wandering past picturesque waterfalls, poling rafts down river rapids, sailing under a tropic moon to the sound of calypsos, snorkeling on coral reefs, Errol would turn on her and savage her in his moods of drunken rage, or, as though he wished to fight the very elements themselves, he would (she wrote) "plunge into mountainous seas and swim far out . . . stand on the deck with the rain pelting him and the ship rolling under him." This was the worst period of his life, when nothing seemed to appease him, when the drugs failed to quiet him and he constantly threatened Nora with savage beatings.

In September, Errol began work on yet another Western, *Montana,* in which he played an Australian sheepherder opposite Alexis Smith. Upset over the disastrous summer in Jamaica, he began drinking heavily on the picture once again.

Alexis Smith recalls that one morning Errol appeared on set literally reeling from the effects of alcohol. The camera operator reported that Errol's eyes were too bloodshot to be photographed. Immediately, his doctor, Frank Nolan, was called for. The doctor disappeared into Errol's dressing room. Soon after, Nolan emerged, dead drunk himself.

At night, Nora had to sponge Errol during his violent spasms and chills; she wrote in *Errol and Me* that she had to straddle him and pin him down by the shoulders so that he couldn't get to the needle. One night he even tried to pump the morphine into her. She told me years later:

> Errol seized me and thrust me onto a couch. I felt sure he was going to plunge the needle into me. I screamed. I didn't know what to do but at last I threw him off. I told him my father would come and get him. I ran up the stairs to my bedroom. He followed me. He burst in, and hit me and hit me. He dislocated my thumb. Then suddenly he realized he was almost killing me and he sobbed and begged forgiveness again, and I didn't have the heart to refuse it to him.

After this horrifying episode, she again tried to kill herself with pills. Errol managed to save her, but by now she had had enough. She fled to Palm Springs.

While Nora was relaxing there, she met the boyish, open-faced young singer Dick Haymes, then just past the height of his popularity as a juvenile lead in Twentieth Century–Fox musicals. Haymes was a bland, soothing tonic after Errol. His marriage to Joanne Dru was breaking up. He and Nora began dating.

Jack Warner hired spies to watch Errol in case he brought alcohol or drugs onto the *Montana* set. One of these men hid in a loft in a stable set. Night fell, and everyone went home. Errol removed the high ladder to the loft and left the man stranded there all night.

Alexis Smith says:

Late one afternoon the director, Ray Enright, wanted a shot of Errol walking down a dusty street. Errol started in a kind of zigzag. Nobody commented because he was such a big star. Ray said to him, "The light isn't good. Let's do it again." Errol did the walk over twice and *still* he zigzagged. Ray tried again and again and finally Ray threw up his hands in despair. Errol said, "I don't know whether I can handle the walk but I can give you the goddamnedest ride on a horse!"

She adds:

One night it was six P.M. and he was loaded and clowning around. I was very angry and thought his behavior terrible. It was difficult for me to concentrate on the scene. Next morning when I arrived at work Jim Fleming brought me a note on Errol's personal stationery. It was a sweet, beautiful apology, very lengthy and personal, and utterly typical of him; I forgave him at once.

There was an incident during the shooting that illustrates the finer side of Errol's character. He had a favorite prop man known as Alabam because of his birth state. Jack Warner felt that Alabam wasted far too much time talking with Errol on the set and so he fired the prop man. Errol called the studio as soon as he got wind of this and announced that he would not be coming in again until Alabam was reinstated. He had a mysterious illness that could only be cured by Alabam.

The studio instituted a desperate search for the missing man. He was not at his home nor in any one of various watering holes he favored. At last, the studio police had word he was fishing off the coast near Malibu. A police launch went out and told him his job had been restored. Alabam whooped for joy, but proudly announced he would complete the day's fishing before returning to the set. Next day, Errol had a sudden recovery and was back at work.

Jealous of Dick Haymes, Errol asked Nora to accompany him on a publicity trip to New York for *Don Juan,* hoping to persuade her to break with Haymes. But the effort was useless. The husband and wife were by now completely incompatible. They quarreled again in New York and moved into separate hotels. Errol's moods changed almost by the hour. One minute, he criticized Nora to his friends, saying he was glad to be rid of her; the next, he called her, begging her yet again to come back to him. But she couldn't go back. She returned to Hollywood in the first week of December.

At the end of that week, Errol and Graham Wahn of Warner Brothers were returning from El Morocco to the Savoy Plaza when a police car began signaling their cab. Its siren screamed and its lights flashed. There had been a number of incidents in the previous weeks in which underage unlicensed drivers had stolen cabs and lured passengers into alleyways to mug them. The policemen following Errol's cab, Joe Bergales and Joe Gardner, thought that Errol's driver was visibly underage. They stopped the cab and questioned the boy, asking for his identification.

He produced it and turned out to be a licensed Yellow Cab driver. Errol, heavily under the influence of alcohol, was furious at the interruption of his journey and shouted four-letter words at the policemen. He began struggling with Bergales, and immediately he was put in handcuffs and driven to the East Fifty-first Street precinct. Once at the police station, Errol went mad. He screamed at the police, "You fucking Keystone Kops!" and he kicked Bergales on the shin. Bergales and Gardner threw Errol into the drunk pen with a bunch of riffraff. Graham Wahn got in a cab and sped to El Morocco, but Errol's friend, owner John Perona, had gone home. Wahn reached Perona, who got out of bed, drove to the precinct with five hundred dollars bail, dragged Errol out of the drunk pen, threw him into a cab, and tucked him into bed at the Savoy Plaza. Errol promised Perona he would turn up first thing in the morning at the magistrates court.

But he failed to do so. The magistrate told Perona he would lose his bail unless Errol made an appearance. Wearily, Perona made his way back to the Savoy Plaza, threw Errol under a cold shower and forced him to come to court. Errol was let off with a caution and a fifty dollar fine. "This is my worst public appearance," he said to the magistrate, who replied, "I hope your next screen performance is better."

The story made headlines in all the papers. It was the last straw for Jack Warner. He sent a lengthy memorandum to his production chief Steve Trilling, saying that he was disgusted with Errol, that public exhibitions of this kind made it impossible to publicize his pictures in a decent way, and that Errol was humiliating the name of Warner Brothers. Warner wrote that it was time Errol got out of the picture business and joined the Red Cross, "or some goddamn thing."

But Errol had a new contract, made the year before, for seven years. It was among the most fabulous in motion picture history. It gave him $250,000 a picture and the right to make one outside feature a year.

He was supposed to be in Hollywood on December 15, to start work as Soames Forsyte in an MGM version of John Galsworthy's famous saga, horribly retitled *That Forsyte Woman*. But he held up the production for almost two weeks by taking off for Cuba and Jamaica. While in Jamaica, he concluded plans to buy a three thousand-acre estate named Boston. One day, he dreamed, he would build a house there, a man's house overlooking the sea. One day, he hoped, he would be buried in the graveyard of the church he would restore, in the island he was more fond of than anything in the world.

He managed to arrive home for a children's Christmas at Mulholland. He lavished gifts on his son and two daughters. He was battling constantly with Lili for even the smallest access to Sean, a battle that increased when, as Jim Fleming vividly recalls, he taught Sean to smoke cigars at the age of eight.

He spent January through March in surprising sobriety, somehow managing to be punctual on the set of *That Forsyte Woman*. He behaved professionally and showed great skill. His interpretation of Soames was acute and deeply intelligent. Repressing his natural vitality and high spirits, he made a convincing figure of Soames: at once cold, heartless, and touching in his isolation. He movingly conveyed the man's inability to express emotions freely in action or gesture. The director, the English Compton Bennett, was a somewhat stodgy craftsman, and the film is heavy and cluttered. But against the striking technique of Greer Garson, adroit and subtle as Irene, Errol was consistently strong and assured. His was a performance in a narrow range, but it was a performance that worked.

Errol told Alexis Smith of an amusing episode that took place daily on the set:

> Each morning, as usual, a boy would come around and bang on our dressing room doors to tell us the scene was ready. We would all assemble on the set, Robert Young, Harry Davenport, all the others. Except one.
>
> We were called to silence. It was like a church. We stood waiting. Finally, and at long last, a tiny, silver bell tinkled in the silence. The first time this happened, I said to the director, Compton Bennet, "What in God's name was that?" And he replied, solemnly, "The silver bell is for Greer Garson. . . ."

Errol's stand-in, Whayne Coalter, recalls other amusing incidents:

> There was a scene in which Errol and Greer were preparing to go to the theatre. They left the set because the scene gave trouble and wouldn't "play." The director called Greer in to rehearse her separately. At the height of the scene, she had to open a large Victorian closet to take out an evening wrap. She opened the closet door on cue, and was astonished to see Errol, clad only in a pair of jockey shorts, standing inside the closet. She screamed!
>
> Soon after that, she got her revenge. There was a scene in which Errol was supposed to sit in a hansom cab, looking very self-important. She had the electricians wire the seat. When Errol sat down, an electric shock ran up through his behind. He jumped in the air.
>
> During the shooting, Errol took a fancy to an elaborate period watch he wore as part of his costume. It disappeared mysteriously. No one could find it. Finally, when he was out, one of the crew snuck into his dressing room and searched it from top to bottom. They found the watch hidden in one of his shoes.
>
> The cast and crew made up for this act of theft in a very lighthearted way. At the end of shooting, they presented Errol with a large, magnificently wrapped box as a parting gift. He took off the wrappers and opened it. It contained a large pile of horse manure. His comment before he walked off the set exactly matched the gift.

Shooting was completed in early March. On March 19, Errol wrote from Mulholland Farm to Jack Warner:

> Having griped, squawked and beefed on our lot for the last fifteen years, I could hardly wait to get over to those distant pastures that always look greener. I guess Metro was okay, and they were very nice, couldn't have been kinder. But, Buddy, I wanted you to know this— just give me the old home lot any time; as far as I'm concerned that's the joint I like working at.

Warner was touched by the note, but Errol was still off his list. He never again presented him with a vehicle worthy of his talents. The delays on *Don Juan* and the outrageous episode in New York had dug Errol's grave at Warners.

Yet Errol did not grieve over it. Although the conventional view is that his life was intolerable from the spring of 1949 on, actually he entered the freest and most expansive time of his life. Warners loaned him out often. He had long periods of leisure. He became a European: more and more, he turned his back on Hollywood, and became a member of the international set, enjoying, in a gigantic binge of pleasure, the fleshpots of the Continent.

That spring, Errol and Nora began divorce proceedings.

In the presence of her father, Jack Eddington, Nora signed an agreement giving her legal custody of the two children but providing that Errol would have "physical custody" of Rory. Rory says, "My father was wonderful to me. He took me on trips with him to New York, he gave me lovely times whenever he could. He did his best to give me a normal childhood."

In late May, Nora moved to Nevada to obtain the regulation six-week divorce from Errol. She alleged that Errol had treated her with extreme cruelty, that he drank excessively, that he behaved badly, that he nagged her and found fault with her, and criticized her to the point that she became humiliated and embarrassed. She said she had lost weight, had become nervous and irritable, and did not feel she could live with her husband and continue to enjoy good health.

There was to be no property settlement. Custody was agreed upon. Errol was ordered to pay three hundred dollars a month for the maintenance of Deirdre until her majority, this amount to be reduced to one hundred and fifty dollars when Nora remarried.

Nine days later, Nora married Dick Haymes under a fragrant orange tree in the garden of his house on North Canon Drive, Beverly Hills.

Errol had gone to Europe at the beginning of June. On June 3, he was dining with Freddy McEvoy at the restaurant Tour d'Argent in Paris. At a nearby table, he noticed the beautiful Princess Irene Ghika, a Romanian of great charm who had lived in Paris as a music student, an exile from her native country following its takeover by the Communists. Freddy saw to the introductions. They got along well from the start. Irene had a lighthearted grace and style, and she and Errol shared a love of classical music. She was a promising pianist and in their many hours together she played some of his favorite themes. It was a tender and warm relationship. But Irene withheld her favors. Like Nora and Linda Christian before her, she declined to go to bed with Errol immediately.

Errol spent a pleasant fall in Europe, breaking his vacation only to make brief returns to Hollywood for additional scenes of *That Forsyte Woman*. MGM asked him to appear as Mahbub Ali, the Afghan horse dealer and spy, in a version of one of his favorite books, Rudyard Kipling's *Kim*. The part offered the intoxicating prospect of a trip to India.

While he began thinking about the trip, his relationship with Irene developed strongly. On November 15, the couple announced their engagement. Irene, with her exquisite blue eyes and dark brown hair, made a ravishing picture for the cameramen. They traveled to London for the Royal Command Performance of *That Forsyte Woman* held before Queen Elizabeth. Errol arrived at the station in London with Irene, an astrakhan coat flung over his shoulders, the inevitable Barrymorean cigarette holder in his mouth, Irene clinging affectionately to his arm. He looked marvelous; he had undergone a cure for the morphine habit, seemed enormously more relaxed since his divorce from Nora, and was not drinking as heavily as usual. Yet it became apparent to friends that the relationship was not as idyllic as it seemed. They reported Errol snarling at Irene about never being on time. And he was equally annoyed with her inability to cook; indeed, he told a reporter that announcements of his impending marriage were premature because Irene was not yet "a mistress of the culinary arts."

Nora obtained full custody of both her children at the time of the announcement of Errol's engagement. Errol called Marge Eddington in California and told her, "I guess Nora is right. The little girls who love each other so dearly should not be separated. I'll be in India for quite a while. It's better that the kids live with Nora." Actually, at this stage it was almost a technicality, because the Eddingtons saw Nora and Dick constantly and Marge kept house at Mulholland Farm.

In Paris, Errol and Irene had a very good time. They were out almost every night, moving from Maxim's to the Tour d'Argent to the great La Coupole and off to Errol's suite at the Ritz in the early morning hours. But just before his departure for India, Errol began drinking again. It seemed as though he had no sooner committed himself to a Greek Orthodox marriage in Paris the following spring than he began to experience his usual fear of involvement.

He and Irene began to quarrel. She, normally stable, became acutely distressed by his behavior, locked herself in a bathroom and slashed her wrists. She was rescued just in time.

Errol left for India without Irene. In director Victor Saville's handsomely appointed, personally chartered DC-3, the pick of company and crew flew to India in the first week of December to start shooting at St. Xavier's School, Lucknow. While there, Errol told Saville a story about the late actress Lupe Velez. Saville recalls:

> Lupe was Errol's neighbor. One day, Errol dropped by to see her. She was attracted and invited him to her bedroom. He took his clothes off and lay on his back on the bed. He closed his eyes. Nothing happened.
>
> He looked up after a few minutes wondering what his hostess was doing. He was surprised to see her kneeling in front of an altar which had an enormous crucifix on it. She prayed for a considerable time until his patience began to run out. Then she crossed herself three times . . . and went down on him.

The weather in India was perfect. It was the end of the monsoon season and the sky was as blue as amethyst. The air sparkled brilliantly. Errol traveled like a prince. The Indians rolled out the red carpet for him everywhere; he was one of their favorite movie heroes. His plane was drenched in rose water in Bombay, a custom reserved only for the most revered visitors. He was entertained at the palace of the Maharajah of Jaipur with a feast, served by thirty-five waiters and presented on gold plate and with gold and crystal flagons and salt and pepper shakers carved from diamonds. He was similarly received by the Maharajah of Mysore.

In preparation for being the guest of a maharajah, Errol was taught the required court etiquette by a representative of MGM in Bombay. He told a reporter later:

> I was told that the first audience with His Highness was to last exactly ten minutes. When I was admitted to the hall, I was to bow, and await the signal to advance. But I was unprepared for the vastness of that first entrance. The door opened and I bowed. Down a room about a block long was a tiny figure in a jeweled white turban. Soon he became a full sized regal figure who rose to bid us welcome.
>
> I found the Maharajah exceptionally kind. He is a brilliant man who writes poetry in Hindu and composes excellent music. One of the last of the absolute rulers, he still has a big domain, though to him four palaces seem a mere few. Once we began talking I found the Maharajah so charming that our allotted ten minutes had stretched to an hour and a half.

To the same writer, an anonymous contributor to *Screen Guide,* Errol described the elephant hunt, known as the *khedda,* in which forty-two wild elephants were rounded up. The idea was to lead the wild elephants out of the jungle so that tame elephants could teach them to be used by mankind. Errol joined the Maharajah of Mysore and the latter's favorite wife, along with a select handful of visitors, on wooden platforms that were concealed behind trees on the river bank. Errol's description conveys his enthusiasm:

> The drive was mapped out like a Normandy landing. Two thousand beaters (guides) slowly herded the elephants toward a crook in the river. The least sound or motion can cause a stampede. Suddenly, a twig snapped! Five enormous elephants swung, climbed the steep bank like cats, and disappeared into the thicket. The rest were maneuvered into the crook of the river, then into a corral. There, five at a time were set to work with five tame elephants. Each beast is given a special mahout (driver) for life. The tame elephants raise and lower the gates of the corral and wallop the wild ones with their trunks to get them into line. This is the country Sabu came from and he was once a beater.

One day the Maharajah announced that I was to go hunting. The Shikar [head of the game reserve] was to go with me as guide, and I was provided with an elephant and guns. I was violently opposed to the idea, [he lied]. I don't approve of it and I had no desire to shoot anything. But the courteous thing seemed to be to go along and just not shoot at anything. An Englishman accompanied me, but he was to shoot only if I had missed my shot and was in mortal danger. On our first day, we ran into a wild boar—and I shot it. A few days later, we spotted a panther and I took careful aim and fired. The panther leaped and ran wildly out of sight. A wounded panther is deadly, you know, so the Shikar gave the signal to take cover. We waited in ambush. Finally, the Shikar sent in the beaters to find the animal. I protested because they had only daggers and I wanted to join them. "No, you cannot," commanded the Shikar. "The Maharajah has said so." Luckily, they found the panther dead. Then, when the danger had passed, I suddenly discovered that I was exhilarated. I loved hunting!

Later, Errol killed a crocodile and was fascinated when he saw it being stuffed. He watched intrigued as the taxidermist removed some bones with bracelets attached to them. The crocodile had evidently swallowed a woman.

Much of the shooting of *Kim* took place in Jaipur. The Maharajah's forty-room guest house—with a servant for each room—was next to the palace. Errol shared a lavish and enormous suite with Victor Saville. At night, to fill in the time, Errol and Saville would visit the Gem Palace, where the Maharajah's fabulous collection of jewelry was on display. While they were there, the nautch girls were brought in to perform erotic dances for the visitors.

One day Victor Saville received a call from the daughter of a member of the English consular corps who had been allowed to live at the palace while her father was in England. She told Saville that the Maharajah and his court had left on a journey and that she was entirely alone in the palace. She asked if she could come to dinner with the film company. She came to the guest house and had dinner. Afterward, everyone went to the Gem Palace. They returned, got out of the car, and Flynn said that he would see the girl back to the palace. Saville went to sleep. He woke up at two-thirty in the morning, certain that Errol was not in his part of the suite. He went to look. Flynn was missing. Saville was extremely upset.

At about three o'clock, Errol walked in. He had a smile on his face like a Cheshire cat. Saville asked him, "Where the hell have you been?"

Errol replied, "Where do you think I've been? I've been with that English girl."

Saville was horrified. He said, "You can't mean it! She's in the Maharani's quarters. That's sacred."

Errol said, "Where else?"

Saville told him, "You must be out of your mind!"

Errol went on smiling. He said, "If you think it's easy to get a hard-on with a sentry with a fixed bayonet walking up and down outside the window, you've made a great mistake." Saville adds:

> How he ever managed to smuggle himself into the women's quarters I'll never know. They were watched constantly. Guarded every minute of the day and night. No man in history had ever entered them. I'm sure no man ever entered them again. Errol Flynn or no Errol Flynn, the guards would have shot him dead instantly if they had seen him. Imagine the scandal!

During several visits to the Gem Palace, Errol became very friendly with the attendants. One of the staff sold him for thousands of pounds an enormous silver St. George, two feet tall and one foot thick. A superb piece of silver. He took it home with him to California when he returned the following year and asked a silversmith its value. The silversmith, with a wry smile took a needle and scratched the surface. The silver began to flake off. The statue was made of silver foil. Underneath it was lead. For once the "gypsy switch" had been performed on Errol.

He in his turn played a marvelous trick on Paul Lukas, who was cast as the Lama in *Kim*. Lukas flew into Delhi late one night. Errol had bribed the security man who inspected passports at the barrier to let Errol take his place. He put on the security man's clothes, including the elaborate turban, and coated his face in the heavy brown makeup he wore in the picture.

Lukas, a correct, rather humorless man, walked stiffly up to the barrier. Errol said, in a heavy Indian accent, "Passport, Sahib!" Lukas handed him the document. Errol took it and examined it, scratching his head. In the meantime, the Flower of Delight, a Eurasian girl Errol had hired, kept tugging Lukas' arm and saying, "Please look this way for your photograph. I am the president of the

Paul Lukas fan club of India." Normally, Lukas would have been flattered, but now all he wanted to do was get through immigration and rest up at the hotel. Errol said, "Do you have your birth certificate with you? Can you prove this is your correct birthdate? When was this photograph taken? You look so much older. Why didn't you have it taken without a beard? Are you still married to your wife? Where is she? How do we know you aren't divorced? Did she give permission for you to travel? Are you politically subversive?" and so on.

By now, Lukas was red in the face and ready to kill. He was about to struggle with his interrogator when Errol flung off his turban, wiped the makeup from his face, burst into laughter and shook Lukas' hand. Lukas rather dubiously accepted the joke, but cheered up considerably when he was presented with the Flower of Delight as his bed companion for the rest of the night.

Errol left India at the end of January. He was fond of telling the following story. The Maharajah of Mysore asked him as he left Bombay, "What do you want?"

Errol said, "An elephant."

The Maharajah told him he could have two, as well as an elephant boy to take care of them. But when Errol discovered the cost of shipping them to Hollywood, he was forced to decline. The Maharajah said, "How about a mouse deer?"

Errol replied, "How about a what, dear?"

The Maharajah laughed. "A mouse deer is a great pet. It takes two hundred people to catch one." It was in fact a rodent rather like a mongoose with a bobtail and two long fangs. The Maharajah presented the creature to him in a small padded cage and it left Bombay with him on the plane. But there was a mishap on the journey from Bombay and the cabin pressure failed. The mouse deer died. There were, of course, those who suspected that no such animal existed in the first place. But Errol never smiled when he told the story.

Errol and Irene had a reconciliation in Paris and flew to Jamaica from New York to visit with his parents. For once, Marelle behaved pleasantly, and was probably fascinated by the idea of being the mother-in-law of a princess.

Back in Hollywood, Errol had a very good time on the set. Victor Saville remembers that he sometimes forgot his lines, and had to be tutored bit by bit in order to read the script correctly. Nevertheless, Saville says, he was most cooperative and never came on the stage so full of liquor he couldn't perform. But Robert Douglas, who played Colonel Creighton, has a different memory:

> We needed an extra scene after the picture was finished. It was an extreme emergency. I had already started another picture about a submarine. We were shooting off San Diego at night when the call came.
>
> I was dressed in a German submarine captain's uniform. I left the submersible by speed boat and drove between two destroyers that were sailing off to the Korean War. I yelled "Heil Hitler" as I shot between the boats.
>
> I got to the shore and a Cadillac rushed me to a plane. MGM couldn't get hold of a single passenger plane so I was the only passenger in a large airliner. Another Cadillac took me from the airfield to the studio. I arrived exhausted. I threw on my makeup and clothes. And after all that—no Flynn!
>
> Ten o'clock—no Flynn. Eleven. Twelve. Victor was furious. I was mad as hell. At 1:00 A.M. Errol rolled in. He was smashed to the eyeballs. Victor screamed at him. He said, "Don't worry, Uncle Victor, we've got the rest of the night!" He went to his dressing room. He came out in costume, completely pie-eyed. He couldn't remember any of his lines. Victor took him through line by line until 5 A.M. Errol kept going back to his dressing room for vodka. Finally Errol had enough. It was 5 A.M. and he couldn't see his hand in front of his face. I changed, flew back to San Diego, shot across the harbor and was on the submarine by 6:30 A.M. Errol never stopped laughing about that.

At the end of shooting, Errol gave a gigantic party on the sound stage. Only men were invited. He had had a gold-painted pyramid constructed by the prop department. Spread all over it dressed in lamé Turkish lounging pajamas were sixty of the most beautiful girls in town. Each one had been paid to be completely available to any man who wanted her.

All the male members of the cast and crew and friends who were willing were invited onto the sound stage where a handmaiden waited to receive their clothes. Errol spent most of the party watching the men perform. At the end, those who had acted most bravely on the pyramid of sex were given his famous gold medal, FLYNN'S FLYING FUCKERS.

Errol provided a variation on the mouse races at Mulholland Farm. He removed his fish from the tank and replaced them with piranhas. Each piranha had a name attached to it with a waterproof label made of plastic: Jack Warner, Michael Curtiz, Lili Damita, Irving Rapper, Nora Eddington, Tenny Wright, Frank Mattison, and Raoul Walsh—with whom he had a falling out. His friends gathered, and he took bets on which one of the piranha would win. "Jack Warner," his favorite, had been starved for a week. He won the bet, and finally only "Jack Warner" was left in the tank.

Shortly thereafter, the actress Helen Walker boasted that she had the best collection of tropical fish in town. One night, she gave a dinner party. Errol arrived and professed to admire the fish. During dinner, he picked up some bread and carried it to the tank. Helen Walker smiled at the gesture. "So adorable," she crooned to the guests. "He loves fish so. . . ."

Errol seemed to drop the bread in the tank. Actually, he slipped a small package into it which opened automatically as it became waterlogged. At the end of dinner, the hostess took her guests to admire the fish once again. There was only one fish in the tank. It was Jack Warner.

Errol had become very close to the British financier and banker Stephen Raphael, and Raphael's fiancée and then wife, Eve. They frequently figured in his personal japes and jokes.

Sometimes, when they stayed with him, he would take pictures of Raphael's ex-wives and girl friends and put them in their bed just before they retired for the night. When he stayed with them in London, he would steal combs, hairbrushes, and robes. One day on a visit to Mulholland Farm, Eve went into his bedroom and began poking about. Errol caught her and was furious. "I'm only looking for the things you pinched from us," Eve said.

One night, Errol was dining with the Raphaels at Le Pavillon in New York. Raphael (as usual) had to foot the bill. It was enormous, almost two hundred dollars for the three of them. He examined it carefully. He was astonished to see listed on it a sterling-silver pepper mill priced at one hundred dollars. Raphael called the maître d'hôtel over. "What's the meaning of this?" he asked. The maître d' replied, "I regret to mention this, monsieur. But I happened to see Mr. Flynn placing the pepper mill in his pocket!" Blushing, Errol put the pepper mill back on the table.

Raphael had asked Errol to bring him back an aquamarine from India because the precious stone was rare and expensive in Europe. In Paris on his way back to Hollywood, Errol had presented the jewel, an enormous gem of twenty or thirty carats, to Stephen and his wife, Eve. Raphael asked, "How much do I owe you?"

"Don't worry, Pappy, I haggled it down from ten thousand dollars to two thousand dollars." To the Raphaels' astonishment—Errol was not noted for his generosity—he announced he would make them a present of it.

Eve kissed him and when she got back to London she took it to Cartier's to have set in diamonds. The jeweler examined it through his special glass. He put the glass down and looked at Mrs. Raphael in astonishment.

"Where did you obtain the gem, madam?" the jeweler asked her.

"It was a gift," she replied.

The jeweler sighed with relief. "I was afraid you might have bought it," he said. "It is made of glass."

In 1950, Erben was still struggling, after five years, to scrape together enough money to get to Shanghai to recover Errol's incriminating letters.

Erben managed to obtain a job in Iran as a medical field worker. He was part of a group composed entirely of doctors who had been Gestapo agents, hired by an Austrian physician to work on behalf of the pro-fascistic government. While in Iran, Erben appears to have done espionage work against rebels who were threatening the throne.

Having accumulated sufficient funds through his work with the Iranian government and the Shah, Erben set off on the most desperate and dangerous mission of his career. Nationalist China was blockading the Communists, who had seized the power in China. The channel between Shanghai and Hong Kong was lashed by gunfire; blockade runners were being sunk every week. But Erben would not be put off. He was going to get to Shanghai and recover the precious documents if it cost him his life.

He managed to sail on the Nationalist Chinese vessel *Union Pioneer* to Hong Kong and thence under a harrowing barrage of gunfire past sea mines through the blockade aboard the Panamanian vessel

Walter to China. He was lucky to reach the port alive. Only a week before, another Panamanian vessel had been sunk by a depth charge sent down by a Chinese cruiser.

On arrival in Shanghai, he operated with incredible courage under the noses of the Communist Chinese, who had orders to kill him on sight. He contacted Austrian residents who were trying to flee the city on any available craft to the free world. He learned as he dodged from house to house, from office to office, that his former friendly landlady, Margaret Hoebich, had been among the lucky ones who escaped to San Francisco. His suitcases, including the crocodile leather case containing Errol's letters, had been handed over by Amos Moscrip to Roland Ott, the incoming Austrian consul, in 1948. The consulate had closed only a few days before Erben arrived. Ott had been transferred to Montreal. Erben became convinced Ott had taken the suitcases with him. He determined at the earliest possible opportunity to make his way to Canada to find them. The first available ship, the *Steel Seafarer,* was bound for Sumatra. But by the time Erben sailed, Nationalist Chinese intelligence had relayed the fact of his presence in the orient to contacts in Djakarta. When his vessel arrived, he was not permitted to land. His ship proceeded via India to Suez. The captain threatened to dump him in Egypt. He was terrified of being seized by the British and begged the captain not to let him land.

It is part of the bizarre black humor of his life that the Egyptians refused to have him. The ship sailed on across the Atlantic to its ultimate destination—the port of Boston.

When Erben arrived there, he was instantly transferred to Castle Island, where he was held in detention. Here he was, only a stone's throw from Canada and his precious missing suitcase, and he hadn't a hope of recovering it!

He was sent back to Europe. Three years later, he applied to Canada as an immigrant, but he was instantly rejected after an examination of the files on him in the various intelligence branches in Washington.

Twenty-two

In early 1950, Errol was in Miami with Freddy McEvoy, staying at the Nautilus Hotel. Irene was in Hollywood. He and Freddy had hired a girl whom they shared in Errol's room. In the morning, after they checked out, the girl was found dead. The police questioned them closely, but a bribe silenced an investigating officer. McEvoy never returned to the United States. Errol gave a deposition for the inquest and the girl's death was put down to a heart attack.

In May, Errol applied to Superior Court to ease the financial burden of Lili Damita's constant claims for back alimony. He said that she had traveled extensively in the United States and abroad and had lived extravagantly without attempting to earn a living. He asserted she had been offered roles that she had rejected and that she was capable of returning to her career. After a considerable battle in court, Errol lost. He had failed to meet alimony payments almost consistently for nine years.

Errol also fought with Nora that spring. She filed suit in Santa

Monica court demanding full custody of both children and increased payment for their support. She wanted $885 a month for the children. Errol, through his attorney, demanded his rights as a father to see his children at reasonable times.

Errol escaped these problems by returning to Jamaica with Irene in April. They came back to Hollywood in May after a pleasant three weeks of swimming, exploring, and commuting between the Titchfield Hotel and the *Zaca*. He was pleased when he heard that the court had made a compromise arrangement whereby both he and Nora would have access to the children; but soon he was in arrears on child-support payments, and Nora was annoyed. In 1953, she threatened that she and her daughters would move into Mulholland Farm because he was five months in arrears; and in 1954, she asked through her attorney that Errol "be sent to jail for non-support and fined $6,000." He tried to appease her by sending her a check for $2,500.

Back in Los Angeles on May 18, 1950, Professor and Mrs. Flynn, who were now living in Los Angeles, met Errol and Irene at the plane. The Professor had recently joined the faculty of the Los Angeles College of Osteopathic Physicians and Surgeons. Irene had no sooner settled comfortably into Mulholland Farm than her mother fell ill in Paris and she had to return at once. It turned out to be a fatal move.

Errol was studying yet another run-of-the-mill Warner Western, *Rocky Mountain*. He went into the studio for costume tests on June 3, curious about the new contract actress who would be co-starring with him in the picture, a young singer and dancer from Kansas named Patrice Wymore. She was tall, with reddish-blond hair, a beautiful face, and a superb figure. She had made her mark on the nightclub circuit and in *Mexican Hayride, Up in Central Park, Hold It!* and *All for Love* on Broadway and on tour. Errol took a look at her in her first movie, *Tea for Two,* in which she danced sensationally with Gene Nelson. He liked what he saw.

She had a remarkable talent as a dancer and singer and had been trained expertly by choreographer Jon Gregory. Her father, who was in the oil business, had spent between seventy-five thousand and one hundred thousand dollars to help launch her career, much of which she had paid back through her own efforts.

Harry Mines, a studio publicity man, introduced her to Errol that early June day. Patrice was sitting in her dressing room without makeup and in curlers, wondering what on earth she was doing in a part that called for neither singing nor dancing.

Errol appeared in the doorway, went in, sat down and chatted happily with Patrice. They hit it off immediately. Patrice had a slightly cool, defensive air, probably because she knew too much about Errol. But underneath she was a warm human being: at once simple and sophisticated, innocent and shrewd. She was extremely disciplined, partly because of her dancer's training. She was detached and sympathetic where Nora and Lili had been fierce-tempered and highly charged. And there was another attraction. She looked like Errol's mother when Marelle had been very young. But she did not have Marelle's temperament.

Errol seemed to have struck gold. But there was a problem. He had just announced his coming marriage to the Princess Irene in September.

The *Rocky Mountain* company left for Gallup, New Mexico, by train at the beginning of June. The princess returned from Paris and joined Errol at the local hotel. But his interest in Patrice was increasing. She had been given only a corner of a tent to dress in; he had made available to her a separate portion of his large trailer. He and Patrice would open cans of salmon for lunch or enjoy simple cookouts while Irene had her meals at the local hotel. He quickly saw that Irene would not fit into his life in America. She was too sophisticated and used to European cuisine. She was hopelessly out of place in the West, whereas Patrice proved so good a sport that working with her in this difficult location was a joy.

He played a practical joke on her that was his own way of indicating his attraction. She was fishing in a local lake when a gamekeeper appeared and charged her with poaching. She was carried off to the local jail before she realized the hoax. She treated it with good humor.

Gallup was the most boring place imaginable, and Irene, grumbling at her discomfort, left for Paris again, the romance over.

Errol and Patrice grew closer. But Patrice had her own problem. She too was engaged to be married—to the Broadway producer Sammy Lambert. And Sammy was in New York.

Patrice spoke to Sammy. Sammy Lambert said to the New York *Daily News:* "People said I was a fool to let Patrice go to Hollywood. I've heard those things happen there. I never believed it until now. Marrying Flynn isn't the best thing in the world for Pat. Maybe he can advance her career. But once he drops her, she's through. Maybe I can make her see things my way again. After all, I helped her get started. The ball game isn't won until the last pitch."

Sammy Lambert was wrong. Errol had already hit the home run.

Patrice Wymore remembers how their relationship developed:

We were like two kids. Having fun. I was twenty-four and Errol was forty-one but we both felt we were sixteen. We laughed at the same jokes. People thought we were mad, but we didn't care. It was all a delightful game. But don't make a mistake. We were madly in love.

The couple flew to Kansas on August 9 to meet Patrice's parents. Her father, a big man in a white hat and short-sleeved white shirt, proved to be a warm and generous human being. The Wymores hit it off with Errol. Patrice says, "You can imagine what happened when two Irishmen got together. They had a glorious time." That week in Kansas was probably one of the happiest in Errol's life. Patrice would present no danger of fury, weeping, or suicide threats. She would not take pills or slash her wrists. Along with her acquired New York polish, she had old-fashioned honest-to-goodness Kansas horse sense.

There was no storm of tears as Errol left for Paris in mid-August to start work on *Bloodline,* renamed *The Bargain,* and later renamed *Adventures of Captain Fabian,* the script for which Errol had written himself. Unfortunately, making the picture proved to be disappointing. Depressed, sick, Errol saw most of his script eroded away in clumsy rewrites on the set. But he liked the director, William Marshall. In a strange *roman à clef, The Deal,* Marshall described a horrifying episode in which Errol raped a girl with a dildo, leaving her to bleed to death in her apartment, during the shooting of the picture. Today, he asserts that this was a true story; that Errol only escaped the guillotine because of his outrageous lies and his great fame.

Patrice joined Errol in Paris on September 23, and the couple decided to marry in Monaco on October 23. Prince Rainier was so anxious to have them wed in his principality that he waived the usual length of residency requirements.

Errol and Patrice occupied different suites at the Hotel de Paris in Monaco, just a step from the Town Hall where they would have their civil ceremony. Prince Umberto de Poliolo, a close friend of Errol's since the 1930s, was also staying in the hotel.

Prince Umberto left the hotel very early the morning before the wedding to supervise some repairs on a small yacht that he had berthed in the harbor. He called Errol from the harbor to tell him to come down for a day of sailing; there was no reply. Worried, he drove quickly back to the hotel. He noticed two policemen standing at the door: French police who were not normally permitted to make arrests in Monaco. The prince asked the hall porter why these men were there. The porter said they had come looking for Flynn.

The day before, a girl working in a perfume shop had gone to the police and accused Errol of having raped her. She was sixteen. The prince knew that if the men arrested Errol he would probably be jailed for life. The punishment for statutory rape was extremely severe both in Monaco and France. He rushed up to the suite and dragged Errol out of bed, warning him that the police were there. He looked out of the window and there were police all around the hotel. They were waiting for Errol to come out because the Monaco government had asked them not to disturb the guests.

Errol said, "Where can I go? I can't fly." The prince told him, "There's another way. During the war, a tunnel was built under the hotel connecting it to the casino. The Gestapo had obtained virtually exclusive use of the casino for themselves and their girl friends. The French used the tunnel so they could get in when the casino was closed.

Errol was delighted. He said, "And where do we go from there?" The prince told him they could jump from a window of the casino into a garden and from there take the prince's car to the harbor, where the prince's boat would sail them into the free-water zone.

Laughing uproariously, Errol flung on a robe and the two men took a back stairway down into the cellars. They ran the fifty yards down the tunnel under the Monaco public square. At last, they reached a large metal door. But to their horror they discovered it was locked from the other side.

The prince said, "Wait here." And ran back through the tunnel, climbed the stairs and raced across the square to the casino. It was already filling with people for the day's gambling. He knew the croupiers and managed to obtain the key to the door. He opened it, and Errol came running into the casino wearing his pajamas and robe at eleven o'clock in the morning to the astonishment of the croupiers and wealthy gamblers.

While everyone in the casino laughed, Errol and Prince Umberto jumped through a window into the garden, ran to the car, and made their way to the yacht. As they sailed out to sea, the French police came running down to the wharf. Errol stood on the deck holding his sides with laughter at their fury.

The Monaco police chief was so amused he let the marriage go on the next day.

Monte Carlo declared a holiday. As a result, more than three thousand people thronged the square and courtyard outside the Monaco Town Hall for the civil ceremony conducted before Mayor Charles Palmaro. For some reason, neither Prince Rainier nor Errol's friend Prince Igor Troubetzkoy turned up for the ceremony.

As Errol and Patrice entered the building, the thousands gathered for the occasion pelted them with rice. Patrice was in a white wool dress, Errol in a blue business suit. Mayor Palmaro read the Monaco marriage laws in French.

The ceremony ended at noon. Immediately afterward, the party was chauffeured in four white-ribboned limousines to the Hôtel de Paris. Patrice had lunch with her parents at the hotel while Errol joined Freddy and his parents on the yacht.

Early in the afternoon, Errol and Patrice and their separate parties drove across the border to Nice for their remarriage in the Lutheran faith. Patrice had changed into an exquisite lace wedding dress and Errol into formal attire. Again, the crowd was tremendous. More than four thousand climbed trees and lampposts, or perched on rooftops. Nice, too, was on holiday for the occasion.

A double row of police in ceremonial uniform lined the street on the way to the tiny Lutheran chapel. Special police outriders had to clear a way for the automobiles, and for the large group of newsreel cameramen stationed outside the doors. Contemporary films show the excitement of the occasion: Patrice smiling joyfully, Errol looking slightly bedraggled. The ceremony was conducted in English. As he entered the chapel, the minister was asked by a reporter why he had granted permission for the twice divorced Flynn to be married in church; he answered that it was acceptable because neither of the previous marriages had been performed by a minister.

The wedding party returned to Monte Carlo for an elaborate reception at the Hôtel de Paris, followed by yet another party on board the *Zaca*. It had been a day of great glamour, rivaled only by Rita Hayworth's marriage to Aly Khan. It was a far cry from the depressing little trip to Yuma with Lili and the marriage by proxy to Nora in Cuernavaca.

But right in the midst of the wedding, a man served a warrant for Errol's arrest, charging him with having had intercourse with the underaged Danielle Dervin. Errol, who thought that the police chief had dropped the charge, was appalled at this reversal of events. Nevertheless, he managed to brazen out the situation and was permitted to enjoy his honeymoon on bail. Next morning, the American Navy fired a salute across the bow of the *Zaca* where Errol and Patrice had spent their wedding night, and when he came out on the deck, feeling groggy, a sailor yelled from a nearby ship, "How was it, Don Errol?"

"Terrific!" he groaned.

He and Patrice spent a noisy day aboard surrounded by catcalls until finally they fled to the shore. After dinner that night in Nice, Errol and Patrice set off for the speedboat. A group of sailors began running after them, making lewd remarks. Hurrying to get away from them, Errol slipped on the edge of the dock as he boarded the speedboat and crashed hard against the scuppers. Patrice knelt at his side and all he could manage to say was, "I'm hurt. Take me to the *Zaca*." Patrice took the speedboat to the nearest warship and asked for the medical officer on board. He immediately accompanied her to the *Zaca* where he made arrangements for Errol to be X-rayed.

The verdict was disturbing. Errol had smashed two lumbar vertebrae and the ilium. He had to lie flat on his back for almost a month. The honeymoon was over before it had begun.

Patrice proved to be a superb nurse, taking care of him like a baby, and the McEvoys were a constant pleasure. But in his bed of pain, Errol had to cope with the knowledge that Danielle Dervin's case against him was being prepared.

On November 25, he faced her in the chambers of the examining magistrate, André Biasset, in Monte Carlo. Painfully limping, he made his way into the chambers with the aid of a stick.

Danielle Dervin made her accusation tearfully, with her mother, the wife of a retired hotel keeper, clinging to her arm. Wincing with pain from his injury, Errol looked, horrified, at the long black hairs on Danielle's legs, knowing that it would have been impossible for him to be attracted to her. Besides, he had not been in the South of France on the date she claimed he had raped her. Taking a leaf out of Jerry Giesler's book, Errol invited the judge to visit the yacht so that he could see that the rape Danielle claimed took place in a shower room would have been physically impossible.

Judge Biasset was intrigued by the idea and did indeed inspect the boat. When he entered the shower, he accidentally drenched himself by turning on the tap. He sniffed the water. It was salt water. Danielle claimed that she had taken a fresh-water shower. The evidence was sufficient. Biasset dismissed the case once and for all on December 31.

The good news was mitigated by Errol's excruciating back pain. Errol and Patrice had to return to Los Angeles for treatment as soon as possible. They managed to enjoy a brief honeymoon voyage to Spain, but even that was marred when a violent storm blew up, ripping off the *Zaca*'s sail and smashing the spars. Despite the fact that Patrice had virtually no experience of sailing, she won Errol's unstinted admiration for her courage under duress. She proved to be a fine ship's mate, and he loved her for it.

The couple, in a surprisingly good mood, flew into Hollywood in mid-January. Errol immediately checked into Burbank Hospital for several days of treatments. In his sickbed he began reading several scripts sent to him by Warner Brothers, all of which were boringly predictable Westerns. The only consolation of the miserable month was that at long last the paternity suit filed against him by Shirley Evans Hassau seven years earlier was dismissed because of lack of prosecution.

Able to walk, though with some difficulty, Errol took Patrice to Mulholland Farm. She was not comfortable there. The chief problem was the presence on the scene of Nora's stepmother, Marge Eddington.

It was a strange situation: the two women uneasily under the same roof, and the constant reminder for Patrice of the presence there for so long of Nora: the odd things Nora had bought with Errol, the nursery she had helped to plan for Rory and Deirdre. And then the two-way mirror, the vibrant echoes of old drinking bouts, rows, orgies. It was a house permeated with the lived-in past as if with the perfume of rotting flowers.

Almost as soon as Errol was up and about, he and Patrice flew to the Bahamas, where he hoped to find ways of setting up a tax-free company or corporation, the interest from which would be payable to him through London. The couple checked into the Windsor Hotel in Nassau on March 10. On the afternoon of March 15, 1951, Pat, Errol, and some friends were sitting in the lobby of the Windsor, Errol sitting stiffly in a chair by a potted palm, his back in a spinal brace. Suddenly, a Canadian millionaire he knew named Duncan McMartin came up to him and began trying to provoke him into a fight.

Normally, Errol would have answered the challenge, but since he was virtually unable to move, he could do nothing except brush McMartin aside with a cutting remark. McMartin responded by striking him in the neck so severely that he collapsed, groaning in pain, to the floor.

All of the months of work on his back had been wiped out by this one vicious blow of a fist. McMartin stalked off.

Errol was barely able to get off the plane at Jamaica. When his attorney saw how badly injured he was, he convinced him he should sue for £80,000 ($223,200).

Jamaica soothed him as it always did. There were many friends to provide consolation for the constant pain. His old friend Niki de Gunzburg and Niki's wife Joycie were on the island, and so was Noël Coward with Cole Lesley and Graham Payn.

Patrice fell in love with Jamaica as deeply as Errol had done. Within the restrictions of his injury, they spent as much time exploring as they were able. They made plans to build a dream house on the Boston estate. They took a deep interest in labor matters and planned to ease the conditions of the workers on the island.

Patrice had good news in 1951: Warner Brothers was so pleased with her, they offered her a two-year contract. She worked under astonishing pressure through into 1952, making, in succession, *The Big Trees,* in which she sang a specialty number as an old flame of Kirk Douglas; *I'll See You in My Dreams,* in which she played a Broadway star singing Gus Kahn songs; *She's Working Her Way Through College,* in which she was a singing coed; and *The Man Behind the Gun,* in which she played a school teacher aboard a stagecoach in the Old West. Despite this grueling schedule, she managed to hold her home together, and attained a rapport with Errol's three children.

In early June, while Patrice began work on *The Big Trees,* Errol left with Jack Benny, Benay Venuta, Marjorie Reynolds, Dolores Gray, and several other performers on his USO tour. The team reached Korea on July 9, where they performed for the troops at the Fifth Air Force's 49th Bomber Wing Base. The rough conditions of traveling by jeep across badly laid roads set back Errol's condition considerably. But despite his physical anguish on the trip, he gave a joking, self-parodying performance wherever he went, combining old and new materials in vivid, Bob Hope-like skits.

Late that summer Errol completed filming *The Cruise of the Zaca,* which was subsequently edited to a usable short and sold to Warner Brothers. Its healthy, vigorous images scarcely suggested the feverish nightmare of the actual voyage to Acapulco or the horror of his disintegrating marriage to Nora. In its finished form the movie was no more than a run-of-the-mill travelogue.

In October, Errol began work on a new picture at Warner Brothers. *Mara Maru* was virtually a B-picture flung at him contemptuously as a way of working out his contract. He was cast as a deep-sea diver in Manila in 1946 trying to find a diamond cross lost aboard a sunken PT boat.

The reason for putting him in the picture would normally have been to show his skill in deep-sea diving. But his back condition made it necessary for all the diving scenes to be done by a double, Clint Dorrington. Errol walked through the picture, his face clearly showing his physical discomfort. The picture was delayed when Ruth Roman, starring opposite him, sprained her shoulder. On November 1 and 2, Errol was in bed with a recurrence of undulant fever.

He had no sooner returned to work than he received news that Freddy and Claude McEvoy had been lost at sea.

Twenty-three

Freddy McEvoy had continued smuggling guns and gold and drugs on Errol's behalf through the West Indies and down to South America, using both the *Zaca* and the *Kangaroa,* his own handsome, Dutch-built yacht.

When things got hot in America in 1950, he shifted his base to the Mediterranean. Rebels in North Africa wanted gun shipments from Nice and Marseilles.

Errol selected Freddy's crew. One of those he chose, a man Errol had known for several years, resembled Errol and Freddy, both in looks and in character. He was a rugged, handsome German named Manfred Lentner, who had been prominent in criminal activity before and during the war. Interpol, the International Police Commission in Paris, had an enormous file on Lentner. He was believed to have stolen atomic secrets from the Russians. Caught, the plans retrieved, he escaped to Berlin where he went underground, living as a pimp. When his prostitute girl friend threatened to expose him as an espionage agent, he murdered her.

He fled to Austria, marrying women bigamously in order to obtain their money. He assumed a new identity as Walter Prexmarer. McEvoy almost certainly used him for agenting against the Russians. His usefulness as first mate and right-hand man for Freddy and Errol in their gun-running ventures to North Africa was that he knew they were on to him. He wouldn't dare double-cross them.

At the end of October 1951, Freddy, Manfred, Freddy's third wife, the lovely Paris model, Claude Stephanie, and a motley crew of cutthroats and thieves set sail from Nice to Morocco, where a rebellion was brewing. The crew was not in on the secret, shared by the three principals: what was stuffed into the large number of whiskey crates in the cargo hold. They suspected guns and ammunition and gold, but they weren't sure. In fact, the cargo was drugs—for Errol to sell in Jamaica. Freddy had the hold key on a chain around his neck. One night, crew members burst into his cabin to try to force the key from him. Their leader stabbed Freddy several times with a knife, but the yacht was lurching so violently, he didn't succeed in making more than superficial flesh wounds. Freddy managed to beat the men off when Lentner came to his rescue and shot at the group.

At that moment, there was a burst of thunder and lightning. A freak storm blew up and sent the vessel heeling over violently to starboard. Waves swept across the decks, sweeping the eighteen-year-old cabin boy to his death. Freddy, Claude, and Manfred ran out onto the deck.

They were all in danger of drowning if the yacht were blown up against the rocks. Freddy called a hasty truce with the mutineers to save all their lives. Suddenly the engine room exploded and the masts snapped off. The ship began drifting dangerously before the gale.

Manfred Lentner dived into the sea and swam almost two miles through mountainous waves to the shore to get help. Freddy and Claude lashed their maid—who was almost insane with fear—to one of the snapped-off masts. Then the McEvoys dived in the sea. Freddy, with his long, hard years of training at the pools and beaches in Sydney, was able to make it to shore. Claude was weaker and struggled behind him, swallowing water. At last Freddy managed to drag himself up the beach. Through the heavy rain he was barely able to make out the form of Moroccan tribesmen. As he staggered up the beach, he saw that the group was screaming across the wind, pointing to Claude who was several yards behind. She was going under, exhausted by the waves. Now Freddy took the one decent action of his life. He dove back to rescue his wife. But he, too, was exhausted. Lentner followed him: it was too late. While the others watched helplessly, Freddy flung up his arms in a strange gesture, pointing at the sky. A moment later, locked in Claude's arms, he was carried away into the sea.

Three days later, Freddy's body, clad only in a black karate belt, was washed ashore in a lagoon. Neither Claude nor the French maid, cabin boy and other crew members were ever recovered.

Errol heard the news while making *Mara Maru*. He fought back the tears and drove home. But there was no time off to mourn his friend.

As soon as *Mara Maru* was finished, Errol went over to Universal to start on another routine picture made strictly for the money. *Against All Flags* was a tired concoction in which he played an eighteenth-century naval officer named Brian Hawke who attacked the pirates of Madagascar.

His task was not eased when, on February 1, he broke his ankle in a dueling scene with stuntman Paul Stader. He finished the day's work in considerable pain. And his back was still troubling him: in October, Duncan McMartin had struck him again during a nightclub party, and this had broken another disc in his spine. He had automatically added one hundred thousand dollars to the lawsuit that was to be tried in Nassau in March.

It was not an entirely bleak period. He made a contact that was to develop into a friendship which would last until the end of his life. Through Jim Fleming and Fleming's new wife, Phyllis, the widow of John Decker, he met a young air-freight merchant named Barry Mahon, who at twenty-eight already had an extraordinary grasp of international finance. He had been a flyer in the Eagle Squadron during the war and had been one of the figures in the famous "Great Escape" from a German prison.

Barry Mahon, through his international contacts, had learned that King Farouk of Egypt wanted Errol to appear in a movie about Mohammed Ali, the Viceroy of Egypt, who built a powerful army and navy, and massacred the Mamelukes. Barry Mahon was asked by Farouk's representatives to approach Errol on the matter. Barry, who had met Phyllis Decker over an art transaction when she was running a gallery in Las Vegas, now asked Phyllis and Jim to introduce him to Errol. They did.

When Barry told Errol of Farouk's idea, Errol dismissed it, and countered that he would like to see Farouk's world-famous collection of pornography; soon, he and Farouk became friends.

Nevertheless, he invited Barry to Mulholland Farm for a chicken and champagne brunch. During that visit in February 1952, Barry told Errol how he could save millions in taxes by spending eighteen months of every two years out of the country, and how he could escape his contract with Warners and all the worthless pictures the studio was forcing him to make.

In the middle of the conversation, Arthur Park and Lew Wasserman of MCA, who had been Errol's agents since the early 1940s, called up. They wanted him to sign a new contract allowing MCA to represent him for ten more years. Errol was already irritated by the agency and felt they had not been protecting him sufficiently from worthless scripts. He looked meaningfully at Barry and announced, "I'm not going to sign."

Barry Mahon says he could hear Wasserman's voice on the other end of the line shouting angrily, "Who's going to represent you, then?" Errol looked at Barry again. "Mr. Barry Mahon," he said. And hung up. He told Barry, "Not only will you be my agent but you'll also be my manager." Barry, who knew nothing about agenting or managing, suddenly found himself handling Errol's affairs, and earning a comfortable fifty thousand dollars a year for the privilege. He earned it. He got Errol out of the contract.

Barry in effect assumed the role in Errol's life that Jim Fleming had occupied since 1935: confidant, adviser, supporter, lieutenant, trusted sidekick. Clelle Mahon, Barry's wife, remembers vividly her first meetings with Errol:

He used to come off the set at Universal in full costume and rather than drive in his beautiful car he would get into our ancient broken down $100 jalopy with its running board. When it stopped, which was often, he would take great delight in getting alongside us and, despite his bad back, he would push it until it started up or get in front and crank it. Every day we'd go to a restaurant in San Fernando Valley for lunch. While Barry and I would be content with simple fare, Errol would search through the menu for unusual delicacies. Food was poetry to him. He spoke exquisitely about it. He would tell the history of each item of food: if it was fish, all about the mating habits, the whole background historically, legends about it . . . and if it was meat he would tell about the mythology and history of sheep, bulls, pigs, incredible stories always: later, when I knew him in Europe, he would swallow sea urchins washed down with martinis; they always had to be alive. He delighted in shocking us with such gruesome gourmet habits.

Barry began to make Errol feel that his future should be in European films.

But in his immediate future was Nassau and the trial of Duncan McMartin for assault.

Patrice was too busy completing *The Man Behind the Gun* to be able to accompany him. She gave a detailed deposition, as did the two doctors, and Arthur Park of MCA added his own to the effect that Errol had lost work as a result of the injuries.

Errol arrived in Nassau on March 17. The heat in the courtroom was insufferable, barely relieved by the large wooden ceiling fans that revolved with painful slowness, merely disturbing the moths and flies. The proceedings went at an equally sluggish pace because Chief Justice Henderson declined the services of a stenographer and insisted upon writing down all of the enormously complex medical and legal evidence in longhand. At the end of each sentence uttered on the witness stand, everyone had to wait until the learned judge's squeaking pen made its way across the large vellum pages. Tempers became extremely frayed, especially Errol's. He would announce that the vicious blows McMartin had inflicted had lost him a part in Darryl F. Zanuck's production of *Lydia Bailey*—only to have to spell "Bailey" to the judge. The trial, which should have taken at the most two days, in fact took twelve because of the interminable writing.

Errol gave his evidence with his usual aplomb, ably represented by attorney Geoffrey Johnstone. McMartin, under oath, told his attorney, A. F. Adderley that he considered Flynn a friend and had simply tapped him lightly on the cheek both at the Windsor Hotel in Nassau and the El Morocco in New York, promising to see him in California. Errol admitted under cross-examination that he knew McMartin, but crisply denied that they had been good friends. He said they had occasionally joined each other for drinks. He added that McMartin had sought forgiveness for his belligerence saying, "When I'm drunk, I don't know who I hit."

Adderley tried to destroy Errol's case by claiming that Errol had been photographed fishing in Jamaica in April 1951, in a brochure issued by the Portland Fishing Club. Errol replied, "I hooked the fish but my wife, Pat, had to reel it in. Everyone knew it was a deception."

Adderley snapped: "So you committed a fraud on the public?"

"Sir, I did not. I simply wanted to help the club which needed funds," Errol replied.

After a severe battle, Errol won damages of fourteen thousand dollars and costs instead of the quarter million he wanted. The jury examining all the papers, decided that he had not in fact been finally cast for *Lydia Bailey,* but only considered for it. This typical example of Flynn fantasizing cost him the substantial judgment he sought.

Errol returned to Hollywood. In July, Patrice made a musical, *She's Back on Broadway,* in which she gave a magnificent display of dancing.

The moment the picture was finished, she and Errol left for England, Scotland, and Sicily, where Errol worked on a version of Robert Louis Stevenson's novel, *The Master of Ballantrae.* As if in an effort to appease their star, Warners mounted the movie with great splendor and for once provided him with a screenplay (by Herb Meadow and Harold Medford) that was literate, well-constructed, and well written. Moreover, the director was his favorite, William Keighley, and the cameraman was Jack Cardiff, whose elegant cinematography for his old friend Ava Gardner's *Pandora and the Flying Dutchman* had greatly pleased him. But a major problem dogged Errol now, and in the years to come. Because of the horrifying facts in the Washington files, he had only been grudgingly granted a passport—and then only for restricted periods. The files until his death reveal a fierce struggle to renew for weeks or months at a time—lies piled on lies in the applications—an appalling record for any American citizen.

Beatrice Campbell, the Scottish actress who played Lady Alison in *The Master of Ballantrae,* recalls Errol's natural skill in the picture:

There was a gavotte that we had to dance in one sequence. I worked for ages with an instructor. So did the rest of the cast. Ex-

cept Errol. There was no sign of him during rehearsals. I was
worried, because he was my partner. I didn't want him to tread on
my feet.

Finally, William Keighley decided to shoot the scene. Errol appeared, and I realized he hadn't learned the steps at all. He simply
made a few movements with me. The result was that I looked like a
cart horse and he looked like Fred Astaire. He had an amazing
knack of making something look good on camera that he hadn't
worked out at all. I could have tried for months and no one would
even have looked at me.

Echoing Ronald Reagan's remarks, she says that Errol would
never allow a scene to slip away to anyone else:

I remember there was a love scene between Flynn and myself.
Again, he hadn't been at rehearsal and we simply played it without
his having prepared anything. I thought the scene went perfectly. But
when the scene was over, Flynn went over and talked to Keighley for
several minutes. The director called me aside and I said, "What's the
matter?" He told me, "I think you should play the scene differently."
I said, "We've discussed it and rehearsed it and we both agreed that
this is the way it should be played." And he replied, "Well, it's like
this. If you play it this way the camera follows you as you make your
exit. Errol wants us to follow him instead." That way, the audience
remembered him at the end of the scene and wanted to know what
he would do in the next scene. Nobody was to take one tiny bit of
limelight away from him.

It wasn't selfishness: the method of a selfish actor in the theatre
who works only for himself to the detriment of the play. Everything
in *The Master of Ballantrae* had to build up and support *Flynn*. He
was clever enough to know that he mustn't give an inch, or he would
lose that mile that made him a star.

At the end of the summer, the entire company shifted to Sicily for
the pirate scenes in which Jamie joined a smuggling crew and raided
a galleon. When it was time to go to London, Errol was reluctant to
leave. Jack Warner sent him a cable demanding he appear in London. Errol sent a telegram reading CABLE INCOMPREHENSIBLE.
PLEASE REPEAT. Warner sent another cable saying GET YOUR ASS TO
ENGLAND. Errol waited two weeks before sending a message which
read YOUR CABLE FULLY UNDERSTOOD AND WILL FOLLOW INSTRUC-
TIONS.

There was no sign of Errol in London for two weeks. Jack Warner sent another cable to the Warner office in Rome. It read WHERE IS HE? Nobody wondered who "he" was. The reply came, HE'S SAILING TO ENGLAND ON HIS YACHT.

The Master of Ballantrae earned Errol his best reviews in years. He decided to embark at once on another picture, this one in Italy. Milton Krims, whose scripts for *Green Light* and *The Sisters* had been among the more literate and intelligent Errol had filmed, had whipped up a new script, *Crossed Swords,* as a vehicle for Errol and United Artists. This was the story of Renzo, a Don Juan-like figure in Italy, who teaches a younger Don Juan the arts of swordsmanship and seduction.

While Patrice and Clelle looked for an apartment in the fashionable part of Rome, Errol went into meetings with his collaborators, working out the details of the script. He clashed initially with the handsome and dashing Cesare Danova who played Raniero, the younger Don Juan, taunting him rather cruelly. But soon the two men became fast friends. Lusty and vigorous, even though past his prime, the middle-aged Errol managed to keep up with the youthful Danova in pursuit of wine, women, and song. They lived out much of the romantic theme of the film in modern-day reality, with the important difference that Danova did not need instruction from his companion.

Shooting began in the freezing January of 1953. Errol went to Naples, where scenes supposed to be taking place in summer heat were shot between flurries of snow falling from a black sky.

Errol's co-star, Gina Lollobrigida, felt no sexual attraction to Errol, and this bothered him. She was cool and distant, and he insisted she, like Olivia de Havilland, was something of a professional virgin.

Nevertheless, liking the picture and Danova, Errol was punctual every day, gave Milton Krims some useful hints, and at first seemed to be avoiding drink and drugs. But a specialist in drug supplies arrived from London in the midst of shooting—a sinister character whom Danova recalls "fixing" Errol constantly. Errol began to show signs of wear and tear, and soon could be wakened from a drug-induced sleep only by a morning jolt of vodka.

Many days were extremely pleasant, others were painful and strange. Perhaps because the needles supplied by the "fixer" from

Bagging a leopard, India, 1949.

From *Kim,* 1950. (From the MGM release *Kim* © 1950 Loew's Incorporated. Copyright renewed 1977 by Metro-Goldwyn-Mayer, Inc.)

Errol and Patrice Wymore at their wedding reception in Monte Carlo, 1951. (Wide World Photos)

Freddy and Claude McEvoy on board the *Zaca*. (Courtesy of Stephen Raphael)

Errol's children Deirdre, Rory, and Sean, 1951. (Pix, Inc.)

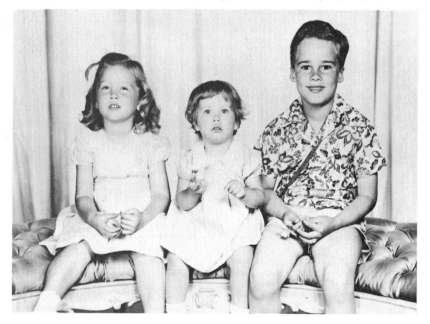

Errol with Paul McWilliams, Jr., 1957. (Courtesy of Paul McWilliams, Jr.)

Errol with Beverly Aadland shortly before his death, 1958.
(Wide World Photos)

With Mickey Rooney, Nora Flynn, and Beverly Aadland.
(Wide World Photos)

Beverly Aadland with Paul McWilliams, Jr., whom she dated after Errol's death, 1960. (Courtesy of Paul McWilliams, Jr.)

Sean Flynn, 1961. (Wide World Photos)

London were infected, Errol came down with hepatitis in February. He suddenly collapsed on the floor of a drafty palace in Rome where he had been playing out a scene with Danova.

A friend of Errol's, Johnny Bash, vividly remembers Errol lying in the hospital:

> He was very sick. Barry Mahon came to the hospital one day and said to the head nurse, "How is he?" She replied, "He probably won't live till morning." And Barry said, "But he can't die before morning. He's making a picture with Gina Lollobrigida!"
>
> Errol shouldn't have drunk a drop or felt like sex. When you have hepatitis you're supposed to keep off alcohol for years and sex for several weeks because you're so contagious. Anyway, who would feel like sex if they were that weak?
>
> Errol was still Errol. He had two girls going up there for oral intercourse every hour on the hour and bringing him champagne which he put in the flower vases. The flowers died, of course.
>
> The result of this crazy behavior was a terrible relapse. Finally I said to him, "This is it, kid. You're going to die." He said, and I saw fear in his eyes for the first time in my life, "Do you really think so, old sport?" I said, "Yes." So he said, "My God. I better see a priest." I didn't find out until later that he was a Protestant.
>
> The priest came in and asked him to make his peace with God. He did. He stopped drinking and sent away the girls who were going down on him. Ten days later he was back at work.

During the shooting, twelve-year-old Sean visited Errol in Italy. Errol asked him if he had had his first erection. Sean replied in the affirmative. Errol immediately went on, "All right, old sport. You're going to feel what it's like to get laid."

He immediately took the twelve-year-old boy to the most lavish and expensive brothel in Rome. The madam shook her head. "It's impossible," she said.

"No, it isn't," Errol assured her. "Sean has told me he's a man now."

"No, that's not what I meant, signor," the madam said. "The authorities . . ."

Errol looked her in the eye. "Fuck the authorities. And get my boy fucked." The deed was done, and Errol was satisfied with Sean's detailed account of what had taken place.

Sean returned to Lili. He never told her what had happened. But he did reveal that Errol wanted him to quit school and join the *Zaca* for a round the world voyage. He also revealed that he had sampled a vodka martini and found it disgusting.

Lili immediately rushed to court to prevent Errol from further access to Sean. She complained that Errol was ruining her son's chances of a decent education. But an amused judge, after talking to Sean in private, decided that Errol should have occasional limited access.

Weakened after his illness, Errol still enjoyed a substantial night life, mingling with a friend, King Farouk, and even with Jack Warner, whom he seemed to have forgiven for everything and joined at several social events that spring in Rome. He and Patrice had a convenient arrangement: they enjoyed the large, rambling, brown apartment they occupied, where Errol installed his monkey, Chico; they spent pleasant hours together at weekends; and Patrice never complained when he went to bed with other women. According to a friend of Mexican days, Jane Chesis, he also dallied, when under the influence of drugs, with Roman hustlers: young, lean, handsome boys who hung around the Spanish Steps or were made available by various call services. Certainly, Pat never knew anything about this. It seems that frequently, the boys would seduce Errol when he didn't know what he was doing, in order to extract money from him, often with threats of blackmail.

Clelle Mahon has vivid memories of those days in Rome:

> Patrice was impeccable. Wherever she went, she would be exquisitely dressed, invariably wearing gloves. She was almost too clean, too perfect for my taste. But I had to admire her.
>
> She was incredibly understanding of Errol. And often, I would come in and see an amusing scene in their bedroom: she reading comic books, he reading *The Wall Street Journal;* and somehow it was very romantic, very charming. She was so ravishingly pretty in her big glasses and her bed jacket.
>
> Errol had a magical talent for perfect gifts, always given with his heart: a meaningful book, one's favorite flower, a lovely mysterious object seen in a store window that would be perfectly suited to the person it was intended for.
>
> In the morning, he would have a wicked look in his eye and call someone out of the depths of a hangover, deliberately to provoke

them to a fight. But he would mellow gradually during the day and by evening he was wonderful. He loved water more than anything. He was happiest of all when he was beside water in Naples or Venice.

Sometimes, when the bad people were getting to him, paving their way into his favors, seeking to get and hold his attention with alcohol, narcotics and gifts, Barry and I would argue and fight with him, trying to struggle for his soul. I would try to help him so intently that I would even try to match him drink for drink in order to get through to him. He would hold my hands tight, and I would see the tears in his eyes you would see in the eyes of a small dog beseeching its keeper not to destroy it. For all his sophistication, he had a blind faith and trust in people. Barry and I never betrayed that trust. We loved him and he loved us.

Clelle Mahon adds of Patrice:

She was a good wife to him up to that point at which she could take no more. The problem was that while she virtually gave up her career to be what he wanted of her, a good housekeeper and cook, she always wanted to be something slightly unreal: a "lady," a princess in a fairy tale. This meant that, in a sense, she was acting out a part, sweetly and kindly, that, because of its unreality, gradually caused a gulf between her and Errol. He wanted a woman to fight with, to brawl with. Somehow, her understanding became intolerable to him.

Clelle Mahon is anxious to make clear that Errol was far from the broken, hopeless drunk he was pictured as being in those days. She says for the most part, he could hold his drink, and even his drugs; he was polished and charming to his friends and at all public occasions. He never disappointed his fans, always seeming stylish even when they would swoop down on him as he left his apartment. He slipped only occasionally. One night, he got into a commotion in a nightclub with King Farouk when Farouk pinched a girl's bottom and she hit Errol over the head with a shoe. The press, she says, made far too much of this.

Twenty-four

Patrice had become pregnant during the filming of *Crossed Swords*, and again, Errol fled from his wife's condition. He had refused to see Lili when she was pregnant with Sean; he had abandoned Nora in Mexico when she was pregnant with Deirdre, and had seen little of her when she was pregnant with Rory. He flew to New York soon after *Crossed Swords* was finished.

Meanwhile, there was the problem of paying for his extravagant way of life. Producer Alexander Salkind became intrigued by an idea, probably suggested by Errol, of filming the story of William Tell. Arthur Krim of United Artists, not entirely happy with the results on *Crossed Swords,* made it clear he would not be interested in making *William Tell*.

Other backers were dubious because they felt Errol was a poor risk: they knew his record of illnesses, in particular of his collapse with hepatitis and his refusal to stop drinking in its wake. They felt he might literally die in the middle of the production.

Barry Mahon and Errol spent weeks going to everyone they could think of in Rome and Hollywood; Salkind appealed to his own connections on both sides of the Atlantic. Salkind obtained $50,000 from a group of Swiss financiers as a guarantee that they would provide support, but soon an insurance report compelled them to withdraw. Errol invested some of his own money. A script was put together, and Jack Cardiff, who had photographed *Crossed Swords,* agreed to direct.

Count Fossataro, the former Police Chief of Naples, would put up $50,000 as his deposit on his part of the investment. Meanwhile, Alexander Salkind found buyers for distribution rights for the Eastern Hemisphere, and the Italian government supplied ninety million lire or $145,800. Errol would provide the raw film stock, cameras, laboratory, insurance costs, and salaries for producer, director, and co-star, who was to be Bruce Cabot, as well as some $430,000 of his own money.

At first, everything went smoothly. CinemaScope was coming in, and everyone agreed it would be necessary to enhance the commercial success of the picture. Barry Mahon took his courage in both hands and went to see Darryl F. Zanuck in Paris, telling him that he wanted to use the CinemaScope cameras. Mahon recalls:

> Zanuck said to me, "Who the hell do you think you are, to ask for CinemaScope? I never heard of you." I told him, "Remember one thing, Mr. Zanuck. There is no law on earth that gives you the right to the exclusive use of CinemaScope. The Monopolies Act forbids any such exclusive franchise. If you don't lease me the CinemaScope cameras and lenses, I will see to it that action is taken against you in Washington." Zanuck saw things my way.

The Italian government money materialized at the same time as the cameras. The script, in which Errol had a hand, was expertly written by John Dighton. A good cast was assembled, including Aldo Fabrizi and Franco Interlenghi. Errol insisted upon a most extraordinary venture: he had a large team of workers literally build the village of William Tell in the foothills of the Italian Alps in full view of Mont Blanc. Meticulously accurate in terms of period, constructed entirely of actual stone and furnished inside and out, the village was a masterpiece of design, supervised closely by Errol, whose passionate interest in history had never been so clearly expressed. The village, visited by tourists, exists to this day in Courmayeur.

The building of the village and the transportation of the large unit to Courmayeur absorbed most of the $145,800 put up by the Italian government. After about two and a half weeks of filming, Count Fossataro's money was needed. Barry Mahon tried to draw on Fossataro's funds in the Bank of Naples: the two men had established a joint bank account.

To Mahon's horror, the bank refused to honor the checks. When Mahon flew to Naples, he was told that there was scarcely any money in the account and that furthermore joint accounts had no legality in Italy.

It seemed that Count Fossataro had removed whatever funds had been deposited in the first place. Mahon confronted Fossataro in Rome. Fossataro apologized and instantly wrote another check. That one also bounced. From then on, no one could reach the reluctant count.

Work continued, but gradually the crew members grew restless, unpaid after the third week. Meanwhile, there was a faint glimmer of hope: Arthur Krim had changed his mind and guaranteed American distribution. But United Artists was not prepared to put up the money that Count Fossataro had failed to supply.

Bruce Cabot strode off the set and refused to continue to work until he had been paid.

In late August, work stopped at Courmayeur.

Errol was devastated. *William Tell* would have followed *The Robe* as the second CinemaScope picture. The film would, he believed, have re-established him as a star of the first rank. The footage shot by Jack Cardiff looked magnificent. But there were less than 30 minutes of it in the can.

Cardiff had to surrender the cameras to pay his rent on his house. Errol put in more money—but it was used up immediately for debts. Creditors seized virtually all of the technical equipment left at Courmayeur. After two months, *William Tell* was shelved.

Then Barry Mahon had an idea. He would raise more money from the Italian government to complete the picture, would approach the Ministers of Finance and Education directly.

In order to give Errol the prestigious image that would insure the picture's protection as a cultural venture, Barry arranged for him to be a distinguished guest of the Venice Film Festival.

Errol left for Venice at the beginning of September. Everything depended on his behaving perfectly on this occasion. But unfortunately there were problems from the outset of his arrival.

While standing with Patrice and the Mahons on an elaborate gondola sailing down the Grand Canal for his arrival at the festival, he was suffering from a miserable case of dysentery. He stood shakily in the stern, smiling at the cameras, puffing at a cigarette, but the moment he reached the wharf he had to make an undignified dash through the cheering fans, desperately asking everyone in sight where he could find a bathroom. From there on, he rushed from screenings to bathrooms with alarming regularity, giving the unfortunate impression that he was totally disinterested in the movie that was unfolding before him.

Worse was to come. The festival organizers gave a giant ball, featuring go-go dancers from Paris who ran riot through the crowd, their scanty clothing barely covering their breasts and bottoms. They darted through the audience seizing every male celebrity they could find and dragging their victims onto the dance floor. One grabbed King Farouk, another Walter Huston, a third the British film chief John Woolf, and a fourth seized Errol. She performed a cartwheel in front of Errol which ended with her legs fastened about his neck, his face buried in her crotch.

The girl's powerful thighs wrenched his neck out of position and dislocated his back. Ever since the accident on the launch in Nice and the slap given him by Duncan McMartin, he had been developing spinal arthritis. The pain was so intense he fell to the floor with the girl on top of him, and many cameramen photographed him in this seemingly compromising position. The girl fled.

Barry helped Errol to his feet, but he collapsed again, crying, "I can't walk. My God, I'm paralyzed. This is going to cost this hotel a bundle." They had to strap him to a table and carry him up to his room. He repeated to anyone who would listen that he would be out of action for months.

Once in the hotel room, alone with Barry, he began to move his legs and Barry knew that although his pain might be genuine, he certainly wasn't paralyzed. It was clear to Barry that Errol was faking with insurance money in mind:

> I told him, "You son-of-a-bitch. You blew everything. Your career is over. Once Lloyds of London find that you're making a false claim, no one will ever give you a picture deal again. No one will ever insure you." It turned out that in terms of the immediate future I was right. Any idea anybody might have had of putting up completion money for *William Tell* was smashed to pieces.

Fortunately, Barry Mahon was not only a loyal friend but an amazingly skillful businessman. He had already managed to protect Errol at least temporarily by making a deal with British producer-director Herbert Wilcox to make two pictures. Wilcox needed a big American star and Errol desperately needed the money: he had lost close to half a million dollars in the disaster of *William Tell*.

Errol and Patrice spent that fall and winter in Rome, looking desperately for some way to salvage the lost production. In November, with Patrice expecting a baby at any time, Errol had to fly to New York to reshoot some scenes of the almost equally ill-fated *Crossed Swords*—and again escaped the sight of his pregnant wife.

Patrice was ill and unhappy at being alone with the Mahons. The birth was delayed all the way to Christmas morning. Errol arrived in the nick of time on Christmas Eve.

The baby was another girl. The smallest of Errol's children at birth, Arnella was just six and a half pounds. Like his other children, she was extremely beautiful, mirroring her mother's as well as her father's spectacular looks.

Errol proved to be a devoted father—always provided that his hectic sex life was not interrupted. In January, he was back in the headlines, trading punches with his stand-in Jack Easton at a party.

In March, Warner Brothers made a settlement with him, canceling forever the contract with him that had been made in 1949.

Errol spent the spring of 1954 in Port Antonio, Jamaica, living aboard the *Zaca*. He had to keep flying to Washington to beg his case in the matter of renewing his limited passport. Jon Gregory, Pat's choreographer, and Jon's fiancée, Helene, arrived to spend the season in Jamaica, frequently visiting the Flynns aboard the yacht.

Dinner parties aboard the *Zaca* were a far cry from the dismal evenings of Errol and Nora. Pat, under some duress, had learned to cook, and prepared delicious traditional Jamaican dishes. Errol had bought the finest silverware and china in England and beautiful Irish lace napkins. The conversation was brisk, and the two couples laughed and drank far into the night.

A main event was the baptism of Arnella, who was now just over four months old. Almost everybody who lived within reach flocked into the beautiful church, in brilliantly colored shirts or dresses, straw-hatted or bandanaed against the sun. A black parson conducted the ceremony. Errol's Nazi racism had been outgrown.

That same month, Errol decided to overhaul the *Zaca* hull and have the barnacles removed preparatory to sailing her across the Atlantic to Spain. The overhauling would be done in Kingston Harbor, less than an hour away by sea.

Just after Pat, Errol, and Jon, with scarcely any crew, left Port Antonio, the weather began to change. The sky grew black and a wind rippled the surface of the sea. Storm birds flew out: harbingers of danger ahead. Errol declined to turn back. Jon, not used to sailing, became extremely nervous.

Telling Pat to take the wheel, Errol hauled down the sails and battened the vessel ready for a heavy blow. Suddenly, it became pitch dark. Errol said, "Jon, sport, we're in bad trouble."

Lightning slashed the sky. Rain beat down on the *Zaca,* and waves, a sinister green, smashed against the hull, causing a violent rolling and yawing. Errol said to Pat and Jon, "There's an L-shaped pattern of lights just off Kingston. If I can find it, I can guide us in." But he could see nothing. Jon, groaning, convinced he was already dead, went down to the cabin and prayed.

Errol strained his eyes through the murk. He and Pat were drenched to the skin. Several times, the *Zaca* threatened to capsize. For a while, it seemed she was completely off course.

Just when Errol was beginning to despair, envisaging a death like Freddy McEvoy's, he caught a glimmering through the rain. He and Pat almost willed the faintly observed lights to assume the form of an L. They did. Errol called Jon up from the cabin. "We're all right, now, sport," he said.

Jamaican boats sailed out to assist the *Zaca* on her passage into the harbor. In the wild wind and storm, scores of people were standing on the wharves to welcome the adventurers.

A few days later, with *Zaca* seaworthy and shipshape, Errol decided to give Jon Gregory a special treat. Secretly, without the knowledge of the police, Errol arranged an Obeya ceremony: a Jamaican version of voodoo at which *ganja* (marijuana) would be smoked. Errol's parents were on the island, and he invited them to the ceremony. Professor Flynn was excited by the idea. Marelle merely shrugged.

After night fell, Errol posted three men at different points on Navy Island to keep an eye open for any approaching constabulary. A fire was built, and the celebrants arrived with the priest. Many of the girls were bare-breasted, and the boys were wearing shorts. The atmosphere was fiercely erotic.

The priest sliced the head off a live chicken and sprayed the blood from its artery over the whirling, dancing figures. The men were visibly aroused. The blood splashed over Errol, Jon, and Professor Flynn, as Marelle, disgusted, stood with her back to the fire. The professor, Errol, and Jon smoked their pot with great pleasure, while Marelle grumbled about the smell. Suddenly, Professor Flynn seized a young girl by the breasts and disappeared with her into the grass. This strictly unacademic behavior greatly delighted Errol. He and Jon took their own pleasures; everywhere they looked, handsome boys and pretty girls were coupling under the trees.

Marelle never let her husband or son forget her scathing displeasure at this incident. Pat dismissed it with her usual good humor.

In late May, Errol and Pat flew to London to begin work with Herbert Wilcox's wife, Anna Neagle, on a picture entitled *Lilacs in the Spring*.

Errol needed every penny he could earn from *Lilacs*. He was involved in battles with the State Department over his restricted passport. In Italy Bruce Cabot had seized Errol's and the Mahons' cars and other belongings, and in London he was preparing a $48,599 suit for unpaid work.

Errol was furious. He had taken Cabot when he was down and had given him a major chance for a comeback. Yet Cabot had proved so disloyal that he even blackmailed Errol, threatening to expose his bisexuality if Errol did not give him the money he asked. He even claimed to have films of Errol in sexual intercourse with boys: whether there was any truth in this will probably never be known. But there was one curious incident that Cabot may have known about: Errol had made a brief voyage down the coast of Italy on the *Zaca* with a young boy named Claud as his sexual companion. For years, Claud, after he joined the Merchant Navy and sailed as a crew member on British P&O Orient ships, showed photographs of Errol with an arm flung around him to prove that they had an affair. It is just possible the "films" Cabot was referring to in fact were copies of these photographs taken aboard the *Zaca*.

Jon Gregory came to London to work with Errol on his duet with Anna Neagle, a soft-shoe version of "Lily of Laguna," and a tango sequence that was not finally used. Gregory recalls that Errol grasped the routines with amazing swiftness, giving the illusion of being an expert dancer.

In April, Patrice arrived from Rome with Arnella. There was a joyous reunion at the Savoy. Errol was extremely circumspect in his nightlife, fully aware of what the yellow press of London would do to him if he slipped even a notch.

In the summer, with shooting not quite completed, Errol traveled to Blackpool to judge a beauty-queen competition. It proved to be an unwise adventure.

He had to be on television on a program called "Holiday Town Saturday Night." Because the organizers were afraid of his drinking, they locked him in his dressing room. Furious when he found out, he banged loudly on the door and when nobody came to rescue him, smashed a window and squeezed his way out of a panel, scratching himself badly in the process.

He hid in the bushes outside the studio while the organizers searched in panic for the star of their live telecast. He was nowhere to be found.

One second before the telecast began, Errol appeared. The only problem was that, though wearing a tuxedo, he was carrying his shoes and socks. The director focused the camera on his head and shoulders while two boys slid along the floor on their stomachs, snatched the shoes and socks from the star, and tried to put them on his feet. Errol fell over.

Somehow, the telecast was completed. When it was ended, everyone cheered.

After the shooting, Errol had to pose with the beauty queens for press photographs. Instead of shaking their hands, he goosed them one by one.

Lilacs in the Spring had little success in the international market. Errol was glad to take on a picture immediately after it.

Originally entitled *The Black Prince, The Warriors* was a feeble-minded affair dealing with the adventures of Prince Edward, son of King Edward III of England.

Many of the scenes were shot in a castle on the back lot that had been built by Metro-Goldwyn-Mayer for the picture *Ivanhoe*. One afternoon after Errol had had too many drinks at lunch, during a break in the shooting, the director gave a signal, and an assistant appeared with a wire hawser with a hook on its end. The assistant attached the hawser to Errol's leather belt and tied it to a flagpole so that the drunken Errol wouldn't fall off the battlements a hundred feet into the moat. Errol was floundering about trying to unhook himself when he saw a car draw up down below. Two girls he had dated the previous night got out, giggling and nudging each other in the ribs. Errol managed to disentangle himself from the flagpole and struggled down the scaffolding inside the tower in heavy armor, a process which took more than half an hour. He identified the girls, spoke to them, then climbed even more laboriously back to the top of the tower where the entire company was waiting at great expense to proceed. The Black Prince addressed his army. "Good news!" he said through his helmet. "It's on with both of them for tonight!"

Soon after that, he was seated on his charger on the drawbridge of the castle carrying a mace, an ax, a shield, a hammer, and several other examples of medieval hardware. The director yelled from the dry moat that the Black Prince must start his progress. "Errol!" he exclaimed. "There are five thousand people in your army! Sit very tall! When I say 'Action!' I want you to lift up your shield and take your battleax and set spur to your horse and raise your sword and say 'Come on men!' and charge over the drawbridge."

Errol sat quietly absorbing this complicated instruction, puffing through the cigarette holder in his helmet. He took the cigarette holder out of his mouth and looked at all the implements in his hands. "What do you think I am, a fucking octopus?" he said, threw all the weapons to the ground and disappeared into the castle to order beer for everyone for afternoon tea.

Errol's next picture for Herbert Wilcox was *King's Rhapsody*, a Ruritanian musical romance about an alcoholic king who falls in love with a princess after an arranged marriage. A ridiculous concoction, the movie held little interest for Errol, but he liked the Wilcoxes and needed the money. Also he was uneasy about Patrice having virtually retired from the screen in her twenties. He convinced the Wilcoxes she would be ideal in the singing and dancing role of the Princess Christiane.

Locations were chosen in and around Barcelona where General Franco had lent a palace.

Errol would rise early in the morning to take his vodka in a Seven-Up bottle or in a cereal bowl in his dressing room when no one was looking. He also used an old trick first developed to escape the attention of the makeup people in Hollywood: injecting vodka into oranges with a syringe.

In many scenes, he had to ride in an imperial coach dressed in his royal finery. One day, he stole the carriage and went careening across the countryside, arriving in a nearby village with a cloak slung over his shoulders and a crown perched on top of his head. He made his way into a local inn. Several peasants who were drinking there pointed a finger at him, announcing that General Franco's police must be informed immediately as it was evident the monarchy had been illegally restored! The police arrived and seized him, announcing that he was a pretender to the vacated throne of Spain. He spent an uncomfortable evening in the local jail.

Late one afternoon, Herbert Wilcox was ready to shoot a special scene in which the king had abdicated in a speech from his balcony. The sun had to set dramatically behind the king's head as a heavy symbol of his resignation as the crowd of five thousand cheered in sympathy.

The company had to leave Spain the following day. If anything went wrong, there was no way that the five thousand extras could be reassembled. Needless to say, Errol was not present as the sun began to go down. Wilcox was almost hysterical. He told his assistant, "Not only won't we get the crowd and the sunset again, but Franco wants his palace back." Just as the sun hit the top of the mountains, there was a commotion below. In a wild swirl of dust and scattered extras, the royal coach came hurtling down the road and its occupant, decidedly the worse for wear, debarked and waved his crown at the infuriated director. "I'll be there in a jiffy, Herbie!" he said. Herbert Wilcox winced.

Errol wove up the stairs and collapsed in the anteroom next to the balcony. Wilcox said, "Errol, I've never kicked anybody in my life. But if you don't come out when I call, I'm going to kick you in the ass so hard you won't sit down till Christmas!"

Errol boozily replied, "Herbert, I'd do anything in the world for you."

Wilcox said, "Don't do anything in the world, just get out on the balcony and give your abdication speech to the crowd when I tell you to do so."

Wilcox called "Action!" Errol did not appear.

Wilcox hauled back and gave him a powerful kick in the seat of his royal pants. He went sailing onto the balcony, recovered himself, and gave a beautifully dignified speech, perfect to the last word. He somehow managed to make his way more or less steadily back to the carriage. And Wilcox said to the driver, "Don't stop till you get to Barcelona. That way he won't hurt anybody."

Errol insisted on dragging Jon Gregory and his fiancée, Helene, off to the bullfights. Helene was sickened by the bloodshed and Jon agreed to take her back to the hotel. Errol, an *aficionado,* was not pleased. Later that afternoon, Jon and Helene were dressing for dinner when there was a knock on the door. Errol produced a package with a flourish. Thinking it was a pleasant gift, Jon unwrapped it. It contained the bull's testicles.

In the midst of the shooting, Jon and Helene decided to get married. They wanted to be wed aboard ship. An American vessel, the *Exochorda* of the Export Lines, was in port in Barcelona for a few hours. Errol took a launch out to the vessel and announced through a public address system, "The captain of the *Zaca* wishes to see the captain of the *Exochorda*."

The *Exochorda*'s master, Captain Ellis, said that he didn't think he could legally conduct the marriage. Errol said, "Do you mean you don't have a Bible?"

Ellis was upset. "Of course I do," he replied. "But you'll have to get permission from the American Embassy and from immigration."

Errol held up shooting for the rest of the day while he and his friends rushed from embassy to immigration and back to the ship, which by now was circling the twelve-mile limit. Somehow, Errol managed to persuade the captain to proceed without further ado. The ceremony began. Exhausted by the hectic afternoon, Jon and Helene could barely stand as the vessel rolled in the waves.

After *King's Rhapsody* was completed, the newlywed Gregorys went to Majorca for a long honeymoon. Errol and Pat joined them, and Sean, on special leave from his mother, was allowed to spend two months there by court order. Sean was fourteen, a fine athlete with his father's looks and a strong physique. He joined in the fishing, scuba diving, and the many pleasures of the island.

One night there was a party aboard the boat. The visitors left in the early morning hours and Errol began to make love to Pat.

Suddenly, they heard a commotion on the deck. A number of holiday makers boarded the vessel in a drunken condition and began shouting Errol's name. He ran up, stark naked, and hit one of the men. The victim responded in kind. A struggle began. One of the visitors bit Errol on the arm.

He succeeded in driving the invaders ashore but he developed a severe infection from the bite. It was impossible to get proper hospital treatment locally or in Gibraltar, so Errol decided to go to Tangier. It was a serious mistake. Tangier was in the grip of political disturbances, and the streets were full of Arabs fiercely fighting the French. Errol somehow managed to get through the military cordons in an ambulance, but the authorities felt it would be too dangerous for Pat to make her way to him through the streets.

She finally arrived there during a brief lull in the revolt. Errol was in his sickbed with bullets bursting against the walls of the hospital. She was only allowed to stay for ten minutes. Then she had to rush back to the *Zaca,* with rebels swirling all about her car.

Errol almost lost his arm. It was several weeks before he was able to return to the *Zaca.*

And while he lay in his bed of pain, he received horrible news. His house, his beloved Mulholland Farm, had been seized.

Twenty-five

Errol had failed to pay taxes on Mulholland Farm for over a year. As a result, the property had been posted for twenty-one days and advertised for four weeks, then been awarded to Robert McIlwaine and George H. Thomas, Jr., for a total of $1,988.62. Its value was well over $700,000, but McIlwaine and Thomas had never been paid for their publicity work on *Adventures of Captain Fabian* and a municipal court had awarded them the property.

Errol redeemed Mulholland Farm by paying the taxes and the fees as soon as he was able to reach Hollywood, but lost it only a few months later to Lili Damita as part payment of back alimony. He was devastated.

At the end of 1955, Errol was in New York fighting charges of owing $150,000 more to Lili. He owed $900,000 to the government. Desperate for cash, he accepted an offer from Universal to appear in a melodrama entitled *Istanbul*. Homeless, he and Pat and Arnella stayed at the Garden of Allah Hotel after a brief stopover in Salina, Kansas, in February 1956. Aware that he would have to behave or be permanently blacklisted in Hollywood, Errol was punctual on the set of the absurd picture and gave no trouble to the director, Joseph Pevney.

But he had to face grueling financial problems piled on the existing ones. MCA Artists and Lew Wasserman were suing him for $13,560 unpaid on a judgment for $38,243 awarded in 1953: Errol had failed to pay 10 per cent on his European earnings before dismissing Wasserman in favor of Barry Mahon.

At least his property in Jamaica couldn't be attached. He had turned the Boston Estates into a corporation in which he had a 51 per cent interest. Patrice and Professor Flynn jointly owned the 49 per cent. He also explained to Commissioner Clarence Johns that his two acres of desert near Apple Valley for which he had paid $10,000 in 1947 were yielding little. He disclosed that his bank accounts in Switzerland, Spain, and Majorca contained only between $3,000 and $4,000 and that Universal was paying him a pitiful $500 a week and deferments.

It scarcely needs adding that Errol's statements of his financial affairs to the commissioner were far from honest. He had substantial holdings in England that he had kept secret, and he had concealed the particulars of holdings in Switzerland.

He finally made a settlement with MCA.

That spring of 1956 Errol and Pat grew even closer. Errol made a special point of giving interviews to both Hedda Hopper and Louella Parsons, assuring them that he was deeply in love.

Paradoxically, no sooner had he decided that Patrice was perfect for the rest of his life than Patrice had to leave for Europe on a concert tour: her voice was now of concert standard. With a small house in Majorca as her headquarters she traveled extensively. She continued into 1957, considerably helping Errol's ailing finances.

During the second half of 1956, Errol made a feeble movie, *The Big Boodle,* in Havana. He had for many years enjoyed this decadent city, with its sleazy bars, exotic hotels, and pornographic films and theatres. Errol had always had a weakness for prostitutes: since his sexual performance was uneven, he liked the fact that they did not subject him to criticism. Always a voyeur, he frequently attended the world-famous performances of Superman, a hugely endowed native of Havana who indulged in prolonged sexual bouts for audiences of international sophisticates.

In the spring of 1957, Errol was delighted to accept the important part of Mike Campbell, Hemingway's heavy-drinking playboy in Darryl F. Zanuck's version of *The Sun Also Rises*. Hemingway was infuriated by his casting, but Errol was perfect for the role. Indeed, in a sense he had almost lived it. There were other attractions. The picture would be shot in Mexico, where he had not been for several years. Pat was on her concert tour. It would present a chance to catch up with old friends like Teddy Stauffer and Ema Fors in Mexico City and Acapulco. He would be working with Tyrone Power for the first time. Power was playing the sexually impotent American reporter Jake Barnes. Ava Gardner was the tragic Lady Brett Ashley.

Errol spent a comfortable spring in Morelia, Mexico, delighted that Pat had influenced him to accept the role. He and Ava and Tyrone met for dinner night after night at the Hotel Bamer, and Errol swam and played tennis with Ava and her current date, the writer Peter Viertel. No reference was made at any time to Errol and Ty's previous relationship.

Errol gave one of his finest performances in the picture. Playing against his natural charm and open-hearted good nature, he allowed his darker side to peep out in the unpleasant scenes of Mike Campbell's drunkenness. He received nothing but praise for his acting when the picture was released in August of 1957.

But he was secretly troubled during the entire length of the shooting. Not only was he suing *Confidential* magazine for libel for lying that he had left his bride for a call girl on his wedding night, but his marriage to Patrice had finally come apart. Just at the time when it seemed to be at its best, it disintegrated. The reason was that Pat, as she says today, could no longer tolerate the sight of Errol unconsciously destroying his health with drink. She saw the deterioration in him and it broke her heart. The correct, tough view then and now is that he destroyed himself deliberately.

Pat's problem was that in her own goodness, she was blind to much that was ugly in Errol. She was so understanding that his intrinsic evil couldn't relate to her in the last analysis. She wanted life to be smooth and clean and sweet, and for that she had emphatically chosen the wrong husband. Nora may have been fiercely defensive, but she was courageous and of the earth: she fought back. Pat, in her blissful sophisticated innocence, tried to give a kind of wedding-cake artificiality to the marriage. Errol could relate more easily to

Lili's fierce temper and Nora's occasional outbursts. It was hard to be married to a woman who "understood" everything. Like many evil men, Errol was drawn to kindness and goodness only as a temporary peaceful refuge from the misery of being himself. Then he grew bored.

As for Pat, she, with her all too gentle sympathy, couldn't understand why Errol would want to destroy himself with drink. They entered a separation that never finally led to a divorce, reconciled, separated again. Pat was in love, Errol was tired of her. He began re-exploring homosexuality in bordellos across the world. He began sleeping with female prostitutes once more. He was more at home in the dark than in the soft light of Pat's bland naïveté.

In the late summer of 1957, Errol received an offer to return to Warners to play John Barrymore in a version of Diana Barrymore's memoirs with Gerold Frank, *Too Much, Too Soon.* The young director-writer team of Art and Josephine Napoleon pleased him with their enthusiasm; they had overruled everybody to cast him. The idea thrilled him, but the role almost proved his undoing. Errol showed the effects of disintegration: his face looked sallow and bloated, and his eyes were glazed. In order to capture the flavor of his old friend, he was all too carefully drinking himself into the stupor of the late Barrymore. He managed to evoke the sadness and desperation of Barrymore's last years, but was unable to meet the discipline called for actually to make the picture.

He was late day after day, and often lost his lines. The Napoleons began seeking his removal but Jack Warner stood by Errol to the last.

The picture turned out to be disappointing, and the reviews, so soon after the excellent notices he had received for *The Sun Also Rises,* were cruelly dismissive. He began to fall apart.

But, with his miraculous good luck, he was saved again. While working on *Too Much, Too Soon,* he was helped by an old friend and a new love affair.

His old friend was the good-natured and intelligent Paul McWilliams, the son of the studio's first aid chief, "Doc" McWilliams. Paul was a fine masseur, and a master at smuggling alcohol into the studio. He would strap small flasks of vodka to his calf and hop over fences right under the nose of the studio police chief, Blainey

Matthews. He would bring Errol vodka in the regulation soup bowl or thermos flask.

He and Errol had the same raunchy sense of humor and enjoyment. Most important of all, McWilliams was an almost exact double, slightly shorter but otherwise perfect for use in dramatic scenes and as a stand-in. One day, visitors to the studio saw a surrealist spectacle: seemingly, five Errol Flynns were walking down the street. Errol and Paul had been joined by Don Turner, Jim Fleming, and Buster Wiles, all of whom at a distance were dead ringers for Errol.

On an adjoining set, *Marjorie Morningstar,* an expensive production featuring Natalie Wood was being filmed. In a tiny concert scene in a summer camp, a pretty young blonde who had just turned fifteen was making her feature-film singing debut. Her name was Beverly Aadland.

Beverly was a product of a Hollywood environment reminiscent of Nathanael West's *The Day of the Locust.* She was conceived on Mariposa Avenue on the day of Pearl Harbor. Her mother had lost her leg in an accident: according to Paul McWilliams, Beverly used to hide her mother's leg in the closet so that she could not be followed to bars or nightclubs where she had made her way despite her tender years.

Beverly was a child prodigy. At three, she imitated Bette Davis in a beauty contest; this unlikely performance won her the prize at the Episcopal Sunday School. At twelve, her singing voice was dubbed in for Diane Varsi's in the movie version of *Peyton Place.* She had previously appeared in something entitled *The Story of Nylon* in which she pursued an Easter egg in the mammoth Technicolor hunt.

Mother and daughter had a curious relationship. Florence Aadland was a brassy woman with an extraordinary range of foul language. She would boozily order her daughter's career, badgering everybody in town until the pretty child obtained work. Her moral behavior was far from ideal, yet, according to Florence's bizarre memoir, *The Big Love,* Beverly managed to hold onto her virginity. In *The Big Love,* Mrs. Aadland gave a hilarious account of a "learned authority on Eastern religions who had lectured all over the world and written many books" who said, "I think men will be terribly affected by this girl . . . men are going to kill over this girl. I have the feeling in my heart that she has the scent of musk on her."

At fifteen, dancing in *Marjorie Morningstar,* Beverly had somehow survived her mother to become a sweet-natured, bubbling extrovert with remarkably few neuroses. She had a strong sense of humor and an affectionate feeling for animals. Errol noticed her walking with her leggy stride to lunch, and asked Paul McWilliams how he could arrange to meet her. Paul knew Orry-Kelly, the homosexual Australian costume designer for *Marjorie Morningstar*. Orry-Kelly found it easy to approach girls he didn't know because his reputation made women feel safe in responding to him. He went up to Beverly and told her that Errol Flynn would like to see her. Errol's reputation had sunk so far that Beverly, who was not a movie buff, scarcely knew who he was.

Orry-Kelly explained; Beverly was fascinated and went over to Errol's dressing room. He received her jovially. He thought she was eighteen; indeed, she had obtained her permission to work in pictures because her mother had been dating a notary public in Las Vegas who had fixed her up with a false birth certificate.

Errol was considerate and charming and talked a great deal, telling Beverly amusing anecdotes. She was petrified. She was so afraid of saying the wrong thing that she said almost nothing at all. But she found him, she remembers, immediately attractive.

The affair of this fifteen-year-old girl and forty-eight-year-old man began that same week. Florence Aadland hysterically described a violent rape, but an actor named John Mohlmann claims he had already taken Beverly's virginity. What is not in question is that Errol ran a very serious risk in repeating his sexual performance with a minor in the wake of his acquittal in the two previous statutory rape cases. Had he been caught on this occasion, he would unquestionably have gone to jail, probably for the rest of his life.

But it was in Mrs. Aadland's best interests not to report the matter as Mrs. Satterlee and Betty Hansen's sister had done. Beverly loyally says her mother knew nothing of this; but it is certain that she did.

Twenty-six

Errol had moved from the Garden of Allah to the loaned estate of the millionaire Huntington Hartford on Fuller Avenue in Hollywood. He and Beverly spent weekends there, Errol greatly pleasing the drunken Florence with his proofs of affections with generous gifts to her. Beverly enjoyed the gardens, with their deer and chipmunks and skunks; and Errol called her Woodsie because she reminded him of a wood nymph. He used to laugh like a child as she chased after the menagerie. Later, she had a variety of pets, including, in various countries, a mongoose, a baby gorilla, a spider monkey, a pig named McTavish, a bird that whistled "Deep in the Heart of Texas," and numerous poodles and cats.

Through Beverly, Errol regained the joy and freedom of his youth. Beverly helped improve his potency. Refreshed by her, he knew the first long period of complete potency he had known since the early 1950s. He cut out drugs completely, except for occasional tranquilizing pills. He even reduced his intake of vodka for a time.

Beverly, with her warmth and generosity, gave him more than she received. She was kindness itself when he had his bouts of undulant fever. She learned much from him, including the pleasure of books, music, and painting. Once again, he was enjoying the role of Professor Higgins that he had enjoyed in the early, ill-fated months of his relationship with Nora.

It would be foolish to pretend that the relationship between this forty-eight-year-old Humbert Humbert and this fifteen-year-old Lolita was a perfect romantic idyll. The age difference created tension, as it had with Nora: Beverly liked to run around with boys her own age, to enjoy the latest dances, and to have the fun of a typical teenybopper. Errol could not keep up with that. Much as she adored him, he was an old man to her. Like most teen-agers, she felt that middle-aged men came from another country. They were mysterious and glamorous aliens, at once dangerous, attractive, and provoking. She and Errol quarreled, sometimes cruelly. Beverly had the ability to let off large amounts of steam, but she was incapable of viciousness: once she exploded she would simmer down quickly, and become cuddly and lovable again.

In the midst of shooting *Too Much, Too Soon* Errol became involved in a brawl at the Screen Publicists Ballyhoo Ball at the Riviera Country Club in Los Angeles. This event featured a number of would-be stars who appeared in curious garb designed to draw attention to them at the studios. A friend of Errol's, press agent Shelley Davis, brought the starlet Sandra Giles in a coffin and a winding cloth. On the coffin was the sign, THE GREATEST BODY IN THE WORLD. Errol arrived at about 10 P.M. He was accompanied by a male teen-ager named Ronnie Shedlo, a fan, secretary, and general factotum, as well as by screenwriter Cedric Kehoe and Kehoe's date, Maura FitzGibbon. Errol began flirting heavily with several starlets and made a pass at Sandra Giles in her coffin. A policeman, William Friedman, asked Errol if he would give his autograph to Mrs. Friedman who was a hatcheck girl. Errol obliged, but asked Friedman whether he was really a policeman, since he didn't look like one. Friedman irritably produced his badge. Errol snatched the badge and slipped it down Miss FitzGibbon's cleavage. She retrieved it and hid it in a glove; a moment later somebody made a pass at her and snatched the glove.

Officer Friedman demanded the return of his badge. Errol refused. Friedman arrested Errol and Miss FitzGibbon, bundled them into a police car, and drove them to the West Los Angeles police station where they were charged as drunks.

Once again, Errol was behind bars. He protested loudly, and his attorney, Robert Ford, had him released. He immediately sued the Los Angeles Police Department for four hundred thousand dollars for false arrest and imprisonment, malicious damage, and humiliation. Actually, his only genuine complaint was against Jack Warner who, when called for aid by Errol's friend columnist Jim Bacon, replied over the telephone, "You just reached a disconnected producer."

Within the month, both sides dropped their charges and the matter was forgotten.

Errol received a script from Huntington Hartford of a play version of *Jane Eyre,* based on Charlotte Brontë's novel. It was a skillful telescoping of the book, and Errol was pleased to be offered the part of the dynamic Edward Rochester. Hartford wanted him to star with Mrs. Hartford, Marjorie Steele, but Errol was convinced Beverly Aadland could play Jane Eyre. It took a great deal of persuasion on both Hartford's and Beverly's part to convince him that the idea was absurd.

Errol was paid $85,000 by Hartford: $10,000 for the play and $75,000 for a possible movie version. No sooner had he committed to the project than Errol began to have qualms. Alcohol had begun to destroy his memory cells. He confessed to Barry Mahon, "I can't remember my own name, let alone a line in a play."

When he arrived in Detroit for out of town rehearsals he was in very poor shape. He asked Hartford's assistant director if he could have teleprompters on the stage. Told this would be impossible, as the audience would see them, he asked if the play could be printed in various books with marked pages scattered on pieces of furniture across the stage so that he could consult them as he moved about. This also was refused.

Hartford told him to keep drink out of the theatre. But during rehearsal Hunt saw him sipping vodka from a glass supposedly containing water.

Amazingly, Errol managed to get through the first night in Detroit without a major disaster. But on subsequent nights he dried up frequently, and it was only Huntington Hartford's help that got him through. Hartford, a good-natured charmer, whom Errol liked very much, protected him through the Detroit run and into a short engagement in Cincinnati. But Errol never made it to New York. He walked out of the production without warning or even a phone call or letter.

He had been offered a script by Zanuck: *The Roots of Heaven,* a story about the preservation of wild animals, set in Africa. The part he was to play, Major Forsythe, was in essence a sympathetic one: a rogue and deserter who redeems himself by aiding the protection of the African elephant.

Before he left, Errol received visits from Patrice, who was trying to patch up their marriage. She was convinced that she was better for him than Beverly. Her efforts proved futile and she finally took steps toward a legal separation.

Meanwhile, Beverly had been with Errol on tour and she and her mother spent a great deal of time with him in New York. Florence continued to benefit from the fact that Errol was sleeping with her daughter.

A curious incident took place just before Errol left for Africa in January. He and some friends were at El Morocco when a lamp manufacturer named Sidney Fuchs came up to him and flourished a fist at him, displaying a forty-five-hundred-dollar ring. Fuchs announced the price of the ring and said rudely, "This is worth more than you make in a week."

Errol calmly invited Fuchs to the table. He engaged him in conversation. Finally, Fuchs rose to leave. Errol firmly shook his hand.

Errol had slipped the ring off the man's finger and pocketed it. When he got home, Fuchs discovered the ring was missing. He charged Errol with having stolen it. Police questioned Errol for a long time. Errol professed himself innocent. He had already taken the precaution of depositing the ring in a local pawnshop.

Beverly was distraught when Errol left her at the airport. Miserably lonely, she obtained a job at the Copacabana nightclub as a chorus girl. Walking by St. Patrick's Cathedral one Sunday she felt a sudden impulse to go inside and pray. Although she wasn't Catholic, she spoke the Lord's Prayer and Twenty-third Psalm and said, "Please, God, let me go to Errol." She arrived home with a bag of doughnuts for her mother and found a telegram on a table. It read: YOU'RE ON THE FLIGHT FRIDAY. GET YOUR SHOTS. LOVE ERROL.

During the previous weeks, he had written to her constantly, a stream of affectionate letters that were later given by Florence

Aadland to the Los Angeles *Examiner*. On the plane from New York across the Atlantic, he wrote: "I seem to be the only one awake—perhaps because I keep thinking of a very strange young soul, whose image is before my eyes as I write this and whose vision is much engraved in my heart." He went on: "I want you to be the fine and intrinsically honorable, decent young'un you are. Tonight there are tears in my eyes—and, yes, my heart, too, is full of deep absymal emotions to explain what I feel about you. Words—mere words, written or even spoken—cannot convey what I feel for you in this all too crusty heart of mine." He warned her of the criticism she would have to face in Hollywood for having loved him, and he urged her to hold her spirits high.

He wrote to her three or four times a week. He was on location at Fort Archambault in French Equatorial Africa; it was stifling, the temperature over 130 degrees and the humidity as intense as it had been in New Guinea. He wrote: "Hi Little Girl Woodsie—I write this by the light of a hurricane lamp. An electric fan is throwing warm hot air at me as I sit on my camp stretcher, and is blowing the paper up my nose.

"BUT—in my throat there is a sort of lump—a hard sort of core that doesn't let you swallow too well. Nothing physical—just pure emotion I guess when I think of you, but very deep and profound—so much so that I find my eyes befogged and glazed and my pen trembles a bit. Of course, it's only sweat that comes from my eyes—perhaps tears of true feeling—feeling for an odd, strange, and different little girl I hold in high regard. Yes, very much so. Please think of this always. I would be crushed emotionally if ever I thought you capable of any behavior that was not fine and honorable and decent as you are!

"You must excuse this—this talk. Perhaps here in the jungle, alone with time to think, with the eerie, strange primitive noises on the air outside, one gets a truer sense of values about people and one's self. Isn't it odd? I mean, you and me, and this true heartfelt, heartwarm thing there is between us that began in so strange a way. And has really to begin. It will—if you want."

His letter went on:

"The other day I was caught staring out over the River Chad, looking down the yellow flow with a hippopotamus sounding off a half-mile down, natives fishing, and this 'friend' whom I won't mention came up behind me and said in a rather kindly manner:

" 'Hey, what's eating you? Are you thinking of what I think you're thinking?'

"I said I was.

"And he said, 'Ten to one she's not thinking of you.'

"I said, 'OK, so what?'

"Said he, 'So you keep muttering you're too old for her.'

"I laughed . . .

"Not too much. . . .' "

He continued:

"Letters are funny things, aren't they? Haven't written one in which I wanted to say so much and suddenly find myself somewhat incoherent—unable to put down on paper those intricate vagaries of feeling that mean so much; if only you could express them to the one small person you want so very badly to understand what you'd like to say. Oh, well . . .

"It won't be too long before I see you, young'un!!

"Please, in everything you do, remember I want to be so very proud of you! When you get mad or sad or depressed or hurt, don't be anything other than the fine young soul you are!"

He wrote again:

"I just bought you some lovely African Moorish embroidered cloth so that we can design something quite different for dresses for you and have it made up."

In this same letter, he wrote:

"Following are the matters on the agenda I will now take up with you . . . Note:

"(1) Your extreme precocity (your adolescence is no excuse) is funny.

"(2) Your almost hedonistic delight in not having any pretense to the rudiments of culture or acquisition of the basic ladylike behaviorism (I think we shall avoid this subject. If I ever find you being ladylike I'll clip you over the side of the ear) is deplorable."

And he also wrote:

"I have much to tell you—so much—but this lamp is fouling up my prose.

"Dear, very dear little girl. I think of you constantly. When I say that there is one constant image in my mind and it seems strange. Strange indeed.

"Both your letters gave me the very strange, very strong, vibrant, vital feeling that you really care for me and I can hardly credit this, but hope and long with this tormented, empty, calloused heart that it is true. Is it? True, I mean, that what you write you mean? That you really love me? It seems incredible! I don't think I'm by any means gullible to the degree that one is overwhelmed by a mere expression of something deep between two people—one so much older than the other and a hell of a lot of other things.

"No, your letters sound real. God alone knows I want to believe you. I want to believe in you. So much.

"This letter is evidently stupid. But it comes from the heart, and that's quite a lot, don't you think?"

One of Beverly's replies was accidentally delivered to Darryl F. Zanuck. Zanuck opened it and doubled up with laughter. He arranged for several African drummers to beat a tattoo as he presented the letter to Errol at lunchtime.

If proof were needed of the joy Beverly brought Errol, then surely proof is to be found in these letters. He longed for her to come to Africa. But no sooner had he sent for her than he was seized by agonizing doubts. He wrote on April 2, 1958: "Woodsie, I feel a bit peculiar—wondering at night, and day too, if I'm doing the right thing. It's no question of conscience, not for a moment, but I worry if I'm not thinking more of myself and selfishly encouraging you to come so very far away . . . anyway . . . I'll be waiting with heart in hand, and hat, too, to greet you . . . Please bring me Oval cigarettes, Emerson's Essays, some quail's eggs in cans and your very darling self." He enclosed a poem:

> Two white leopards, in the heat of the day,
> Under the shade of a tree lay.
> Panting. Heart. Panting, they were.
> They knew these leopards, that no leopard is white . . .
> Knew, too, they were different,
> Like a dark shade is to the light . . .
> Or thought they did—for leopards have spots . . .
> And these two were white—one old, one young.
> So when the rifle flashed
> Hard at the drinking hole,
> At dusk, in Africa,
> The old one hit the dust . . .

Beverly flew to Paris via Shannon, Ireland, and checked into the Prince de Galles Hotel. She had never seen a bidet before and put her roses in it. She spent Easter Sunday trying to find an orchid to send her mother for an Easter present. She obtained her outfit for Africa, complete with bush hat and feathers, and metal trunk with her name on it. Then she flew on Easter Monday to French Equatorial Africa.

She arrived sixteen hours later. Errol met her at the plane. It was the Greek Orthodox Easter, and Errol took her to a party in Fort Archambault, given by the only white people in town. There were Ukrainian painted eggs and special breads and hot cross buns. Errol enjoyed the feast, but Beverly was desperate for a hamburger.

For a fifteen-year-old girl, Africa was a wonderful adventure. But there were problems. She says:

> The bugs were like B-29s. A moth six inches wide was nothing. If you didn't eat, breathe, and sleep bugs, you had no place in French Equatorial Africa. They were in everything. They crawled over your skin and in your hair. They were in the food. Winged beetles, spiders, roaches, and then on the ground horrible things crawling. Most of the time you couldn't see what they were, the grass was so thick. Thank goodness.

> Like the rest of the unit, Errol and I lived in a tent or sometimes in a mud hut or an outhouse. We were under mosquito nets. I was full of shots and we took quinine pills and salt tablets all the time. We were allowed no water, only Perrier. I got amoebic dysentery because I brushed my teeth after two weeks with tap water. I was delirious. When I came out of my fever the first thing Errol said to me was, "Now, see, I told you so. You should have used a dry Sauterne!" I didn't think it was funny at all!

Despite the atrocious conditions, Errol and Beverly managed to have a good time. Errol, so often sick in the pleasant milieu of southern California, was scarcely ill at all in this hell in the middle of nowhere. He ordered the finest food to be flown from Paris and he and Beverly sat at a sumptuously laid table in the middle of the jungle. The actor Trevor Howard recalls that while the rest of the cast looked crumpled, Errol emerged from his tent or hut impeccably dressed in his jungle uniform, his clothes knife-pleated. He had not had his long experience in New Guinea for nothing.

Errol had to undergo many dangerous experiences. He had to cross a stream hanging onto the tail of a horse. Halfway across, he noticed several logs moving: they were crocodiles. Director John

Huston said, "Don't worry, Errol. We'll fire and they'll scatter." "Yes," Errol replied, "but suppose one of them is deaf?"

One time, Errol was completely covered with leeches. John Huston said, "If they drink your blood, they'll fall off anyway." Errol replied, "You should know. You've been a leech all your life!"

Sometimes, despite the fact that the picture concerned animal conservation, Huston and Zanuck would hunt wild game. Errol, with his strong sense of irony, was fascinated by this, but not amused by it. Finally, he agreed to go on safari. Every time the animals appeared, he fired at random, scaring them so that they disappeared. This act of conservation was greeted as a sign of pure drunkenness by the others. They would glare at Errol and say something a good deal more colorful than "How could you?" He would respond with, "Sorry, sport, my finger slipped on the trigger. Better luck next time!" He was not invited on the next safari.

For Beverly, the experience became more and more poetic and marvelous. She says:

> The river with its crocodiles was dangerous but often I would take a boat out and paddle into beautiful little coves. Errol and I went on a picnic I'll never forget as long as I live. The trees were so dense that the light filtering down from the sun made the glade look just like a cathedral. Errol said, "Woodsie, get over there, I want to take a picture." I waved and made funny faces and just when I got to the clearing and the sunlight shone on my hair, millions of multi-colored butterflies whirled out of the trees all around me in a cloud and I was catching them and touching them. It's all lost now: that magical, beautiful moment.

One actor after another was stricken in the later weeks of the production. Juliette Greco was flown back to Paris, suffering from a severe intestinal disorder. Eddie Albert, who had been taking photographs on a mountain slope, got sunstroke for his pains.

Finally, Zanuck called a halt and the entire unit was flown to Paris. Just before they left, Beverly made a special journey to see the pygmy tribes. Her mother had given her two filled saltshakers against heat prostration and when she presented these to the pygmies they were overawed. Salt meant a great deal to them; it was like manna. They wanted Beverly to share their dinner with them in return. She agreed until she saw that the meal consisted of a rat and a cockatoo. She got in her jeep and fled.

Beverly and Errol flew to Paris at the beginning of May. Shooting continued. One evening, Errol decided to revisit a lesbian nightclub where he and Lili had gone in 1937. More than twenty years later, it had scarcely changed. The columnist Jim Bacon accompanied Errol and Beverly. A powerful, leather-clad dyke seized Beverly and began dancing with her cheek-to-cheek. Errol stood up and argued with the lesbian. The woman, who was the size of a truck driver, struck him in the chin. He flew out the door and landed in the gutter. As the former Gentleman Jim miserably rubbed his jaw, he said to Bacon, "For Christ's sake, don't put this in the paper, sport. If they find out I've been knocked out by a woman, I'll be through in Hollywood."

Errol had to report on the set very early one morning for shooting. He had been up all night and had a severe hangover. Without warning, the director let a large, growling hyena out of a cage. It was supposed to chase Errol in a scene to be matched into the jungle footage in Africa later.

Errol looked at the hyena. The hyena looked at him. Errol said, "If that isn't the DTs, I'm going back to the hotel." And he did.

The Roots of Heaven turned out to be a worthwhile examination of the problems of animal conservation, intelligently written by Romain Gary, the author of the novel on which it was based, and by Patrick Leigh-Fermor. But it was too long and flat, lacking in action and conflict until the last quarter. Errol's performance as the broken ex-army officer with his Mexican jumping bean in a box and his weary calls for "Just one more jig, old boy" is a rather cruel instance of type-casting, but he plays the part with dignity and charm. In some scenes, he looks ancient, battered, bloated; in others, he looks remarkably handsome, the features still retaining their elegance and strength. Whether propping up a bar with a straight scotch at his elbow or charging into the jungle with a rifle, he was a good actor in a role worked out carefully for his talents and his range.

Errol and Beverly traveled south to Marseilles and Provence. While they were in Nîmes, they saw some gypsies by the road, and Errol decided to have Beverly's fortune told. But the gypsies were so busy exclaiming "Captain Blood!" that they forgot to tell Beverly her future.

The couple continued on to London. Errol was held at Heathrow Airport for possession of drugs and questioned for hours, but fortunately, Stephen Raphael could prove that Errol was registered with the Home Office as a drug taker. He had brought large quantities of cocaine in his luggage. Errol and Beverly traveled across England— happily at first. But some hotels refused to book them into a double room and the clerks expressed horror at Beverly's age. The Stephen Raphaels refused to receive her. Mrs. Flynn also declined to meet her, though Professor Flynn dined with them and was fascinated by her.

The happy couple sailed to New York, where Florence joined them. Errol was amazingly youthful, dancing about their hotel suite naked in a gray fedora hat with a rose in his teeth. Diana Barrymore, who had very much admired his performance as her father, was constantly present.

And, in August 1958, Errol picked up the threads of a memoir, *My Wicked, Wicked Ways* that he had started under contract to Putnam two years before in Mexico.

He needed a collaborator, and Putnam recommended a journalist named Earl Conrad. Conrad turned up at the Park Lane Hotel, and Errol liked him. Errol began weaving a fantastic, imaginary version of his young life. It made good reading, but very little sense. It didn't matter: his readers wouldn't know the difference, and fiction was always more entertaining than truth.

He and Beverly and Conrad continued work in Jamaica in the fall. Fortified by large amounts of vodka, Errol struggled with the book for several months. There were many distractions: voodoo ceremonies, river raft trips with Beverly down the rapids of the Rio Grande; crocodile hunts with flashlights; fishing for shark and marlin; and comfortable drinks at the Titchfield Hotel, now very ramshackle and run-down, whose resident doctor had the delightful name of Wesley Clutterbuck. Beverly caused a sensation as she skipped noisily through the hotel in her bikini, watched in horror by the ancient and stuffy colonial residents.

For the first time in many years, Errol's sister Rosemary came to visit him in Jamaica. They had run into each other only briefly in New York during the 1940s. Now in her thirties, quite unlike Errol because she was quiet, subdued, and eminently respectable, she liked Beverly and Beverly liked her.

That fall of 1958, Errol became fascinated by Batista's government in Cuba. He visited Batista twice, and was intrigued with him; his old fascistic sympathies were still intact. But Errol was, like the rest of the world, aware of Fidel Castro. He worked out a fantastic plan which he described to his friend Charles Pilleau, to invite Castro on a hunting expedition with bow and arrow along with Howard Hill. Howard would fire an arrow in the wrong direction—and that would be the end of the great rebel in Cuba.

Ironically, the FBI took the view that Errol was pro-Castro and investigated him thoroughly. He conceived the idea of making a movie about the young women who accompanied Castro. The title would be *Cuban Rebel Girls* and Errol would star in it with Beverly.

He had been eaten for years by jealousy of Hemingway who had stolen his thunder in Spain and who had poured contempt on Errol's hopeless venture in the cause of fascism. Now that Hemingway was in Cuba and had failed to see Castro, Errol would compete with him and fly to Castro in person.

With this new scheme in mind, he once more tried to act as he had done in Spain. This time he did interest the Hearst press in a possible series of articles. Then he flew to Havana with Beverly and began to use contacts in restaurants to find out where Castro was, all this under the nose of Batista. He made connections with a well-known agent of Castro's. Along with a good friend, photographer and actor John MacKay Elliott, he flew to Castro's stronghold, leaving Beverly behind in Havana. The two men were ushered into the room. Castro was cool: he wasn't convinced by Errol's pleas of interest in his cause. Subsequent meetings were planned, but Errol was usually too drunk to attend them. There was one brief encounter in which Errol almost rose to the occasion: the two men talked about the balance of power in the Caribbean.

It was a pathetic expedition. Errol cooked up an absurd incident for the press in which, as in Spain, he pretended to be wounded, this time not in the head but in the leg. He and John took a small bruise Errol had gotten stepping out of a jeep and covered it in scarlet nail polish that looked like blood. They later gave a press conference in which the wound was the center of attention.

While Errol was away, Havana fell to the rebels, and Errol could not reach Beverly. There was no way to get through to her by phone. He charmed his way onto a flight to Havana on an old plane which he described as "built for small boys by a firm that makes erector sets."

Alone and frightened, unable to reach Errol, Beverly had been stranded at the Hotel Nacional when Batista abandoned the city and the young insurgents swept through it, killing and looting at random. They pillaged shops and shot windows out; they butchered people in cold blood; food and electricity were cut off. Beverly scarcely ate for four days and there was no drinkable water. The toilets in the hotel would not flush. The lobby was packed with panic-stricken Americans trying to find some way of escape to the mainland.

Beverly, aged fifteen, became the leader in the evacuation scheme. She managed to help some six families out to the airport where they were flown home on planes supplied through the influence of J. Edgar Hoover. People offered her mink jackets, hundred-dollar bills, expensive cigarette cases to insure their freedom. She refused any rewards for her help.

People were shot right in front of her in the lobby of the Nacional. She knew she would have to escape. She was determined to make her way to the Capri Hotel where she knew George Raft managed the casino. She says:

> There was a long circular driveway that led out of the Nacional. I took my small suitcase and started walking. The next thing I knew men were shooting on either side of the wall. I got down on my hands and knees and crawled like a Marine to the Capri Hotel. I was lucky to live through it. George Raft cleared me when the soldiers frisked me. He gave me warm beer, sardines and dry English biscuits to eat. It was all he had. I felt like Scarlett O'Hara in *Gone With the Wind*. I swore I'd never be hungry again.

At last, Errol arrived in Havana. It was a profoundly grateful reunion. He flew at once with Beverly to Jamaica, where Earl Conrad wove his day-to-day account into publishable articles for the Hearst press, and then on to New York.

By the time he reached Manhattan, Errol was very ill. As long before as 1954, he had confessed to Jon Gregory that he had cancer of the tongue. Radium needles had been used, and the condition had been halted. But in those last days in Cuba, he had felt pains in his throat and at the back of his tongue. He got hold of a mirror and looked—he saw chilling evidence that the lesions had returned.

In Manhattan, he checked into Presbyterian Hospital. Incredibly, he had no sooner undergone a painful but successful operation to remove the growth than an obliging nurse gave him an expert example of fellatio.

Errol and Beverly returned to Jamaica to start work on *Cuban Rebel Girls*. The story was weak: Beverly was to play a girl searching for one of her friends, a boy in the rebel army. John MacKay Elliott played the part, and Errol was virtually himself as a war correspondent. It was a clumsy home movie, shot around Havana.

One night, while the unit was shooting in a sugar mill, John MacKay Elliott was experiencing a restless night. It was very hot, so he went up to the roof to try to sleep. He describes what happened next:

> I heard a sound. The moonlight was very intense: as intense as it can only be in the Caribbean. Against the sharp white light, a man was standing on a high battlement. My heart almost stopped when I saw it was Errol. He was duelling. With an invisible sword and an invisible opponent. Waving his arm gallantly: this puffy, overweight man of almost fifty trying to be young again. He parried and thrust and leapt up and down. I went back to my room. I was heartbroken.

By now, Errol had become convinced despite Castro's protests that this new demagogue was a Communist. Castro's spies in the film unit told their leader that the movie was no longer a propaganda picture made to support Castro's cause but was in fact a criticism of him.

Castro was furious. Errol and Barry Mahon, who was assisting in the production and direction, decided to leave Havana before Castro had them shot. A storm broke out, with violent thunder and rain, as Errol, Beverly, the Mahons, MacKay and the rest of the cast fled aboard an ancient, rusty tub that sailed to Key West. Castro's police were hot on their heels and they barely made it in time. They had shipped the blank film to Castro for inspection; the real film was stuffed into oil cans and placed in the hold of the oceangoing ferry. Castro exploded with rage when he saw the blank film.

The journey to Key West was horrific. For the first time in his life, Errol was seasick. He leaned over the rail in his captain's cap, retching miserably. Beverly, sick herself, was so amused by the sight of this world-famous master mariner surrendering to *mal de mer* that she took a picture of him. He snatched the camera from her and flung it far out into the sea.

Twenty-seven

Sometime in July 1959, Errol was stricken with a heart attack. He recovered, but doctors told him he had only a year to live. His liver, kidneys, and spleen were in very poor condition. He had hardening of the arteries and there seemed some indication of a recurrence of the cancerous lesions on his tongue and in his throat.

The press treated him cruelly, describing his gray complexion and sagging, overweight body. Yet his spirits were unquenched. He was as full of mischief and humor and laughter as ever. Beverly recalls that his impish, romantic soul remained despite the rapid decline of his body.

They spent weeks together in Jamaica, correcting the proofs of *My Wicked, Wicked Ways,* walking to some of the lovelier spots in the island. Over several visits, they had started to build a house that was a reflection of their dreams. In front of the house stood an oak tree that had been there since Captain Bligh had landed near the spot. This echo of Errol's ancestral past reminded him of the days of Fletcher Christian and Edward Young. He told Beverly he wanted to

be buried in its shade, so that his bones would one day mingle with
its powerful roots. He also told her he wanted to be married under
the spreading branches, so that their relationship would be secure as
long as he lived.

They even had a tiny ceremony of their own, pretending the tree
was a minister. It was a joyful, slightly mad moment, typical of Errol
in its humor and extravagance.

The rest of the summer was divided between New York and
Hollywood. When the couple returned in mid-August to the West
Coast, Beverly was wearing an engagement ring. Nora met Errol at
the airport with Deirdre and Rory. Beverly went off with a friend.
On the way to the hotel, Errol told Nora he had only a few months
to live. He told her he had disinherited Patrice in favor of the
children.

Errol, who had managed only scattered meetings with Deirdre and
Rory over the years, saw them more often in those weeks. Despite
his frequent neglect of them and the miserable court battle with Nora
over money for their support, they retained a deep love of him. They
longed to go to Jamaica with him and Errol promised he would arrange it. They both liked Beverly immensely; they were about the
same age.

In Hollywood, Errol appeared in *The Golden Shanty,* a "General
Electric Theatre" teleplay co-starring Patricia Barry, in which he
played a traveling quack in the sticks, and on a Red Skelton Show as
a tramp, with Beverly as a hippie and Red Skelton as another bum.
Errol could not resist one more practical joke. On his instruction, a
member of Skelton's talent team took Beverly into a schoolroom
with numerous children and placed her at a tiny desk with the words,
"You're just in time for milk and cookies." Beverly was so furious
she broke into Errol's dressing room and socked him in the jaw.

Errol was equally impish over the matter of his will. He had told
Nora on their car journey from the airport that he had left everything to his children in trust. Now he told Patrice and Beverly that
each was the sole heir. Nobody knew who would be getting the
money. It was characteristically perverse of him to kick up a contro-
versy that he knew would only be resolved after his death.

He also disclosed yet another joke to Ida Lupino. He told her that
his autobiography was devised in order to make sure the public
would know absolutely nothing about him. He said, "My closest
friends are not mentioned in it. I've done them the honor of leaving

them out of it. You're one of them. If I had put you in, you'd have suspected the book was full of truths about Errol Flynn. It isn't."

He gave a valedictory interview to one of his favorite reporters, Vernon Scott, of the Los Angeles *Herald Express,* in September. He told Scott, "I've squandered seven million dollars. I'm going to have to sell the *Zaca.* I need the money, old bean. But don't grieve for me when I go. The way of a transgressor is not as hard as they claim. I suppose I'll be criticized, but it's a question of living life the way you see fit, and I've been careless of other people's opinions. I never thought the public would be interested in my so-called antics.

"Years ago it was a matter of choosing which road to travel. After all, there is only one road to hell, and there weren't any signposts along the way. I've taken the human disasters in the same stride as the good times. And I hope I managed to face it all with a brave front. You shouldn't distress your friends or have them feel the disasters.

"I've lived hard, spent hard and behaved as I damn well chose. You'd think I'd be ready for the wheelchair after the last twenty years of hell raising, but I never felt better."

A gallant statement of his philosophy, followed by a gallant lie to conclude it: it was a marvelous last interview.

In September, Errol and the publicist Majorie Walker supervised a party in honor of Beverly's birthday. It was also a feeble attempt to attract attention to *Cuban Rebel Girls* which Barry Mahon had induced Errol to try to publicize, though Errol had begged him to shelve it. Marjorie pulled together Errol's friends old and new. The cake was adorned with tiny figures of Cuban rebel girls and a replica of a motion-picture camera.

In the second week of October, Errol decided to accept an offer for the *Zaca.* She was moored in Majorca and was being used for charters. A Vancouver businessman named George Caldough was offering $150,000. The money would bail Errol out with Pat and would clear the way to his marriage late that fall to Beverly in Jamaica.

Errol's friend, Shelley Davis, his new press agent, Helene Heigh, and his last agent, Dick Irving Hyland, all confirmed that, during those last weeks in Los Angeles, Errol's homosexuality again came to the fore. Helene Heigh, who also handled Beverly, says: "I happen to know that Errol was having an affair with a young male admirer of his at the same time as his affair with Beverly."

Just before they left Los Angeles a good friend of theirs, Marilyn Hinton, gave a farewell party for Errol and Beverly. She remembers:

> During the party, Beverly wandered off to an indoor pool with a waterfall and a little rubber boat. She climbed into the boat and began paddling about happily like a little child. Ronnie Shedlo was upset. He seized hold of the boat to pull it in, telling Beverly she was making a fool of herself at a sophisticated gathering. In doing so, he accidentally capsized the boat and Beverly fell in the water, ruining her dress. She wept and wept. It was so sad and pathetic. She ran to the bathroom. Errol went in to console her. He held her very close. I never saw such tenderness in a man's eyes. He was almost in tears himself because of her embarrassment. That night was the last time I ever saw Errol.

Beverly and Errol flew to Vancouver where they had an agreeable stay with the Caldoughs and saw some of the sights.

On October 14, with most of the negotiations for the sale of the *Zaca* completed, they were on the way to the airport when Errol felt acute pain in his back and legs. George Caldough, who was driving, suggested he take Errol to a doctor friend's apartment.

When the party arrived at Dr. Grant Gould's apartment, Gould made an examination. Errol told Beverly he would have to lie on the floor of the bedroom to ease the pain.

He lay there for some time, while Beverly, the Caldoughs, and the Goulds talked away in the living room. Then Beverly went in to see how he was. She noticed he was trembling and that his face was blue. She put a coat over him and bent down to kiss his lips. The sight of her beautiful face, eyes full of love, was almost certainly the last thing he ever saw.

He did not seem to be breathing. She felt his pulse; it was ticking very faintly. She put her ear to his heart. There was scarcely a sound. She screamed and ran into the living room. First Dr. Gould, and then George Caldough ran in and began pounding his chest. Beverly tried mouth-to-mouth resuscitation, desperately forcing her breath into his throat. "He's having a coronary," Dr. Gould said.

While the others worked on the dying man, Beverly ran onto the balcony and looked up at the sky, which was dark with clouds. She cried out, "Take me, please Lord, not him."

The ambulance team arrived. They gave Errol oxyen and carried him on a stretcher to the ambulance. Beverly was hysterical. She began pounding her head against the balcony railing. The Caldoughs were afraid she would throw herself the thirty feet to the ground. They managed to drag her back and take her down to the ambulance.

Errol never regained consciousness. Beverly was crying miserably in the hospital when the doctors told her, "We're sorry, we did all we could." She says:

I went into a little curtained-off room and saw that Errol had a very large bruise on his forehead. It was explained that when you pump oxygen into a corpse, it blows things up in the brain.

I remember going out of the room. I was screaming for them to wake him up. At my age, I didn't know what death was. When my cat died, Mother told me a rich lady stole it.

They took me off and set me down in a chair someplace to get a shot. I fell to the floor beating my hands on it until they were bloody. Four or five stones rolled out of my engagement ring. I began looking for them, scrabbling across the floor.

They put me in a straitjacket. I woke up in a room, locked up tight, with that terrible thing on me. I couldn't move.

At last they let me out of it. I drove away from the hospital in the back seat of the Caldoughs car with their huge dog beside me. The news came on the radio of Errol's death. The voice said, "We're sorry to announce that veteran actor Errol Flynn died tonight in Vancouver of a major coronary." I said to the Caldoughs, "They're crazy. What are they talking about? He isn't dead. He's off doing something. He'll be back." I couldn't believe he was gone. I couldn't accept it for six months. If one of his movies came on TV, I'd go across and kiss his face on the lips. And, for me, he's still alive. Sometimes I wake up in the night, and feel he's there.

Jim Fleming told me in 1970: "I haven't wanted to say this until now. But I had conclusive evidence from somebody who was very close to Errol at the end that he deliberately killed himself by overdosing himself with morphine. I suppose he had had enough. The cancer had returned and life was no longer a pleasure. Feeling himself to be a burden to Beverly and everybody else, he took the fastest way out. Suicide."

The death certificate, dated October 23, indicated myocardial infarction, coronary thrombosis, coronary atherosclerosis, liver degeneration, liver sclerosis, and diverticulosis of the colon as the causes of death.

Up to the last moment of his life, Errol had worn around his neck the key to the safe-deposit box in Switzerland that contained numerous personal papers, stock certificates, bonds, and some half million dollars in cash. The key disappeared from his neck sometime between the apartment and the autopsy room. Nobody knows who stole it. Three weeks later, when Justin Golenbock authorized someone in Switzerland to open the box, it was empty. The mystery has never been solved.

Ronnie Shedlo flew to Vancouver to accompany Beverly on the flight to Los Angeles. The flight stopped at several airports, and they had to change planes in Seattle. At every airport, crowds rushed in on them, trying to catch a glimpse of Beverly. In Seattle, she ran into a bar, only to be ejected because she was underage. When several reporters cornered her, the only refuge she could find was in the ladies' room.

At the Los Angeles airport, newspaper men had been lined up behind a protective barrier. In drenching rain they broke through it and swept down on Beverly. She collapsed, soaked to the skin. Shedlo, who had become equally hysterical under the pressure of the journey, stood over her prone figure waving his cane and shouted, "You barbarians! I'll hit you with this! Why don't you leave us alone?" Then he helped Beverly to her feet and stumbled off with her through the storm.

Florence Aadland, press agent Helene Heigh, Mrs. Melvin Belli, and a friend of Beverly's named Linda Tartar surrounded Beverly and Ronnie as they fought through the mob. Beverly, with a black cloak flung over her head, was so heavily sedated that she lost her shoe. Linda Tartar rescued it. A fan magazine woman said to Beverly, "Can I have an interview?" Ronnie Shedlo told her sharply that she could not.

But Beverly's mother proved equal to the occasion. Florence Aadland gave a small press conference saying with more than one eye at the photographers, "Patrice Wymore, the widow Flynn, may have his body. But Beverly has his love and her dreams forever."

Beverly, Ronnie, Helene, Mrs. Belli, Linda, and the reporter Joe Finnigan of United Press International made their way to Mrs.

Belli's car and drove off into the storm. To protect Beverly from further harassment, she was taken to San Francisco and became a temporary ward of the Bellis.

Patrice heard the news as she was leaving the stage of a Washington, D.C., nightclub. She was deeply distressed but stoical as always. She dried her tears and, pale and trembling, flew to Hollywood at once to supervise the funeral arrangements.

Patrice arranged with Buster Wiles to transfer the body to Los Angeles by train.

The corpse was laid in a plain pine box marked "Please handle carefully" and deposited in the freight car.

Wiles accompanied it on the long journey south. He sat on the coffin, swallowing several drinks. He was sure Errol would have wanted him to enjoy himself.

About halfway to Los Angeles, Buster was still sitting on the coffin slightly the worse for wear, swaying gently with the movement of the train, when suddenly, he heard a shattering sound that made him jump in the air, every hair on his head on end. He was convinced Errol was beating his fists against the coffin lid. Actually, a freight-car door had blown open.

Much to the annoyance of Beverly and Nora, Patrice ignored Errol's own wishes for his last rites. She refused to ship the body to Jamaica for interment under the old oak tree. Nor would she countenance burial in a Jamaican churchyard or cremation with the ashes scattered at sea.

She was determined to have the funeral at Forest Lawn, and she refused the pleas of everyone, including her stepchildren, to have a marker on the grave. Even she cannot explain why. In 1979, Deirdre, Rory, and Arnella at last supplied the marker.

Nora had always known that Errol hated the idea of being buried in a suit, but Patrice insisted on a gray suit, formal white shirt, and dark tie. When Nora went into the slumber room to inspect the body in its open casket, she was disgusted and deliberately loosened the tie. She couldn't face going to the funeral.

Worse still, the coffin was completely covered in yellow roses, Errol's least favorite flower. Beverly sent a single red rose with a message attached.

Beverly, too, stayed away from the funeral—as did Lili. Sean flew in from Palm Beach. Jon Gregory escorted Deirdre and Rory. Patrice, disgusted by the circus accompanying Tyrone Power's funeral the year before, had tried to discourage people from coming. Dennis Morgan sang a version of Robert Louis Stevenson's poem that began, ironically in this context, "Here he lies where he longed to be."

And the bitterest irony of all: Jack Warner was chosen to deliver the eulogy.

Epilogue

Within days, the tragicomedy went into its second act. Nora, Beverly, and several other heirs began instituting claims against the estate, though Errol's will, dated April 27, 1954, left everything to Patrice except for small legacies to the children.

His American assets, some $430,000 in all, were controlled by Justin Golenbock, who was to disburse them to the various creditors, notably the Internal Revenue Service, which also obtained the rights and royalties on *My Wicked, Wicked Ways*. Stephen Raphael, by skillful use of investments, saved $850,000 for the estate in London. Justin Golenbock tried to have this money sent to America to meet further debts for taxation and unpaid bills; Patrice fought to retain the funds on the ground that British authorities were not compelled to pay American taxes out of an estate. She won; and the money was obtained by her, less substantial deductions, including $100,000 to Huntington Hartford, and legacies to the children and to Professor and Mrs. Flynn. Sean was left $15,000 which he never lived to collect. After seven years his share reverted to his half sisters.

To this day, Nora is convinced that there was another will, revoking the one which left everything to Patrice. But there is no evidence that Errol was telling Nora the truth when he led her to believe that. Deirdre, through her guardian, Curley C. Hoffpauir, also became a litigant. She asserted that Justin Golenbock had either misplaced, lost, or destroyed the will revoking the one favorable to Patrice. The charge further claimed that the will favoring Patrice was procured by fraud and undue influence practiced on him by Patrice or person or persons unknown acting in concert with her. Sean and Rory also claimed against the estate on the same grounds. The court decided, after hearing all complaints, that there was no reason to believe that the will referred to existed, or had been destroyed. It was Errol's last cruel black joke at Nora's expense.

Beverly and her mother sued the estate on February 27, 1961. Beverly charged that Errol had "debauched and corrupted her through repeated or persistent immoralities," and asked for five million dollars in settlement, a sum far in excess of that remaining in the estate. Patrice called for a dismissal. In refusing to grant the Aadlands even a minimal settlement, Judge Samuel Hofstadter made a number of points. He referred to the charge that Errol had "led Beverly along the byways of immorality, accustomed her to a life of frenzied parties, subjected her to immoral debauchery and sex orgies . . . and roused within her a lewd, wanton and wayward way of life, and deep unripened passions and unnatural desires inimical to the interest, welfare and fulfillments of her normal youth." The document went on to state that Flynn "deprived her of the God given opportunity of coming into bloom as a normal woman. He robbed her of all the beauty, wonder and joy of her youthful years of normal growth and development . . . [he forced her] to conform to [his] overpowering and magnetic demand for a loose and carefree companion who would adopt his unhealthy, his unwholesome and perverted philosophy of wringing every pleasure out of life today, regardless of the cost, for there might not be a tomorrow."

There seems no doubt that the author of this extraordinary document was Beverly's outrageously florid mother. As though her use of language were catching, Judge Samuel Hofstadter embarked on a no less extraordinary response. He stated:

> Doubtless, the unfortunate young woman has been victimized—but
> by whom? Even during the pendency of this motion, she has been

exploited by being paraded at various nightclubs for the unwhole-some edification of their patrons. To be sure, Flynn was the immediate occasion for her degradation. But was he the sorcerer's apprentice who evoked a demon in her—or, was he not himself the issue of an evil spirit—one of the creatures which "never remains solitary (because) every demon evokes its counter-demon" in an endless moral chain reaction? In an ultimate sense, was not Flynn the victim of the deep social contamination? For we live in a climate of physical violence compounded by moral confusion. The drive for power and possession has generated talent without scruple, contesting for ascendance—of which Flynn was but an egregious exemplar.

The judge launched into an elaborate attack on crime, television, and movies, blaming the effect of these morally corruptive instruments for the decline of the young. Then he pronounced judgment. He dismissed Beverly's suit without even a minimal settlement.

By 1963 Patrice was in complete possession.

Many people believed, and believe today, that in some mysterious way Errol visited them after his death. They heard his laugh, his footstep, just around a corner. Ida Lupino, who had shared so many discussions with Errol of psychic matters, recalls an extraordinary event that took place some months after Errol's death. She was at the home of director and actor Richard Whorf and his wife on Christmas Eve when she was seized by a strange feeling. She felt that Errol was standing next to her and telling her that her mother, Connie Emerald, was not going to live through the night. Ida said to her husband, Howard Duff, "Errol is here. And father now. Mother is going to be killed." They left the party and drove back to their home. As they opened the door, the phone was ringing. Duff answered it and dropped it to the table. He looked pale as he said, "My God, you were right. Connie has been smashed to pieces in a car crash and the hospital is calling."

Ida takes up the story from there:

> We drove off into the night. We tore into the ward and my poor little mother was indeed smashed to pieces. Someone had driven her from her business in Las Vegas on that wet night on the wrong side of the road. Howard went to fetch a doctor friend and I sat by mother's bed. Amazingly, the book at hand was Errol's autobiography. She begged me to read it to her and I did until she slipped off into sleep.

Eventually, she opened her eyes and said, "This is it. I'm going to Errol. He always said he would be waiting for me. He's outside the window. Would you and the Little Scout, Doctor, carry me to the window? You remember in *Wuthering Heights* how they carried Cathy to the window to look out at the moors before she died? I'll try to imagine the moors and Errol waiting for me like Heathcliff." We carried her to the window and just as she reached it, she said, "Errol is here. Goodbye, Little Scout. I'm going to join Errol now." And at that moment she died.

Errol had always dreamed in his precognitive dreams that Connie would be buried beside him in Forest Lawn. And amazingly, the place they found for her in the Garden of Everlasting Peace was right next to his grave. There's a tree that blooms over both their graves. Whenever I go there, I put flowers on them. Errol hated that place. But at least he and Connie, the Duchess, are together there now. Or wherever they are. . . .

Lili Damita did not remarry until 1962. Her husband is a prominent Iowa dairyman. She divides her time between Fort Dodge, Iowa, and Palm Beach.

In 1962 also, Patrice announced her forthcoming marriage to Texas insurance executive Mack Caudle, but the union never took place. In 1968, she returned to Jamaica and managed the estate, building it up from a run-down condition to its present prosperity.

In 1965, Nora married Richard Black, a wealthy businessman. They had a son, who died of leukemia at the age of twelve.

Sean had an abortive movie career, imitating his father in a feeble epic named *The Son of Captain Blood.* Sean, though physically handsome and dashing, lacked his father's style and magnetism. Disappointed, he became a *Time-Life* photographer and traveled to Vietnam to cover the war. He disappeared in April 1970, and has not been seen since. Until 1978 Lili was convinced he was still alive and spent a fortune searching for him. His bedroom in her home remained fully furnished; his clothes in the closet, awaiting his return. She told me in 1979 she had given up hope.

Deirdre became a stunt girl in pictures and Rory spent much of her life as a model in London, where she became involved with a member of the "Yes" rock group, after a brief marriage to a man named Kyle Lind.

Her half-sister, Arnella, is a successful New York model.

Professor Flynn died at the age of eighty-five in 1968. Shortly before, the unhappy Marelle stepped in front of a car near the English town of Brighton and died as a result of her injuries.

Beverly scarcely knew what she was doing for the next six months. When she was still only seventeen, she was plunged into a series of sordid events. One night, a young hoodlum she was dating burst into her apartment and raped her at gunpoint; in the struggle, his gun accidentally discharged and a bullet entered his brain. Beverly was not charged, but her mother was tried and sentenced for contributing to the delinquency of a minor. One accusation was that she had watched while her daughter had sexual intercourse. Florence was placed on probation but when she broke her janitor's shinbone with her wooden leg in an outburst of rage, she was sentenced to serve out the remaining days of her probation in jail. She died two years later. Beverly had three marriages, only the last of which brought her happiness.

Dr. Erben's latter day history was as remarkable as that which preceded it. He kept turning up in the most unlikely places, including Iran, Saudi Arabia and, after the first refusal, Indonesia. He tried to re-enter the United States in 1968 with the aid of Senator Louis Wyman—but failed because of his espionage record. He was awarded the Golden Cross for his work in Afghanistan on behalf of the Austrian government on March 21, 1973. At the very moment he received this important honor, he was on trial for negligence in causing the death of an ambulance patient in Vienna. He was given a suspended sentence.

In the Philippines, Erben was still the subject of speculation. There were rumors that he was being investigated for criminal activities. My correspondent in Manila, Marcos Agayo, reports: "Erben is not really under criminal investigation. He was just asked, informally, by the Chief of Police of Sagada what he was doing since there was a rumor about him being an agent of a company running guns to Rhodesia and South Africa.

"The questioning of Dr. Erben by the Chief of Police is one of several cases of mild harassment by some people of Sagada who do not like him. It is perhaps hard for many of the people of Sagada to like him because he is very undiplomatic in giving out criticism and, at the same time, has not accomplished, to any considerable degree, what the people *think* he is in the Philippines for—to establish

Sagada as a base, a hospital for Aborigines who do not have access to medical services.

"Dr. Erben is here, as he said to me many times, for a 'fact-finding mission' for the establishment of a hospital; it is not really very definite that a hospital will be established. The distinction between a fact-finding mission and a definite plan to establish a hospital has been overlooked by most of Dr. Erben's critics."

Dr. Erben is today reformed—for years devoted to leprosy study among aboriginal tribes.

What is the solution to the great mystery of the missing Flynn letters written to Erben during the war? I at last found out in Fall, 1979.

In 1948, the Austrian Consulate was reopened in Shanghai. Consul Ott was in charge. He received Erben's cases, including the crocodile leather one containing Errol's letters, from Amos Moscrip of the OSS. Ott had them opened and found them filled with a jumble of old diary pages, canceled tickets, and dirty laundry as well as the letters, damaged by the tropical heat. None of them seemed to him of any significance. He would not have identified Errol from his signature.

Outside the Austrian Consulate in that terrible postwar period, hordes of scavengers, destitute because of war and civil war, crawled in rags along the streets, desperate for food and clothing in the severe cold of the Shanghai winter. Ott had the suitcases emptied and flung to the scavengers. The tangled mass of dirty clothes, tickets, and letters whirled off forever into the darkness.

When last heard of, the *Zaca* lay rotting, abandoned and forgotten, in the South of France.

Errol left a final joke. For years, he told people *Zaca* was the Samoan word for peace. But the Samoan alphabet does not contain the letters Z and C. The word comes from no known language. It means nothing.

ACKNOWLEDGMENTS

Certain minor names in the book have been altered for privacy reasons.

I should like to thank the following for their help in preparing the book.

Jeanne Bernkopf edited it brilliantly.

Charles Pilleau was my main source on the Australian upbringing, and Edward Ashley filled out many more details.

Roy Moseley in London and Northampton did a magnificent job of interviewing all of Errol's British friends and colleagues. He was my reliable sounding board. His was an invaluable contribution to the book. So was the director Philippe Mora's.

I must thank my two kind and considerate helpers throughout the writing: Jim Fleming and Paul McWilliams, Errol's devoted friends, who never ceased to answer a host of difficult questions. Paul in particular unearthed more vanished people than I could possibly count, earning himself the honorary title of Sherlock Holmes of Atwater, Los Angeles.

My assistant Peter Lev heroically took on the task of newspaper and photographic research and shared with me hour by hour the amazing adventure of discovering the truth about Dr. Erben.

Janet Hayman tackled the hard job of Washington archival research. Frances Rowsell helped her in Washington.

Joel Greenburg in Sydney, Australia did an equally good job of tracking down Errol's Australian friends at school and after.

Rudy Behlmer read the manuscript carefully for errors on films and gave indispensable editorial advice.

Pat Guadagno, Maggie Starr, and Judy Keefer were my intrepid typists.

Jon Gregory was a great source on the last years. So were the Barry Mahons.

David Bradley screened some hard-to-find films.

Dr. Robert Knutson was generosity itself in giving me access to the Warner archives.

Kathie Nicastro of the National Archives was most helpful in copying scores of documents. Jeanne Giamporcaro of the State Department was very cooperative.

Retired Colonels Frank Farrell (of the OSS) and William E. Williamson were major sources on Dr. Erben. Others were Chauncey Tramutolo, the late Johnny Meyer, Frederick Justh, Marcos Agayo, Jim Fleming, Margaret Hoebich, C. J. Wood, E. O. Jellinek III, and Hellmut Schuetze. John Hammond Moore helped in Washington.

Kevin McCormick in New Guinea was most useful establishing many of Flynn's local connections.

On the subject of Errol's bisexuality, I received confirmation from Jane Chesis, the late Dick Irving Hyland, Helene Heigh, Shelley Davis, the late Johnny Meyer, Irving Rapper, Justin Golenbock, Truman Capote, and John Marven.

The National Archives Diplomatic Branch Records staff released under the Freedom of Information Act a great volume of material. More came from George Shalou of the General Archives Division in Maryland, and the Departments of the Navy, Army, Air Force, and the State Department. Records of the American consulates in Mexico, Chile, Panama, Argentina, Brazil, and Uruguay were consulted. Intelligence Division records of the Office of Chief of Naval Operations, Office of Censorship Records, CIA Records, telephone intercepts and intercepted letters and telegrams were filed and analyzed. Most helpful of all, Jerry Donohoe and Ed Grimsley of the Federal Bureau of Investigation released documents quickly. I thank, among hundreds of others, Lili Damita, Nora Eddington Black, Patrice Wymore, Beverly Aadland, Rory Flynn, Truman Capote, Olivia de Havilland, Ida Lupino, Alexis Smith, Dame Flora Robson, Dr. Hermann Friedrich Erben, Lillian Hellman, Jim Bacon, Richard Winter, the late George Brent, Louis C. Wyman (former congressman for New Hampshire), Robert Wolfe, Francis R. Stewart, Gerard Schiappa, Louis Mercado, Stuart Thompson, George Raho, John Harcourt, Max Darling, Enid McKoy, Marie Dechaineux, Angus Brammall, Alan Crosland, Edward Ashley, Ken Hunter-Kerr, Patricia Potter, Carl Schencke, Dr. Dexter Giblin, Robert

Young, Freda Jackson, Zillah Gray, Irving Asher, the late Jack Warner, Louis Hayward, Dick Carlin, Dolores Del Rio (my main source on the marriage to Lili Damita), "Iron Eyes" Cody, Victor Jory, Margaret Lindsay, the late Robert Florey, the late Lyda Roberti, Casey Robinson, Jean Muir, Hal Wallis, Minna Wallis, Jerome Zerbe, Michel Carmel, James Roosevelt, Franklin D. Roosevelt, Jr., Patric Knowles, Mrs. Laurance Stuntz, the late Dr. Frank Nolan, Mushy Callahan, Dr. Lee Sieger, William Keighley, Alex Pavlenko, Irving Rapper, "Limey" Plews, David Lewis, C. J. Wood, Vernon Wood, Oscar R. Cummins, the late John Ford, Al Wetzel, Marilyn Hinton, John McKay Elliott, Robert E. Ford, Robert Neeb, Phyllis Decker, Jean Howard, Ladislas Farrago (source of the information on, and interview with, Theodore Herstlet), Miliza Korjus, Ronald Reagan, Frank Angell, Thomas Hood, Raoul Walsh, Professor Carl Hubbs (whose letters to his son provided the log that gave me the details of the voyage of the *Zaca* in 1946), Jerry Courneya, Teddy Stauffer, and Robert Douglas.

BOOKS, FILMS AND PLAYS

Only four works, *The Films of Errol Flynn,* a lavishly illustrated book on the movies by Tony Thomas, Rudy Behlmer, and Clifford McCarty; *The Young Errol,* a highly specialized but fascinating analysis of the early years by John Hammond Moore; Nora Eddington's touching and accurate *Errol and Me* and Linda Christian's equally enjoyable *Linda* are of use. A list of Flynn's pictures with brief credits follows:

IN THE WAKE OF THE BOUNTY. Mayne Linton. Expeditionary Films, 1933.

I ADORE YOU. Margot Grahame. Warners, 1933.

MURDER AT MONTE CARLO. Eve Gray. Warners, 1935.

THE CASE OF THE CURIOUS BRIDE. Margaret Lindsay. Warners, 1935.

DON'T BET ON BLONDES. Claire Dodd. Warners, 1935.

CAPTAIN BLOOD. Olivia de Havilland. Warners, 1935.

THE CHARGE OF THE LIGHT BRIGADE. Olivia de Havilland. Warners, 1936.

GREEN LIGHT. Anita Louise. Warners, 1937.

THE PRINCE AND THE PAUPER. The Mauch Twins. Warners, 1937.

ANOTHER DAWN. Kay Francis. Warners, 1937.

THE PERFECT SPECIMEN. Joan Blondell. Warners, 1937.

THE ADVENTURES OF ROBIN HOOD. Olivia de Havilland. Warners, 1938.

FOUR'S A CROWD. Olivia de Havilland. Warners, 1938.

THE SISTERS. Bette Davis. Warners, 1938.

THE DAWN PATROL. Basil Rathbone. Warners, 1938.

DODGE CITY. Olivia de Havilland. Warners, 1939.

THE PRIVATE LIVES OF ELIZABETH AND ESSEX. Bette Davis. Warners, 1939.

VIRGINIA CITY. Miriam Hopkins. Warners, 1940.

THE SEA HAWK. Brenda Marshall. Warners, 1940.

SANTA FE TRAIL. Olivia de Havilland. Warners, 1940.

FOOTSTEPS IN THE DARK. Brenda Marshall. Warners, 1941.

DIVE BOMBER. Fred MacMurray. Warners, 1941.

THEY DIED WITH THEIR BOOTS ON. Olivia de Havilland. Warners, 1942.

DESPERATE JOURNEY. Ronald Reagan. Warners, 1942.

GENTLEMAN JIM. Alexis Smith. Warners, 1942.

EDGE OF DARKNESS. Ann Sheridan. Warners, 1942.

THANK YOUR LUCKY STARS. All-star cast. Warners, 1943.

NORTHERN PURSUIT. Julie Bishop. Warners, 1943.

UNCERTAIN GLORY. Paul Lukas. Warners, 1944.

OBJECTIVE, BURMA! William Prince. Warners, 1945.

SAN ANTONIO. Alexis Smith. Warners, 1945.

NEVER SAY GOODBYE. Eleanor Parker. Warners, 1946.

CRY WOLF. Barbara Stanwyck. Warners, 1947.

ESCAPE ME NEVER. Ida Lupino. Warners, 1947.

SILVER RIVER. Ann Sheridan. Warners, 1948.

ADVENTURES OF DON JUAN. Viveca Lindfors. Warners, 1949.

IT'S A GREAT FEELING. All-star cast. Warners, 1949.

THAT FORSYTE WOMAN. Greer Garson. MGM, 1949.

MONTANA. Alexis Smith. Warners, 1950.

ROCKY MOUNTAIN. Patrice Wymore. Warners, 1950.

KIM. Dean Stockwell. MGM, 1951.

HELLO GOD. (Alternative title *The Man Who Cried*.) William Marshall Productions, 1951.

ADVENTURES OF CAPTAIN FABIAN. Micheline Presle. Republic, 1952.

MARA MARU. Ruth Roman. Warners, 1952.

AGAINST ALL FLAGS. Maureen O'Hara. Universal-International, 1952.

CRUISE OF THE ZACA. Warners, 1952.

DEEP SEA FISHING. Warners, 1952.

THE MASTER OF BALLANTRAE. Beatrice Campbell. Warners, 1953.

CROSSED SWORDS. Gina Lollobrigida. United Artists, 1954.

WILLIAM TELL. Bruce Cabot. (Unreleased.)

LET'S MAKE UP. (Alternative title *Lilacs in the Spring*.) Anna Neagle. United Artists, 1955.

THE WARRIORS. (Alternative title *The Dark Avenger*.) Joanne Dru. Allied Artists, 1955.

KING'S RHAPSODY. Anna Neagle. United Artists, 1955.

ISTANBUL. Cornell Borchers. Universal-International, 1956.

THE BIG BOODLE. Gia Scala. United Artists, 1957.

THE SUN ALSO RISES. Ava Gardner. Twentieth Century–Fox, 1957.

THE CRIMINALS. Danielle Darrieux. William Marshall Productions, 1958 (Unreleased.)

TOO MUCH, TOO SOON. Dorothy Malone. Warners, 1958.

THE ROOTS OF HEAVEN. Juliette Greco. Twentieth Century–Fox, 1958.
CUBAN REBEL GIRLS. Beverly Aadland. Exploit Films, 1959.

STAGE APPEARANCES

Northampton Repertory Theatre

1933 THE THIRTEENTH CHAIR. Bayard Veiller.
      JACK AND THE BEANSTALK. Pantomime. Anonymous.

1934 SWEET LAVENDER. Arthur Wing Pinero.
      BULLDOG DRUMMOND. "Sapper."
      A DOLL'S HOUSE. Henrik Ibsen.
      ON THE SPOT. Edgar Wallace.
      PYGMALION. George Bernard Shaw.
      THE CRIME AT BLOSSOMS. Mordaunt Shairp.
      YELLOW SANDS. Eden Phillpotts.
      A GRAIN OF MUSTARD SEED. H. M. Harwood.
      SEVEN KEYS TO BALDPATE. George M. Cohan.
      OTHELLO. William Shakespeare.
      DR. FAUSTUS. Christopher Marlowe.
      THE GREEN BAY TREE. Mordaunt Shairp.
      THE CARD. Arnold Bennett.
      FAKE. Frederick Lonsdale.
      THE FARMER'S WIFE. Eden Phillpotts.
      THE WIND AND THE RAIN. Merton Hodge.
      SHEPPEY. William Somerset Maugham.
      THE MOON ON THE YELLOW RIVER. Dennis Johnson.
      THE SOUL OF NICHOLAS SYDERS. Jerome K. Jerome.
      THE DEVIL'S DISCIPLE. George Bernard Shaw.
      PADDY THE NEXT BEST THING. Gertrude Page.
      9:45. Owen Davis and Jewell Collins.

Malvern Theatre

1934 A MAN'S HOUSE. John Drinkwater.

(Despite his frequent claims, Errol Flynn did not appear in the West
End of London. Nor did he make films in New Guinea.)

DECLASSIFIED SECRET DOCUMENTS:

ESPIONAGE:

Errol Flynn and Dr. Hermann Friedrich Erben

(1926–68)

NOTE: Certain important documents on the above individuals have been declared unreleasable by various departments because, after all these years, they are still considered
to be dangerous to the national security. Also, very important telephone intercepts of Flynn's have vanished along
with certain FBI documents. The following is a fraction of
the thousands of documents declassified under the Freedom
of Information Act.

1926

Nazi party records. Rejoining of party by H. F. Erben. Berlin documents
center. Supplied, June 1979.

1927

Visitor's card. Presented to Rockefeller Foundation. Attached record of
rejection of Erben for grant. January 27, 1927.

1930

Department of State. Application for renewal of passport. H. F. Erben.
November 15, 1930.

1931

Consulate General, Montevideo, Uruguay. Application for new passport.
H. F. Erben. January 19, 1931.

State Department. Memorandum to American Consul General, Montevideo, Uruguay. February 28, 1931.

American Consulate. Montevideo, Uruguay. Memorandum to the Secretary of State. March 25, 1931.

State Department. Memorandum to Passport Agent, San Francisco. April 24, 1931.

Department of State. Passport agency. San Francisco. Memorandum to Ruth Shipley, Passport Office, Washington. June 15, 1931.

Memorandum. H. F. Erben to Ruth Shipley, State Department. July 8, 1931.

Department of State. Passport agency. San Francisco. Memorandum to Ruth Shipley, Passport Office, Washington. August 13, 1931.

State Department. Refusal of travel facilities. H. F. Erben. December 1, 1931.

1933

State Department. Refusal of travel facilities on grounds of alleged narcotic smuggling. H. F. Erben. April 6, 1933.

1934

U. S. Consulate General. Vienna. Report to the Secretary of State. H. F. Erben. August 1, 1934.

Application for passport. H. F. Erben. Vienna, Austria. August 8, 1934.

U. S. Consulate General. Vienna, Austria. Letter to the Secretary of State. August 9, 1934.

Ruth Shipley, State Department. Letter to Collector of Customs, San Francisco, California. August 20, 1934.

Treasury Department, Washington. Memorandum to U. S. Consul General, Vienna, Austria. September 24, 1934.

Memorandum from State Department to Department of Commerce. September 24, 1934.

Seaman's Protection Certificate. H. F. Erben. 1934.

U. S. Consulate General, Vienna, Austria. Memorandum to Secretary of State. November 12, 1934.

U. S. Consul General, Vienna. Report to the Secretary of State. November 16, 1934.

Federal Police Department, Vienna. Report on H. F. Erben. November 17, 1934.

Bundespolizeidirektion Wien. Arrest document. H. F. Erben. Police Department, Vienna. Arenbergring, Vienna. November 19, 1934.

U. S. Consul General, Vienna, Austria. Memorandum to the Secretary of State. Arrest and release of H. F. Erben. December 11, 1934.

1935

Letter to Department of State. H. F. Erben. Application for renewal of passport. Vienna, Austria. March 5, 1935.

Division of Foreign Control. Memorandum to U. S. Consulate, Paris. April 13, 1935.

American Consulate General, Vienna. Memorandum to the Secretary of State. H. F. Erben. Citizenship. April 19, 1935.

American Consulate, Trieste, Italy. Memorandum to the Secretary of State. H. F. Erben. Investigation on drug smuggling. April 23, 1935.

Division of Foreign Control. Memorandum to U. S. Consulate General, Paris. May 8, 1935.

CID London. Report on activities of H. F. Erben in Palestine. Jerusalem. June 8, 1935.

U. S. Legation. Baghdad. Memorandum to the Secretary of State. H. F. Erben in Iraq. Baghdad. June 27, 1935.

U. S. Consulate General. Jerusalem. Presence in the Near East of H. F. Erben. Report. June 28, 1935.

Legation of U.S.A. Teheran, Iran, memorandum: Afghan series. Fourteen. To the Secretary of State. July 9, 1935.

Letter. William H. Hornibrook, to Wallace S. Murray, Chief, Division of Near Eastern Affairs, State Department. July 20, 1935.

U. S. Consulate, Teheran, Iran. July 20, 1935. Dr. Erben passes through Iran. Teheran. July 20, 1935.

Memorandum. In German. Dr. Skubl. Official Representative Schuschnigg Government. Vienna. Report on Erben as Nazi and drug and money smuggler. August 19, 1935.

U. S. Consulate General, Vienna, Austria. Letter to the Secretary of State. Encloses police report. Vienna police. August 23, 1935.

Letter. Murray to Hornibrook. September 3, 1935.

Confidential report. Consul General of the U.S. Vienna, ⌗1738, to the Bureau of Narcotics. H. F. Erben. Vienna. August 23, 1935.

Secretary of State memorandum to U. S. Consul General, Shanghai. H. F. Erben. September 12, 1935.

U. S. Consulate General. Calcutta, India. Memorandum to the Secretary of State. H. F. Erben. Suspicious activities. Calcutta. September 19, 1935.

U. S. Consulate General, Calcutta, India. H. F. Erben. Drugs and espionage activities. Gun possession. Contains confession by Erben of Nazi activities in Austria. Calcutta. September 14, 1935.

Telegram. U. S. Consul, Calcutta, India. The Secretary of State. Warning about H. F. Erben. October 18, 1935.

U. S. Consulate General, Calcutta, India. Strictly confidential dispatch to the Secretary of State. Statement of Erben's Nazism and terrorizing of the governor of Bengal. Calcutta. October 18, 1935.

Memorandum. Secretary of State to Secretary of Labor. H. F. Erben. Confidential. November 16, 1935.

Secretary of State. Memorandum to U. S. Consul General, Vienna, Austria. H. F. Erben. Nazism. November 16, 1935.

Memorandum. H. F. Erben to Ruth Shipley. Washington. December 6, 1935.

U. S. Consulate General, Vienna, Austria. Memorandum to the Secretary of State. H. F. Erben. December 10, 1935.

Ruth Shipley. Memorandum. Addressed to Secretary of State. H. F. Erben. Accusation of murder. December 11, 1935.

Letter to Fred W. Jandrey, U. S. Vice Consul, Calcutta, India. H. F. Erben. At sea aboard *City of Rayville*. December 19, 1935.

1936

U. S. Consulate General, Vienna, Austria. Report to the Secretary of State. H. F. Erben. January 8, 1936.

Bestatigung. German document. January 16, 1936.

Deutsche Gesandtschaft. NAU permission to enter Germany. H. F. Erben. January 27, 1936.

U. S. Consul General, Berlin, Germany. Report to the Secretary of State. H. F. Erben. March 18, 1936.

Court Case. Expulsion of H. F. Erben. National Socialist Activities. Transcript. Vienna. March, 1936.

U. S. Consul General, Berlin, Germany. Report to the Secretary of State. H. F. Erben. April 27, 1936.

Department of State. Instructions to American Consulate, Pernambuco. Brazil. November 16, 1936.

Memorandum. U. S. Consul, Pernambuco, Brazil, to Secretary of State. H. F. Erben. Suspected espionage. November 16, 1936.

U. S. Consulate General, Rio de Janeiro, Brazil. Report to State Department. H. F. Erben. December 5, 1936.

Headquarters, Ninth Corps Area. Military intelligence, San Francisco. Report. December 10, 1936.

U. S. Consulate General, Buenos Aires, Argentina. Report to Secretary of State. H. F. Erben. December 22, 1936.

1937

U. S. Consulate General, Rio de Janeiro. Report to McCormick Steamship Company, San Francisco. January 10, 1937.

Report from seven crew members and Captain E. A. Jensen, *West Mahwah,* Bahia Blanca. January 10, 1937.

Memorandum from Ruth Shipley to the Secretary of State. Reference to Erben's SS activities. January 15, 1937.

American Consul General Emil Sauer. Private and strictly confidential memorandum. To Department of State and to U. S. Consul General, Buenos Aires and American Embassy, Rio. January 15, 1937.

Office of Naval Intelligence. Report. January 28, 1937.

Office of Naval Intelligence. Report. January 29, 1937.

Confidential telegram. Secretary of State, Cordell Hull to U. S. Consul General, Shanghai. January 29, 1937.

Office of Naval Intelligence. Report. February 1, 1937.

Letter. H. F. Erben to Ruth Shipley. February 17, 1937.

U. S. Consulate General. Rio de Janeiro, Brazil. Report. February 19, 1937.

Letter from Ruth Shipley to H. F. Erben, c/o Errol Flynn. February 19, 1937.

Memorandum from Ruth Shipley. Somerset Owen, Passport Agent, San Francisco. February 19, 1937.

Telegram. H. F. Erben to Ruth Shipley. Los Angeles. February 19, 1937.

Letter. Errol Flynn to Ruth Shipley. R.M.S. *Queen Mary* in New York Harbor. February 24, 1937.

Letter. H. F. Erben to Ruth Shipley. R.M.S. *Queen Mary*. New York Harbor. February 24, 1937.

Letter. R. F. Hoyt, Passport Agency, New York City, to Ruth Shipley. February 24, 1937.

Letter. Ruth Shipley to F. Willard Calder, American Vice Consul, Southampton, England. February 26, 1937.

Executive Officer, General Staff, War Department. Military Intelligence Division. Memorandum to Asst. Chief of Staff, G-2, Ninth Corps Area. H. F. Erben. March 1, 1937.

War Department G-2. Report. H. F. Erben. March 1, 1937.

Foreign Service of the United States. Memorandum to U. S. Consul General, London, England. H. F. Erben. March 8, 1937.

Spanish Medical Aid Committee. Letter to H. F. Erben, Berlin. March 15, 1937.

Affidavit. Signed Errol Flynn. U. S. Consulate General, Paris. March 19, 1937.

Affidavit. Signed H. F. Erben. U. S. Consulate General, Paris. March 19, 1937.

Application for Passport to be marked "Not Valid for Travel in Spain." H. F. Erben. U. S. Consulate General, Paris. March 19, 1937.

U. S. Consulate General, Paris, France. Report to the Secretary of State. H. F. Erben seeks new endorsement to enter Spain. Paris. May 11, 1937.

U. S. Consulate General, Berlin, Germany. Memorandum to Secretary of State. H. F. Erben seeks permission to re-enter Spain. Berlin. May 21, 1937.

U. S. Consulate General, Paris, France. Memorandum to the Secretary of State. Erben's sons fighting for Franco in Spain. June 1, 1937.

Memorandum from John C. Wiley, U. S. Consul General, Vienna, to the Secretary of State. H. F. Erben in China. Vienna. November 9, 1937.

1938

Department of State. Passport Division. Report by A. J. Nicholas on Erben's Nazism, spying on the Lincoln Brigade, and on his and Flynn's mission for the Nazis in Spain. April 26, 1938.

Nazi party card. H. F. Erben. Applied for May 1, 1938. Issued 1939. Application forms. Card ⌗6378730.

Department of State. Division of European Affairs. E. F. Kennan. Erben's Nazism. Internal office memorandum. May 13, 1938.

Letter. H. F. Erben to A. J. Niklas (Nicholas) from Dr. H. F. Erben. Vienna. May 15, 1938.

Memorandum. Unsigned. To all U. S. consular offices in China, Russia, and Holland. Restrictions on Erben's travel. His connection with German Secret Police/Gestapo. Washington, undated. (Probably December, 1938.)

1939

McCormick Steamship Company. Reports, 1937–39. Privately issued.

Information lists. German-American coordinating intelligence. Buenos Aires. November 13, 1939.

Travel Document. Permission by Nazi and German military headquarters offices in Buenos Aires for H. F. Erben on Gestapo clearance to travel on non-German vessels. Deutsche Botschaft, Bescheinibung. December 1, 1939.

1940

U. S. Consulate, Antofagasta, Chile. To the Secretary of State. Enclosed statement from British Consul indicating Erben is on British list of Nazi agents. Antofagasta. January 26, 1940.

U. S. Consul General, Buenos Aires, Argentina to Secretary of State. Forwarded to J. Edgar Hoover. H. F. Erben. Detailed report. Intelligence report on connections with Tito Martens of Nazi Party in Buenos Aires. Buenos Aires. January 26, 1940.

U. S. Consulate, Valparaiso, Chile. Detailed report. 18 pages. H. F. Erben. Espionage. Valparaiso. January 19, 1940.

American Embassy, Valparaiso, Chile. Confidential memorandum. H. F. Erben. Activities as German agent. Valparaiso. February 5, 1940.

FBI. Report. February 15, 1940.

Army Information Service. New York. Report. February 28, 1940.

FBI report. 18-page statement by H. F. Erben. Confession of Nazi membership. Reveals Flynn connection. March 5, 1940.

Department of State. American Consulate. Pernambuco. Brazil. Report. March 13, 1940.

FBI. Report. March 16, 1940.

FBI. Report. March 18, 1940.

FBI. Report. March 20, 1940.

FBI. Report. March 26, 1940.

Memorandum. U. S. Consul General, Buenos Aires, Argentina, to the Secretary of State. Whereabouts of H. F. Erben. March 26, 1940.

FBI. Report. March 29, 1940.

Department of State. New York Division. Report. March 30, 1940.

Letter. J. Edgar Hoover to Chief of Staff, G-2. April 2, 1940.

FBI. Report. April 2, 1940.

Assistant Chief of Staff, G-2. Washington. Report. April 4, 1940.

War Department, G-2. Report. April 4, 1940.

Office of the Assistant Chief of Staff, Headquarters, Ninth Corps Area, G-2. Report. April 4, 1940.

FBI. Report. April 9, 1940.

Ninth Corps Area, San Francisco, G-2. Report. April 11, 1940.

American Consulate. Antofagasta, Chile. Report. April 17, 1940.

U. S. Consulate, Antofagasta, Chile. To the Secretary of State. H. F. Erben. Activities in the Panama Canal. Antofagasta. April 17, 1940.

Confidential Dispatch 383, American Consul, Valparaiso. April 26, 1940.

Embassy of the United States of America. Panama City. Memorandum. Encloses FBI report and report by Chief, Civil Intelligence Section, Panama Canal. Activities of H. F. Erben. Panama. May 1, 1940.

Headquarters, Second Corps Area, Governor's Island. New York. Report. May 10, 1940.

War Department, G-2. Report. May 10, 1940.

Department of State. Confidential Dispatch. May 13, 1940.

FBI. Report. Baggage Search. May 13, 1940.

Office of the Assistant Chief of Staff, G-2. San Francisco. Report. May 14, 1940.

War Department. Military Intelligence Division, G-2. Report. June 10, 1940.

Secretary of State Report. J. Edgar Hoover. June 17, 1940.

U. S. Consulate. Buenos Aires. Report. June 21, 1940.

Department of State, Washington. Buenos Aires. Report. June 21, 1940.

Embassy of the United States of America. Santiago, Chile. The Fifth Column in Chile. Report. June 26, 1940.

Memoranda to Brigadier General Sherman Miles, Acting Assistant Chief of Staff, G-2, War Department, Captain Nixon, Military Intelligence Division, J. Edgar Hoover and others from Adolph A. Berle, Assistant Secretary of State. Enclosure: Report of the Embassy of the U.S.A., Buenos Aires, Argentina, June 21, 1940, strictly confidential dispatch, linking Flynn with Erben and detailing Flynn's defense of Erben. July 2, 1940.

Trial transcript. Erben's citizenship revocation. U. S. District Court. San Francisco. December 8, 1940.

1941

Coast Guard Report. Los Angeles. January 18, 1941.

Erben Case. Revocation of Citizenship. Fraudulent Procurement. U. S. District Court, San Francisco. January 29, 1941.

Office of G-2. San Francisco. February 4, 1941.

Lieutenant Colonel, GSC, G-2. Report. February 4, 1941.

Federal Bureau of Investigation. Report. Hans Adolph Mosberg with Aliases. April 18, 1941.

Report of Federal Bureau of Investigation Agent H. Frank Angell. October 16, 1941.

1942

Testimony. Martin Fischer. Consul General. Shanghai. 1942.

Report: Denaturalization of H. F. Erben on Grounds of Disloyalty and false statement. United States Government Report. 1942.

1943

Report Card. CIC. February 9, 1943.

Naval Investigative Service. Report. December 15, 1943.

1944

FBI report. Erben's Nazi connections with Errol Flynn. Informer for OSS Pootung Camp. Shanghai. May 11, 1944.

1946

Sworn Statement: H. F. Erben to Captain Frank Farrell. Shanghai. February 28, 1946.

Sworn Statement. H. F. Erben to Captain Frank Farrell. March 4, 1946.

Sworn Statement. H. F. Erben to Captain Frank Farrell. March 15, 1946.

Sworn Statement. H. F. Erben to American Consulate General. Shanghai. May 27, 1946.

Interrogation Reports. Civilian Internment Enclosure. Ludwigsburg. June 15, 1946.

Signal Corps, U. S. Army. Report. Shanghai. September 3, 1946.

Transcript. U. S. War Crimes Trials. Shanghai. September 1946 to January 1947. 3,350 pages. Testimonies of H. F. Erben, Louis Siefken, and twenty-three others.

1947

American Consulate General. Shanghai. 1947. Biographic reports on obnoxious Nazis repatriated to Germany on USAT *General William Black*.

Autobiography. H. F. Erben. Submitted Document. USAT *General William Black*. September 8, 1947.

Confession of Treason. H. F. Erben. September 8, 1947.

Report to CIC. H. F. Erben. September 12, 1947.

Letter to Captain Frank Farrell. Signed H. F. Erben. September 18, 1947.

H. Q. German Repatriation Detachment. Report. September 30, 1947.

1948

Report. S. Mardyks, Chief, Intelligence Detachment, U. S. Screening Center, Ludwigsburg. From H. F. Erben. January 6, 1948.

Letter to Major W. E. Williamson. H. F. Erben. Ludwigsburg. February 9, 1948.

Commanding Officer. U. S. Screening Center. Ludwigsburg. March 17, 1948.

EUCOM. Intelligence Division. Report. April 22, 1948.

Letter from Colonel A. M. Moscrip to CIC. May 22, 1948.

Code Letter. Ludwigsburg, Germany. June 4, 1948.

Agent Report. Communist Activity. July 26, 1948.

CIC Region One. U. S. Army Report. August 9, 1948.

U. S. Political Advisor for Germany. Intelligence Report. H. F. Erben. October 19, 1948.

1949

Department of the Army. Office of the Chief, Chemical Corps. Report. October 7, 1949.

1950

Military Intelligence Section. U. S. Army. Report. January 5, 1950.

Letter from Dr. Berger-Voesendorf. United Nations Club, to H. F. Erben. March 15, 1950. Intercepted and censored.

Central Intelligence Team. Report. Iran. March 28, 1950.

430th CIC. Reports. June 30, 1950. (Further records of Erben's Nazi and SD memberships)

430th CIC. Report. July 26, 1950.

CIC Salzburg. Report. August 9, 1950.

Central Censorship Group, Austria (U.S.). U. S. Army. Vienna. Report. August 25, 1950. Intercepted Mail: Berger-Voesendorf.

430th CIC Det., Headquarters, U. S. Army. Report. September 22, 1950.

Secret File. Chief of Operations. Iran. Report. September 22, 1950.

Report to U. S. Consulate, Medan, Indonesia. H. F. Erben. December 1, 1950.

Letter to Lieutenant Colonel W. E. Williamson. H. F. Erben. Port Said. December 30, 1950.

1954

Canadian Government Documents, Immigration Department. Reasons for rejection of Dr. Hermann and Mrs. Joan Scott-Smith Erben.

1968

Senator Louis C. Wyman. Files relative to Erben's rejection for readmittance as immigrant to the United States; evidence of Erben's espionage from all departments and deposition report on his espionage by Colonel W. E. Williamson, Colonel Amos Moscrip and Colonel Jeremiah J. O'Connor, etc. Erben refused visa to enter United States (State Department dossier still classified).

Index

Aadland, Beverly, 4, 350, 359
  background of, 322–23
  Flynn and, 323–42
    claims against Flynn's estate,
      346, 347–48
    in Cuba, 335–37
    death of Flynn, 341–45
    letters of, 327–30
    marriage plans, 339, 340
    in motion pictures, 322–23, 335,
      336–37, 340
    television shows, 339
Aadland, Florence, 324, 331, 332,
    334, 342, 343
  moral character of, 322, 323,
    327–28, 347, 350
Abwehr, the
  Erben and, 147, 149, 170–71,
    222–23, 250

Flynn and, 159
McEvoy and, 179
in Mexico City, 147, 149, 170
in Shanghai, 138, 170–71,
    222–23
Acapulco, Mexico, 179–80, 218,
    221–22, 231–32, 245–46,
    248–50, 320
Acapulco Yacht Club, 222
Action in the North Atlantic, 245
Adams, Trelawney, 35
Adderley, A. F., 299, 300
Addison, Honorable Christopher,
    95
Admiral Graf Spee (battleship),
    138–39
Admiral Nulton (freighter), 146
Adventures of Captain Fabian,
    288, 318, 358

Adventures of Don Juan, 233–34, 239, 259, 260–67, 271, 274, 358
Adventures of Robin Hood, The, vii, 3, 101–9, 239, 266, 357
Afghanistan, 350
Against All Flags, 297, 358
Aga Khan, 18
Agayo, Marcos, 7, 350–51
Alabam (prop man), 270–71
Alba, Duke of, 51, 94, 97
Albert, Eddie, 332
Alden, John, 113
Alexander's Ragtime Band, 119
All for Love, 286
All-Star Melody Master Bands, 245
Aly Khan, 291
American Pioneer Lines, 73
Anders, Glenn, 249
Anderson, Gertrude, 5, 130–31, 164, 192–93
  FBI and, 192–93
Anderson, Sir John, 73
Anderson, Mrs. Ruby, 212, 213, 214
Annabella, 119
Another Dawn, 83, 87, 357
Anti-Semitism
  in Australia, 10, 47
  in Austria, 45, 47
  in England, 52
  of Erben, 44, 45, 74
  of Flynn, 10, 47, 52, 142
  in Tasmania, 47
Araner (ketch), 114
Archer, Claude, 174
Argentina, 90, 91, 93, 119, 139, 144, 188, 253
Arlen, Richard, 114
Armour, Norman, 144
Arno (Schnauzer), 84, 116, 117, 128–29, 156, 157, 210
Asher, Irving, 55–56

Ashley, Edward, 22, 125
Australia, 8–27, 34–35, 38–39, 161, 171
  all-white policy in, 47
  anti-Semitism in, 10, 47
  Flynn's anti-Australian feelings, 10, 47–48
  Flynn's first motion picture made in, 38–39
  Flynn's short wave broadcast to, 124–25
  sadomasochistic repressed homosexuality in, 47
Australian Department of Aborigines, 45
Austria, 6, 44–45, 50, 72–73, 76, 111, 252, 284, 296, 350, 351
  anti-Semitism in, 45, 47
  Erben deported from, 76
Ayres, Lew, 178

Bacon, Jim, 326, 333
Bahamas, the, 112, 159–60, 293
Bahia Blanca, Argentina, 139
Bailey, Lady, 166
Baird, William S., 226–27
Barcelona, Spain, 95–96, 159, 314–16
Bargain, The, 288
Barry, Patricia, 339
Barrymore, Diana, 321, 334
Barrymore, John, 24, 64, 68, 69, 84, 154, 185, 258, 321
Bash, Johnny, 303
Batista, Fulgencio, 334–35
Bauer, Erna, 135
Beam Ends (Flynn), 84, 132, 216
Beckman, Mrs., 202
Beery, Wallace, 105
Behlmer, Rudy, 357
Belli, Melvin, 344
Belli, Mrs. Melvin, 343–44
Bengal, India, 73

Benjamin, Henry Rogers, 242
Bennett, Compton, 273
Benny, Jack, 294
Bergales, Joe, 271
Berkeley, Busby, 109
Bermuda, 242
Bernstein, Dr. Maurice, 168
Berry, Wallace, 247–48
Biasset, André, 291–92
Big Boodle, The, 319, 358
Big Love, The (Aadland), 322
Big Trees, The, 293, 294
Bishop, Julie, 358
Black, Morrie, 184
Black, Richard, 349
Blackpool, England, 313
Black Prince, The, 313
Black Wars, 47
Blanchard, Mari, 221, 250
Blondell, Joan, 357
Bloodline, 288
Blue, Mrs. Emily, 201–2
Bodine, Lieutenant Colonel, 250
Boehm, Lorene, 201, 202
Bond, Ward, 176, 177
Bondi Lifesavers' Club, 23
Bonet, Marcel, 225
Borchers, Cornell, 358
*Borrah Minevitch and His
    Harmonica Rascals*, 245
Borzage, Frank, 83
Boston, Massachusetts, 112, 113,
    219, 284
Boston Daily Record, 219
Bowling, R. W., 184–85, 186
Boyd, Mrs., 55
Boyd, Charles, 213
Boyer, Lynn, 183, 198, 200–1,
    202, 210
Brammall, Angus, 16
Brazil, 90–91, 119, 144
    Erben deported from, 91
Bredell, Woody, 259
Bremen (liner), 98

Brent, George, 67, 88, 114, 115,
    181
Brewster's Millions, 57
Bridge of San Luis Rey, The, 57
Brisbane *Courier-Mail*, 27
Brontë, Charlotte, 326
Brown, Harry Joe, 64
Brown Derby, 59, 80
Browning, Robert, vii, 133
Buckner, Robert, 225
Budlong, Ralph, 155
Buenos Aires, Argentina, 90, 91,
    93, 119, 139, 144, 253
Bulletin, The, 35, 39, 40
Burbank Hospital, 292
Burma, 231
Burt, Charlie, *see* Pilleau, Charles
Butler, David, 195, 232

Cabot, Bruce, 122, 181, 182, 307,
    308, 358
  sexual exhibitionism of, 238–39
  threatens exposure of Flynn's
    homosexual activities, 312
Cagney, James, 57, 114, 193
Calcutta, India, 73
Caldough, George, 340, 341, 342
Caldough, Mrs. George, 341, 342
California, University of (San
    Francisco), 45–46
California Yacht Club, 157–58,
    202
Callahan, Mushy, 100, 176–77
Campbell, Beatrice, 300–1, 358
Campbell, Campbell, and
    Campbell (solicitors), 39
Canada, 172, 284, 341–43
Capote, Truman, 227
Captain Blood, 3, 64–69, 75, 77,
    88, 108, 357
  special appeal of, 68, 69
Captain Blood (Sabatini), 64
Captains of the Clouds, 193
Cardiff, Jack, 300, 307, 308

Carlin, Dick, 58, 61, 76
Carmel, Max, 74, 148, 242
Carroll, Ruth, 227
Carstairs, Harry, 160
Cartwright, Beatrice, 161–62, 179, 242
Case of the Curious Bride, The, 60–61, 64, 357
Castro, Fidel, 334–35, 337
Cathcart-Jones, Owen, 193, 197, 205, 208
Caudle, Mack, 349
Cavens, Fred, 233, 239, 259
Cedars of Lebanon Hospital, 257
Cedros Island, 247
Central Intelligence Agency (CIA), 5, 148
Ceylon, 50
Chao-Kung, Abbot (Lincoln), 46, 49, 51, 171
Chaplin, Charlie, 225
Charge of the Light Brigade, The, 75–82, 357
Chasen's, 59, 80, 99, 154
Chauvel, Charles, 38, 39
Chauvel, Elsa, 38, 39
Chesis, Jane, 3, 250, 304
Cheyenne, 239
Chiang Kai-shek, 98, 251
Chichibu Maru (vessel), 46
Chile, 119, 140, 141, 144
China, 46, 47, 49, 98, 147, 148, 149, 152, 241, 250, 251, 283–84, 351
  the Abwehr in, 138, 170–71, 222–23
  Erben deported from, 251
Choo-Choo, 249–50
Chow, Captain, 251
Christian, Fletcher, 10, 11, 192, 338
Christian, Linda, 179–80, 192, 200, 211, 214, 231, 238, 250, 275, 357

FBI and, 192
  marriage to Power, 250
  origin of the name, 192
Chums, 81
Chungking, China, 223
Churchill, Viscount, 94, 96, 97
Churchill, Sir Winston, 94, 124, 149, 180
CinemaScope, 307, 308
Cinesound Studios, 39
Ciro's, 163
City of Rayville (freighter), 46, 73–74
Civilian Conservation Corps (CCC) camps, 145–46
Cleminshaw, Dr. C. H., 210–11
Clutterbuck, Wesley, 334
Coalter, Whayne, 273
Cocaine, 86, 220, 231–32, 261, 333–34
Cochran, Thomas W., 197–202, 205, 207–9, 214, 226
Cockeyed World, The, 57
Coconut Grove, 59
Cocos Island, 253–54
Cody, "Iron Eyes," 59–60
Cody, Jim, 59
Cohn, Harry, 114
Communism, 99, 283–84, 337
Confidential, 320
Conrad, Earl, 334, 336
Conrad, Joseph, 133
Conte Verde (vessel), 46, 171
Cooper, Edward Ashley, 22–23
Cooper, Gary, 114
Copacabana, 327
Corbett, James J., 176–77
Cosmopolitan, 93, 95
Count of Monte Cristo, The, 64
"Country Gardens" (Grainger), 130
Courmayeur, Italy, 307–8
Courneya, Jerry, 244, 245, 263

Covering the Mexican Front
    (Kirk), 159
Coward, Noël, 293
Criminals, The, 358
Crocker, Templeton, 240
Crosland, Alan, Jr., 258, 259–60,
    263, 266
Crossed Swords, 302–6, 307, 310,
    358
Crude Oil, Inc., 172
Cruise of the Zaca, The, 268, 294,
    358
Crump, Owen, 256, 257
Cry Wolf, 244, 358
Cuba, 87, 272, 319, 334–37
Cuban Rebel Girls, 335, 336–37,
    340, 359
Cuernavaca, Mexico, 85–86, 160
Curtis, Warren, 213
Curtiz, Michael, 45, 56, 64, 68,
    78–79, 127, 134, 150–51,
    174
    Flynn and, 61, 65–67, 76, 79,
        82, 100, 108, 124, 127–28,
        217
    Wallis and, 78–79, 107

Dale, John, 194
Dalgety's, Ltd., 21–22
Damita, Lili, 3, 45, 89, 98, 243,
    287, 349
    Flynn and, 58–59, 60, 64, 65,
        123, 124, 133, 134, 179,
        215, 217, 238, 272, 303–4,
        333
        birth of son (Sean), 153, 306
        death of Flynn, 345
        financial aid to Flynn, 66,
            69–70
        first meeting, 56–57
        honeymoon, 87–88
        marriage, 62, 63, 69, 74, 84,
            99, 101, 109, 114, 116, 120,
            153, 291, 321

    property settlement and
        alimony, 171–72, 227, 285,
        318
    reaction to rape charges and
        trial, 187
    separation and divorce,
        156–57
    jealous nature of, 62, 63, 81,
        132
Danova, Cesare, 302, 303
Darjeeling, India, 73
Dark Avenger, The, 358
Darling, Max, 12
Darrieux, Danielle, 358
D'Artagnan (liner), 49
Darwin, Charles, 132
Davenport, Harry, 273
Davies, Marion, 99
Davis, Bette, 115, 124, 178, 217,
    322, 357
Davis, Shelley, 325, 340
Davis, William Rhodes, 164
Dawn Patrol, The, 115, 357
Dawson, Douglas, 115, 116, 133,
    135
Day of the Locust, The (West),
    322
Deakin, Prime Minister Alfred, 9
Deal, The (Marshall), 288
Dechaineux, Mrs. Marie, 15
Decker, John, 165, 167–68, 244,
    246–49, 257, 297
    background of, 154
    death of, 257–58
Decker, Phyllis, 154–55, 298
Deep Sea Fishing, 358
De Gunzburg, Joycie, 293
De Gunzburg, Niki, 293
De Havilland, Olivia, 68, 69,
    79–81, 99, 101, 107, 124,
    127, 302, 357, 358
    romantic relationship with
        Flynn, 65–66, 80–81, 105,
        122–23, 132, 238

De la Mora, Constancia, 96
Delnorte (vessel), 91
Del Rio, Dolores, 59, 63, 64, 114
Delta Lines, 91
Dervin, Danielle, 291–92
Desperate Journey, 173–75, 193, 214, 358
Detroit, Michigan, 326–27
Díaz, Apollonio, 221–22, 250
Dickens, Charles, 133, 165
Dickey, Dr. C. D., 264
Dieterle, William, 83
Dietrich, Marlene, 59, 178
Di Frasso, Countess Dorothy Dentice, 163, 164
Dighton, John, 307
Di Poliolo, Prince Umberto, 161–62
Dive Bomber, 150–52, 358
Dixon, Campbell, 231
Djibouti, French Somaliland, 50
Doctor Faustus (Marlowe), 54, 359
Dr. Jekyll and Mr. Hyde (Stevenson), 133
Dodd, Claire, 357
Dodd, Jimmy, 227
Dodge City, 117, 118, 122–23, 357
Dollfuss, Engelbert, 71, 73, 91
Donat, Robert, 64
Don't Bet on Blondes, 61–62, 357
Dorrington, Clint, 294
Dorsey, Tommy, 216
Douglas, Kirk, 293
Douglas, Lloyd C., 82
Douglas, Robert, 262, 266, 281
Dromgold, George, 37–38
Dru, Joanne, 270, 358
Drug smuggling
  by Erben, 46, 47, 50, 72, 98
  by Flynn, 27–28, 126, 242, 245–46, 248, 295–96
  by McEvoy, 242, 295–96

Duff, Howard, 348
Duncomb, William, 12–13
Dupaine, William, 37

Easton, Jack, 310
Ecker, Alois, *see* Erben, Dr. Hermann Friedrich
Eddington, Jack, 215, 216, 228, 237, 239, 248, 269, 274
Eddington, Marge, 216, 228, 237, 238, 239, 248, 256, 268, 275–76, 292
Eddington, Nora, 3–4, 24, 214–15, 287, 292, 349, 357
  expedition to collect marine specimens, 243–46, 248, 249
  Flynn and, 215–18, 220–22, 237–38, 240, 258, 267, 275–76, 325, 339
    birth of daughter (Deirdre), 233, 236, 306
    birth of daughter (Rory), 255, 306
    child-support payments, 285–86, 339
    claims against Flynn's estate, 346, 347
    death of Flynn, 344
    divorce, 237, 255–56, 274
    on Flynn's homosexual activities, 3, 215, 222, 260
    marriage, 228, 231–32, 291, 294, 310, 320–21
    rape by Flynn, 220–21
    violence between, 239, 248, 268–69
  Haymes and, 269–70, 271, 274–76
    marriage, 274–75
  resemblance to Flynn's mother, 215, 256
  suicide attempts, 268, 269

Edge of Darkness, 180–81, 184, 186, 187, 189, 358
Egypt, 284, 297–98
Ehrhardt, Ludwig, 222–23
Einfeld, Charles, 192–93
Eldridge, Florence, 99
Electrolux industries, 159
Elizabeth, Queen, 275
Elliott, John MacKay, 335, 337
Ellis, Captain, 316
El Morocco, 163, 227, 271, 299, 327
Emerald, Connie, 167, 169, 348–49
England, 51–56, 88, 254, 313, 333–34
    anti-Semitism in, 52
Erben's anti-British feelings, 45, 73
    Flynn's anti-British feelings, 10, 48, 101
    motion pictures in, 51, 55–56, 231, 310, 311–14
    theatre in, 51–55, 359
    Warner Brothers in, 51, 55–56, 231
    World War II, 124, 138–41, 160, 195, 231
Engling, Alfred, 96
Enright, Ray, 270
Enterprise (aircraft carrier), 150–52
Epstein, Julius, 67–68
Epstein, Philip, 68
Erben, Dr. Hermann Friedrich, vii, 4–7, 133, 350–51
    admiration for Hitler, 44, 73, 91, 93, 145
    alias of, 149
    anti-American attitude, 90–91
    anti-British feelings, 45, 73
    anti-Semitism of, 44, 45, 74
    arrested for treason, 241

in assassination of Dollfuss, 71, 73, 91
background of, 44–47
becomes U.S. citizen, 45
contrast in personality of, 48
deportations
    from Austria, 76
    from Brazil, 91
    from Hong Kong, 98
    from India, 73
    from Shanghai, 251
drug smuggling of, 46, 47, 50, 72, 98
efforts for voluntary trial for treason, 252
FBI and, 90–91, 141, 145–46, 148, 152
Fleming on, 74
Flynn and, 4–5, 43–50, 71, 74, 75, 76, 91, 110, 144, 146–50, 152, 170, 171, 250–52
    adventurous travels, 48–50
    escape to Mexico, 147–48
    Roosevelt (Eleanor) used for protection, 142–43, 144, 145, 252
    the Spanish Civil War, 92–98, 149, 335
    uncensored wartime letters, 223, 241–42, 283–84, 351
as a Gestapo agent, 72, 90–91, 250–52, 283
    the Abwehr and, 147, 149, 170–71, 222–23, 250
    arrest in 1934, 71–72
    declassified secret documents, 361–70
    photographic espionage, 72, 90–98, 138–41, 143, 152
    in the service of German ships, 138–43, 171
    the Spanish Civil War, 92–98, 110–11, 149, 335

interest in leprosy, 6, 43, 45, 48, 351

in the Nazi Party, 71–73, 76, 138, 140

joins and re-joins, 45, 111, 138

passport problems, 45–46, 71–73, 93–98, 111, 139, 141–42, 146

Revocation of Citizenship proceedings, 142, 146–48

State Department and, 5, 45–46, 90–91, 95, 96, 97, 98

U.S. citizenship revoked, 149

Ernst, Bud, 62, 109–10

Errol and Me (Eddington), 215, 221, 228, 231, 268, 269, 357

Escape Me Never, 358

Esperanza (vessel), 46

Espiritu, Pio, 156

Ethiopia, 75

Exochorda (vessel), 316

Export Lines, 316

Fabrizi, Aldo, 307

Farago, Ladislas, 164

Farmer's Wife, The (Phillpotts), 53, 359

Farouk, King, 297–98, 304, 305, 309

Farrell, Captain Frank, vii, 241–42, 251

Faulconer, Judge Oda, 187

Federal Bureau of Investigation (FBI), 5, 44, 144, 170

Anderson and, 192–93

Christian and, 192

Erben and, 90–91, 141, 145–46, 148, 152

Flynn and, 90–92, 126, 130, 135, 143, 148, 159, 163, 173, 174, 218, 335

action on extortion threats, 191–92, 219–20

attempts to establish "white slavery" charges, 221–22

deportation threat, 76–77

Federal Bureau of Narcotics, 46

Fields, W. C., 154

Fight Fish Fight, 245

Films of Errol Flynn, The (Thomas, Behlmer, and McCarty), 357

Finnigan, Joe, 343

FitzGibbon, Maura, 325–26

Fleming, Frances, 62–63

Fleming, Jim, 3, 66, 69, 75, 86, 89, 118, 174, 216, 241, 242, 256, 261, 270, 272, 297, 298

on death of Flynn, 342

designs stables for Flynn, 166

on Erben, 74

expedition to collect marine specimens, 245, 246

in Flynn's rape charges and trial, 157–59, 183, 188, 189, 190, 209

as Flynn's stand-in, 63, 177, 229, 230, 322

hired as a live-in houseman, 62–63

sees reporters for Flynn, 132, 228

sexual exhibitionism of, 238–39

Fleming, Phyllis, 297

Florey, Robert, 61, 233

Flynn, Arnella, 310, 313, 318, 344, 349

Flynn, Deirdre, 236, 237, 244, 255, 256, 258, 274, 286, 292, 306, 344, 345, 349

claims to father's estate, 347

relationship with father, 238, 272, 275–76, 339

Flynn, Errol
  on acting, 217, 261
  adolescence and early years,
      18–43
    con games, 28–29, 31
    headhunter scheme, 34
    as a lifeguard, 23
    as a model, 35
    as a procurer of native labor
      in New Guinea, 32, 34, 42
    as a wharf laborer, 21–22
  amorality of, 2, 42, 48
  anti-Australian feelings, 10,
      47–48
  anti-British feelings, 10, 48, 101
  anti-Semitism of, 10, 47, 52, 142
  appeal to men as a symbol, 3, 68
  appearance of, 19, 55, 69
    clothing, 69–70, 110
  Arno (Schnauzer) and, 84, 116,
      117, 128–29, 156, 157, 210
  Barrymore (John) and, 24, 68,
      84, 154, 185, 258, 321
  birth of, 9, 11
  boats owned by
    Little Sirocco (launch), 222
    Sirocco (yacht), 87, 112–14,
      115–17, 126, 133, 135–36,
      147–48, 156, 157–58, 169,
      173, 187, 189, 190, 194,
      202, 209, 211, 240
    Sirocco (yawl), 34–35, 84, 87
    Zaca (yacht), 240–41,
      243–49, 252–55, 268–69,
      286, 291, 292, 295, 304,
      310–11, 312, 316–17, 340,
      341, 351
  childhood of, 8–18
    punishments, 11, 12
    sexual precocity, 12
  claims against estate of, 346–48
  conflicts with mother, 12, 24
  cruelty to animals, 17, 27, 166
  Curtiz and, 61, 65–67, 76, 79,

      82, 100, 108, 124, 127–28,
      217
  death, thoughts about, 167–68,
      169, 187
    contemplation of suicide, 200,
      230, 248
  death of, 341–45
    funeral and burial place, 167,
      344–45
    mystery of key to safe-deposit
      box, 343
    question of suicide, 342
  De Havilland and, 65–66,
      80–81, 105, 122–23, 132,
      238
  desire to be a star, 55, 61, 67, 87
  draft evasion, 172–73, 195, 227
  drinking, 100, 104, 132, 174,
      178, 184, 208–9, 212, 220,
      256–63, 266, 269, 270, 276,
      281, 302, 305, 313–16,
      321–22
    arrest in Los Angeles, 325–26
    arrest in New York City,
      271–72
    drunken driving charges, 124
    memory impairment from,
      326
    as self-destructive, 320, 321
  drug smuggling of, 27–28, 126,
      242, 245–46, 248, 295–96
  drug use, 86, 99, 132, 133, 178,
      212, 220, 239, 248, 249,
      253, 256, 259, 305
    cocaine, 86, 220, 231–32, 261,
      333–34
    hepatitis from, 302–3
    kif, 86
    marijuana, 86, 178, 231–32,
      311–12
    morphine, 205, 212, 231, 246,
      256, 269
    opium, 86

personality change from, 220,
    231, 248
education, 12–13, 16–20
Erben and, 4–5, 43–50, 71, 74,
    75, 76, 91, 110, 144,
    146–50, 152, 170, 171,
    250–52
  adventurous travels, 48–50
  escape to Mexico, 147–48
  Roosevelt (Eleanor) used for
    protection, 142–43, 144,
    145, 252
  the Spanish Civil War, 92–98,
    149, 335
  uncensored wartime letters,
    223, 241–42, 283–84, 351
expedition to collect marine
    specimens, 243–49
extortion charges, 242
false report of death of, 97–98
FBI and, 90–92, 126, 130, 135,
    143, 148, 159, 163, 173,
    174, 218, 335
  action on extortion threats,
    191–92, 219–20
  attempts to establish "white
    slavery" charges, 221–22
  deportation threat, 76–77
financial problems, 56, 59, 63,
    88, 112–13, 214, 306–10,
    312, 319
  attitude toward creditors, 75,
    99, 125
  divorce settlements and
    alimony, 171–72, 173, 318
  income taxes, 172, 318, 346
  sells *Zaca*, 340, 341
gambling by, 22, 24–25, 31, 35,
    66, 104–5, 169
gold smuggling by, 126, 245–46,
    252, 295
gun running, 126, 295
health of, 115, 156, 167, 189,
    225, 229–30, 256

cancer of the tongue, 336,
    338, 342
collapses on set, 88, 176–78
depressive aspect of, 131–32
as a deterrent to raising
    money, 306
emphysema, 81–82
given one year to live, 338
headaches, 14, 33, 74, 127,
    156, 158
heart attacks, 338, 341–42
hemorrhoids, 229–30, 231,
    259, 261, 264
hepatitis, 302–3
insomnia, 66, 132
neck and back problems,
    291–93, 294, 297, 309
production delays due to, 83,
    88–89, 167, 174–78, 218,
    229–30, 232–33, 264–65,
    302–3, 306
spinal arthritis, 309
tuberculosis, 173–78
undulant fever, 11, 74–75,
    117, 144–45, 229, 237, 264,
    294
Virus X, 264–65
home on Mulholland Drive, 123,
    165–66
loss of, 317–18
sexual jokes in, 165, 238–39
homosexual activities of, 3, 19,
    30, 78, 85–86, 87, 110, 112,
    119–21, 215, 260, 321,
    340–41
acting out the "hambone," 19
Cabot threatens exposure, 312
Capote and, 227
Díaz and, 221–22, 250
Eddington on, 3, 215, 222, 260
Mexican hustlers, 85–86, 133,
    160
Power and, 119–20, 250, 320

repressed sadomasochistic, 47
Roman hustlers, 304
insecurities of, 63, 87
kleptomania/stealing, 11–12, 14,
  22, 30–32, 35, 85, 154–55,
  245, 273, 282–83, 327
  jewelry, 39–40
  lugger, 42
lack of cooperation in early days
  of World War II, 124–25
love of Jamaica, 234–35, 243,
  272, 293
as a male prostitute, 30, 52
manslaughter charges against,
  48–49
motion pictures (Australia and
  New Guinea), 37–39
  first film role, 38–39
motion pictures (England), 51,
  55–56, 310, 311–14
motion pictures (Hollywood)
  acting talents, 65, 68–69,
    108–9, 115, 155, 266,
    272–73, 320
  arrival in Los Angeles, 58
  decline of career, 294, 310,
    318–19, 321
  first picture, 60–61
  production delays due to
    health, 83, 88–89, 167,
    174–78, 218, 229–30,
    232–33, 264–65
  salaries, 58, 68, 82, 83, 87–88,
    99–100, 109, 123, 131, 133,
    180, 214, 272
  social standing, 114, 132, 142,
    155, 159–60
motion pictures (independent
  productions), 133–37,
  224–26, 228, 239–40, 244,
  263–64, 268, 294
motion pictures (international),
  275–82, 300–3, 306–10,
  312–16, 319

production delays due to
  health, 302–3, 306
salaries, 319
motion pictures (list of), 357–59
musical taste, 48, 216, 275
Nazi (fascist) activities and
  sympathies, 37, 47–48,
  51–52, 74, 75, 90–92,
  98–99, 114, 130–31, 133,
  144, 152, 159–64, 223,
  250–52
the Abwehr, 159
admiration for Hitler, 92, 160
affair with Gertrude
  Anderson, 5, 130–31, 164,
  192–93
aids in Erben's escape to
  Mexico, 147–48
declassified secret documents
  on, 361–70
first detected evidence of, 4–7
Pearl Harbor photographs,
  118, 133, 149, 151–52
plot to kill Castro, 334–35
Roosevelt (Eleanor) used for
  protection, 142–43, 144,
  145, 252
sexual fascination, 37
socializing with Nazis in
  Mexico, 78, 159, 218
the Spanish Civil War, 92–99,
  149, 335
U-boat refueling bases, 164,
  241
uncensored wartime letters,
  223, 241–42, 283–84, 351
as a parent, 153, 172, 234, 236,
  255, 268, 272, 303–4, 316
passport problems, 48, 77–78,
  252, 300, 310, 312
paternity charges against,
  226–27, 292
personal philosophy of life, 340
practical jokes of, 15, 17, 18,

79–80, 109, 128, 129, 151,
169–70, 262, 273, 279–80,
287, 339–40, 351
radio shows, 117, 129–30, 159
rape charges and trial
(Monaco), 289–92
rape charges and trial (U.S.),
157–59, 182–214
appearance on witness stand,
208–10
bail, 188, 189
depression caused by, 200
escape plan if found guilty,
188, 212
extortion threats regarding,
191–92, 218–20
financial cost of, 214
Hollywood's reaction to, 187,
188
nervousness about, 187,
191–92, 212, 213
press relations, 188
public reaction to, 188–89,
191–92, 196, 209, 211, 213
the verdict, 213–14
reactions to snobbery, 14–15
reading habits, 14, 33, 40–41,
132–33
real estate investments, 123–24,
133, 214, 234, 272, 319
religion and, 11, 14
as a sexual athlete, 19, 239
sexual exhibitionism of, 19, 53,
56, 86, 110, 126–27, 132,
238–39, 258, 281–82
Shakespearean aspirations, 68,
84, 168–69
short wave broadcast to
Australia, 124–25
South American tour for Warner
Brothers, 143–45
special charm of, 2–3
sports
boxing, 19, 24, 25–26, 28, 36,
52, 60

fencing, 24
swimming, 19, 23, 24, 49, 52
tennis, 18, 19, 23, 49, 58–59,
81
wrestling, 25–26
State Department and, 90–91,
98, 143, 312
deportation threat, 76–78
sues McMartin for assault, 293,
297, 299–300
the supernatural and, 131,
252–53, 311–12, 334,
348–49
television shows, 313, 339
theatre
England, 51–55, 359
U.S., 326–27
tour of Alaskan army bases,
227–28
tradition and, 16–17
treasure hunting, 253–54
U.S. citizenship of, 177, 178
USO tour, 294
violence by, 17, 50, 54, 61, 79,
220–21, 236, 239, 248,
268–69, 288, 310, 316
virility, decline of, 259–60, 319,
324
Wallis and, 65, 67, 68, 69, 78,
82, 88, 107, 115, 127, 187
Warner Brothers' cover-up
activities for, 130–31, 144,
178, 192–93
will of, 339, 346–47
work ethic of, 2, 41
writings of, 35–36, 84, 132,
216–18, 288, 307
diary, 40–41, 42
See also Aadland, Beverly;
Christian, Linda; Damita,
Lili; Eddington, Nora;
Warner, Jack; Wymore,
Patrice

Flynn, Lily Mary (Marelle), 10,
    11–18, 89, 244, 268, 280,
    286, 287, 290, 311–12, 334,
    346, 350
  anti-Semitism of, 10, 47
  financial aid to son, 35
  reaction to son's success, 69
  sexual infidelities, 11, 13, 18,
    215
Flynn, Rory, 255–56, 258, 272,
    274, 275–76, 286, 292, 294,
    306, 339, 344, 345, 349
  claims to father's estate, 347
Flynn, Rosemary, 17, 18, 89, 334
Flynn, Sean, 153, 156, 172, 187,
    234, 255, 268, 272, 294,
    303–4, 306, 345, 349
  claims to father's estate, 346,
    347
  taken to brothel by father, 303
  visits father on Majorca, 316
Flynn, Theodore Leslie Thomson,
    10–18, 22, 24, 89, 263, 268,
    286, 290, 311–12, 319, 334,
    346, 349
  correspondence with son, 41, 47
  expedition to collect marine
    specimens, 243–49
  financial aid to son, 49
  reaction to son's success, 69
Flynn and Thomson, Inc., 172
Footsteps in the Dark, 358
Forbes, Mrs. Elaine, 201–2
Ford, John, 114
Ford, Robert E., 185, 187, 188,
    189, 201, 210, 213, 219,
    242, 264, 326
Forest Lawn, 167, 344, 349
Fors, Ema, 320
Fossataro, Count, 307, 308
Foster, Preston, 114
Four's a Crowd, 109–10, 112, 357
France, 50, 94, 161–62, 289, 290,
    291, 295

Francis, Kay, 56, 80, 83, 357
Francis, Lee, 239
Franco, Francisco, 51, 92, 94, 97,
    314, 315
Frank, Gerold, 321
Frank, Harriet, Jr., 256
Franklin, Sidney, 98
Freeman, Justice Ernest A., 62
French Equatorial Africa, 328–32
French Indochina, 49
French Somaliland, 50
Friderun (tramp steamer), 44, 46,
    47, 48
Friedman, William, 325–26
Friedman, Mrs. William, 325
Frischauer, Willi, 5
Frisco Kid, 57, 61
Frontiersman, The, 240, 243
Fuchs, Sidney, 327

Gable, Clark, 39, 69, 70, 178
Galapagos Islands, 243
Galsworthy, John, 272
Gardner, Ava, 300, 320, 358
Gardner, Erle Stanley, 60–61
Gardner, Joe, 271
Garfield, John, 115
Garson, Greer, 273, 358
Gary, Romain, 333
Gem of the Breakwater (vessel),
    114
General William Black (vessel),
    251
Gentleman Jim, 176–79, 187, 214,
    245, 358
George V, King, 88
German-American Bund, 111
Germany, 51–52, 71, 161
  Nazi Party, 45, 71–73, 76, 111,
    138, 140
  World War II, 124, 138–41,
    160, 251, 252, 289
  See also Hitler, Adolf

Ghika, Princess Irene, 275–76, 280, 286, 287
  suicide attempt, 276
Gibbons, Cedric, 59, 114
Giblin, Mrs., 36–37
Giesler, Jerry, 159, 185–214, 226, 228
  disarming methods of attack, 186, 198–200
  methods of uncovering information, 186, 194
  smearing dubious witnesses, 186, 193–94, 205, 207
Giles, Sandra, 325
Goebbels, Joseph, 161, 163
Goering, Hermann, 160, 163
Goiaribari, the, 36
Golden Shanty, The (TV play), 339
Goldie Gets Along, 57
Goldman, Harold, 233
Gold smuggling, 126, 245–46, 252, 295
Golenbock, Justin, 343, 346, 347
Gone With the Wind, 124
"Good Companions, The" (Priestley), 41
Good Samaritan Hospital, 156, 178
Gould, Dr. Grant, 341
Goulding, Edmund, 115, 120
Grace Lines, 140
Grahame, Margot, 51, 357
Grainger, Percy, 130
Gray, Dolores, 294
Gray, Dr. Etta, 194, 208, 214
Gray, Eve, 357
Gray, Zillah, 54
Greco, Juliette, 332, 359
Green Light, 82–83, 302, 357
Green Light (Douglas), 82
Gregory, Helene, 310, 316
Gregory, Jon, 286, 310–12, 316, 345

Grieg, Edvard, 216
Gross, Chuck, 244, 245
Guadalupe Islands, 246
Guatemala, 74
Gun running, 126, 295
Gurney, Noll, 82
Guthrie, Colonel William, 92, 150
Gyssling, George, 130, 147

Habenicht, Bodo, 171
Hagenbeck Wild Animal Reserve, 50
Haines, William, 86, 119
Haiti, 252–53
Hakluyt, Richard, 132
Hale, Alan, 104, 174, 262–63
Halifax, Lord, 149
Hamilton, Ward, 107
"Hamlet" (Nazi agent), 138, 171
Hamlet (Shakespeare), 169
Hampden, John, 38–39
Hansen, Betty, 182–86, 189, 193, 197–200, 209, 210, 214, 323
  reputation of, 193, 200
Happy Harry, 21
Harcourt, John, 10
Harding, Jack, 191–92
Hartford, Huntington, 324, 326–27, 346
Hartman, Joe, 135
Haskin, Helen, 46
Hassau, Marilyn, 226, 227
Hassau, Shirley Evans, 226–27, 292
Havana, Cuba, 319, 335–37
Hawaii, 117–18, 131, 133, 135, 150, 153, 172
  Flynn's photographs of Pearl Harbor, 118, 133, 149, 151–52
Haymes, Dick, 269–70, 271, 274–76

Hays, Will, 77–78, 91–92
  power of, 77
Hayward, Louis, 56, 166
Hayworth, Rita, 249, 291
Hearst, William Randolph, 78, 93,
  178
Heart of Darkness (Conrad), 133
Heigh, Helene, 340–41, 343–44
Heinze, Wally, 115, 117
Heiyo Maru (vessel), 46, 140
Hellerman, Hans, 96, 159
Hellman, Lillian, 99
Hello God, 358
Hemingway, Ernest, 95, 96, 97,
  99, 141, 320, 335
Henderson, Chief Justice, 299
Henry V (Shakespeare), 169
Hernshaw, Giles, 260
Heroin, 251
Herstlet, Theodore, 164
Heydrich, Reinhold, 96
Hides, Eileen and Jack, 36
Hill, Howard, 101–7, 116, 123,
  133–34, 136–37, 245, 247,
  335
Himmler, Heinrich, 45
Hinton, Marilyn, 341
Hitchcock, Alfred, 130
Hitler, Adolf, 45, 49, 51–52, 72,
  92, 138, 159–60
  Erben's admiration for, 44, 73,
  91, 93, 145
  Flynn's admiration for, 92, 160
  Marsh on, 161
Hobart, Tasmania, 8–17, 18, 24
  anti-Semitism in, 47
  description of, 8–9
Hoebich, Margaret, 284
Hoffpauir, Curley C., 347
Hofstadter, Judge Samuel, 347–48
"Holiday Town Saturday Night"
  (TV show), 313
Hollywood (Los Angeles),
  California, *see* Motion

pictures (Flynn),
  Hollywood; names of
  motion pictures,
  personalities, and
  organizations
Hollywood Athletic Club, 59
Hollywood Canteen, 194
Hollywood Tennis Club, 59
Homosexuality, 3, 19, 30, 78,
  85–86, 87, 110, 112,
  119–21, 215, 259, 260, 321,
  323, 340–41
  acting out the "hambone," 19
  Cabot threatens to expose Flynn,
  312
  Capote and, 227
  Díaz and, 221–22, 250
  Eddington on, 3, 215, 222, 260
  Mexican hustlers, 85–86, 133,
  160
  Power and, 119–20, 250, 320
  repressed sadomasochistic, 47
  Roman hustlers, 304
Hong Kong, 48, 49, 98, 283
  Erben deported from, 98
Honolulu, Hawaii, 117–18, 150
Hood, Richard, 143
Hoover, J. Edgar, 142, 144, 145,
  164, 191, 219, 221–22, 242,
  336
Hopkins, John, 209–12
Hopkins, Miriam, 99, 127, 357
Hopper, Hedda, 132, 188, 319
Horn Blows at Midnight, The, 232
Howard, Jean, 119
Howard, Trevor, 331
Hubbs, Professor Carl, 243–49,
  263
Hubbs, Mrs. Carl, 246
Hudson, W. H., 165
Hughes, Howard, 118, 120–21,
  160
Hull, Cordell, 149
Hull, Henry, 229

Hunter, Ian, 88, 101
Hunter-Kerr, Ken, 22–23, 31, 35
Huston, John, 132, 237–38,
    331–32
Huston, Walter, 309
Hutton, Barbara, 51, 161
Hyland, Dick Irving, 250, 340

I Adore You, 51, 357
I'll See You in My Dreams, 293
India, 50, 72, 73, 171, 275,
    276–80, 283
  Erben deported from, 73
Indonesia, 350
In Old Chicago, 119
Interlenghi, Franco, 307
International Brigade, 94–95
International Police Commission
    (Interpol), 295
In the Wake of the Bounty, 38–39,
    357
Iran, 72–73, 283, 350
Iran, Shah of, 283
Iraq, 72
Ireland, 48, 69, 343–44
Istanbul, 318–19, 358
Italy, 302–5, 307–10, 312
It's a Great Feeling, 358
Ivanhoe, 313
Ivens, Joris, 99

Jack and the Beanstalk, 53, 359
Jackson, Freda, 53
Jacobsmeyer, Homer, 213
Jacoby, Abraham (Michel), 75
Jaipur, Maharajah of, 276–77
Jamaica, 87, 252, 268–69, 280,
    286, 296, 299–300, 310–12,
    319, 334, 338–39, 344, 349
  Flynn's love of, 234–35, 243,
    272, 293
  voodoo in, 311–12, 334
James II, King, 51
Jane Eyre, 326–27

Japan, 98, 114, 159, 251, 252
  concentration camps, 223
  print of *Dive Bomber* shipped
    to, 150, 151–52
Jasin, Gene, 173
Jerusalem, 72
Jezebel, 245
Joby R., The (vessel), 114
Johns, Clarence, 319
Johnson, Nunnally, 245
Johnstone, Geoffrey, 299
Jory, Victor, 60
Jupiter Laughs, 132

Kahn, Gus, 293
Kahner, Gerhardt, 46
Kangaroa (yacht), 295–97
Kazanjian, Reginald B., 91
Keats, John, 133
Keeper of the Flame, 163–64
Kehoe, Cedric, 325
Keighley, William, 89, 101, 104,
    107–8, 134, 300, 301
Kiel, Bill, 135
Kif, 86
Kim, 275–82, 358
Kim (Kipling), 275
Kingsley, Captain Hayward, 135,
    156, 157, 190, 207, 240–41,
    244
King's Rhapsody, 314–16, 358
Kings Row, 174–75, 245
Kipling, Rudyard, 165, 275
Kirk, Betty, 159
Knapp, Armand, 182–83, 184,
    193, 197, 200
Kniemeyer, Jack, 81, 260
Knights of Columbus, 99
Knowles, Enid, 109
Knowles, Patric, 2, 76, 81, 88,
    104, 105–6, 107, 109, 125
Knowlton, Speed, 105
Koko Maru (vessel), 46
Kolowrat, Count Sascha, 45

Korea, 294
Krim, Arthur, 306, 308
Krims, Milton, 302
Kuku-Kukus Tribe, 35–36
Kurnitz, Harry, 259

Lacey, William, 16
Ladies in Retirement, 166
Lady from Shanghai, The, 249
Lady Vanishes, The (radio show), 129–30
Lambert, Sammy, 287–88
Landis, Carole, 109
Lane, Charles, 60
Langille, Federal Agent, 141
Langsdorf, Captain, 139
Larson, Mrs. Jennie, 212
Latorre (battleship), 141
Laval, Pierre, 161
Leahy, Mrs. Mildred, 212
Leigh, Rowland, 75
Leigh-Fermor, Patrick, 333
Lejeune, C. A., 231
Lentner, Manfred, 295–97
Lesley, Cole, 293
Let's Make Up, 358
Lev, Peter, 5–6
Levy, Benn W., 52
Lewis, David, 110
Lewis, Ed ("Strangler"), 176
Liberty, 93, 95
Life, 157, 204
Lilacs in the Spring, 312–13, 358
Lincoln, Ignatius Trebitsch (Chao-Kung), 46, 49, 51, 171
Lincoln Brigade, 110–11
Lind, Kyle, 349
Linda (Christian), 180, 357
Lindfors, Viveca, 261–62, 358
Lindsay, Margaret, 61, 357
Lindsay, Norman, 217–18
Linton, Mayne, 357
Little Sirocco (launch), 222

Litvak, Anatole, 115
Lloyds of London, 309
Loeb and Loeb (law firm), 171
Loesser, Frank, 195
Lollobrigida, Gina, 302, 303, 358
Lombard, Carole, 99
London, England, 51, 54–55, 230–31, 275, 283, 301–2, 312–14, 333–34, 346, 349
London, Jack, 33
London *Daily Telegraph,* 231
London *Observer,* 231
London *Times,* 154
Long-Innes, Rex, 35
Longstreet, Stephen, 256
Loper, Jack, 100
Lord, Robert, 84, 151–52
Los Angeles College of Osteopathic Physicians and Surgeons, 286
Los Angeles *Examiner,* 188, 328
Los Angeles *Herald Express,* 340
Los Angeles Juvenile Control Division, 184
Los Angeles Police Department, 84–85
Los Angeles Tennis Club, 58
Los Angeles *Times,* 188, 237
Louise, Anita, 83, 357
Lourenço Marques, Mozambique, 138, 171
Loyalists (Spanish Civil War), 92–97, 99, 110–11
Ludwigsburg Repatriation Prison, 252
Lukas, Paul, 225, 279–80, 358
Lupino, Ida, 166–70, 187, 339–40, 348–49, 358
Lurline (liner), 117
Lydia Bailey, 299, 300
Lynn, Jeffrey, 115

Macbeth (Shakespeare), 159
McCarty, Clifford, 357

McCormick Lines, 90
McCrea, Joel, 109
McEvoy, Claude, 294–97
McEvoy, Freddy, 5, 149, 161–64,
    179–80, 221, 227, 231, 275,
    285, 290, 291
  the Abwehr and, 179
  death of, 294–97, 311
  declassified secret documents,
    361–70
  drug smuggling of, 242, 295–96
  extortion charges against, 242
  in Flynn's rape charges and trial,
    181–83, 188, 195, 208, 210
  U-boat refueling bases and, 5,
    164, 241
McIlwaine, Robert, 318
McKoy, Enid, 12–13
McLaglen, Victor, 25
McMartin, Duncan, 293, 297,
    299–300, 309
MacMurray, Fred, 358
McWilliams, "Doc," 230, 321
McWilliams, Paul, 3, 230, 321–22
Madrid, Spain, 96–97
Magnet, 81
Mahon, Barry, 3, 297–99, 303,
    305, 306–10, 312, 319, 326,
    337, 340
  Fossataro and, 308
  Zanuck and, 307
Mahon, Clelle, 3, 298–99, 302,
    304–5, 310, 312, 337
Mahoney, Jock, 266
Majorca, 316–17, 319, 340
Malone, Dorothy, 358
Maltese Falcon, The, 238
Man Behind the Gun, The, 293,
    299
Mann Act, 222
Manolete, 180
Man's House, A (Drinkwater), 54,
    359
Mantz, Paul, 188, 263

Man Who Came to Dinner, The,
    245
Man Who Cried, The, 358
Maru Maru, 294, 297, 358
March, Fredric, 99, 114–15
March of Dimes, 142
Marcos, Rossi di, 69
Marie Antoinette, 119
Marijuana, 86, 178, 231–32,
    311–12
Marjorie Morningstar, 322–23
Marsh, Tara, 160–61
Marshall, Brenda, 357, 358
Marshall, William, 288
Martha (vessel), 114
Marx, Samuel, 77
Masefield, John, 14
Massey, Raymond, 131
Master of Ballantrae, The, 300–2,
    358
Matthews, Blainey, 321–22
Mattison, Frank, 229, 232
Mauch Twins, 88–89, 357
Mayberry, Dick, 262
Mayer, Louis B., 77, 86
MCA Artists, 298, 299, 319
Meadow, Herb, 300
Medford, Harold, 300
Melbourne, Australia, 25, 38–39
Melville, Herman, 14, 133
Mendoza, Harry, 227, 228
Mercado, Louis, 146, 147
Merchant of Venice, The
    (Shakespeare), 169
Messageries Maritimes, 49
Metro-Goldwyn-Mayer, 64, 68,
    119, 245, 272, 274, 275,
    277, 281, 313
Mexicali, Mexico, 77–78
Mexican Hayride, 286
Mexico, 77–78, 110, 114, 116–17,
    123, 126, 144, 156, 159,
    160–61, 164, 179–80, 188,
    231–32, 248–50, 320

Erben's escape to, 147–48

Flynn's socializing with Nazis in, 78, 159, 218

homosexual hustlers in, 85–86, 133, 160

Mexico City, Mexico, 78, 148, 160–61, 179–80, 221, 236, 320

the Abwehr in, 147, 149, 170

Meyer, Johnny, 3, 19, 81, 118–21, 130, 143–44, 148, 227, 242, 250

death of, 118

Miami, Florida, 242, 285

Midwick Country Club, 108

Milder, Max, 231

Milestone, Lewis "Millie," 181, 187

Miller, Bill, 105

Minear, Mrs. Nellie, 213

Mines, Harry, 286–87

Mr. Peabody and the Mermaid, 245

Mitford, Unity, 51–52

Moby Dick (Melville), 14

Mohlmann, John, 323

Mohr, Hal, 64

Monaco, 288–92

Monopolies Act, 307

Monroe, Marilyn, 227

Montana, 269–71, 358

Monte Carlo, 288–92

Montesano Hospital, 264

Montevideo, Uruguay, 46, 139

Montgomery, Robert, 99

Moon in the Yellow River, The (Johnson), 54, 359

Moore, Erin O'Brien, 55

Moore, John Hammond, 18, 357

More, Pat, 84

Morgan, Dennis, 177–78, 345

Morocco, 296–97

Morphine, 46, 205, 212, 231, 246, 256, 269

Mosberg, Hans Adolf, 91, 147, 152, 170

Moscrip, Colonel Amos, 251, 284, 351

Moseley, Roy, 5

Motion pictures (Flynn)

Australia and New Guinea, 37–39

first film role, 38–39

England, 51, 55–56, 310, 311–14

Hollywood

acting talents, 65, 68–69, 108–9, 115, 155, 266, 272–73, 320

arrival in Los Angeles, 58

decline of career, 294, 310, 318–19, 321

first picture, 60–61

production delays due to health, 83, 88–89, 167, 174–78, 218, 229–30, 232–33, 264–65

salaries, 58, 68, 82, 83, 87–88, 99–100, 109, 123, 131, 133, 180, 214, 272

social standing, 114, 132, 142, 155, 159–60

independent productions, 133–37, 224–26, 228, 239–40, 244, 263–64, 268, 294

international, 275–82, 300–3, 306–10, 312–16, 319

production delays due to health, 302–3, 306

salaries, 319

list of, 357–59

See also names of motion pictures, personalities, and organizations

Moxom, Fred, 213

Mozambique, 138, 171

Muir, Jean, 64, 65

Munitions sales, 159–60
Murder at Monte Carlo, 55, 357
Mussolini, Benito, 75, 163
Mutiny on the Bounty, 69
Mysore, Maharajah of, 277–79
My Wicked, Wicked Ways
    (Flynn), 2, 334, 338
  deceptions in, 4–5, 339–40
  royalties on, 346

Naldi, Aldo, 233, 234, 239
Naples, Italy, 302, 305, 308
Napoleon, Art and Josephine, 321
National Archive, 5
National Socialist Colonial Bund,
  139
Nazi Party, 45, 71–73, 76, 111,
  138, 140
Neagle, Anna, 312, 358
Neeb, Robert, 208–9
Nelson, Gene, 286
Neutrality Act, 139
Never Say Goodbye, 240, 358
New Britain, 32–33, 37, 42–43, 48
New Guinea, 21, 32–34, 35–38,
    40–42, 47, 48, 77, 331
  German population in, 37
  headhunting, 33–34
New South Wales, 21, 26, 29
New York, N.Y., 57, 68–69, 73,
    74, 75, 87, 93–94, 113, 227,
    261, 282–83, 287–88, 299,
    306, 327, 334, 336, 349
  Flynn's arrest in, 271–72
  Nazi activities in, 110–11,
    162–63
New York *Daily News,* 287
New York *Herald Tribune,* 69, 74,
  75
Nice, France, 290, 291, 296, 309
Nicholas, A. J., 92, 93
Nicolaus, George, 159
Nietzsche, Friedrich Wilhelm, 48
Nightingale (vessel), 140–41

Niven, David, 81, 82, 115, 125
Nolan, Dr. Frank, 88, 229–30,
    261, 264–65, 269
Northern Pursuit, 218, 358
North German Lloyd, 44, 48
Norway, 180
Now, Voyager, 245

Oakes, Sir Harry, 160
Oakie, Jack, 114
Objective, Burma, 228–31, 358
Obringer, Roy, 77, 88, 89, 172,
    178, 180, 187
O'Driscoll, Martha, 227
Office of Strategic Services (OSS),
    vii, 148, 152, 241, 251, 351
O'Hara, Maureen, 358
Oliver, Hubert, 194
Olivier, Laurence, 124
Olympic Games (1936), 161
Opium, 27–28, 86
Oppenheimer, George, 259
Orry-Kelly, 323
Ott, Roland, 284, 351

Pacific Institute of Tropical
    Medicine, 45–46
Palestine, 72
Pallette, Eugene, 106
Palmaro, Charles, 290
Palm Springs, California, 265,
    269–70
Panama Canal, 90, 110, 139–40,
    141, 143, 243, 253
Panama Lines, 143
Pandora and the Flying
    Dutchman, 300
Pantages, Alexander, 186
Paris (liner), 56
Paris, France, 94, 95, 161, 162,
    275–76, 280, 287, 288, 307,
    330–31, 332, 333
Park, Arthur, 125, 298, 299
Parker, Eleanor, 358

Parrakoola (vessel), 46
Parsons, Louella, 188, 232, 319
Patterson, Elaine, 157–58, 194, 202, 203
Pavillon, Le, 282–83
Pavlenko, Alex, 184, 187–88, 192, 200, 214, 216, 220, 230, 237, 256
Payn, Graham, 293
Pearl Harbor, 118, 131, 149, 151, 152, 172
  Flynn's photographs of, 118, 133, 149, 151–52
Peerschke, Heinz, 139
Pepper, Claude, 145
Perfect Specimen, The, 99–100, 176, 357
Perino's, 214
Perkins, Frances, 98–99, 142
Peron, Eva, 253
Peron, Juan Domingo, 253
Perona, John, 227, 271–72
Pete Smith Specialty, 245
Pevney, Joseph, 319
Peyton Place, 322
Philip Morris Playhouse, 129–30
Philippines, the, 6–7, 171, 350–51
Phoenix, Arizona, 265
Photoplay, 99, 132, 232
Picard, Jean, 224–25
Pilleau, Charles, 3, 24–25, 35, 38, 41–42, 188, 253, 335
  trip to Queensland, 27–30
Planetta, Oskar, 71
Plews, Limey, 79, 80, 81, 151
Ponder, Mrs. Harriet, 201
Pootung Civil Assembly Center, 223, 241
Port Antonio, Jamaica, 310–12
Portland Fishing Club, 300
Port Moresby, New Guinea, 35–38
Potter, Pat, 24
Power, Tyrone, 119–20, 178, 320, 345

  homosexual affair with Flynn, 119–20, 250, 320
  marriages, 119, 250
President Garfield (vessel), 46, 146
Presle, Micheline, 358
Prexmarer, Walter, 296
Priestley, John, 41
Prince, William, 358
Prince and the Pauper, The, 87–90, 357
Prince and the Pauper, The (Twain), 87–88
Pringle, Eunice, 186
Prinz, LeRoy, 195
Privall (vessel), 141
Private Lives of Elizabeth and Essex, The, 123–24, 357
Puritanism, 11, 23–24

Queen Mary (liner), 93–94, 98
Queensland, Australia, 21, 27–30, 39–40, 45, 84

Rabaul, New Guinea, 32–33, 48, 77
  German population in, 37
Rachmaninoff, Sergei, 216
Radio shows, 117, 129–30, 159
Raft, George, 336
Rainier, Prince, 288, 290
Rains, Claude, 101
Raphael, Eve, 282, 283, 334
Raphael, Stephen, 181, 234, 254, 282–83, 333–34, 346
Rapper, Irving, 217
Rathbone, Basil, 67, 68, 69, 101, 109, 115, 357
R. C. Hargon, Ltd., 35
Reagan, Ronald, 174–75, 301, 358
  Wallis and, 175
Reed, Dr. Alfred C., 45
Republic Pictures, 240
Reynolds, Marjorie, 294

Rhodesia, 350

Ribbentrop, Joachim von, 51

Rich, Hugh, 3

Rimsky-Korsakov, Nikolai, 216

Rio de Janeiro, Brazil, 91, 119, 144

Robb, Captain James, 149

Robe, The, 308

Roberti, Lyda, 62

Robinson, Ann, 105, 132

Robinson, Casey, 64

Robson, Flora, 128–30

Rockefeller Institute, 45, 73, 74

Rocky Mountain, 286–87, 358

Roman, Ruth, 294, 358

Rome, Italy, 302–5, 307, 310
  homosexual hustlers in, 304

Romeo and Juliet, 68

Romilly, Esmond, 94

Roosevelt, Eleanor, 92, 98, 126, 148
  used for protection by Flynn and
    Erben, 142–43, 144, 145, 252

Roosevelt, Franklin D., 77, 91, 92, 98, 148, 149, 159, 180, 252

Roosevelt, Franklin D., Jr., 142, 232

Roosevelt, Mrs. Franklin D., Jr., 232

Roots of Heaven, The, 327–33, 359

Rowe, Mrs. Gussie Alliet, 201

Rowntree, Seebohm, 49

Rubirosa, Porfirio, 161

Russell, Rosalind, 99

Sabatini, Rafael, 64

Sagada, the Philippines, 7, 350–51

Salamaua, New Guinea, 40–42

Salkind, Alexander, 306, 307

San Antonio, 232–33, 358

San Benito Islands, 247

Sanders, George, 129

San Diego Naval Base, 150–52

San Francisco, California, 45–46, 90, 93, 94, 118, 130, 146, 147, 344

San Simeon (Hearst ranch), 178–79

Santa Fe Trail, 131–32, 174, 358

Sarcoxie (vessel), 46

Saschafilm, 45

Satterlee, Mrs., 158, 207–8, 323

Satterlee, Mickey June, 208

Satterlee, Peggy, 157–59, 184, 186, 187, 189, 190, 193, 197, 200, 202–8, 209, 210, 211, 214
  reputation of, 193–94, 205

Saudi Arabia, 350

Sauer, Emil, 91

Saville, Victor, 163–64, 276, 278–79, 280–81

Scala, Gia, 358

Scarf, Frank, 26

Schaefer, Carl, 144, 192–93

Scharf, Dr. Rudolph, 140

Schellenberg, Walter, vii

Schencke, Carl, 37

Schuetze, Hellmut, 139

Schwab's Drugstore, 63

Schwartz, Arthur, 195

Scott, Vernon, 340

Scott, Sir Walter, 133

Screen Actors Guild, 107

Screen Guide, 277

Screen Publicists Ballyhoo Ball, 325

Scripps Oceanographic Institution, 243, 244, 263

Sea Fever (Masefield), 14

Sea Hawk, The, 3, 127–29, 143, 357

Selznick, David O., 78, 124, 237

Selznick, Myron, 68, 82, 83, 87

Senaja, George, 133

Shackleford, James, 37

Shanghai, China, 46, 47, 49, 147, 148, 149, 152, 241, 250, 251, 283–84, 351
 the Abwehr in, 138, 170–71, 222–23
 Erben deported from, 251
Sharman troupe, the, 25–26
Shedlo, Ronnie, 325, 341, 343–44
Shelley, Percy Bysshe, 133
Sheridan, Ann, 181, 187, 257, 258, 358
Sherman, Vincent, 259, 260–63, 265–66
Sherman, Mrs. Vincent, 266
She's Back on Broadway, 300
She's Working Her Way Through College, 293
Shipley, Ruth, 93, 94, 140, 141, 146
Shourds, Sherry, 67, 124
Showdown (Flynn), 216–18
Siefken, Louis, 138, 170–71, 222, 250, 251
Siegel, Buggsy, 163
Silver River, 256–58, 267, 358
Sirocco (yacht), 87, 112–14, 115–17, 126, 133, 135–36, 147–48, 156, 157–58, 169, 173, 187, 189, 190, 194, 202, 209, 211, 240
Sirocco (yawl), 34–35, 84, 87
Sisters, The, 114–15, 302, 357
Skelton, Red, 339
Sloan, Everett, 249
Smith, Alexis, 187, 232, 269, 270, 273, 358
Socorro Island, 247
Son of Captain Blood, The, 349
Sorge, Richard, 46
Southern Cross (vessel), 91, 160
Spain, 159, 292, 311, 314–16, 319
Spanish Civil War, 92–99, 110–11, 149, 335
Spanish Earth, 99

Spanish Medical Aid Committee (S.M.A.C.), 94–97
Spotlight, 51
S.S. *Panama,* 143
S.S. *Triton,* 110
Stackpole, Peter, 157–58, 207
Stader, Paul, 297
Staghound (vessel), 147
Standard Oil Company, 140, 162, 164, 242
Stanwyck, Barbara, 358
State Department, 5, 45–46, 92–93, 111, 148
 Erben and, 5, 45–46, 90–91, 95, 96, 97, 98
 Flynn and, 90–91, 98, 143, 312
 deportation threat, 76–78
Stauffer, Teddy, 231, 244–45, 247, 320
Steed, Captain, 84–85
Steele, Freddie, 176
Steele, Marjorie, 326
Steel Seafarer (vessel), 46, 284
Stevenson, Robert Louis, 14, 133, 300, 345
Stewart, Francis R., 76
Stewart, Jimmy, 105, 178
Still, Judge, 200, 202, 208, 211, 212, 213
Stockwell, Dean, 358
Story of Nylon, The, 322
Street, Robert, 219–20
Street, Mrs. Robert, 220
Sullivan, Jack, 107
Sullivan, John L., 176–77
Sun Also Rises, The, 320, 321, 358
Superman, 319
Sweden, 159–60
Switzerland, 319, 343
Sydney, Australia, 17–27, 34–35, 38
Sydney Church of England Grammar School, 19–20

Tacoma (vessel), 139

Taiping (vessel), 27–28

Tangier, Morocco, 317

Tartar, Linda, 343–44

Tasmania, 8–17, 18, 24
  anti-Semitism in, 47

Tasmania, University of, 10, 24

Taylor, William H., 231

Tea for Two, 286

Teddington Studios, 55

Teheran, Iran, 72–73

Television shows, 313, 339

Tempest, The (Shakespeare), 169

Thaelmann Brigade, 92

Thank Your Lucky Stars, 194–95, 358

That Forsyte Woman, 272–74, 275, 358

"That's What You Jolly Well Get" (Loesser and Schwartz), 195

They Died with Their Boots On, 155–56, 158, 159, 169, 170, 198, 242, 358

Thirteenth Chair, The (Veiller), 53, 359

Thomas, George H., Jr., 318

Thomas, Tony, 357

Thomson Inc., 172

Thomson Productions, 224, 239–40, 244

Tiajuana, Mexico, 81

Tilden, Bill, 181, 182

Tone, Franchot, 115

Too Much, Too Soon, 321, 325, 358

Toone, Geoffrey, 54

To the Last Man, 218

Toupes, Chi-Chi, 183, 202

Tramutolo, Chauncey, 148, 149

Treasure in Yucatan, 244, 245, 249

Treasure Island (Stevenson), 14

Trieste, 72

Trilling, Steve, 233, 256, 272

Triton (vessel), 46

Trocadero, 59

Troubetzkoy, Prince Igor, 290

Truffaut, François, 225

Truman, Harry S, 252

Turner, Don, 259, 266, 322

Turner, Lana, 250

Twain, Mark, 75, 87–88, 89

Two in the Campagna (Browning), vii

Two Lugs on a Lugger (Dromgold), 37–38

Typee (Melville), 133

U-boat refueling scheme
  Flynn and, 164, 241
  McEvoy and, 5, 164, 241
  Wenner-Gren and, 160

Umberto di Poliolo, Prince, 289–90

Uncertain Glory, 224–26, 358

Union of Soviet Socialist Republics, 251, 252, 295, 296

Union Pioneer (vessel), 283

United Artists, 302, 308

United Press International, 343

U. S. Naval Air Corps, 150–51

U. S. Selective Service Board, 173

Universal Pictures, 297, 298, 318, 319

Up in Central Park, 286

Uruguay, 46, 139

Ussukuma (freighter), 46, 138–39

Valencia, Spain, 93, 95, 96, 98

Valparaiso, Chile, 119, 140, 141, 144

Vanderbilt, Gloria, 227

Varsi, Diane, 322

Veimauri (liner), 37

Velez, Lupe, 276

Venice, Italy, 305, 308–9

Venice Film Festival, 308–9
Venuta, Benay, 294
Vienna, Austria, 6, 44–45, 50, 72, 252, 350
  anti-Semitism in, 45, 47
Vienna, University of, 45, 46
Viertel, Peter, 320
Vietnam War, 349
Vincent, Robert P., 244, 246
Virginia City, 126, 127, 357
Voesendorf, Dr. Berger, 95–96
Von der Decken, Leopold, *see* Decker, John
Von Miorini, Dr. Albert, 46, 241
Von Reichenau, Baron, 241
Von Wallenberg, Consul General, 149
Voodoo
  in Haiti, 252–53
  in Jamaica, 311–12, 334
Voyage of the Beagle (Darwin), 132
Voyages (Hakluyt), 132

Wagner, Richard, 48, 216
Wahn, Graham, 271
Wald, Jerry, 233–34
Walker, Edward, 184
Walker, Helen, 282
Walker, Marjorie, 340
Wallis, Hal, 83, 88, 104, 256
  Curtiz and, 78–79, 107
  Flynn and, 65, 67, 68, 69, 78, 82, 88, 107, 115, 127, 187
  Reagan and, 175
Wallis, Minna, 68
Wall Street Journal, The, 304
Walsh, Raoul, 155, 167, 170, 174, 175, 177, 180, 225, 229, 230, 233, 234, 256, 257, 258, 282
  in Flynn's rape charges and trial, 187, 189, 212, 213–14
Walter, Judge Byron, 187, 189

Warner, Jack, 3, 55–56, 63, 68, 115, 124, 144, 233, 239, 259
  Borzage and, 83
  Flynn and, 64, 65, 68, 69, 76, 80, 82, 83, 86, 88, 98, 108, 110, 123, 150, 169, 194–95, 217, 239–40, 265, 304, 345
  animosities between, 262–63, 272, 274, 301–2, 326
  cover-up activities, 92, 126
  defends Flynn, 321
  in deportation threat, 77, 78
  distrust between, 256–57, 270
  drugs forbidden by Warner, 261, 270
  fear of Flynn, 125–26
  reaction to rape charges and trial, 187, 214
  skepticism of Flynn's illness, 88, 174, 175
  power of, 77, 150
Warner Brothers, 3, 59, 61, 64, 75, 79, 85, 98, 101, 113, 124, 133, 174, 180, 227, 238, 252, 274, 292, 293, 294, 298, 321
  cancels Flynn's contract, 310
  cover-up activities for Flynn, 130–31, 144, 178, 192–93
  in England, 51, 55–56, 231
  political influence of, 144, 150
  reaction to Flynn's rape charges and trial, 187, 196–97, 214
  skepticism regarding Flynn's health, 167, 174, 175
  South American tour by Flynn for, 143–45
Warriors, The, 313–14, 358
Warwick, John, 38
Washington, D.C., 92, 93, 98–99, 114, 142, 310, 344
Washington *Post*, 159
Wasserman, Lew, 298, 319

Waverly, Lord, 73
Weigon (vessel), 138
Welles, Orson, 168, 249
Welles, Sumner, 148–49
Welter, Blanca Rosa, *see* Christian,
    Linda
Wenner-Gren, Axel, 159–60
West, Nathanael, 322
West Mahwah (freighter), 46,
    90–91, 92
Westmore, Perc, 264–65
West Notus (vessel), 46
Westside Tennis Club, 58
Wetzel, Al, 115, 117, 133–37
Wetzel, Mrs. Al, 133, 134
Weyl, Carl Jules, 103
"What Really Happened to Me in
    Spain" (Flynn), 99
White Rajah, The (Flynn), 132
Whorf, Richard, 348
Wicklund, Toivo, 244, 248
Wiedemann, Fritz, 118, 130, 135,
    147
Wilcox, Herbert, 310, 312–16
Wiles, Buster, 133, 134, 136, 174,
    177, 195, 215, 216, 219,
    229, 230, 233, 242, 322,
    344
  in Flynn's rape charges and trial,
    157–58, 183, 188–90, 194,
    202, 203, 209, 213–14
Williamson, Colonel William E., 5,
    148–49, 251
William Tell, 306–10, 358
Winchell, Walter, 219, 220
Windsor, Duke and Duchess of,
    160
Wood, C. J., 113, 136, 147–48,
    322
Wood, Natalie, 322
Woodbury Program (radio series),
    117
Woods, Donald, 61
Woolf, John, 309

Woolley, Monty, 169
World Championship Bobsled Run,
    161
World War I, 45, 49, 154
World War II
  England, 124, 138–41, 160, 195,
    231
  Germany, 124, 138–41, 160,
    251, 252, 289
  U-boat refueling scheme, 5, 160,
    164, 241
  U.S., 124–25, 142–52, 162–64,
    170–74, 223, 227–28,
    241–42
Wright, Tenny, 83, 173, 175, 187,
    233–34, 264
Wrightsman, Irene, 221, 231, 242,
    285
Wuthering Heights, 349
Wylie, I. A. R., 164
Wyman, Louis, 350
Wymore, Patrice, 4, 24, 349, 358
  in Broadway musicals, 286
  concert appearances, 319, 320
  Flynn and, 286–94, 299, 300,
    302–5, 310–19, 339, 340
    birth of daughter (Arnella),
      306, 310
    death of Flynn, 343, 344, 345
    estate battles, 346–48
    financial aid to Flynn, 319
    marriage, 288–91, 304–5
    separations, 320–21, 327

Yachting, 112
Yachting Association, 135
Yankee Doodle Dandy, 245
Yellow Sands (Phillpotts), 53, 359
Young, Edward, 10, 338
Young, Robert (actor), 273
Young, Robert (English
    producer), 52–53
Young, Mrs. Robert (English stage
    manager), 54

Young, Robert (slave trader), 10

Young Errol, The (Moore), 357

Yuma, Arizona, 62

Zaca (yacht), 240–41, 243–49,
    252–55, 268–69, 286, 291,
292, 295, 304, 310–11, 312,
    316–17, 340, 341, 351

Zanuck, Darryl F., 299, 307, 320,
    327, 330, 332

Zerbe, Jerome, 74

Zobell, Professor Edward, 244

Flynn, Errol Leslie

DATE DUE
